PENGUIN BOOKS

WHAT NEXT?

'There are good reasons why even the most sceptical should read it. One reason is that it contains one of the best analyses in print of where we are now' Jonathan Sumption, *Spectator*

'Beautifully written, sharp and ironic . . . acutely observed and full of insight, anecdote and sardonic observation' Rod Liddle, *Sunday Times*

'A coherent and utterly credible assessment of what is wrong with the world and how we might fix it . . . Patten has succeeded in grasping the complexity of the political and economic challenges facing the world' Misha Glenny, *Irish Times*

'The book benefits from Patten's sure familiarity with the places he's writing about, and his asides – the "weak handshake" of a Sri Lankan rebel leader, the taste he shares with Helmut Kohl for the products of Chinese brewer Qingdao – set it apart' Simon Robinson, *Time Magazine*

'An enjoyable book . . . well-informed, with many surprising details, it rattles along' Peter Oborne, *Literary Review*

'*What Next?* is the work of a convinced and clever democrat; it is a good book and worth reading, crunch or no crunch' Henry Porter, *First Post*

ABOUT THE AUTHOR

Chris Patten is currently co-Chair of the International Crisis Group, and of the UK-India Round Table, and Chancellor of Oxford and Newcastle Universities. As a British MP from 1979 to 92 he served as Minister for Overseas Development, Secretary of State for the Environment and Chairman of the Conservative Party, being described afterwards as 'the best Tory Prime Minister we never had' (*Observer*). In 1998–9 he chaired the Independent Commission for Policing in Northern Ireland, and from 1999 to 2004 he was European Commissioner for External Relations. He is probably best known for being the last Governor of Hong Kong (1992–97), about which he wrote in *East and West* (1998). Both that and his most recent book, *Not Quite the Diplomat: Home Truths about World Affairs* (2005), were No 1. international best-sellers. He was made a Companion of Honour in 1998 and a life peer in 2005.

CHRIS PATTEN

What Next?

Surviving the Twenty-first Century

PENGUIN BOOKS

PENGUIN BOOKS

Published by the Penguin Group
Penguin Books Ltd, 80 Strand, London WC2R ORL, England
Penguin Group (USA), Inc., 375 Hudson Street, New York, New York 10014, USA
Penguin Group (Canada), 90 Eglinton Avenue East, Suite 700, Toronto, Ontario, Canada M4P 2Y3
(a division of Pearson Penguin Canada Inc.)
Penguin Ireland, 25 St Stephen's Green, Dublin 2, Ireland
(a division of Penguin Books Ltd)
Penguin Group (Australia), 250 Camberwell Road, Camberwell, Victoria 3124, Australia
(a division of Pearson Australia Group Pty Ltd)
Penguin Books India Pvt Ltd, 11 Community Centre, Panchsheel Park, New Delhi – 110 017, India
Penguin Group (NZ), 67 Apollo Drive, Rosedale, North Shore 0632, New Zealand
(a division of Pearson New Zealand Ltd)
Penguin Books (South Africa) (Pty) Ltd, 24 Sturdee Avenue, Rosebank, Johannesburg 2196, South Africa

Penguin Books Ltd, Registered Offices: 80 Strand, London WC2R ORL, England

www.penguin.com

First published by Allen Lane 2008
Published in Penguin Books with updated material 2009
1

Copyright © Chris Patten, 2008, 2009

The moral right of the author has been asserted

Printed in Great Britain by Clays Ltd, St Ives plc

A CIP catalogue record for this book is available from the British Library

978-0-141-02145-4

www.greenpenguin.co.uk

Penguin Books is committed to a sustainable future
for our business, our readers and our planet.
The book in your hands is made from paper
certified by the Forest Stewardship Council.

*This book is written above all for Isabella, Elodie, Willow,
Max and Samuel: this is their century.*

Contents

List of Illustrations

Photographic acknowledgements are given in parentheses.

Acknowledgements

My gratitude for help in writing this book runs wide and deep.

As ever, my thanks go first to my editor and friend Stuart Proffitt, who is diligent, learned and the most creative critic. He constantly prods me into trying harder without ever destroying my morale. This book would not have been written without him. My agent, Michael Sissons, brought his legendary wisdom to my support at every difficult turn in the road.

When I began research for the book, I needed help to assemble the raw material in order to educate myself about several subjects on which initially I knew too little. I had the assistance of two doctoral students at Oxford University, Taiye Tuakli-Wosomu and Richard Pan. Their help was invaluable.

As I started writing, my dependency level rose steeply. Two other postgraduates at Oxford, again recommended like the original two by Professor Sir Adam Roberts, came to the rescue. They provided overviews of complex issues, commented wisely on my draft and answered my questions with speed and accuracy. I cannot thank Emily Paddon and Andrew Baker enough. They are very clever, smart and sensible beyond their years, and exceptionally nice and decent people. They will have distinguished academic or public-service careers themselves. If you were ever to feel depressed about either the academic world or the future of free societies you would only need to meet either Emily or Andrew to cheer yourself up.

Several people have read and commented on parts of the draft, including Professor Roberts, for whose wise advice I am particularly grateful. I would also like to thank Anthony Cary and Edward Llewellyn. Professor Paul Younger of Newcastle University gave me excellent advice on the chapter on water and Professor Angela McLean of Oxford University told me what I should read about epidemic disease.

My favourite bookshop, alongside the Elliott Bay in Seattle, is in our London neighbourhood. The Barnes Bookshop, easier to get to than the one in Seattle, is the best possible example of the case for small bookstores. It is run by people who both love books – Isla Dawes and Mark Brighton – and have been hugely helpful in tracking down very quickly what I need and want to read. Their shop is one of my principal indulgences.

I write the first drafts of books by hand, which creates huge problems of translation for those who type the manuscript. Most of the work was done by my friend Jane Sigaloff in between writing her own witty novels. She was a friendly adviser and critic as well as an extraordinarily accurate interpreter of my tiny script. My youngest daughter Alice also typed parts of the book and my wife Lavender volunteered her services whenever we were under pressure. My eldest daughter Kate did the research for the chapter on drugs. My middle daughter Laura would have helped too had she not been looking after Elodie and having Willow.

So this volume has really been a 'family and friends' business, but full responsibility for all its failings must be taken by the capo di capi himself. Any plaudits should be widely shared.

The book is dedicated to my grandchildren, which is as good in a way as dedicating it to their loving and much-loved grandmother. Lavender has once again had to cope with a writing husband whose papers are scattered across desks, dining and kitchen tables and most available flat surfaces throughout the house, who loses the only one he needs with regularity and who is not much of a companion when in full flow. She deserves a medal, but all that I am now going to give her back is me.

I have understood that the world is a vast emptiness built upon emptiness. And so they call me the master of wisdom. Alas! Does anyone know what wisdom is?

Song of the Owl from *The Thousand and One Nights*

While all other sciences have advanced, that of government is at a standstill – little better understood, little better practised now than three or four thousand years ago.

John Adams, 1813

I

Funny Old World

All the people like us are We,
And every one else is They.
Rudyard Kipling,
'We and They', 1926

Governments can do so little and prevent so little nowadays.
Power has passed from the hands of statesmen, but I should
be very much puzzled to say into whose hands it has passed.
It is all pure drifting.   Lord Salisbury, 1895

My policy is to be able to buy a ticket at Victoria Station and
go anywhere I damn well please.   Ernest Bevin, 1951

As Margaret Thatcher famously observed at her last cabinet meeting, 'It's a funny old world.' She might have added that it seems to get funnier by the year, to be sliding out of order. Gone are the day before yesterday's certainties, when the mutual assurance of destruction yoked together in a brittle truce what we called the Free World and its communist adversary. Gone too, apparently, is what followed those perilous decades: the acclaimed global triumph of liberal economic and political values, with the modernization of the world in America's and Europe's image and nothing much more to worry about. Gone over the last year the vanity of a purported New Economy of credit card riches, as a long boom explodes into a painful bust. So what is it – blind but blogging – that slouches onstage instead? Is it denial of the authority of nation-states, which have been so far the political building blocks of our modern world? Is it the overthrow of the notion of sovereignty, which for over three and a half centuries has been 'the organizing principle of international relations'?[1] Is it the rejection of the Western world's view of modernization? Does economic globalization – and the social and environmental changes that accompany it – run too far ahead of the ability of politics to cope? Are the excesses of unregulated financial markets going to turn back the clock from global integration to national economic protectionism? What on earth is happening to us, and is it really new at all, or simply more of the drifting spied in his world-weary way by the late-Victorian statesman Lord Salisbury over a century ago?

This book will try to suggest what answers to these questions, and a number of others, might look like. I was motivated to write it by a number of factors. First, without ever believing that before the Bush administration there were no problems in the conduct of foreign relations, like so many others I reacted with consternation and occasional rage to the policies pursued by Washington from 2000 to 2004. The partial retreat in the last four years from the more mindless and dangerous forms of unilateralism was a welcome though insufficiently comprehensive recognition of the costs of earlier failure and the impossibility for even the world's greatest power of tackling every global problem on its own, or at least on entirely its own terms. President Bush and his vice-president are not ever-present visitors to these pages, but they do put in occasional appearances (when I discuss terrorism in Chapter 4 for example) and what they represent is never far away. But democracy in America has turned the page. A new administration has arrived in Washington, wreathed in hope, weighed down by expectations of success that would challenge miracle workers. My book describes the contemporary problems which President Obama and his team now have to tackle. When I began writing it in early 2007 I felt like the unpopular fellow who first hears the sound of distant thunder at a picnic. By the time of publication of this paperback the heavens are dark with clouds and the rain is lashing down.

More important to me than the personalities and policies of an era of hapless dogmatism now fortunately subjects for the past tense, have been four lessons – not especially original ones, it has to be said

– that I have learned over the years about international politics. I suppose they pretty well define me. I am not a particularly angry old man, and I have during a fairly long career at the heart and on the fringes of politics been called a lot of abusive things. I recall, for example, the prodigally right-wing Canadian columnist Mark Steyn (to his credit, a journalist who stood by his old patron Conrad Black in bad times as well as good) calling me 'Chris Pétain' because of my rather moderate criticism at the time of the invasion of Iraq. Mr Steyn believed that its easy accomplishment had vindicated Donald Rumsfeld. Rather like this author on the tennis court, Mr Steyn and others like him must get tired of saying 'sorry'. One can shrug off straightforward abuse such as 'Pétain', but I did bridle when regularly described by others with a knowing sneer as a 'liberal internationalist' as though it were some sort of rash intellectual deformity or defect in my patriotism. To my mind there is nothing else for a sensible person to be. So I thought I should set out what this liberal internationalist thinks, and what he believes liberal internationalism means today. What are to me its main themes – all of them especially germane to coping with the problems of the twenty-first century – run like threads through the different chapters of this book.

First, liberal internationalism should encompass a strong belief in the rule of law, democratic government, open markets and free trade. I also reckon that it is a proper aim of foreign policy to pursue these desirable outcomes consistently, coherently and without a constant parade of double standards or a precisely delineated template into which every country has to fit. Many of the problems of the poorest parts of the world are the result of them being shut out of, or shutting themselves out of, competitive global markets. They also stem from bad governance, which is both a cause and a consequence of political instability and violence. Dependence on easily lootable resources like diamonds and oil, and the proliferation of small arms (Chapters 6 and 7) stoke and pay for conflict. We need to avoid future conflicts over water (Chapter 8).

Second, the global order established after the Second World War on the sort of lines advocated by Woodrow Wilson after the First, has been challenged in two major ways. Its institutions – the United Nations (UN) above all – work much less well than they should, and the power balances between countries especially in economic terms have recently changed with the re-emergence of Asian economic strength. We should not resile from trying to reform and reinvigorate the UN. But we cannot postpone international cooperation until a perfect UN has emerged from its chrysalis. Regional and global collaboration is essential to deal with issues like epidemic disease (Chapter 13) and, above all, the biggest challenge to the world: global warming and climate change (Chapter 12). America and Europe can no longer set the global agenda on their own. They have to involve China, India and others like Brazil and South Africa in the management of the world's problems. Crucially, China has to be found a place at the table without the democracies accepting the validity of that country's implied and sometimes explicit critique of the guiding values and standards of plural, free societies.

Third, I am convinced that good domestic policy is often the best foreign policy. Failure to deal adequately with the supply of drugs from broken-down states such as Afghanistan is, for example, part and parcel of the failure of domestic drugs policy in the West (Chapter 10).

Fourth, I am not convinced – liberal internationalist lapel badge notwithstanding – that the state has withered away because of globalization (Chapter 3), nor that it should. But I do not believe either that the definition of the state assumed in the seventeenth century (Chapter 2) is appropriate today. Individuals have rights as well as states. Nation-states continue to be the crucial links in any chain of effective global action against problems that cannot be dealt with by a single government. The authority and effectiveness of nation-states should come because we trust them to safeguard and represent 'us'.

So who do I mean by that conveniently all-purpose, unexplained 'us'? Who am I talking about? Who are 'we'? The 'we' who are both formed by events and capable of forming them, too. The definition of 'we' is one of the starting points on any historical or political journey, and it is therefore at the heart of this book. 'We' starts small and ends big, though when used by an individual these days it will never go quite as far as Alexis de Tocqueville thought it travelled for French kings before the Revolution. These Bourbons assumed that the state was simply an extension of themselves. 'L'Etat, c'est moi,' Louis XIV, the Sun King, is claimed to have remarked in 1655 – apocryphal this may have been, yet he certainly believed it. For most of us today, the question is which 'we' when? Small children delight in writing galactic addresses for themselves: 'A. Smith, 10, Station Road, Oxford, Oxfordshire, England, United Kingdom of Great Britain and Northern Ireland, Europe, Earth, Solar System, Universe.' Even that leaves out plenty of identification marks that are not contained in any address: 'C of E' or Muslim, Arsenal supporter or Chelsea fan, Boy Scout or Girl Guide. We are all members of several groups, with mixed loyalties and muddled connections.

These are the borderlands in which I have spent much of my political life. A Catholic conservative from Irish immigrant stock, my first ministerial post was in Northern Ireland, where I quickly caused a stir by making the sign of the cross after grace at a civic lunch in Derry, something I had done ever since childhood. This apparently was a public signal of my Catholicism. Did not Protestants cross themselves? And was I actually in Catholic Derry – Catholic, that is, unless you were a Protestant playing for the Derry rugby team – or was I in Protestant Londonderry – Protestant that is, unless you were a Catholic member of the Londonderry Chamber of Commerce? No wonder it was called – London/Derry – 'stroke' city. Inadequate sensitivity to these theological niceties meant that I badly misjudged denominational differences in kneecappings on my first visit to the Accident and Emergency Unit at a hospital in Belfast. When I protested at reference to a 'Protestant' kneecapping, it was patiently explained to me that there really was a tribal though admittedly not a liturgical difference. Catholics, I was told, used a shotgun for this system of unofficial 'justice'; Protestants used a Black and Decker drill. These were not issues that concerned papal authority, but they did differentiate 'our' knees from 'theirs'.

As the last governor of a large British colony (we called it a territory, which sounded a little more neutral) I found myself wielding authority over mainly ethnically Chinese men and women, in an exercise of anonymous sovereignty that was recognized in quiet practice, though not in public declaration, by the future sovereign power in Beijing, a sovereign power from whose authority a large proportion of Hong Kong's population had once fled. Having handed over a colony, I then went to Brussels to hand over a nation-state to foreign rule: at least, that is how it played in Rupert Murdoch's biggest selling British newspaper. My appointment in 1999 as a European Commissioner was marked by a 'cartoon' in the *Sun* showing two sketches – in the first I wept over the Union Flag in Hong Kong; in the second I surrendered it to the nameless bureaucratic führers in Brussels. A Commissioner's life at the heart of the European Union (EU) certainly brought me into sharp contact with what exactly national sovereignty means today, how it can be made more effective by being shared, and how disengaged political rhetoric about this whole process can be from public practice and private emotion.

Plainly, whatever the defects of national institutions, we identify with them before we connect with the organizations established to manage shared or pooled sovereignty, from the Commission in Brussels to the World Trade Organization (WTO) in Geneva to the UN in New York. Nation-states, which are both the reason for and the result of the modern world, have absorbed our tribal memories; they subsume our narrower identities; they have become our 'imagined communities', the main (if occasionally crumbling) pillars in our political world.[2] They often make bogus claims to historical integrity and tribal cohesion. Consider, for instance, the question of borders, and take the example of the country whose name – Ukraine – literally means 'borderland'. Joseph Conrad, the novelist, was born south-west of Kiev. His earliest surviving work is a note to his grandmother, thanking her for some cakes. It is signed 'grandson, Pole, Catholic, gentleman', though there is no reference to the continent or the planet.[3] Conrad, of course, the Pole from the Ukraine who wrote his famous novels in English, died in Kent and is buried in Canterbury. Kent, bordered on three sides by the Thames Estuary and the English Channel, has not known the dramatic border reconfigurations that have been the stuff of Ukrainian history, its customs posts and defensive fortifications moving hither and yon over the Carpathian mountains and Galicia. Lviv, lying fifty miles east of today's Polish–Ukrainian border, was Lemberg when part of the Austro-Hungarian Empire; it became Lwów when Polish from 1918 to 1945, Lvov when the Russians took it after the Second World War and Lviv when Ukraine became independent in 1991. Go there and while chewing your poppy-seed bun, ask who are 'we'? In Lviv, if you ask me, 'we' are Mitteleuropeans.

For all the often fake claims of nation-states, and for all the vast mistakes that they made in the last century, they remain the principal arbiters of politics. We are prepared to accept that their actions in our name – we, the citizens of Britain, or Australia, or the United States, or India, or China – can still secure our best interests as individuals and as members of a national group. For example, we expect our states to take adequate measures to respond to the present economic crisis. Increasingly, we also understand (borrowing from Lord Palmerston) that while our nation-states may not have permanent friends, they do have permanent interests which include cooperation to cope with problems that one state cannot deal with on its own. The 'we' crosses frontiers. There is increasingly a 'we' that is global, a 'we' that feels itself part of the international community, a 'we' that knows about the big issues on the international agenda. These larger problems, which form the main part of this book, are often the product, as though part of a Hegelian dialectic, of the solution of previous problems. We have today lost the order brought on by our response to xenophobic nationalism and preserved in an uneasy truce for forty years between two mightily armed powers, one democratic, the other totalitarian. A major challenge over the next years will be to prevent domestic calamity – jobs lost, homes abandoned, businesses bust – luring us bit by bit into the sort of economic nationalism that less than a century ago had such terrible political consequences.

Today's problems can be solved, doubtless at the cost of the emergence of new problems. There is no inevitability about disaster, even though some predict that survival until the end of the twenty-first century is now no better than an even-ways bet.[4] We – nation-states working together in different and varying formations – have to steer a course between all too many rocks and hard places. There is no simple formula for survival, no global plan waiting to be set in place, no institution that will provide compass and captain for the world. But there is hope and there is reason. As ever in human affairs, there are better and there are worse ways of going about coping with the predicament of living together on this planet. So do not expect this book to provide a manifesto or manual for survival. What it aims to do is to suggest ways in which realistic liberal internationalists should try to answer today's and tomorrow's principal problems and shape a better future.

As I have already argued, the state is pivotally important in political life. It binds a society to territory, which is clearly delineated on every map. See, for example, the border of Iraq, drawn above all by Britain with an eye to the discovery of oil reserves as she shared out Ottoman territory with France after the First World War. This invented border defines a state that presently runs from Kurdistan in the north across the plateau that separates the Tigris from the Euphrates to the flood plains and marshlands in the south. Turkey, Iran, Kuwait, Saudi Arabia and Syria are on the other side of the Iraqi state's borders, and they too have borders of their own marked out by geography, chance and the retreat of old empires. The society and the territory that in human and geographical terms comprise the state are in their turn bound to the exercise of authority. What the German political economist Max Weber regarded as the state's internal monopoly of the use of force (theoretical at least, though not, as in Iraq, always actual) gives it the principal element for government across its territory and the basis on which the fundamental political identity and loyalty of individuals living within its borders are defined. With the ultimate authority to govern – that is to tax, regulate, protect and defend – states have traditionally been the cause and the community for which people 'mobilize, kill others and commit their lives'.[5]

Because of their supposed ability to impose order within their territories – their jurisdictions, as the lawyers put it – states have been the main recognized actors in international affairs for five hundred years. Each state accepts other states' authority and supreme discretion over their jurisdiction. Relations between states rest on the theoretical premise of recognized equality such that 'none is entitled to command; none is required to obey'.[6] States may agree to share their sovereignty up to limits that they themselves determine: the limits are pushed a fairly short distance in the UN, rather further in the EU. But the state itself is the authority that determines where and how the sharing is done. The state is supreme within its territory, and outside it states are theoretically equal though plainly not always so in practice.

The flags that flutter bravely outside the UN's skyscraper in Manhattan's September breeze, when heads of state and government from all around the world attend that body's annual General Assembly, represent the 192 countries which are members. Each has its own national anthem, few as stirring as Italy's 'Fratelli d'Italia'; each its own symbols and system of governance; each its own pretensions to authority. Bogotá and Tirana claim to control their own national frontiers; Kinshasa and Mogadishu feign to levy taxes and dispense justice across their terrain; Queen Elizabeth's writ purportedly runs in Northern Ireland's Crossmaglen and President Hu's among the Uigurs in China's far north-west. When states cooperate, their jointly exercised authority fills in the cracks that may appear from time to time between the manifestations of individual state sovereignty, so that a threat that one state on its own cannot overcome may be resolved by collective action by several states. In taking such action, although the United States, Bangladesh and Belgium are notionally equal, the power – especially the military and economic muscle – of the world's only superpower gives it a greater authority than others in shaping the world for better and conceivably for worse. The super-power can, like every previous big country in history, throw its weight around and get its own way. It has been a feature of what communist apologists first called American hegemony – a feature that has served to sustain it since the Second World War – that the US has usually been extraordinarily restrained in using its own power.

Unswerving belief in the efficacy of states and sovereignty seems to have been scattered like thistledown in a gale as the last century turned into the present one. How much these days can states do and achieve on their own? Can they secure the welfare and safety of their citizens, policing borders, regulating economic activity, preventing financial ruin, protecting public health, avoiding environmental catastrophe? As the vocabulary of state aspiration becomes more ambitious, with political leaders promising almost every sort of fulfilled happiness, the capacity of states to deliver on these promises appears to become ever more suspect. A peaceful life, let alone a happy one, often seems more problematic than rhetoric suggests should be the case.

America's Institute for National Strategic Studies (INSS) underlined this point in its assessment of the last year of the last century. It raised, for example, the threat of organized crime, noting that criminal groups were involved in buying, selling and moving around the world humans, narcotics, arms, metals, minerals, endangered flora and fauna, and even Freon gas (a chlorofluorocarbon used in commerce and industry). It went on to note that these groups were engaged in large-scale money laundering, fraud, extortion, bribery, economic espionage, smuggling of embargoed commodities, multinational auto theft, international prostitution, industrial and technological espionage, bank fraud, financial market manipulation, counterfeiting, contract murder and corruption. This insidious threat, as the Institute calls it, 'covertly challenges the state's prerogatives and control over its own activities'.[7] I'll say. All this is complex and baffling, though we see every day its consequences in our newspapers and in our own lives. We read about poisonings and the murky activities of 'retired' KGB agents in London restaurants and on London streets. A friend of mine from Hong Kong, visiting Beijing, found by identifying cigarette burns on the leather upholstery that he was being chauffeured in the Chinese capital in his own car, recently stolen back home. Driving from the centre of Tirana to its airport five years ago, I counted one by one over 350 Mercedes – a limousine crop harvested by Albanian entrepreneurs (of a sort) in Europe's rich north. In Naples, our fellow Europeans in vain awaited the nod from the Mafia to collect the mounds of refuse from the gutters. It took the army and interventions by Prime Ministers Prodi and Berlusconi over several months to begin shifting the stinking garbage.

Crime groups organize networks of drug producers, processors, traffickers and street sellers which often work closely together. The INSS cited an example identified by French researchers which described a network involving criminals from Latin America, eastern Europe, Israel, Africa and Pakistan. Hashish that came originally from Pakistan was carried to Mombasa, Kenya, where it was put into cargoes of tea and reshipped to Haifa, Israel, through Durban, South Africa. The drugs were then put on to a ship that carried cargo to Constanza, Romania, every two weeks. From Constanza it was transported by way of Bratislava, Slovakia, to Italy for consumption there. The head of the network was a German citizen of Ugandan origin who worked for a Romanian company. Each of the countries through which the hashish was moved has its own border police, internal police, customs regulations, drug-enforcement agencies and other manifestations of sober and serious sovereignty.

Organized crime and the trafficking of drugs – a more valuable traded international commodity than iron and steel – are only two examples of a more general phenomenon: the impact of globalization on the pretensions of the nation-state (Chapters 9 and 10). What can states do on their own to cope with the problems that threaten their citizens, for instance epidemic disease, the threat of which causes so much apprehension? I recall flying through Singapore at the height of the SARS scare in 2003. My plane to Australia was almost as empty as the *Mary Celeste*. The globalization of threats comes in many forms. We recall the antecedents of the 9/11 terrorists, all citizens of a new, more open and interdependent world. The leader of the terrorist cell, Mohammed Atta, for example, was an urban planner from Cairo who worked in Hamburg with the three friends who trained with him in Afghanistan for the murderous attacks in the USA. Recent environmental surveys estimate that about one third of the toxic mercury pollutants (produced by the burning of coal) that get into American soil and waterways come from other countries, especially China.

The 'father' of the Pakistan nuclear weapon, A. Q. Khan (whose activities are covered in Chapter 5), toured the world in the late 1990s trying to peddle home-made tool kits to construct weapons of mass destruction. He helped Iran, among others. North Korea, shorn of anything to sell save counterfeit money and drugs, was thought to harbour the ambition to hawk bespoke if primitive bombs to any state or terrorist group that could afford to buy. Globalization was said to be a principal vector of the triumph of pluralism in the last century. But today the dark side of globalization seems to be a threat to the sovereignty of all states, including those that have embraced liberal values.

Even the mighty have taken a tumble. Well before its blood and treasure drained away so incontinently into the sands of Mesopotamia, American leadership and technological hubris had already been discomfited. After al-Qaeda's attacks on the American embassies in Nairobi and Dar-es-Salaam in August 1998, Washington rained Tomahawk missiles on suspected terrorist sites in Sudan and Afghanistan.

Over three-quarters of a billion dollars' worth of cruise missiles destroyed a pharmaceutical factory near Khartoum and a terrorist training camp near Afghanistan's border with Pakistan. At the latter, probably six terrorists were killed. Many of the missiles failed to explode. Russian intelligence reported that Osama bin Laden sold a number of these unexploded missiles to China for over $10 million. Other missiles landed in Pakistan. Two Pakistanis were killed, according to General Hamid Gul, the former head of his country's military intelligence, and the Pakistanis are believed to have used the missiles that failed to explode in their country for designing their own missiles. This abortive venture was entitled Operation Infinite Reach.[8] The reach may be infinite, if inaccurate, but the hegemony can no longer be exercised with confident and magisterial military swagger.

Economics appeared for a time to pass all this political turbulence and uncertainty by, heedless of headlines. The five years after the attacks on the Twin Towers and the Pentagon saw further bombings in Bali, Casablanca, Istanbul, Madrid and London. There were wars in Afghanistan and Iraq and heavy fighting between Hezbollah and Israel, primarily in Lebanon. Iran and North Korea were locked in arguments with America and other countries about their nuclear ambitions. The Middle East peace process was deadlocked. Russia's relations with her neighbours grew increasingly fractious. The price of oil soared. Yet the world economy during this period grew faster than in any comparable period since the mid-seventies. GDP growth per head went up by 3.2 per cent a year, the highest figure that has ever been recorded. What did markets then know that worried political leaders overlooked? They recognized perhaps that growth in China and India was leading a deflationary boom similar to that triggered by Chicago and the American Midwest in the late nineteenth century. And what did markets know as an asset bubble grew and grew in America and the princes of banking harnessed their glittering wagons to its effervescent ascent? But before America's banking crash in late 2007 and 2008 the global economy had swept tens of millions of the hitherto poor into relative prosperity. They could eat better, dress better, live longer, be better educated, buy their children Nikes and iPods. What did the crumbling of age-old political truths matter to them? Why should they worry about the fragmentation of the political authority that had once kept them safe by the globalization that apparently made them better off?

Political scientists have their own explanations for what has happened, shaping meaning out of random events, conceptualizing from incidents enacted by individuals. Is this really a science at all? It has method, but how much do the docketing and enumeration capture the essence of what is happening? We know that political science cares little for the length of Cleopatra's nose, so how much can it comprehend what Jorge Luis Borges called an 'impulse more profound than reason'?[9] We can trace the origin of the modern state to the seventeenth-century Peace of Westphalia. We can study the accumulation of capital, the development of central banking, the rise of centralized bureaucracies, the industrialization of war in the eighteenth and nineteenth centuries. We can tick off the great changes in our democracies – winning the right to vote, mass education, the coming of welfare capitalism. But how do we explain the psychological mood of investors as euphoria and panic follow hard on each other's heels in one financial crash after another? Isaac Newton, one of the greatest minds in the history of the world, lost a fortune speculating in South Sea stock in the early eighteenth century. 'I can calculate the motions of the heavenly bodies,' he said gloomily, 'but not the madness of people'. Or how should we interpret the events of St Vitus' Day 1914 in Sarajevo, the Archduke Franz Ferdinand's Graf & Stift limousine that took the wrong turning, the mental state of the 19-year-old consumptive student Gavrilo Princip, who suddenly found the archduke and his wife in the sights of his revolver? According to Claud Cockburn, there used to be a game played at the end of each year in the 1920s and 30s in the editorial room of *The Times*. Journalists would compete to devise the most improbable imaginary headline. The winner one year was – 'Archduke Found Alive; First World War Fought In Vain'. No Princip, no car losing its way – would history have been different? 'The terrible Ifs accumulate', as Winston Churchill wrote.[10]

So how do we interpret what is arbitrary, villainous, poetic, unique? Was it only long-term economic weakness and bureaucratic overreach which brought down the Berlin Wall? To be sure, there were short- and long-term sources of Soviet malaise and colonial weariness;

there was also more immediately Hungary's announcement in 1989 that its recently undertaken obligations under the UN Convention on Refugees were incompatible with its secret treaty on refugees with East Germany. But the action itself, the destruction of the wall stone by stone, the unwillingness of the soldiers to open fire, makes no more sense than Luther on All Souls Eve in 1517 nailing his arguments against indulgences (so tradition tells us) to the door of Wittenberg's castle church. At least, these actions make no sense unless we recognize that they were personal, emotional, passionate, in a sense lyrical. They were the poetry of the deed. Ultimately, while some prescient individual scholars predicted what would happen, most theories and branches of political science failed miserably in 1989. They failed too, when well-educated, middle-class Muslims from strongly governed states – not poor, uneducated, unemployed boys from failed states – turned civil aircraft into precision guided weapons and flew them into the symbolic heart of America's global commercial and military power. So political scientists rarely tell us more than part of the story. But they still help to explain how the world got to where it is today, and why the gap between presumption and reality is growing, as nation-states so often flex and flail their imagined autonomous sovereignty like boxers beating the air with their gloved fists.

2

The Journey So Far

We ... made you into Nations and tribes, that ye may know each other. (Not that you may despise each other.)

The Quran

Nations, like men, do not have wings; they make their journeys on foot, step by step.   Juan Bautista Alberdi, 1837

Who are the Slovaks? I can't seem to place them.

David Lloyd George, 1916

The disadvantage of men not knowing the past is that they do not know the present.   G. K. Chesterton, 1933

The search for the origins of the state, for the opening up of the modern world, yields numerous answers. Adam Smith, in Book IV of *The Wealth of Nations*, in the second half of the eighteenth century, decided the clock should start at the end of the fifteenth century, with the momentous discoveries of the Americas and of a passage to the East Indies via the Cape of Good Hope – in Smith's words, 'the two greatest and most important events in the history of mankind'. This great age of European sea power was later to be dubbed the 'Columbian Age', ended only by the invention and spread of the railway and telegraph.

For Machiavelli the starting point for the modern age was Charles VIII's invasion of Italy in 1494 with a French army that looked like a professional force. The French cavalry was not the feudal host of old, even though its members might ape past codes of chivalric conduct. They moved and fought in formation, with clear lines of command, ready to deliver the *coup de grâce* to opposing infantry formations once their gunners had scattered these pike-men. Cities long considered strong surrendered at the approach of the new bronze cannon that Charles brought in his train. Charles's soldiers were not mercenaries, paid bands under the command of a contractor (*condottieri*), rather like today's navvies on a building site, though there were many such operating in Italy at the time. They were officers of the French Crown paid out of the royal treasury and deployed in organized and mutually supportive formations and combinations. It was an army whose composition would later have been recognized by Marlborough and Wellington.

In *The Art of War*, the only book that Machiavelli published in his own lifetime, he argued that the ability to wage war depended less and less on a small professional class – whether made up of aristocrats or mercenaries – and more and more on the ability of a whole society to put effective military forces into the field. He reacted strongly against the predominance in Italy in his own time of mercenary forces, the *campagnie de ventura*, led by a *condottiere*. The richest of the great powers in Europe in the fourteenth and fifteenth centuries were the Italian city-states; their mastery lay in their treasuries which were filled to the brim with ready cash. This made Italy a magnet, an El Dorado, for the mercenaries, the 'free lancers', who were useful to trading states like Florence or Milan which lacked the vast agricultural hinterlands necessary to feudalism and the feudal knight-based military. But by the end of the fifteenth century, it was obvious – at least to Machiavelli – that the mercenary era was ending. The careers of some of the most notable of these soldiers of fortune showed why. The Essex man Sir John Hawkwood, the most notorious mercenary of his age (the second half of the fourteenth century), had extorted money from terrified city-states, offering his bloody sword to the highest bidder.[1] Disloyalty, dishonesty, greed and unheroic caution were usually associated with men like Hawkwood, who nevertheless was immortalized in a magnificent fresco by Paolo Uccello in the cathedral in Florence – the city fathers wanted him, for their own purposes, to represent civic virtues rather different from the reality of his life. Machiavelli regarded the Englishman as a typical example of the military system that could not and should not last: the *condottieri* were unreliable; they were blackmailers; they were deserters; when they were unemployed, off the books of a city-state, it was difficult to distinguish between them and brigands. For the *condottiere*, his company of armed men was an irreplaceable investment. He was therefore reluctant to get them to do what they were paid to do, namely to fight. They were cautious professionals, with a wary, even comradely regard for others in their trade. The ability to wage war successfully clearly depended more and more on the power to put an army of the state into the field, to maintain it and to command it. This required states with the sort of immense power commanded by Francis I of France and Charles V, the Holy Roman Emperor. Machiavelli worried about how a republic could survive in a world like this. He rightly thought it would need an army of well-drilled conscripts.

This is the point of modern departure. Between the end of the fifteenth century and the beginning of the seventeenth, the distinction grew between those states able to keep up to date with the latest military technology, the latest fortifications, the latest tactics – all of which called for huge cash investment – and those states unable to do so. As a result of their weakness, the poorer states that were left behind in this military revolution were subjugated or destroyed. This was the ultimate military means test. Those that passed the test emerged as strong states having suppressed, usually violently, those feudal relics that might try to rival their own power. The mercenary story does not, incidentally, end here. We shall come back to the use of mercenaries when we consider later the deployment of modern military forces by states that cannot afford to put in the field traditional armies of the size needed to accomplish their security objectives, or cannot persuade enough young men and women (now that the draft is largely ended) to serve professionally in the uniforms of the state at the price that the state is prepared to pay them.

The second great dividing line to emerge between the medieval and the modern world – it follows from the first – was money. As Robert de Balsac, a veteran of the Italian campaigns of Charles VIII, wrote: 'Most important of all, success in war depends on having enough money to provide whatever the enterprise needs.'[2] It was cash that saved some of the smaller nations of Europe, such as the United Provinces, from being swept away entirely by the bigger states. Money in the sixteenth century came from trade, and the control of trade became the critical precondition of war. Making war and trading were therefore almost synonymous. The privateer with his 'letter of marque', giving him an official warrant to raid and capture the merchant shipping of an enemy nation, was the maritime equivalent of the *condottiere*, and it was hard to tell the difference between privateer and pirate. I recall a tour of the great cathedral in Santiago de Compostela that contains a plaque referring to Sir Francis Drake. Our Spanish guide introduced him to us as 'the English pirate', hardly surprising since he had raided the Galician coast. 'I think you mean the seafaring hero and explorer,' an English friend intervened. The exploits of privateers were given official licence by mid-sixteenth-century negotiations that proposed two great 'Amity lines', establishing zones west of the Azores and south of the Tropic of Cancer where naval warfare could take place, in the name of trade, without jeopardizing the peace of Europe. In the Cold War, there was a similar understanding that proxy wars could be fought in the Third World without disturbing the uneasy peace between East and West in Europe.

Trade was only part of the picture. How could a sixteenth-century warrior prince turn the wealth gained from trade into power? It was possible to bring spices from the New World to the Old, but what happened then? Traditionally, a prince raised money through sacking an opponent's cities or foraging in enemy countryside, which defrayed the costs of campaigning. This provided the ready resources to pay mercenaries until there had been a military victory. As borders were to some extent stabilized (though in many places they remained pretty fluid until the Second World War), order was established and trade was developed; taxation became the rationalized means of legal despoliation. But neither pillage nor (as became clear in the seventeenth century) taxation really provided the certainty and continuity that a prince needed. The breakthrough came with the development of credit and finance.

The early masters of this evolution were the Dutch. The bankers of Antwerp lent money, for example, to the famous merchant family, the Fuggers in Augsburg, Bavaria, who in turn used it to finance the Spanish war effort against their rebellious Dutch subjects in what later became the independent United Provinces. The bankers of the Low Countries did not seem to bother too much about this, so long as future deliveries of American silver were available as collateral. Nothing should be allowed to get in the way of business. The Fuggers went bankrupt when Philip II of Spain defaulted on his debts in the 1550s. He was not the first prince to take the money and run, but this was a short-sighted princely policy. The most effective leaders, for instance in England and in Holland, decided that the best way to ensure for themselves a steady supply of money at a reasonable rate of interest was to pay what they owed on time. Moreover, they also learned that it was better – and less costly – to tax at home than to borrow abroad. This required the presence of financiers and merchants for them to tax in the first place. The cash-rich Dutch were more adept than others – with the French learning fast – at creating a capital market with state bonds, backed by tax revenues, available for purchase by their burghers at safe rates of interest. Was it pure chance that the English, who founded the East India Company in 1600, only began to succeed as a new world power, beating the Dutch in the process, when they acquired a Dutch king of their own, William of Orange, at the end of the seventeenth century and founded the Bank of England?[3]

Steadily, the ability to make both war and money emerged as two of the key indicators of political success, but there was never an umbilical link between success in finance and success in war. Warriors did not always make good businessmen. In the early modern age, Spain – the land of the conquistadors, which was to give the word 'guerrilla' to the world – was good at making war. Yet it became a backwater for two centuries, isolated, impoverished, backward, worn out by the sun and scraping by in history's shade. Nor did financial success guarantee political success. Venice and Genoa were cash fort-resses, like the Dutch. Like them, too, they used public credit to raise their military forces. Unlike them, they did not become successful modern states because they did not have large enough populations. So it is misleading to draw a straightforward connection between money and war. What really linked money and war, and gave direction to both, was political organization.

The sixteenth and early seventeenth centuries – the age of the Reformation and Counter-Reformation, Copernicus and Bacon, the arrival of syphilis and the departure of the *Mayflower* – produced an extraordinarily diverse political landscape in Europe. There were sovereign city-states like Florence, Genoa, Venice and Dubrovnik. Some could barely cling on to their independence; others ran their own empires. There were leagues of city-states. The cantons of the Swiss Confederation specialized in providing the mercenaries for European princes. The Hanseatic League focused on trade. There were the sprawling domains left over from the Middle Ages, most prominent among them the Holy Roman Empire. Finally, there were what we would recognize as proto-nation-states – notable among them France, England, Holland and Portugal.

Among these different kinds of political organization, those which we can call states, whether of the city or the proto-nation kind, were distinguished from their competitors first by the development of a well-defined internal hierarchy. The same authority had control over weights and measures, taxation and coinage. There were the makings of what we would today call a level playing field. Individuals, companies, guilds, aristocrats could not absent themselves from the duties they disliked, defecting from the provisions of trade treaties or from military obligations. The state also developed credibility externally. The territory within which it laid down the law was by and large fixed. This provided greater certainty in negotiating with outside polities and in redressing external grievances or violations. More important, it established a credible link between the threat of war and the means to wage it. Here lay the problem for city-states, city-leagues and medieval empires. The multiplicity of relationships that they covered produced immediate and abiding uncertainties. Who could tell exactly what duties and rights bound together princes and vassals in the Holy Roman Empire or the Diet of the Hanseatic League? How could one fathom who exactly owed what responsibility or obligation to whom at any given moment in the murky politics of Venice? Machiavelli did not know whether the men of Pisa would fight for Florence if he were to arm them; Charles V could not be certain whether his German princes would fight for him in his titanic struggle with Francis I; in the event, many of them declined to do so. The principal key to political success in that era, from which success in war and finance derived, was whether a prince was capable of binding together all the political interests of a defined territory in a credible manner. It was a very modern challenge.

At the turn of the seventeenth century Europe was divided between Catholics and Protestants and between sovereign rulers who were jockeying for power. Though the Holy Roman Empire was the dominant political force on the continent, it was a fragmented dominion of duchies, counties, cities and bishoprics which professed only a notional fealty to their Habsburg emperors. As Catholics, the Habsburgs also had to deal with the expansion of Protestantism within their realm. This had been tolerated in the second half of the previous century but had now become politically contentious with the outbreak of sectarian violence and the emergence of alliances along religious lines. The Thirty Years War (1618–48) saw Emperor Ferdinand II bidding to revive Catholic universality, to stamp out Protestantism and to assert control over his empire. For the Habsburgs, and for central Europe in particular, this war was a disaster. C. V. Wedgwood, still the conflict's most humane historian, wrote of it: 'Almost all [the combatants] were actuated by fear rather than lust of conquest or passion of faith. They wanted peace and they fought for thirty years to be sure of it. They did not learn then, and have not learned since, that war only breeds war.'[4] By the war's end, Germany was ruined, with between a third and half of its people dead, its trade wiped out, its culture ravaged. The new political reality in Europe was codified in the Treaties of Münster and Osnabrück which are popularly known as the Peace of Westphalia, sometimes known also as the Peace of Exhaustion. These treaties settled territorial disputes between the Holy Roman Empire, France, Sweden, and the German Princes; most important, they finally accepted that, while there was some protection for minorities, each ruler could determine the religion of his own state as first laid down at the Treaty of Augsburg in 1555.

From this terrible war only the fittest European polities emerged intact, but the war also gave birth so far as many historians (including Henry Kissinger) and political scientists are concerned to the rudiments of the modern state system. The Thirty Years War demonstrated that it was no longer enough to pay soldiers for the campaign season.

They needed to be paid throughout the year. The practice began in Holland, which could afford the tremendous expense. When the state paid soldiers for the whole year, it could for the first time make them do three things. It could make them drill; it could make them dig; and it could make them disciplined. Drill transformed the infantry into the most important unit on the battlefield. It taught them to fire in time, to countermarch and to reload, while each successive rank fired and countermarched. In this way they could deliver a continuous stream of fire on the battlefield; they projected more lead for every minute of fighting. Drill also ensured that they could withstand the withering power of opposing gunnery, hold firm in the face of the cavalry charge and deliver the bayonet charge, their ultimate weapon. Digging transformed the face of Europe as vast new fortifications, pioneered by the French under Vauban and the Dutch under Coehorn, proved able to withstand the heaviest guns, to silence any artillery that drew too close and to enfilade approaching infantry.[5] Defending or besieging a fortress like one of Vauban's was a long-term commitment. Discipline, finally, could only be imposed when soldiers themselves were fully professional, no longer free agents but subject to courts martial. These three developments in the conduct of war were pioneered by Holland and especially by Prince Maurice of Orange (1567–1625). This helped Holland to survive and prosper in a century of conflict, rapine and brutality, even though it was in a state of war for most of the time. Others imitated the Dutch, centralizing state power and finding new ways to raise money. In the 1630s Cardinal Richelieu in France, for example, established control over the whole country, including the aristocracy, appointing a civilian bureaucracy (the *intendants*) and turning independent liveried aristocratic soldiers into musketeers in the service of the Crown. The famed disciplinarian in Louis XIV's army was Lieutenant Colonel Martinet.

The Peace of Westphalia consolidated a recognizable system of states, in which each one possessed and recognized in the others essential characteristics of organization, capacity and legitimacy. As we have seen, sovereignty became a territorial monopoly with state boundaries and an internal administrative infrastructure, comprising a bureaucracy and the means of tax collection and the levying of armed forces. States sent permanent diplomatic representatives abroad. At the same time that political boundaries were being redrawn, society within these state frontiers was also changing. Before the Thirty Years War citizenship had been multidimensional. There were two currents of political authority, one ecclesiastical, the other feudal. Before the sixteenth century the dominion of the Catholic Church in Europe was largely uncontested; the Church was present everywhere and the picture of medieval citizenship and government was complex. 'Emperors, kings, dukes, knights, popes, archbishops, guilds and cities exercised overlapping secular power over the same territory in a system that looks much more like a modern three-dimensional network than the hierarchical state order that replaced it.'[6] The Peace of Westphalia excluded the Holy See; it effectively ended the Holy Roman Empire, by recognizing the sovereignty of many of its members. So by the middle of the seventeenth century the universal communion of the Catholic Church was overthrown and the temporal power of Christendom was undermined. This underlined what had in a sense been the great political problem for Europe since the Reformation: if sovereignty did not derive from the Universal Church – with all the symbolism of coronation, chrism, orbs and sceptres – then whence did it derive?

There were three answers. For Machiavelli, it was simple. Power justified itself. You had sovereignty because you could exercise power and the end of protecting or enhancing that capacity justified whatever means you used. *Raison d'état* could explain away whatever the state did in order to hang on to its prerogative of applying authority. Machiavelli still enjoys a vogue today among those who like to be regarded as sophisticated realists, taking the world for what it is rather than for what we would like it to be, accepting that we – hard-boiled citizens of the world – do the least harm by setting our sights on moving the political caravan from one moral lowest common denominator to another. The second, less specific answer was that sovereignty could be identified when others in the community of states recognized your own existence as a state, and saw that you were capable of exercising authority in your agreed space. Third, and more subtly, the Dutch jurist Hugo Grotius, 'generally reckoned to be the first major theorist of international law',[7] argued in the 1620s that there was a natural law, based upon shared humanity, which joined together those separate bands of people who also had their own group laws. He described the emergent states of Europe as being part of a system in which there existed *popular* sovereignty – sovereignty vested in the people, at least to the extent that citizens could disobey a tyrannical ruler.

A further change in international relations began in the middle of the seventeenth century though it was not enshrined until the Treaty of Utrecht in 1713, which ended the War of the Spanish Succession and separated the crowns of France and Spain for ever. This was the belief in the balance of power. Henry Kissinger has written that 'Europe was thrown into balance-of-power politics when the first choice, the medieval dream of universal empire, collapsed and a host of states of more or less equal strength arose from the ashes of that ancient aspiration . . . The balance-of-power system did not purport to avoid crises or even wars. When working properly, it was meant to limit both the ability of states to dominate others and the scope of conflicts. Its goal was not peace so much as stability and moderation.'[8] The balance of power reflected one of the core values of what we now call the Enlightenment. Reason replaced the medieval geocentric universe with God on his throne managing everything. This helped us to discover that all spiritual and physical phenomena taken together formed a stable and ordered whole. We could in due course find the causes for everything, patiently applying Francis Bacon's scientific method, and one thing – like the elements in the American constitution, one of the greatest products of the Enlightenment – always balanced another. The balance of power endured as a theory of international relations for 200 years, though it was put under severe strain by the Napoleonic Wars and by the rise of Italy, Germany, the United States and Japan; some historians argue that even the First World War represented a proper functioning of the balance of power, with most of the rest of Europe going to war to prevent German domination of the continent.

From Utrecht to the beginning of the First World War the political order of Europe – based on the balance of power – remained essentially stable. There were, it is true, numerous wars in those two centuries, and some testing shocks to the system. But it managed to adapt to external changes and suppressed or integrated those who challenged the system itself. The decapitation of Louis XVI in 1793 was one of the most dramatic of the events that helped end the Age of Enlightenment, but the European state system and the elite who ran it remained committed by and large to the political doctrines of the Enlightenment for another century. Throughout the nineteenth century Europe's aristocracy worked hard to preserve the rational, often absolutist states of the Enlightenment age, curbing the demands of democrats and nationalists and ensuring that the traditional system of states functioned harmoniously. Where nationalist and democratic demands could not be thwarted, for example in Italy and Germany, revolutions were made acceptable by the wiles of statesmen – Cavour and Bismarck – who moulded them just as Talleyrand had rehabilitated post-Napoleonic France.

The competition between these European states in the nineteenth century would often be channelled into the scramble for land and resources in Africa and Asia. In the last quarter of the nineteenth century over a quarter of the globe's land surface was grabbed by six European countries. Even the polar regions were nominally brought under European sway. It was not only European weapons and the successful bureaucratization of violence that enabled Europe to bring weaker African and Asian polities into their system. As William H. McNeill has pointed out, the application of fossil fuels to the problem of deploying and supplying troops – the launching of steamships and construction of railways – helped Europe to project power to previously remote and impenetrable places.[9] When European doctors developed an effective prophylaxis against malaria, a main barrier to imperial expansion was overcome. Where Europe led the way, the USA by the end of the nineteenth century followed into what Henry Cabot Lodge (the US senator who led the opposition to his country's participation in the League of Nations) called 'the waste places of the Earth'. The colonial powers in Africa tried to establish governable communities – drawing lines in places that seemed convenient, pulling together tribes and clans with different languages, interests and cultures into a pattern that resembled a continent of subordinate states. They haggled over places of which they were wholly ignorant in the scramble for real estate. Lord Salisbury, Britain's prime minister for much of the 1890s, observed, 'We have been giving away mountains and rivers and lakes to each other, only hindered by the small impediment that we never knew exactly where they were.'

This brief history has so far focused on Europe. The reason is simple. The development of the nation-state was very much a European phenomenon. That is not to deny that there were other forms of governance, other bonds of obligation, other sorts of community elsewhere. In Asia, for example, the empire of the Qing, the Mughal dominions in India and the development of princely states there, and the feudal shogunate system in Japan, all had their own distinct characteristics – aspects of what Christopher Bayly calls 'archaic globalization'.[10] But in the nineteenth century the European 'gunpowder states' and their colonial appetites reshaped the world order. Mughal power in India had begun to fall apart in the eighteenth century; in the words of a Mughal poet 'the face of the sky and earth was changed'. The East India Company and then the British colonial regime slipped and, when necessary, bludgeoned their way into the vacuum. In China, within not much more than forty years of Lord Macartney's ignominious embassy there in 1793 to try to open up its market to British trade, Britain's gifts in Macartney's words hiding 'their diminished heads', the Chinese were demolished in the first Opium War. For China, a century of humiliation followed. Commodore Matthew Perry forced Japan to open its doors to foreign trade in the 1850s, the real catalyst for the Meiji restoration when imperial power was re-established and the industrialization and militarization of the country was accelerated. So the West imposed its way of doing things on even the most ancient civilizations. In the case of the United States and the white dominions of Canada, Australia, New Zealand and South Africa, Britain exported it wholesale along with the infantry who helped to build those new countries.

Why did the European order collapse in 1914? Doubtless demography played a part in the political convulsions in Europe in the twentieth century, with a growing population hitting the buffers of traditional rural ways of life in central and eastern Europe. There were proximate political causes too. First, the Habsburg dynasty, already smarting from the blows of nationalists in Italy and Germany, felt its grip slipping in the Balkans, where the Serbian nationalist movement denied the essential legitimacy of one of the great European empires. It became increasingly difficult to reconcile the competing claims of European nationalists to Europe's conservative, aristocratic order; the ascent of new states, especially outside Europe, jeopardized the harmony of the overall system; and the rise of new technology, especially the railway, created an imperative to take rapid action in the event of war. Speedy mobilization was one of the clear lessons of the Russo-Japanese War. In the summer of 1914 traditional diplomacy proved too slow to deal with a crisis speeded up by this technology which happened to provide the preconditions of survival. Military action no longer seemed subordinate to political control. While diplomacy was too slow to avert the crisis, once war had begun, how could it be stopped?

Carl von Clausewitz, the great Prussian conceptualizer of military activity at the beginning of the nineteenth century, found it difficult to distinguish between limited and total war. But he was clear that war was an extension of politics, and a means to an end. So why did the European war not end after the first battle of the Marne in the autumn of 1914, which killed off any chance of a decisive German victory (albeit at heavy cost to the French)? The German chief of the general staff, Moltke, suffered a nervous breakdown with the failure of his gamble to deliver a swift knockout blow. Why was there no immediate peace? The terrible problem for Europe's elites was that they were riding a tiger – nationalism – and they could not clamber off its back. National passions had been aroused. National honour was at stake. National survival hung in the balance. 'Your Country Needs You' – it needed you to be part of mass attacks that appeared, while making scant military sense, to set the national will of one side against the national will of the other. The victor was the machine gun. There could be no exit from this Gethsemane, no end to this bloodshed, partly because Europe's elites dared not incite the wrath of their own peoples. Europe's leaders were as frightened of their citizens, whom they had armed, as they were of one another. So the war ceased in a sense to be political, and became metaphysical, with awesome consequences. The French Republic and the German Empire collapsed. The Russian, Austro-Hungarian and Ottoman empires were ruined. What was the sentiment that held reason in its grip, squeezing the life from it? What was the dreadful romance that drove a stake into the heart of old Europe? Nationalism! For what had changed in the preceding century was not the means of government, but the relationship between government and the governed. Now there were not just states, but *nation-states*.

In the eighteenth century the American Declaration of Independence had explained in its magnificent preamble the distinction between mankind and man as citizen. 'When in the course of human events, it becomes necessary for one people to dissolve the political bonds which have connected them with another, and to assume among the powers of the earth, the separate and equal station to which the Laws of Nature and of Nature's God entitle them, a decent respect to the opinions of mankind requires that they should declare the causes which impel them to the separation.' For residents of the American colonies it was George III's misdemeanours and those of the ministers who governed in his name that sealed their sense of common citizenship and nationhood and 'impelled them to the separation'. (It should also be remembered, though it has no place in America's founding myth, that the colonists disliked the Crown asserting its prerogative to deny them the right to take over Indian lands.) For the colonists, their ruler had lost his right to the loyalty of his subjects and with it his possession of sovereignty because of his bad and tyrannical government. The contract described by Grotius had been broken.

A common language, family and clan ties, a sense of shared roots, the popularity of well-known ballads and stories, commercial co-operation, religious affinities – all these could create a deep and rewarding kinship within a state. This point was strongly made by John Jay, first Chief Justice of the US, in the Federalist Papers, the essays published in the late 1780s advocating ratification of the new American Constitution. The neighbourhood was where men and women felt most comfortable and the extension of neighbourhood provided them with a political and cultural habitat. All this could be natural and unforced; it produced patriots like Ignacy Paderewski, the Polish composer and pianist who became prime minister of his country in 1919 in time for the Versailles Conference. It could also be a response to bad government by those seen as outsiders. The seeds of national sentiment were often planted by a government that could appear or be made to appear tyrannical and the representative of an external authority and set of interests. The development of a distinct cultural identity in Finland, for instance, was partly a response to rule first by Sweden and then by tsarist Russia. German nationalism was kindled by resistance to Napoleon with Herder and Fichte supplying the ideas. But national sentiment was also something that could be manufactured and force-fed. In 1861, at the opening session of the parliament of a united Italy, Massimo d'Azeglio (Piedmontese painter, politician and patriot) observed: 'Now that we have created Italy, we must start creating Italians', a process that arguably continues to this day as Italians still struggle to demonstrate that their country is more than Metternich's insulting description of it as 'a geographical expression'. Nation-states have from the start needed a language, grammars, dictionaries, folklore, a history of triumphs and betrayals. In the nineteenth century eugenics could also give them a notion of racial solidarity and racial superiority. Blood brought a spurious homogeneity, not least in wartime. The body of the unknown soldier at the Arc de Triomphe was exhumed from an area at Verdun thought to be free of Jewish and Negro corpses. In Britain, Lady Desborough – wife of the politician known before the award of his peerage as William Grenfell – gave a lunch party in 1919 'to meet the mother of the unknown warrior'.

In Britain, the Act of Union of 1707 (or 'Treaty' as Scottish historians would have it), which hammered England and Scotland together into the United Kingdom, was followed by an effort to create a sense of British identity with a heavy English tilt under a German king. At the beginning of the nineteenth century Scotland was transformed by a splurge of cultural invention worthy of its chief impresario, Sir Walter Scott. This produced tartans, kilts, trews, the fake poetry of Ossian, 'Burns Night' suppers (from speaking at any more of which, may the Lord preserve me) and Queen Victoria's Balmoral.[11]

The term 'nation-state' is now so common that it has almost become a banality. But it is a mass of contradictions. The state itself is a supremely rational organization, but it has had to contain the particular attachments of language, culture, race and blood that go to make up the nation. These are more than the stuff of romance. They are thought to reflect a higher order to which man must subjugate himself, and that act of subjugation has a spiritual intensity. The

British ambassador to the United States during the First World War, Cecil Spring-Rice, wrote the hymn 'I vow to thee my country', familiar to those who attend funerals and memorial services in Britain. (It was sung, for example, at Princess Diana's funeral and also with proper commercial reverence as a B-side to 'Jerusalem' by the English cricket team after they had improbably defeated Australia in the Ashes series in 2005.) The second verse is a reminder of man's Christian duties to 'another country' whose 'ways are ways of gentleness and all her paths are peace'. But the first verse, nearer to home, lauds love of country:

> The love that asks no questions, the love that stands the test,
> That lays upon the altar the dearest and the best;
> The love that never falters, the love that pays the price,
> The love that makes undaunted the final sacrifice.

Spring-Rice was clearly thinking of those who had died from 1914 to 1918. They had certainly stood the test, paid the price, made the final sacrifice in obscene numbers. They had done it for King and Country, for Kaiser and Country, for Tsar and Country, for President and Country but not for Reason and not, as it turned out, for a better country and a better world.

Whatever was done by the nation, reflecting its romantic tryst with history, would find its apologists – the terror in revolutionary France, the purges and show trials in Russia, the rise of fascism in Italy, and the rise of Nazism in Germany. They were all celebrated, not least abroad. Milan Kundera described how, in Stalinist Czechoslovakia, the French poet Paul Eluard renounced a friend in Prague who was going to the gallows. Kundera noted, '. . . when an executioner kills, that is after all normal; but when a poet (and a great poet) sings in accompaniment, the whole system of values we considered sacrosanct has suddenly been shaken apart'.[12] Sartre, Gide and Pound were among those writers who at one time or another placed their literary talent at the service of evil. What accounts for their hymns to horror? Did these men know what was really going on? Perhaps they had no inkling of the truth, though we can catch a whiff of wilfulness in their ignorance. Yet surely the real reason for their songs of praise was that they were romantics. They agreed with the spirit of what was being done without bothering to know, inconveniently, too much about it. Whatever it was exactly, it sat well with their sense of history and destiny. And this romantic will, the will of the nation, what Marxists would come to call the will of history, gaining control of the ultimate political tool, the modern state, inflicted dreadful misery on the people of Europe and the world. When these people refused to bend the knee to the zeitgeist or the overriding moral exactions of the national clan, when they refused to acknowledge the spirit of history, when they refused to forget their common humanity, they became, so far as their rulers were concerned, superfluous. They passed from numbers to noughts. Tragically, the same fate sooner or later affected those who were swept away by the intoxication of nationalism.

Maybe we have identified the wrong heroes in our history. Perhaps like Kissinger we should give more praise to those like Metternich and Talleyrand who tried to restrain the tide of nationalism and romanticism. So long as the state remained true to its own early Enlightenment principles – with its sense of virtue and restraint – it was a relatively benign entity; infused with the romantic will, it quickly became murderous, a point which I suppose Margaret Thatcher was making in 1989 when she made a song and dance about going to Paris to celebrate the French revolution and the nationalism it unleashed. It is ironic that we condemn today Metternich and Talleyrand as cynical reactionaries who foolishly obstructed the development of nations, and in the next breath decry the deadly nationalism of the twentieth century's world wars. The heroes in every nation are invariably those who could summon the spirits of the nation-state. These were men who knew one big thing about politics. The big thing they knew – Napoleon and Garibaldi and even (in a wholly different class) Hitler with his virulent wickedness – was that the nation was bigger than the state, that it embodied more than the jurisdiction within borders. So they became compelling symbols, their words aphorisms, their deeds examples; they helped to form the popular idea of how citizens should behave as political entities.

The nation-state then is no grand resolution of government and identity. It is an entity in perpetual tension, a constant struggle for supremacy between a romantic national will and the rationale of good government. The contradiction was well understood by the Founding

Fathers of the United States, who tried to resolve it in the Constitution they drafted for their new nation-state.

Those nation-states which buried their young men in the cemeteries along the Somme and the Marne had not yet completed their own destruction. After the 1914–18 war and the Peace of Versailles, a new problem emerged in Europe with the disintegration of the last continental empires and the emergence of new nation-states. How could Europe in these circumstances deal with minorities? The question of how to protect minorities who found themselves on the wrong side of new state boundaries kept the peace talks going until 1923. The League of Nations that emerged from Versailles found that much of its time was spent arbitrating between states that were trying to protect members of their own nationality, who were maltreated by other states, or else transferring populations from one state to another, as in the case of Greece and Turkey. A new international principle appeared to have emerged: every nationality had final recourse not to international or national law, but to the protection of whatever state represented its nationality. Hitler used this principle with consummate skill in his brinkmanship of the 1930s. It was not only the Germans that behaved in this way, nor were German Jews alone in being regarded as an 'insoluble' problem for their lack of a state – whatever their understandable aspiration for one. Germany simply provided the most barbaric and wicked example of ferocious, domineering nationalism. Hannah Arendt has argued that the Holocaust could never have taken place without the whole-hearted cooperation that was accorded the Nazis right across Europe. The complicity of the Vichy regime in France in the terrible crimes against the Jews has been well documented, for example, despite the lamentable and self-serving efforts of President Mitterrand to hide it. Both during and after the Great War, murderous nationalism was not just a German phenomenon. Nor was the medicine prescribed by the League of Nations – open arbitration, public diplomacy and ultimately world opinion – sufficient to deal with it.

The political leaders and the diplomats who framed the League knew that nationalism and minorities would be a problem. What they did not anticipate was that they would also have to cope with economic isolationism or autarky. Who could blame them for overlooking this? Every liberal critique of imperialism had begun with the assertion that the principal goal of empire is the suppression of free trade. From Cobden to Hobson the world had been told that if you got rid of empire, trade would flow freely, and if that were to happen you would remove at a stroke a principal cause of war. How could such a view survive the experience of negotiating at Versailles, where it became obvious that states as well as empires were jealous of their trade? The US, for example, dug in its heels and refused to write off any European debts. Not surprisingly, Britain used the negotiations to rob Germany of her merchant marine, and France seized German coal and gold. Both saddled Germany with a huge reparations bill that was, in the event, partly inflated away rather than paid in full. In his classic *The Economic Consequences of the Peace* in 1919, J. M. Keynes saw the disaster that was to come and sounded the alarm. Since European peace and prosperity depended on widespread economic recovery, it was essential to encourage the free movement of goods, resources and currency, and foolhardy to try to beggar one's neighbours. Keynes's book, a runaway best-seller, was used cynically as a way of denouncing the whole peace settlement and of advocating inaction in its defence. What Keynes had wanted to do was to promote a better peace. Instead, he found that his arguments were used as a justification for turning a blind eye while the peace was demolished bit by bit.

There are two sorts of autarky: first, there is the attempt to practise economic self-sufficiency – an aspiration of several economic illiterates including Ireland's Eamon de Valera and Jamaica's Michael Manley – and second, there is the effort to dominate or control a necessary resource in order to deny it to other states. Both represent attempts to gain power and control, in much the way that Vladimir Putin recently tried to use Russia's oil and gas reserves for strategic political purposes (see Chapter 11). The practice of autarky in the twenties and thirties was particularly problematic. Half of Europe, which had until recently been organized in broad empires, was now dominated by squabbling states. Each one was set on controlling its own 'vital' industries. So half the European chain of supply, manufacture and finance was reorganized at the price of efficiency. Reorganization was followed by hardship, protective tariffs, punitive measures, the freezing of assets, the seizure of the property of now this, now that minority, followed by further seizures. When economic recovery from the Great War did finally come in the second half of the twenties, it was so fragile that the withdrawal of long-term American credit, especially to Germany, brought the first signs of depression to central and eastern Europe before the end of the decade.

This triggered the second problem of autarky as Europe's economic plight spread to the rest of the world. The Wall Street Crash led to the US raising trade barriers, through the infamous Smoot-Hawley tariff, and establishing a dollar bloc, including Canada, in the western hemisphere. Britain responded in kind, introducing the sort of protectionist measures within the sterling area that imperialists like Joseph Chamberlain and Leo Amery had been advocating since the turn of the century. With the US and Britain leading the way in trying to restructure their trade and finance so as to become self-sufficient and therefore 'strong', most of the world soon lived behind high economic walls.

This could be made to look like a viable proposition for the Soviet Union, the United States and Britain who could procure most of the resources vital to a modern economy – aluminium, bauxite, chrome, petroleum and zinc – within their broad economic zones. The gulag in the Soviet Union helped with the extraction of resources from that country's vast Siberian and central Asian hinterlands. The US was able to get most of what it wanted from the western hemisphere and Britain from its colonies and dominions. It may have been inevitable, and was certainly an indication of the failure of post-First World War diplomacy, but in these circumstances other great nations like Germany and Japan expressed their aggressive, expansionist plans in terms of racial and national survival, combined with the search for resources, trade and living space. The fierce economic competition of the Depression years tempted the Japanese 'to cast the samurai sword into the mercantile scales' that were unfairly weighted against them.[13] Prime Minister Tanaka in the 1920s argued that the successful invasion of China would provide a jumping-off point for conquests across the rest of Asia and beyond.

After Versailles, many democratic politicians assumed that the end of empires, and the transnational aristocracies that controlled them, would bring the triumph of liberalism and the arrival of a new world in which every nation controlled its own destiny, expressed itself freely and openly in a global forum (the League), and pursued its natural and rational interests in peace and tolerance, with open borders and freely flowing trade. In 1919 a new order was founded in the belief that the nation-state pointed the peaceful and prosperous way forward. By 1945 it was quite clear that nation-states were, if anything, even more aggressive, violent and irrational than the empires which had in part preceded them. The order that was founded at the end of the Second World War was still based on the political credibility of nation-states, but clearly recognized their many shortcomings.

The most successful of the pillars of post-Second World War order were those that shored up economic recovery and trade. They included both US-sponsored and European initiatives ranging from the International Monetary Fund, the World Bank, the United Nations Relief and Rehabilitation Administration and the Marshall Plan to the European Coal and Steel Community. The keystone of this order was the establishment at the Bretton Woods conference, in July 1944 while the war still raged, of the dollar as the premier trading currency, linked to gold. All these initiatives recognized the folly of the economic nationalism of twenty years before which had intensified during the Depression.

The global institutions dedicated to the preservation of order and security met with less success because, in the service of universality and reflecting the power balance at the end of the Second World War, they included the Russians. The United Nations was a far better institution than the League of Nations. Its Security Council and the veto accorded to permanent members (a narrowing down of the veto rights enjoyed by the members of the League of Nations Council) did a better job of recognizing the political realities of a world dominated by great powers. But many of the original executive components of the UN – an international air force, the military staff committee, 'security agreements' between states and the Security Council – quickly withered and died. One result is that the UN has often appeared to be surviving rather than resolving the great crises of world affairs; Cuba, Vietnam and Iraq are among the many which come to mind. It has too often been a well-intentioned actor in the drama, not the author of its conclusion. Palestine and Israel have been on the

Security Council's agenda for over fifty years, but the few glimmers of hope for a resolution to the bloody quarrel have not usually come as a result of UN action – indeed sometimes UN statements or resolutions have complicated the search for peace there. Nevertheless, the UN has done as much good as its member states will allow; indeed, thanks to the Herculean efforts of some who serve it, rather more. It has developed useful functions, for example peacekeeping and focusing attention on some of those economic, social and environmental issues that its members should take more seriously. Where the UN is flawed, the problems lie primarily with its members, not with some fundamental weakness in the ideas that inspired its creation. We need a better UN, not a weaker UN or no UN at all.

Since 1945 security has relied more on regional than global arrangements. In eastern Europe, this first took the form of the Soviet Empire, with Russian-backed thugs and assassins fomenting revolution and with Moscow sustaining the communist regimes that emerged as a result. (Unhappily, America's CIA sometimes responded in kind around the world.) In western Europe, security was provided by the North Atlantic Treaty Organization, anchored by the United States, with European countries paying a political price for the US commitment by responding positively to Washington's pressure for economic and political integration. The attempt to create a similar regional security organization in the Middle East, the Baghdad Pact (launched in 1955), never amounted to much, since its purpose seemed rather obviously to be the maintenance of British influence in the region. The Pact crumbled away with the changes of regimes in Iraq and Iran, ending with the Iranian revolution in 1979. SEATO, an organization in South-East Asia formed after the withdrawal of France from Indo-China in 1954, fared little better. The United States, Australia and New Zealand put together a more enduring mutual defence treaty in the early 1950s, from which New Zealand has for some time been semi-detached because of its refusal to allow access to its ports by US nuclear-powered or nuclear-armed vessels.

While the design of the post-war settlement sought to deal with some of the shortcomings of nation-states, the years since have seen the unprecedented spread of states – with those who hold membership of the UN increasing by 141 from the initial 51 – and the triumphant march of many different forms of nationalism. The twentieth century opened as a world of vast, transnational empires – for instance, the British, French, Portuguese, Ottoman, Austro-Hungarian and Dutch. It closed as a world of nation-states. There were numerous alternative political arrangements along the way: some empires endured in shadow more than substance with variations of theme embodied in UN trusteeship and the British Commonwealth – an organization in which (as one wag put it) all roads led to Washington. Soviet communism provided a more bruising system, yet it failed to brutalize nation-states into accepting that, according to its own doctrine of historical materialism, they were fundamentally illegitimate. There were ethnic coalitions like Yugoslavia and the United Arab Republic. But just as it did in the seventeenth century, the sovereign state has seen off all challengers, while inventing methods of regional co-operation (like the EU) which enable states to work together for individual benefit and the common good.

Since 1945 there have been numerous waves of decolonization, the most recent of which was in central and eastern Europe, and in the former Soviet Union, from 1989 to 1991. The number of states in the international system has expanded exponentially, and if nationalists in many parts of the world (for example, the Kurds, Basques and Scots) have their way, the number will continue to grow. In Europe and North America, the state developed classically, both as the expression of a philosophy of human relationships and as the best way of surviving politically in a very competitive environment. In the last half-century, the development of many new states in Asia and more particularly in Africa, that seized their independence from the European colonial powers and often had to cope with some enfeebling consequences of a colonial legacy, has been very different. Unlike the states that emerged in seventeenth-century Europe, they are not so much the products of strategic competition as fugitives from it, protected by the current international norms of behaviour against conquest, imperialism and increasingly against total collapse. This has encouraged some writers to become a little wistful about the days when the rich and powerful had suzerainty over palm and pine, providing firm albeit colonial government in these countries. They often, it should be remembered, also helped to plant the seeds for future terrible violence, Tutsi against Hutus, Muslims against Christians, Igbos against the rest of Nigeria. Empires are not going to enjoy a revival, even shorn of their more combative aspects. Today's newish states are often sustained by international welfare – soft loans, development assistance and NGO activity – and have become creatures rather than shapers of the international system. Their elites do not have to bother much about competing with other states; they can focus their energy upon retaining power and suppressing dissent while enjoying a non-competitive equality in the UN that will even allow them to lecture other less-abusive states on their human-rights records. The Peace of Westphalia may not come very often to the lips of those who represent some of these states, but the principle of national sovereignty that it incorporated is regularly asserted.

The triumph of the nation-state has resulted in two problems that interact. The first is that we have today a very conservative global order, which has created in the post-Cold War era a new political dilemma. If we continue to recognize the nominal sovereignty and equality of all states, there is a risk of sustaining and subsidizing an unjust order in parts of the world, presided over by a class of corrupt and sometimes vicious petty tyrants with all the problems – economic stagnation, environmental degradation, poor public heath, forced migration and so on – that entails. Take as one example the Democratic Republic of the Congo, a country that has suffered from serious problems of corruption virtually since it became independent in 1960. After vicious fighting, in part for control of mineral deposits in Katanga, a brave but ultimately unsuccessful intervention by the UN and the murder (with American and Belgian complicity) of the lawful, if foolhardy, prime minister in a coup, a Belgian-trained general seized power. President Mobutu then ruled the country for thirty-two years. A grotesquely shameless predator, he was supported as a pawn in the Cold War by France, Belgium and the USA. Maybe he was a corrupt bastard, but he was on *our* side. Following Mobutu's fall in 1997, the DRC was ruled (a not altogether adequate or accurate word) by Laurent Kabila, who was just as corrupt as his predecessor. Kabila had earlier disappointed the Cuban revolutionary hero Che Guevara, who had come to the Congo to help him foment revolution only to discover that he and his supporters were more interested in booze and brothels than in fighting. Kabila was in turn followed by his son. Years of fighting between rival factions drew in the Congo's neighbours (especially Zimbabwe, Rwanda and Uganda), who joined in this struggle for control of the DRC's mineral wealth, especially copper, cobalt, diamonds, gold, coltan and tin. The Congo's history has been one of pillage and massacre – it is a story told in more detail in Chapter 7. In a World Bank survey, Congolese citizens were asked, 'If the State was a person, how would you interact with him?' The response was often, 'Kill him'.[14] But that is not, of course, an option. We keep this state and others alive, in part with the transfusion of development assistance, and have no obvious or defensible alternative.

As is the case in the Congo, many of the problems faced by these weak states cannot be confined within state borders. Because of the suffering caused to the local population, the state's political order is intrinsically unsustainable and liable to cause regional chaos. Intervention by the international community to press for greater justice and administrative order in newish young states risks undermining what little order exists already, and creating a system without local roots, heavily dependent on the outside world. Yet the rest of us cannot seal off this Fourth World of failed and impoverished states, a ghetto that we can ignore, avoid, pass by. The problem is not simply the weakness of some states, it is also the weakness of the 'nations' that they are supposed to represent, usually a colonial leftover. They are like the new states in central and eastern Europe after the First World War, often heterogeneous, divided societies struggling to cope with badly drawn borders, national minorities, bad political theory, even worse economic theory, squabbling self-interested elites, short-sighted grudges against neighbours and a complete absence of the sort of technocratic bureaucracy which would allow them to identify and pursue their rational self-interest.

How did the old states of the West – North America and western Europe – get to the much happier condition that they enjoy today? We should confess to the fact that it was a long and hazardous business that took us from wars of religion, through wars of empire, trade wars, atrocities, more wars of conquest, wars of unification, national wars, genocide, a cold war, more wars of empire (particularly in the Balkans) and numerous proxy wars. Somewhere along the way we became more or less civilized, with more or less stable sovereign governments. We were helped by the fact that by 1991 in Europe almost everyone who did not speak the correct language in the correct place had moved, adapted or died (except in the Balkans). Even in Northern Ireland, where people were the same colour and spoke the same language, we tried to rehouse them in religious blocs or deal with the consequences of their vicious discord in other ways. (The first political decision that I had to take as a junior minister there was to build a higher wall – three and a half metres was not thought to be high enough – between two communities who would have seemed more or less identical to any outsider but who worshipped, at least in theory, the same Christian God in slightly different ways: it was well known down Belfast's Shankill Road that Jesus Christ was an Orange Man, and in the Falls Road that he was a Green Fenian.) Perhaps we were also helped in creating today's European civilized order by the fact that in the second half of the last century the bigger modern states had established the means of annihilating one another outright. They dwelt between the promise of the UN and the catastrophe of nuclear war. They got used to living in peace, since the alternative was Armageddon. Today is surely better than that. Whatever the failures of international society now, and the problems encountered by so many new states, we should not overlook an occurrence of momentous proportions, namely the relatively peaceful and orderly adoption by countries in eastern Europe, some of the states of the Indian Ocean and many of the states of the Pacific Rim (with China the great hold-out) of liberal democracy and market economics. More people live in successful states than in failed and failing ones.

The second of the two interacting problems is one that tests the philosophy and ingenuity of these successful states in particular. We have devised some institutional solutions in the last half-century to facilitate cooperation and to avoid the wars of the past. Yet our belief in the sharing of sovereignty required to make those solutions work was weakened, not least by the behaviour of President Bush's US administration, at exactly the time when we – the 'we' of nation-states – need to do more together rather than less. Why is deeper and wider cooperation required? The rest of this book explores possible answers to that question in a number of different areas. But above all, it is needed because the world has changed; distance has been sharply reduced (though not eliminated); borders, rather than solidifying, have been honeycombed; pretensions to the authority of states acting on their own have been shredded; and American leadership of globalization has been questioned, undermined by financial extravagance and stupidity, and even in the area of trade liberalisation deliberately withdrawn. There is a rapidly growing gap between the de jure sovereignty of states and their de facto control over their own circumstances. This does not mean the withering away of states, but it means their competence is in some respects diminished, and requires more forceful and imaginative cooperation between them.

We do not face the imminent end of the state, but a new age of the state. Increasingly, politics as we have typically understood it, structured in old-fashioned terms of states and sovereignty, is not the politics that is actually practised. Nor perhaps should it be. This has important consequences for how we think about citizenship, both in and beyond the state, and for what should be expected of individual citizens in a world where responsibility, authority and control do not wholly, or even partially in some cases, lie with the state any more, except in the sense that states have to make the choices and carry the consent to act in concert. How can we develop a broader civic sense that will stop globalism becoming anarchic? How are we to persuade individuals that ultimately sovereignty rests with them?

Next we turn to some of the issues surrounding globalization. First, we examine the concept itself, whose very meaning attracts controversy. Then we look later in the next chapter at the way in which the ill-understood and largely unregulated excesses of financial globalization have brought economic integration around the world into disrepute. After that in subsequent chapters we will go on to look at some of the dragons that threaten us all, from terrorism to climate change.

3

Les Big Macs and the Crash

If we want a platitude, there is nothing like a definition.
John Morley, 1905

The WTO kills; kill the WTO.
Chant of protestors in Seattle, 1999

The World Is Flat
Title of a book by Thomas Friedman, 2005

Why did no one see this coming?
Queen Elizabeth II, November 2008, asking the question
about the crash that puzzled most of her subjects

I have just done the shopping at one of our local supermarkets in the Tarn region of France. At the entrance to the Leclerc car park in Gaillac there is a McDonald's. Today it looked full. It looked full last time I drove past too, with cars queuing at the outside takeaway hatch. McDonald's. In France. Full.

Listen to many politicians and anti-globalization campaigners in France and the fast-food choices that so many French families make must be collective acts of culinary treason. At the very least, in a country where restaurants serve snails, fast food is clearly culturally aberrant. More than that, much more than that, McDonald's represents to these critics all that is worst in globalization: indeed, it represents all that is worst, full stop. It stands for big, brutal, unethical business, for US imperialism, for environmental despoliation, for loss of jobs and local identity, for the rape of familiar *terroir*, for the further impoverishment of the downtrodden, and so on . . . and on and on. The world is a bad place run by neo-liberal ideologues. (The precise relevance of the 'neo' in that word is rather lost on me, except that it has become a popular synonym for plain nasty.) The state has allegedly been overthrown by roistering banks and grasping multi-nationals.

How can it be that at the same time as all this fuss and fury, McDonald's Golden Arches have formed the pediments of the theory of a global village peacefully grazing upon Big Macs? No country with Golden Arches, it used to be said, would ever fight another blessed with similar edifices. This admittedly flawed theory crumbled at the edges when the Serbs waged their genocidal wars in the 1990s, and when NATO aeroplanes bombed Serbia. With a restaurant chain standing for so much, good and bad, I must admit that nevertheless (even in pursuit of a little more knowledge about the world) I have not actually eaten a Big Mac, the extraordinary burger from Uniontown, Pennsylvania that stands on both sides of the world's Manichean dividing line. Shame on me!

The vilification (or lionizing) of McDonald's is illustrative not only of the dissembling cant – in view of its origins we might better call it Tartuffery – of political discourse in France and elsewhere, but also of the extent to which the subject of globalization reflects whatever it is that we want to think about the world, its joys and miseries, its bold ventures and its dark conspiracies, its hopes and fears. Let us begin with France, a country that, like many of my countrymen, I love even as it puzzles and exasperates me.

The French are, of course, very effective closet globalists as Michael Veseth has pointed out.[1] French business – public utility companies, aerospace firms, luxury-goods manufacturers, retailers – are globally very successful. Louis Vuitton Moët Hennessy owns New Zealand's Cloudy Bay wine. How's that for respect of *terroir*? Carrefour comes second only to Wal-Mart in size as a mass-market retailer. France is the third largest recipient of foreign direct investment in Europe, and McDonald's – before we finally leave burgers – is one of France's biggest foreign employers, counts its French operation as one of the most profitable of any of the 120 countries in which it works, and is more popular in France than in any other country in Europe. But France also has a strong Colbertist tradition, named after Louis XIV's most important minister for twenty years in the mid-seventeenth century who built a mercantilist economy on industrial subsidies and high tariffs, all designed to pay for his royal master's army and his Versailles court. This tradition is often at the root of French attacks on free trade and on the idea of an open global economy. While President Sarkozy looked initially to be at the more liberal end of this philosophy, he soon began to wobble, recalling the behaviour of his Conservative and Socialist predecessors and adversaries who were protectionist through and through. President Chirac equated liberalism with communism. Can even this cynical, old populist have really believed this? His one-time opponent for the presidency, Edouard Balladur, asked, 'What is the market? It is the law of the jungle, the law of nature. And what is civilization? It is the struggle against nature.' To this sort of Frenchman, who represents the law of the jungle? The United States, the hyper-power, as the French were the first to dub it? And who represents civilization? France. The former French foreign minister Hubert Védrine, an intelligent realist in foreign policy, has argued that 'the foremost characteristic of the United States, which explains its foreign policy, is that it has regarded itself ever since its birth as a chosen nation, charged with the task of enlightening the rest of the world.' Change the name of the country, take out 'United States' and insert 'France', and the sentence is an unexceptional statement of the truth. We only need recall the then foreign minister Dominique de Villepin's rhetorical tour de force at the UN in February 2003, before the Iraq war (on the substance of which France was correct) to get the point. 'France', he concluded, 'has always stood upright in the face of history before mankind.' It sounds better in French.

As a colonial power, France inculcated its territories with French-ness – the food, the language, the education, the urban planning. In parts of Hanoi even today, there is a thoroughly French feel about the place, the squares, the boulevards. The croissant is as widely travelled as the burger. So it is not commercial or cultural imperialism itself that the French political class abhors; there is only a problem when the stamp does not bear the words 'Made in France'. The messy, open world outside France is a threat to French culture; it mocks French reverence for the state and its institutions; it menaces French identity. France has so much to be proud of, but which parts of itself is it going to lose as the world becomes less French? The Canadian journalist Adam Gopnik, in his charming book *Paris to the Moon*, describes his puzzlement at the French public's support for striking students and railway workers in 1995 protesting against social security reforms proposed by Prime Minister Alain Juppé.[2] Gopnik finds French attitudes to economic policy and competitiveness beyond his comprehension; and yet he manages, while observing the damage done by the strikes, to buy the best turkey he has ever eaten for his family's Thanksgiving dinner. Maybe there is some inward relationship between these things that you can only fully understand if you are French. Speaking to the rôtisseur who has sold him the turkey, he senses that the man believes that somehow the *cheminots*' strike will keep out the frozen turkeys and the supermarkets where you buy them: a wish perhaps as vain as the idea that a ghost dance could bring back the buffalo but 'no less fervently held'.

There is a sense in which it is the French themselves who have been damaging those things that are identifiably French, while the globalized economy dominates their supermarket shelves. Look at the white goods in Leclerc, the electronics, the cheap clothing – made everywhere but in France, and mostly in Asia. Then ask someone trying to run a small business – a patisserie, a butcher's, a cheesemaker, a restaurant – how easy it is to do their job and you see how French social and tax policies have been destroying these magnificent examples of French identity. Perhaps President Sarkozy, if he can avoid becoming a celebrity figure of fun, frantically chasing after 'l'amour' one moment and launching dramatic policy gimmicks the next, will change all this as he promised during his bold election campaign – the planning policies that drive commerce out of towns and villages into shopping malls on greenfield sites, the social charges on employers that make it so expensive to hire staff, the regulations that protect monopolies and cartels from banks to taxi-drivers and which inhibit competition. The Asterix-like hero of the French anti-globalization movement is José Bové, though he was displaced for a time in French affections by Jérôme Kerviel who helped to lose his bank, Société Générale, a cool 5 billion euros. Bové is a sheep farmer and cheese-maker who was first provoked into violent protest against the world when, in retaliation for Europe's ban on American beef, Washington imposed tariffs on European products including the Roquefort cheese that Bové makes. Now a veteran of trashing McDonald's and destroying GMO crops, Bové stands out as a heroic opponent of free trade, of industrialized farming (about which I sympathize with him) and of so-called 'Frankenstein foods', in other words the sort of application of biotechnology to agriculture which carries the promise of more nutritious, disease- and drought-resistant crops for the world's poor. But the menace to his Roquefort cheese – of which, unlike Big Macs, I have eaten a lot – is not American imperialism, big business or fast food; it is the domestic policies of French governments and the political prejudices of too many of his fellow citizens. When French polls show that almost twice as many young French between the ages of 20 and 25 fear globalization as see some hope in it, when usually well-heeled French students protest against modest reforms introduced to cut youth unemployment (whatever the cost of their protest to jobless youngsters in the *banlieues*), and demonstrate too against any adjustment to civil service pensions because they are focused on receiving them one day, a Francophile outsider like me realizes that President Sarkozy has his work cut out to make his remarkable country a more competitive part of an open world economy. To succeed, he has to encourage the French to be more honest with themselves. To borrow from Tancredi in Lampedusa's great novel *The Leopard*, about the Sicilian Prince of Salina, 'If we want things to stay as they are, things will have to change.'[3] In the years of the Risorgimento, things in the social structure as well as the economy had to change even in Sicily, though it should be admitted that nothing has altered very much in that beautiful and pitiless island.

Those political and economic upheavals in Italy in the nineteenth century are a useful reminder that globalization is not new. Nor are the business cycle, downturns and recessions, something apparently confusing to commentators who cannot decide whether the present recession is the worst since 1974, 1929 or simply (for those lacking historical imagination) the worst ever. What does globalization actually mean? Much of the literature on the subject concentrates heavily on this, and on how whatever it is should be studied. Platitude and cliché seep from use of the word. We all live on the same planet. We are all in this together. No man is an island. The world economy is globalized, or maybe it is the globe's economy that is worldized. We know that there are networks of interdependence that link people wherever they live, to deeper or shallower degrees, through their own movement, and that of trade, money, ideas and information. With time, these networks have become wider and deeper, and technology makes all the interconnections operate faster. In 1453 it took forty days for the pope to hear of Constantinople's fall to the Turks. India and China were once joined to Europe by camels, sailing ships and monsoon winds. Vice-President Henry Wallace in the later years of the Second World War thought that air power would transform the world and flatten national borders. What would he have made of fibre-optic cables, of Google, Yahoo, browsers and outsourcing? All this is globalism; to employ the sort of metaphors that come to distort the debate about it, the wired world is smaller, flatter. What globalization really means is how much of all this globalism there is; it is in a sense simply a statement of how the world is, a set of disparate phenomena which suddenly appear to generate connections like the butterfly's wings in chaos theory. A bank goes bust in America or Britain and the world rocks. Poor home owners in Florida default on their mortgages and men and women up and down England's high streets queue for hours to withdraw their savings from their bank. A man sneezes on a plane and the world catches a deadly cold.

As is obviously to be expected, the roots of globalism are as old as the world itself. Deliberate if unconscious globalization began with the first migration out of Africa 60,000 years ago. These hunter-gatherers (*Homo sapiens*) moved across continents over the next 50,000 years, crossing, for example, the Bergia land bridge to the American continent. As Nayan Chanda has reminded us, DNA research in the last twenty years or so has confirmed our common African parentage.[4] Some Chinese assertions that their own distinctive *Homo sapiens* emerged from intercontinental gene exchanges after the passage from Africa of *Homo erectus* a million years ago can be discounted as in part an intellectual reluctance to accept that the antique civilization of the Middle Kingdom could possibly have had its origins in East Africa.

It was only in the last millennium that humans reached the Pacific Islands and New Zealand, but the slow pace of global migration was transformed by the European conquest of the Americas and Oceania from the sixteenth century onwards, followed by the colonization of much of Africa and parts of Asia. Then came the terrible forced migration of the slave trade, until the middle to late nineteenth century, of between 9 and 12 million Africans. Even more substantial was the voluntary mass migration in the century after 1815, when 60 million people emigrated from Europe to settle in the Americas, Oceania and southern and eastern Africa; there were also substantial migrations from Asia to the USA, Canada and European colonies and from Russia to central Asia and Siberia. International migration fell sharply during the First World War; the Second and its aftermath saw forced and voluntary migration in central Europe, the Indian subcontinent and Korea. Jews fled the Holocaust, and the European racism that produced it, to settle in Palestine and create the state of Israel. The arrival in Britain from Jamaica of the SS *Empire Windrush* in 1948 signalled the beginning of waves of migration from former colonies to Europe to help drive the fast-recovering economies of the post-war years. Migration to the USA today – legal and illegal – from the Latin countries to the south and from Asia raises the country's population by 1 per cent a year, in comparison to the European continent's declining numbers (predicted to fall in total from 730 million to 660 million by mid-century). Canada aims as a matter of government policy to let in immigrants equivalent to about 1 per cent of its population each year. British eating habits have been transformed by travelling Chinese from Hong Kong's New Territories, and by Indians, Pakistanis and Bangladeshis who have made the chicken tikka masala ubiquitous. There are more Scots living outside than within Scotland's borders. Ten per cent of Swedish nationals were born outside the country. The largest Greek city outside Greece is Melbourne. *Homo sapiens* has been a great traveller.

All these travellers have been biological vectors wherever they have gone, spreading epidemic diseases with increasing fatal speed. In the mid-fourteenth century the Black Death, which seems to have originated in China, travelled the routes of land and marine commerce to and through Europe, laying the population waste. Smallpox, carried to the New World by an African slave accompanying him, helped Hernando Cortez defeat the Aztecs and establish Spain's empire in the Americas in the middle of the sixteenth. In the last century, Spanish flu killed tens of millions of people, from Eskimos to Samoans, in a few months after the end of the First World War.

But pioneers, settlers and soldiers have spread much else besides disease around the world. They traded new technologies like firearms and steel; they found and disseminated new flora such as tomatoes, maize and potatoes, and new fauna including buffalo and horses. Some military and political leaders like Genghis Khan and the nomadic Mongols seized land and plunder and left little but fear in their wake. Others from Alexander to the Romans to the European imperialists also bore ideas, notions of government, languages and religions with them. Islamic generals carried their religion and culture to the heart of Europe, to the walls of Tours in the eighth century and the gates of Vienna in the seventeenth, and their traders took Islam to the Malabar and Coromandel coasts and beyond to the Malay Peninsula and Indonesian islands. Buddhist missionaries transported texts and teachings along the Silk Road. Jesuits such as Francis Xavier and Matteo Ricci travelled to southern India and China; the Franciscans took the Bible to Japan. David Livingstone explored and evangelized Africa.

The sort of colonialism which followed rapaciously in Livingstone's footsteps led to environmental degradation as traders exploited natural resources to satisfy consumer demand in Europe and the US. Forests were cut down in Africa, Asia and the Americas; species were extinguished; soil was eroded. These local consequences of a growing international appetite for resources have become more obviously global with the fast polluting growth, the surge in population and the industrialization of hitherto mostly agrarian economies in the last half-century. Man has tried to establish his dominion on, in and above the earth; in California today even river currents are controlled by computers. The baleful results of this reckless and imperious aspect of globalization will be explored later.

At the heart of today's debate about globalization is the connection between the growth of populations and the development of the economies that sustain them; trade is both an effect and a lubricant of this relationship. The economic historian Angus Maddison has argued that in the first millennium AD the world's population and average standard of living barely changed. In the second millennium the world's population increased twenty-two-fold, while global domestic product went up thirteen times as fast.[5] This economic growth has been uneven; some countries have done much better than others. But regardless of where the growth has been concentrated, it has been accompanied by an increasing flow of goods and money, as well (as we have noted) of people. Between 1500 and 1800 world trade grew at about 1 per cent a year; since 1820 it has increased by about 3.5 per cent a year (in real terms). In the nineteenth century European trade went up forty-fold. We have come a very long way from the oared galleys built in Venice's shipyards in the twelfth century to connect this city-state commercially to the markets of the Mediterranean; from the fifteenth-century expeditions of Zheng He's great Chinese armadas around the Indian Ocean and along Africa's eastern coast; and from 'King Cotton's' reign in the nineteenth century when American farmers fed their fibre crop to Britain's mills.

The intellectual case for growing free trade among nations, the rejection of mercantilism, was made most famously by Adam Smith in *The Wealth of Nations* at the end of the eighteenth century. He argued from his theory of the division of labour, demonstrated by the practical example of the manufacture of pins, to the maximization of labour productivity through the creation of the widest possible market, not one limited by national boundaries and aggressive tariffs. He believed that what was good within a country was also good for a country. The 'invisible hand' of the market should operate across oceans and continents. This was contested in the nineteenth century not least by American advocates of protectionism. The difficulty of putting the case for free trade was noted by Thomas Macaulay in 1824: 'Free trade, one of the greatest blessings which a government can confer on a people, is in almost every country unpopular.' But as the century wore on, the 'free traders' won the debate in Britain, at the cost to the oldest political party in the country – the Conservative Party – of division and decades in the wilderness. The repeal of the British Corn Laws of 1846, which led to the import of cheaper food, and of the Navigation Acts in 1849, which had hitherto limited foreign shipping, brought in a period of free trade on the back of Britain's global commercial potency. British liberal free traders had won the argument internationally. In 1860 Britain signed free-trade agreements with France and other European countries, though protectionism grew again later in the century with the raising of European tariff barriers against exports of American grain. Nevertheless, the way had been cleared for the huge trade boom of the years before the First World War, generally assisted by the cheapening and speeding up of communications – the steamship, the telegraph, the railway. As has happened again with the recent global boom in trade, the reduction of the barriers created by distance was a key factor. In the first years of the last century trade represented a similar proportion of national GDP in the main European economies as it did at the century's end. In Japan, trade took a smaller share, and in the US a much larger one, a reflection of the increasing strength and openness of the US economy.

The claims made for and against what was happening to the global economy were as extravagant in earlier days as they are in the contemporary world. In the *Communist Manifesto*, published in 1848, Karl Marx and Friedrich Engels argued that 'The need of a constantly expanding market for its products chases the bourgeoisie over the entire surface of the globe . . . In place of the old wants, satisfied by the production of the country, we find new wants, requiring for their satisfaction the products of distant lands and climes. In place of the old local and national seclusion and self-sufficiency, we have intercourse in every direction, universal interdependence of nations.' A brutal capitalism showed an 'enormous werewolfish hunger for surplus labour' in its drive for profits – profits for business whatever the cost to the rest of society, particularly its poor and its environment.

On the other hand, Norman Angell, the Nobel Peace Prize laureate, wrote in the first edition of his widely praised *The Great Illusion* in 1909, that war in the century ahead was 'economically unsustainable'. Should Germany invade England, 'German capital would, because of the internationalization and delicate interdependence of our credit-built finance and industry, also disappear in large part, and German credit also collapse, and the only means of restoring it would be for Germany to put an end to the chaos in England by putting an end to the condition which had produced it.' The argument sounds today quite familiar: prosperity will efface patriotism; war between great states is obsolete; interdependence is much too far advanced to be reversed. As Martin Wolf points out, to be fair to Angell, where he was saying that war would be a disaster for all concerned he was entirely correct. But human stupidity knows no bounds.[6]

The imperfections of the period of globalization a century ago produced countervailing forces which in their turn wrecked what was manifestly beneficial about the process, and left us with the struggle against fascism and communism, the twentieth century's discredited alternatives to liberalism. That experience should perhaps remind us that the defence of liberal values – of open markets, regulated properly to prevent abuse and excess – requires vigilance, and that without it the process of globalization can prove surprisingly fragile. For the sensible liberal internationalist, the question is not how to defend whatever is currently described as globalization, but to define terms rigorously, avoid exaggeration, win arguments issue by issue and try to make the whole process work better for the spreading of prosperity and the preservation of peace. The demand for this approach has been increased by the financial crash of 2007–9, brought on principally by uncontrolled greed and unsupervised stupidity. There is nothing inherently illiberal about the regulation of banks and the banking system which has failed so spectacularly. Transparency is as vital to the working of a free market as the sanctity of contracts.

In one sense, the globalization that is transforming our world in the twenty-first century is nothing more than the most recent movement of people, ideas and technologies, taking advantage of a new era, politically and economically, of relatively easy travel, relatively easy communication and relatively open opportunities for education, self-betterment and self-aggrandizement. It is not far-fetched to locate the 'modern' variant of the process of 'globalization' in the Enlightenment which, uniquely, endows this mundane human quest for safety, prosperity and good government with a sense of grander purpose. It is identified unequivocally with progress and given a universal stamp. Hence, the quest to realize the rights and freedoms of the individual, the belief in social and scientific advance, the constant race to open new frontiers, exploit new resources, and pioneer new innovations, has become today systematic rather than accidental. We debate aspects of the Chinese invention of gunpowder, the European development of the clock and the Arab devising of algebra. But it was not gunpowder, nor clocks, nor algebra, nor even the discovery of a route to America which made the modern world: it was the invention of new ways of recognizing and utilizing those discoveries, in the methodical service of personal profit and the public good, making things more efficiently, selling them more competitively. We might expect, therefore, that the society which (by and large) has most cherished, indeed venerated, the Enlightenment, is today the most quintessentially global society: the United States. The US did not become a global society by worldwide expansion or domination; rather, it created the right conditions to become the globe in microcosm, to attract the poor, the oppressed, the young, the ambitious and talented from every country. The Latin Americans striving to enter there today, whatever the alarm this generates, make up only the latest wave of this immigration. They want to join the 41 million Latinos who are already there.

The anti-globalization movement is closely associated with the modern counter-Enlightenment (as well as with modern anti-Americanism). These forces from the political wings of left and right converge rather curiously. The romantic right, speaking from a communitarian tradition, argues that globalization destroys community and *terroir*, erodes tradition, undermines custom, and brings lots of strange people into our country – wherever it may be – who eat the wrong food, worship the wrong gods, speak the wrong language and cannot be trusted to root for the national team. The romantic left, speaking from a cosmopolitan tradition, argues that globalization makes the strong stronger and the weak weaker, undermining individual freedoms by eroding the welfare state in the developed world, leaving individuals everywhere – as Marx warned – exposed to the remorseless exploitative force of capital. Both sides of this debate have their own philosophical systems, and their own tensions and contradictions. But they have a tendency to converge particularly in their opposition to liberal principles, opening up countries to do more business with one another, with governments that allow markets to operate with the minimum of interference under the rule of law. Their criticism of globalization has been reinforced by the recent financial meltdown and recession. Opposition to globalization rarely takes the form of a credible alternative approach; too often it is simply a bellow of rage. Nayan Chanda tells the story of a young demonstrator at the aborted WTO meeting in Seattle in 1999 hurling a trash can at the glass door of a Starbucks coffee shop. 'Stop it,' an elderly woman passer-by called out. 'You're making fools of our country and our city.' 'It's self-defence,' the protester retorted. 'What are you defending yourself against?' the woman exclaimed. 'The window?'[7] The left–right convergence helps to explain why old-fashioned communists seem to tolerate Islamic fascists, and why skinheads seem happy marching alongside socialists at anti-globalization rallies. It also explains that very contemporary odd couple of anti-free-trade Democrats and anti-immigrant Republicans in the US Congress, apparently eager to resurrect the glorious Hoover years. Those who defend globalization, even when they also choose to criticize certain elements of it, stake out the territory of liberalism, the liberalism of free choice and expression, the liberalism that believes that individuals will usually make sensible choices within an open market which benefit both themselves and their societies.

So globalization is ultimately about choices exercised on a global level: economic choices, lifestyle choices and identity choices (particularly important in relation to terrorism). The real dividing line between those for and against globalization has less to do with right and left than it does with a particular stance on the wisdom of leaving as many choices as possible to individuals: individuals like Nobel laureate Jody Williams campaigning with considerable success for a world free of landmines from her kitchen with no more than a phone, a fax and a computer. What defines the anti-globalization radicals, whether Jean Marie Le Pen, José Bové or Pat Buchanan, is an extraordinary lack of faith in human beings like Ms Williams. The movement of people from one country to another will apparently destroy national cohesion and integrity. Individuals will be ground down along with their local identity by an impersonal global capitalist machine. Consumer choice will be distorted by and subjugated to the marketing of brands. The 'comparative advantage' of poverty will lead to the export of jobs from rich countries, impoverishing white-collar as well as blue-collar workers. Globalization is something 'out there', a pitiless, inexorable process, or else a shadowy, threatening conspiracy. The irony of anti-globalization, even at the extremes of ecological Druidism, Islamic radicalism, skinhead isolationism or Marxist irredentism, is that all the activists are more than happy to use the means of globalization – cheap air fares, internet communication, blogging, money transfers – even as they damn them. I once saw in London at a demonstration someone (presumably without a sense of humour) holding a poster announcing the presence of 'The World-Wide Movement against Globalization'. This may be one of the ironies of globalization, that the foundation of a truly global civil society will begin in the activists, organizations and charities of the anti-globalization movement. They can certainly use the technologies and methods of globalization to try to change the choices people make. For all the talk about power-lessness, those who reject globalization have the power to shut it down if they build up a sufficiently large critical mass, if they are able to put themselves in control of the right levers of power. It is salutary to remember that those who came so close in Europe to shattering belief in democracy and the values of reason and liberalism in the 1930s and 1940s began life as bands of extremists. Lenin, Stalin and Hitler rose out of the wreckage of liberalism.

There are two other 'isms' that we need to watch carefully even as we try to mould a better and more inclusive globalization. The first of these is technological determinism. The distinguished American columnist Thomas Friedman, who has written two very successful and entertaining books on globalization, has been accused of arguing that technological developments ensure that the only route to success lies in being more like the United States. One of his most recent books is called *The World Is Flat*,[8] a proposition that he substantially qualifies by its end. His argument is that until 1800 economic competition pitted country against country, that in the subsequent two centuries technology set company against company, and that since then infor-mation technology in particular has empowered individuals to compete and to collaborate, especially non-white men and women principally in Asia. This has gone so far that these days, for example, increasing numbers of American workers outsource the preparation of their tax returns to workers in India. Outsourcing and insourcing, browsers and Internet Relay Chat, Google and Yahoo, Bill Gates and Nandan Nilekani (co-chairman of India's information technology company Infosys) are the heroes of this Whiggish view of onward and upward progress. Like Friedman, I have visited the Infosys campus just outside Bangalore. It is extremely impressive: brand-new buildings like an Ivy League campus and (when I was there) 14,000 young Indian software engineers. For Europeans worried by competition from Polish plumbers, this looked like the real McCoy. But it did not convince me that the world is entirely flat. Nor do I think Mr Nilekani takes this view. Driving to the Infosys campus, there are all too many examples of how uneven the world is, even in a booming and often shining India, with too much poverty on view. Moreover, the road to the Infosys campus is anything but flat, the sort of incongruity that is still so present in India for all its progress. Friedman is wholly right to argue that technology today can liberate and connect individuals to an unparalleled degree; we now also know that it can help them to lose amounts of money so vast that no one seems able to track or count them. We should not exaggerate, however (and, to be fair, Friedman doesn't), the impact of the internet, air travel and container ships in comparison with that of the technological developments in the last century; nor should we forget that most people do not live in a cyberworld. They possess neither phone, nor modem, nor computer, though these technologies are spreading rapidly.

The suggestion that modern technology means that no one is in charge of globalization, and that – to borrow a proposition effectively assaulted by Martin Wolf – the combination of powerful markets means that politicians are left powerless, overlooks all the paradoxes of technology with which political leaders have to deal.[9] Globalization may flatten parts of the world, perhaps, but it increases the bumps too. The gap between those with access to the new technologies and those without it has widened. Globalization increases trade in goods and services yet also encourages protectionism. It speeds and facilitates capital flows and investment and yet dries them up everywhere when one part of the system goes wrong. It disseminates the truth while spreading disinformation and lies. It makes businesses more competitive and also subjects them to greater competition. Through the transmission of information, it can make us more conscious of individual freedom and civil liberties, but it can also give a global soapbox to hate groups and a pervasive outlet to pornographers. It bridges the divides between countries and continents and increases those between the old and the young. Yes, globalization is about choice, but sometimes it seems as though we have more choice than we can easily handle. So technology is not destiny. We can and should control its development and its application, not least to save the environment. Technology and globalization have not done away with politics, nor, as we shall see, with the nation-state. The French can relax.

The second 'ism' to reject is anti-Americanism. As Robert Keohane and Joseph Nye have argued, 'globalism is not intrinsically American, even if its current phase is heavily influenced by what happens in the United States'.[10] The whole history of globalism, which we have briefly noted, speaks to the wealth of causes, effects and influences of the process. The hated symbols of American cultural expansion – loathed even while consumed in prodigious quantities – are testament to America's German past. We eat hamburgers and frankfurters and wash them down with the peculiar coca mixture spiked with the kola caffeine plant whose medicinal properties were first publicized by a German.

We should beware of overstating the case that global civilization is American civilization. David Beckham may be a global sporting superstar, known from Birmingham to Beijing to Borneo, but in Baltimore he is 'David who?' The Italian culinary magazine *Gambero Rosso* asserts that, while there may be 17,000 McDonald's outside the United States, there are 54,000 decent Italian restaurants outside Italy.[11] What the US does contribute is as much a distinctive and at least for most of the time successfully competitive way of doing things as a distinctive civilization: how to combine, for instance, several cuisines to produce a fast fusion food on a miniature assembly line (miniature, so that it can be called hand-made), purchased from a corner franchise, with a French name, financed by a multinational corporation that also handles strategy and advertising, while outsourcing cleaning to the lowest bidder and data entry to a firm in Mumbai. Such is the genius of the US. The export of the McDonald's model is a much greater component of globalization than the export of actual McDonald's, while the uptake of both the model and the McDonald's is entirely about choice within the free market. There is nothing imposed or imperial about this aspect of American culture, any more than there is in the spread of Italian restaurants. Neither the burger nor pasta manifests a colonial hegemony.

In other words, while the US itself is the product of a long-term process of globalization, the recent expansion of global society has less to do with the expansion of American society than it does with America's contribution to the structure of world affairs. The US has been a powerful enabling factor in globalization (for example, buying so many goods from emerging economies) rather than its sole driving force. But America did more than any other nation to frame the rules and form the institutions that shaped the global economy in the last half-century, aiming for a global emporium rather than a global imperium. Just as it advocated capitalism and – usually – free trade, it also used its military might to support a system of world security that was not so much the extension of American control as it was the extension of a zone within which the US denied control to any other potential contender. This occasionally led to terrible errors: overlooking lessons of history; judging some security issues entirely in terms of whether or not a country fitted into America's zone or into a potential contender's; forgetting that other people had their national pride and national interests, too. Sometimes a single bilateral relationship, like that with Iran, was wrecked by all three of these mistakes.

The United States is often compared to an empire. This is not a particularly good comparison. American military power is orders of magnitude greater than that of any empire ever to exist, which makes the US invincible in any global high-tech conflict. But Iraq shows the limitations of even this measure of 'hyper-puissance'. Moreover, an empire is usually an assertion that nothing short of the full formal occupation and control of a territory is sufficient to secure its cultural, economic and political integration into a given system. America imports rather than exports people. There is no trained cadre of American officials sedulously schooled to run the world like Britain's imperial civil service. (Almost 350 alumni of my own college, Balliol, at Oxford served the Raj in India from 1853 to 1947; two were killed by tigers.) In most cases, all the US has to do, to win the process of integration into the world system that it moulded, is to deny individual territories to any aggressive contenders. That is what America's global network of bases, its eleven active carrier groups, its array of special forces, its elite Marine and army battalions, its fleet of heavy-lift aeroplanes and ground-attack helicopters, its long-range bombers and orbital surveillance technology, are all there to achieve. When managed and deployed with sophistication and an assured touch, and on the basis of innumerable agreements and guarantees, these forces have denied large swathes of the earth's surface to every kind of aggression and conquest. They have protected Israel, western Europe, South Korea, Kuwait and Taiwan. It has helped that other states with global strike capabilities have been allied to the United States. Most of the remaining states capable of developing such military power, for instance Japan and Germany, have not sought to do so and are anyway also allies of America. At its most subtle, America has operated rather like a good central bank, one which deals in security rather than securities. It has maintained the global balance, not by brute force, but by managing debts, liabilities and withdrawals and cultivating a special relationship with other such banks.

While Americans are more likely (as are the rest of us) to be moralistic rather than moral, and while (again like the rest of us) they are not especially consistent, they do measure themselves against the extent to which they foster freedom and democracy successfully in other nation-states, and protect those states from other pernicious forms of influence – such as imperialism, communism or theological radicalism. The failures and disasters of US foreign policy are regarded and recorded, not as the result of bad luck, or challenging circumstances, or insurmountable obstacles (Americans do not believe in insurmountable obstacles), but rather as catastrophic deviations from the traditional ideals of America. Even many trenchantly critical accounts of US policy, for instance Gabriel Kolko's accounts of the US in Vietnam, or Arthur Schlesinger's criticism of the 'imperial' presidency, are essentially catalogues of the failure of Americans to live up to the proper ideals of America.

So a world in which the United States is the only superpower, a world whose principal economic dynamism has in the past reflected the American way of doing things and running businesses, is not an American empire to be hated and fought. You can criticize US policies or attitudes without believing that America is the Great Satan or the wild-eyed driver of the great machine that provides William Greider's metaphor for globalization: 'It is huge and mobile, something like the machines of modern agriculture ... Think of this awesome machine running over open terrain and ignoring familiar boundaries ... It ... throws off enormous mows of wealth and bounty while it leaves behind great furrows of wreckage.'[12] To be hostile to America is very often to be hostile to the decisions that the rest of us make – the decision to buy this or that product in the marketplace, to follow hugely risky financial fads, to run our affairs in this or that way or the decision as taxpayers not to spend as much as we should on security. If Europeans, for example, want a world in which the international rule of law is preserved, they need to accept that this sometimes requires the use of force, and unless they can provide their own military contribution to this, America will either do it on its own or it will not be done at all. The European propensity for offering every sort of assistance short of real help may prove – unless it changes pretty radically – as much a trans-Atlantic problem under President Obama as it has often been in the past.

For the US to avoid the headache of anti-Americanism, except on the political fringes, it is necessary first for it to stop hitting its head against the wall, a point understood by President Obama, though not apparently by his predecessor. Those outside America forget about its soft-power – the way of life, the land of opportunity, the political values, the culture, the media, the higher-education system – when hard-power is used injudiciously and when the US appears hypocritical in its international security policy. There are other things America will need to do. First, it has to remember that it is usually the only country capable of assembling the consensus and the alliances necessary to meet many of the problems thrown up by globalism. There is scarcely an international challenge to which we can rise without enthusiastic US support. Secondly, its status as the world's only superpower is not threatened by the ascent of India and China. Yet the resurgence of Asian economic clout, and with it political influence, obliges the US to search for ways of sharing the leadership of global problem-solving, albeit as first among equals. What has dynamized the world economy more than any other factor in the last few years has been the fact that China and India have joined it, breaking out of their own developmental cul-de-sacs and bringing more than 2.5 billion people into the world's economic system. Both these issues will be explored later in this book.

There is a third point that confronts the US with diplomatic and security dilemmas, not least since the American humanitarian intervention in Somalia in 1993. How can it cope, as the guardian of global balance, with the dangerous small fry who choose not to participate in the enormous, stable, generally secure portion of the world that is more or less happily a part of the American-led system? Can we perhaps leave those whose behaviour is beyond the pale exactly where they are – beyond it? When conflicts are rarely globalized and mostly ghettoized, can the rest of us not simply wall up the ghettos and drive around them?

Whatever small if cynical hope may have remained that people would be content to set their own 'ghettos' alight and leave the rest of us unchallenged in peace (one of the theoretical guarantees of a world of sovereign states, after all) was blasted away on 11 September 2001. Globalization means that the smoke from a burning ghetto degrades the regional environment; it means that the stream of people fleeing the destruction must crowd and aggravate other people; it means that the guns used to perpetuate the destruction, and the drugs and diamonds and slaves used to finance it, will find their way into the global marketplace; it means that damaged and brutalized people will wander the earth inflicting damage and brutality without remorse; it means that deranged fanatics can enact fantasies of alienation, frustration and rage upon a global stage. The former Soviet diplomat Georgi Arbatov once warned the West as the Soviet Union fell to pieces, 'We are going to do something terrible to you. You will no longer have an enemy.' Compared to the Cold War world, when all the US had to do was to deny states to an enemy (which was a state, the Empire of Russia, in fact if not in name) in order to create security and stability, this world is much more complex and threatening. The security of each state remains the cornerstone of global security. But this security and therefore the whole edifice of globalization faces threats, depredations and degradations which could undermine it and bring it crashing down.

The main threat to globalization comes, however, from the rich and powerful states losing their nerve and their belief in markets and failing to make the corrections in the system that would benefit all. The scale of this threat has been magnified as the ruin of so many banks has taken its toll on the wider economy. A defence of economic globalization does not require an ideological refusal to accept any criticism of it; the rout of Western banks in 2007–9 underlines that. Nor should we feel any necessity to defend to the last ditch the global institutions which at present manage the process – the World Bank, the WTO and the International Monetary Fund (whose reform will be considered later). Much as it grieves me to write this, Prime Minister Mahathir of Malaysia appears to have been more correct about many aspects of dealing with the Asian financial crash in the 1990s than the IMF, for all its claims of infallibility. High-handedness reigned on both sides of this debate but when Mr Mahathir asked, 'Why not leave us to do the wrong things we want to do?' he turned out to be right. The defence of free trade does not oblige its advocates to believe that all is for the best, any more than that the world is now entirely flat. What the case for a liberal global economy does entail is belief in markets, in regulating them so that they work better rather than fail to work at all, in the effect that growth in trade and growth itself have on poverty though not always on inequity. The liberal will also recall the discrediting of socialism and central planning. As Australia's former Labour prime minister Paul Keating once put it, 'Today governments are more interested in . . . steering the boat rather than rowing the boat.'

The growth in world trade in the last century was substantial. It doubled as a proportion of world output in that period. More trade means more economic activity, more jobs, more investment and more prosperity. By the last decade, a quarter to a third of the growth in trade was between the 60,000 multinational corporations and their 820,000 foreign subsidiaries. In less than four decades, the exports of manufactured goods from developing to developed countries rose twelve-fold. The countries of east Asia have done conspicuously well.

Foreign investment reached extraordinary levels in the period before the First World War, particularly from Britain. For forty years the UK's capital investment abroad represented 4.6 per cent of GDP, and at its highest was twice this size. While today's comparative figures for global financial investments may not seem exceptional, they have been growing exponentially especially in the last quarter-century. On the foreign exchange markets daily turnover exceeds $1.5 trillion. Most of the investment from rich countries – the members of the Organisation for Economic Cooperation and Development (OECD), founded in 1961 – goes to about thirty newly industrializing economies. As a result São Paolo, for example, has been described as one of Germany's largest industrial cities, home to Volkswagen and more other German industrial firms – so it is argued – than any other foreign city in the world.

Increases in trade and investment have triggered growth which has lifted unprecedented numbers of people out of poverty, especially in Asia. The number of people in east Asia in extreme poverty (that is, living on less than a dollar a day) fell during the 1990s from 486 million to 275 million; in China itself the decline was from 376 million to 222 million.[13] Poverty also fell in south Asia as the Indian economy opened up to the world. Later we will look at sub-Saharan Africa, where the story was very different. The figures for India would be much better if reform had been pushed further and faster. There is now in the country a strong consensus in favour of not very strong reforms; this is largely a consequence of a fractured political system rather than of the constraints of the democratic process itself. To form governments, it is necessary to mobilize support from a wide variety of splintered parties, which increases the power of lobbies to block reforms and increases the temptation of politicians to appeal to bigotry. As happens everywhere else – look at examples of the middle-class welfare state in Britain – the pressure from interest groups is particularly effective in stopping radical changes in public spending priorities. It is generally reckoned that 10 per cent of India's GDP – roughly 40 per cent of all public spending – goes into subsidies to cut the food, water and power bills of the relatively prosperous.

The evidence is overwhelming that faster trade and economic growth in the last quarter-century has taken hundreds of millions out of poverty. Globalization has not been an impoverishing conspiracy by the rich against the poor. But globalization has not helped every country, because some countries have excluded themselves by accident or design from the whole liberal project; some have been excluded from it by its imperfections; and some have governments that are just too incompetent to take advantage of it. Nor has globalization reduced social inequity within every society that has benefited from it. Indeed, the gap in rewards in a more open global economy between better-educated and better-trained workers and those with fewer skills is bound to grow (as it usually has in the past) as higher value-added industries enhance their competitiveness and industries further behind fall back. Moreover, weakened trade unions in richer countries have not had the muscle to extract a bigger share of the rising profits that technology has earned for the corporate sector. But domestic policies can abate or aggravate these problems in both richer and developing economies. A good example of this is China, where, largely because of the differences between urban and rural households, inequality has been rising. Measured by the internationally accepted indicator of income and equality (the Gini coefficient), inequality in China is actually higher than in the United States. Incomes are more evenly spread in Asia's development pioneers Japan, South Korea and Taiwan. It should be emphasized again that these are issues that the governments of states can tackle. The outcomes are not ordained by the inexorable forces of globalization. Visiting Beijing recently, I toured a three-level shopping mall beneath my hotel complete with its own ice-skating rink. Doubtless developed with visitors to the Beijing Olympics in mind, it contained all the most expensive Western retailers selling the most famous Western designer labels. Even someone as addicted as I am to retail therapy was put off purchasing anything by the steep prices. There were very few Chinese in the mall, and even fewer purchasing goods in any of the shops. I suppose there must have been a few thick Chinese wallets about. Nevertheless, quite what a peasant farmer from Yunnan province would have made of it, or a factory worker from Wuhan, heaven alone knows (though to be fair they would both almost certainly have been better off than their peer groups in India). If it is not already, Mao's corpse will soon presumably be spinning like a top in its mausoleum as the shopping malls open across China. Yet Mao is the beginning if not the end of the point.

There was less social inequity in Mao's day when everyone was dirt poor, and when many were starving – 38 million starved to death in the Great Famine of the 1960s. That sort of grim equity was not obviously preferable to recent spectacular growth, nor preferable to the inequity that it has brought in its train. Whereas the real Chinese leap forward – the quasi-capitalism unleashed by Deng Xiaoping's dash for growth – began in the countryside, it has primarily benefited the urban areas, especially those in the maritime provinces. There is a real east–west divide in China, a country so big in any case that there was bound to be an uneven distribution of the benefits of its transformation into the workshop of the world. There is not the sort of effective central tax, benefit and spending system that would allow for redistribution of wealth to poorer groups and poorer regions. To their credit, the present Chinese leadership of President Hu Jintao and Prime Minister Wen Jiabao have tried to implement policies that would bridge some of China's social divisions. One of the reasons for the dramatic sacking in 2006 of the powerful party boss in Shanghai, Chen Liangyu, was that he contested these policies, arguing that the right approach to dealing with poverty was to continue creating wealth in cities like his own, allowing it to trickle down to those in need. Chen must be the first Communist Party apparatchik to be sacked for supporting the 'trickle-down' theory advocated by many right-wing politicians and economists in the West.

In China it seems perverse to blame globalization for increasing the gap between rich and poor, rather than to give the process credit for the substantial reduction in poverty. Economists continue to debate whether or not free trade, which most concede is good for growth, is neutral as to income distribution or whether it always advantages the richer, more educated parts of society. As I have just suggested, it would not be surprising if in the early stages of a trade boom in a more open economy, those with the best connections to the process, through education or existing economic well-being, were to do best. But as overall income rises, so the middle-income and poorer groups should gain in comparison to the richer members of the community – unless domestic tax and benefit policies impede this process, as has happened in the US, where not only has the gap between rich and poor widened but also the gap between the rich and middle-income families.

Globalization is blamed in the USA for this growing gap between rich and poor largely because of alleged job losses to poorer countries. Most people now acknowledge that better education and training could help to close the gap. At the top end, the fact that the rich are doing better than at any time since the Roaring Twenties helps fuel the resentment about inequality. Corporate earnings have surged, partly as a result (as we have noted) of technology, while lower incomes have stood still in a weak labour market. But it was the Bush administration's tax and spending policies that made the inequalities far deeper. They made corporate greed seem patriotic. From time to time that greed turned into theft. At least Enron fell eventually to regulatory rigour, though so great had been the scale of the dishonesty that this was hardly an astounding outcome. The greed of the few inevitably leads to the envy and indignation of the many. A chief executive officer in Japan typically earns eleven times as much as one of his average workers; the full compensation package for a typical American in the same position is very substantially greater. Some estimate the multiple as 170; more recently the *Washington Post* calculated the figure at 360. You do not have to be a socialist to regard this as pretty grotesque. No wonder that in the United States the top 1 per cent of families hold more wealth than the bottom 90 per cent. No wonder, too, that this has caused growing anger, directed unfortunately and largely unfairly at globalization. One of the results of globalization has been to nurture a new super-rich class in fast-developing economies plagued by their own social equity problems. Of the 178 newcomers to the 2007 *Fortune* list of billionaires, 19 were Russians, 13 Chinese and 14 Indian. The world's richest man in this list was the Mexican billionaire Carlos Slim.

Hostility to free trade is on the rise in the US and Europe, largely because it is seen as a threat to jobs and livelihoods, especially as recession bites. Switch on Lou Dobbs's news programme on CNN and you hear about the hollowing out of the American middle class. Not only have blue-collar workers – in the textile and automobile industries, for example – lost their jobs to foreign competition, but now white-collar jobs are threatened mainly by outsourcing. Moreover, while all this is happening, immigrants are allegedly streaming into the United States, partly at the behest of big business, to keep the labour market weak. Figures for the first quarter of 2004 suggested that less than 2 per cent of layoffs in the US were the result of relocation overseas. A survey for McKinsey showed that every dollar spent on outsourcing in India led to a larger benefit back home. Others suggest that jobs are not on the whole lost to India or China, they are simply lost to the past. They disappear because technologies change. Protectionism is invariably about protecting the losers from this process, pinning labour down in low value-added, low-paid jobs at a high cost to consumers and taxpayers.[14]

This is not how it seems, nor how it is portrayed. The result is that surveys indicate that globalization is viewed a lot more favourably in poor countries than in rich ones. A survey for the *Financial Times* in July 2007, measuring views on globalization in the USA and Europe, showed that in none of these countries was it believed that globalization had a more positive than negative effect. In Spain, Britain and the USA less than a fifth of respondents thought that globalization had been beneficial to them; the respondents were plainly affected by resentment at growing income disparities and low regard for company bosses.

Having pressed the benefits of globalization on poorer countries, it now seems that their richer cousins are rejecting a process which has increased the competition that they inevitably face. 'Twas ever thus. The rich pressed free trade and open markets on the poor, who have in many cases benefited from them, as have the OECD countries. Now many in developed countries want to constrain free trade because of the purported unfairness – to the West – of dealing with 'coolie' labour.

Growing protectionist sentiment in the US and Europe is particularly noisome because it reeks of so much hypocrisy. We preach free trade to the poor while shutting their own goods out of our markets, or slapping prohibitive tariffs on them. The most notorious examples of this are in agriculture, though some politicians are in denial on the issue. I was privy to the row at a European Council meeting when Tony Blair and Jacques Chirac went head-to-head over the impact of agricultural protectionism on poor African countries. In response to a rather mild critique by Mr Blair of the disjuncture between French expressions of concern about the poverty in sub-Saharan Africa and French support for agricultural protectionism, President Chirac blew a Gallic gasket. Presidential rage was excited by the observation, as it were, that the vicar was committing adultery behind the presbytery. But the story about agricultural protection in the US, Europe and Japan is true. At the beginning of the new century the EU provided in subsidies more than a hundred times as much money for each Union cow as for each sub-Saharan African human being – $913 in contrast to $8. Japanese cows enjoyed an even bigger, almost 2,000-fold advantage. Americans spent more than three times as much a day on subsidizing the domestic US cotton farmers as on the poor of sub-Saharan Africa. Overall, assistance to rich farmers in the OECD has run at a level six times as great as total development assistance. Subsidies in rich countries, which invariably go to the better-off farmers, disrupt global markets and cut back the exporting prospects of poor farmers in poor countries. Non-tariff barriers also reduce poor countries' exports through what are often excessive food-safety requirements. Martin Wolf has pointed out that the world's least-developed countries face tariffs that are four to five times higher than those faced by the richest economies.[15]

The early days of the latest trade negotiations under WTO auspices, dubbed the Doha development round (an allusion to the much-advertised objective of the rich countries to correct some of the trade disadvantages faced by the poor), more or less coincided with the US in 2002 slapping a 30 per cent tariff temporarily on steel imports in order to safeguard a handful of congressional seats in the mid-term elections. American pressure in the talks for liberalization of financial services, where OECD countries are strong, was matched by resistance to opening competition in sectors like construction and maritime services, where developing countries often have an advantage. The tough defence of the intellectual property rights of rich-country companies, for instance in the pharmaceuticals sector, has gone well beyond what is necessary to secure their commitment to large research budgets. The poor have often suffered in the past through having to pay higher prices for drugs and other patented products. Fortunately, the most egregious example of this, the cost of AIDS medicines in Africa, has been resolved. Poor countries also resent what is called 'biopiracy', the patenting of traditional medicines and foods by international companies.

These are the sort of issues that should be resolved in the present round of multilateral negotiations; success, however, seems unlikely. This is not entirely the fault of the US, Europe and Japan. India and Brazil have hung very tough, making progress difficult, and are probably not too fussed about whether there is an agreement at all. But if there had been more political energy and support in OECD countries for further trade liberalization, the outcome would almost certainly have been different. There is insufficient recognition of the huge boost to world trade predicted by the World Bank (benefiting the rich as well as, principally, the poor) from liberalization of trade in agriculture, services and textiles; there is also growing resistance to those measures of liberalization that are already in place. The main fight today is not to make faster progress, desirable though that would be, but to avoid a protectionist retreat. The ending of the Multi-Fibre Agreement in 2005 – a measure originally brought in to protect the textile industry in rich countries – was followed by a long-predicted and wholly predictable surge in textile imports to rich countries from the developing world, in particular China. Europe immediately resiled, at least for a time, from its free-trade commitments, slapping restrictions on imports and launching a brief and humiliating 'bra war', as it was called, against China. European politicians talk more and more about protecting their industries against Asian competition and occasionally do so. The debate in the US on the issue has become much louder and more aggressive than this. Americans have already used spurious security arguments in 2006 to block the sale of six port-management businesses in the country to a Dubai-based company. Opponents of the deal included Senator John Kerry and the then Senator Hillary Clinton. There is growing protectionist sentiment even in those parts of the Democratic Party which piloted the North American Free Trade Agreement through Congress and which should know a lot better. There was a general sentiment, especially in Asia, before the November 2008 presidential election, that a change of administration in Washington from Republican to Democrat, should bring a more sensitive multilateral approach to security issues, but set against this was the fear that it might also lead to a ham-fisted and unilateralist policy on international economic affairs. American politicians might recall the impact of the protectionist Smoot-Hawley legislation in 1930, that helped to tip the US and the world over the edge into depression and a slump in world trade. As noted in the previous chapter, the setback to economic globalization helped produce military globalization ten years later. Perhaps the fall in the value of the dollar and the surge in US exports that it engendered in 2007–8 will help to cool protectionist fever.

The increase in the number of multinational corporations, which account for over 20 per cent of world production and 70 per cent of world trade, has attracted the wrath of the anti-globalization movement. This has been aggravated by the growth of investment instruments like hedge funds and private equity companies. Private equity companies now employ through their investments in Europe about the same number of people as the population of the Netherlands. There are serious issues about the role of these new financial instruments, touching on transparency, the taxation of profits, the driving down in the past of the price of risk and the driving up of the amount of credit in the marketplace. But these questions, which ignore the fact that the main investors in these vehicles tend to be the organizations that manage pensions for you and me, do not really add to or subtract from the rage about big capitalism.

More international tension is likely to be caused by the rapid growth of sovereign funds. These are the state-run investment riches which have been accumulated by countries replete with oil wealth, like the Gulf States, Norway and Russia, or foreign-exchange reserves acquired from export surpluses by countries like Singapore and China. They are thought to total between $2 and $3 trillion, with the likelihood of rising to between $6 and $9 trillion by 2015. The subject of their strategic deployment is heavy with hypocrisy and paradox. Countries with large trade and budget deficits have been perfectly content for these funds to be used to purchase low-yielding American and European government bonds, bailing us out of the consequences of over-consumption. But the US, Germany, France and others have been very nervous about foreign government funds, opting instead for more exciting investments than Treasury bonds, buying large stakes in companies regarded as 'strategic'. There is an understandable if somewhat incoherent hostility to privatizing assets owned by the state in one country, only to see them snapped up in effect by a government from another country. The answer is pretty straightforward: not to block foreign investment but to insist that everyone plays by the same rules. If Singapore, Russia, Dubai, China or any other country wants to invest in American or European telecommunications, power, airlines, banking or shipping companies – to take a few examples – it should be open to our investment in similar industries in its own territory. For Russians to take advantage of the relatively open European market to buy up energy assets should require them to allow our investment and competition in their own backyard. The danger of losing control over strategic industries – the American populist case against the Dubai ports deal for instance – is exaggerated. We should not block foreign investment but insist on reciprocity and on transparency over the composition of these funds and over their strategic objectives. Norway has shown how to do this. The danger of arguments over the role of sovereign funds turning into an excuse for protectionism may have been obviated by the effects of 2007's subprime mortgage crisis. Most of the biggest banks lost so much money in this debacle – estimates of total losses climbed rapidly to a trillion dollars and even higher – that they had to turn to sovereign funds to help bail them out of the consequences of their foolish imprudence. Beggars, of course, cannot be choosers, even when they inhabit the banking palaces of Wall Street and the City of London.

Part of the argument against capitalism is unanswerable. Money often confers power – market power, political power. Is life fair? No. Have collective attempts to make it more fair been successful? No – unless equality of misery and oppression is regarded as desirable. Can the rich enjoy themselves more than the rest of us? Well, they can spend more money, that's for sure, but quite why they choose to do this in places like Monte Carlo has always puzzled me. Can a lower tax bill ever make it worth living somewhere so expensively tacky? Yet it is not simply envy and resentment about money that drags the corporate world into the centre of the debate about globalization. After all, there would be rich people even if we lived in a world where there was wide-scale protectionism, and as we know socialism often generates both poverty and extreme inequality.

The two other charges that need to be answered are, first, that globalization leads to a race to the bottom in the conditions of workers and environmental quality and regulation and, secondly, that the economics of globalization threaten the end of the nation-state.

Concern about 'the race to the bottom' was not the reason for labour unions joining the demonstrations in Seattle. They were not concerned principally about the conditions experienced by workers in poor countries. They wanted to protect their own jobs in a rich country. Wages are lower and working conditions usually worse in poor countries. Growth raises pay levels and improves conditions. There is scant evidence that wages are driven down by multinationals, nor that they help perpetuate indefinitely bad working conditions. As growth accelerates, child labour falls. Any multinational, if it is sensible, will try to ensure that its factories everywhere meet high standards, something which makes good business sense not least since the consumers and the workforce in their countries of origin increasingly demand it. While there are many things wrong with China, it is not obvious that the lack of a strong trade union movement is the biggest of them. Strong trade unions would represent a welcome development of civil society in that country, but they might also have held back economic development, as has happened in India. Indian trade unions have been all too effective in imposing conditions on governments and employers that inhibit growth and give too many people the privilege of continuing joblessness and poverty.

There are terrible examples of corporate capitalist recklessness in developing countries; the chemical leak in the Union Carbide plant in Bhopal, India, in 1984, is an often-cited instance. Capitalists are not always wrong, as was shown in 1995 when Shell and the British government, under pressure from Greenpeace activists, gave up a perfectly sensible plan to dump the Brent Spar oil platform at sea in favour of a more expensive and less environmentally friendly disposal on shore. Nor does the record of central planning suggest that it offers benefits to living conditions or the environment. A visit to central Asia – for example to the shrinking and polluted Aral Sea – provides evidence of that. It is true that growth affects the environment; that is not a problem to lay at the door of globalization, unless we embrace the full eco-totalitarian position that everyone – everyone else, that is – has an inalienable right to live in a primitive state of nature. A World Bank study in 2003 showed that with very few exceptions companies did not choose to invest in poorer countries in order to avoid the costs of pollution abatement in richer ones.

The other charge, which takes us back to the discussion in the first chapter, is that globalization kills off the state, at least the state that we know today. Does economic globalization mean the end of sovereignty and the creation of new kinds of governance, perhaps by global corporations with what John Ralston Saul describes as their own royal court, their own fool, at Davos, the annual World Economic Forum?[16] Will we see nation-states giving up the ghost and subjecting themselves lock, stock and barrel to regional super-state organizations like the EU? Will the United Nations, hitherto at the mercy of its member nation-states, turn – caterpillar to butterfly – into real global government? Davos, Brussels and New York will not destroy the nation-state. Nor should they.

When discussing globalization, the greatest danger time and again is in letting the word itself run far ahead of the thing it is supposed to describe. We know that a central feature is greater trade between more open economies brought closer together by technology. But global corporations – Exxon Mobil, General Motors, Wal-Mart and the rest – that are able to coordinate and control operations in more than one country even where they do not own them, are still operating within structures that influence and constrain what they do. They have to be aware for a start of a network of other firms and businesses, producers and customers. The principal regulator of any production line or enterprise remains the nation-state, though there are other supranational institutions, such as the IMF, the WTO, or regional groupings like the EU or the North American Free Trade Agreement (NAFTA), which also contribute to regulating companies. States have set up an expanding number of suprastate organizations with their own growing jurisdiction.[17] Shipping laws are written by the International Maritime Organization; air safety laws by the International Civil Aviation Organization; many food standards are set by the Food and Agriculture Organization. There are expanding networks of influence and control from banking and accountancy to health and water. Many corporations inevitably try to shop around for lighter regulation; many states seek to provide it. The fact remains that all big corporations continue to operate within national and international regulatory frameworks, even if some are ingenious in manipulating them to reduce their tax burden. From an economic standpoint, globalization is defined not by the obsolescence of the state, not by the rise of new 'mega corporations' with greater value than the GDPs of many states calling all the shots. What really defines what has been happening are the new interactions between corporations and national and international regulatory regimes.

When national regulators in particular do their job properly, the market – producers, consumers, investors, employees – benefits. What came to be called the sub-prime mortgage crisis was a good example of the importance of credible states, governed by people doing the right things, in cooperation with the governments of other states, with the help of more informal networks. There is no particular magic about this. It has been true systemically, and not just in relation to the recent crisis.

As an example, we can look at Latin America, something which is done all too rarely in discussions of international relations. Why is this region so frequently ignored? First, because it does not really threaten us, though we worry about drugs and illegal immigrants. Two of the larger states, Brazil and Argentina (which recently agreed to construct a nuclear reactor together), opted voluntarily some years ago not to translate their intellectual capacity into the development of nuclear weapons. So there is no Latin American bomb to disturb our sleep. Countries in Latin America do not on the whole fight one another. Nor are they as dirt poor as many Africans; there are no photos of emaciated pot-bellied South American children in our news-papers. The countries of the region are not yet economic powerhouses. Indeed, their record is one of flattering to deceive. It is said of Brazil, for example, that it is the country of the future – permanently. As for Argentina, it has been a lesson in how to engineer a long decline, like a football team that is demoted season after season from the top division to one of the lower leagues. It is not a developing country; it is a developed country that hit the skids and stayed on them. The reasons for parking Latin America in history's lay-by were partly matters of governance. It had bad governments and weak institutions; the governments either seemed to be run by right-wing corrupt gen-erals or by left-wing corrupt populists. The former were backed by conservative Catholics and the latter by conspiracy-hugging socialists. Sometimes, the conspiracies were real, as when an elected President of Chile, Salvador Allende, was deposed partly as a result of economic chaos, partly because of US machinations. But Chile shows what can happen with good government and sound policies. Under President Lagos, a moderate socialist elected some time after the retirement of General Pinochet, Chile recovered its economic vitality as well as its democracy. It has buttressed economic success with the development of social programmes. It is a well-governed state which now enjoys the rule of law. Brazil has also started to fulfil some of its huge potential as one of the region's two giants (the other one is Mexico) and as the world's fourth largest democracy. It has vast natural resources, sophisticated industries and a great cultural self-confidence. The Amazon tropical rainforest gives it enormous importance in global environmental policy. Goldman Sachs believes that if it continues to follow the path mapped by Presidents Cardoso and Lula, it will grow strongly and have a bigger economy than France by 2031. Right across the continent, where the quality of government rises, economies grow, social programmes develop and support for democracy increases. Good governments make the most of globalization. If this continues, much of Latin America will at some time become today's success story, not always remaining tomorrow's.

The absence of good government – taken hostage in America, Britain and elsewhere partly by a deep, allegedly philosophical prejudice against too much regulation of financial markets – led directly to the financial crash in 2007–9 which overwhelmed the global economy. So destructive was the turmoil and so comprehensive across countries and continents its effects, that not only was financial globalization discredited but also the global integration described in this chapter of trade, markets, labour and investment. It became increasingly and alarmingly obvious that the gains made around the world with the liberalization of trade were at risk as fear of foreign competition replaced the arrogant assumption that the good times would roll on forever, bought on tick in America and Britain. The UK's Prime Minister, Gordon Brown, had even bragged when managing the British economy before its breakdown, that he had abolished boom and bust. Thanks to him, the business cycle was apparently a subject for books on economic history. As banks and their shadowy counterparts collapsed, and the credit markets around the world dried up, bankrupting hitherto profitable businesses and thwarting trade, the totems of recent years were laid low one after another. Bankers were figuratively borne away in tumbrils; no humiliation seemed too great for them though some were able to assuage their suffering with the bonuses – now routinely described as 'obscene' – which they had salted away or sometimes still claimed. Government, which had once been regarded as the enemy of market omniscience, opportunity and growth, suddenly found itself the only potential saviour of prosperity. Maybe globalization had not destroyed the state after all. The Massachusetts Democratic Congressman, Barney Franks, chairman of the House Banking Committee, opined that it would be some time before anyone told again the Republicans' favourite joke, so often on the lips of the late President Reagan. The most terrifying nine words in the English language, the president used to say, were 'I'm from the government; I'm here to help you.' Now the help was demanded thick and fast, indeed it could not come thick and fast enough. Billions of dollars, pounds, euros, yuan and yen were thrown at the world's biggest economies. Deficits soared and more billions were thrown. In the deficit democracies of the West, like the US and Britain, while hoping that in future people would save more and spend less, for the time being they were urged to spend today in order to save their economic prospects tomorrow. With homes, jobs and savings in peril because of too much spending and too much debt, it was a rather counterintuitive message. Where necessary, which proved to be an elastic concept, governments tossed aside old shibboleths and took over industries and economic activities themselves. Banks were nationalized by governments that had hitherto believed in free enterprise and markets; politicians took over housing finance, too. Manufacturing industries carried their begging bowls to the heart of government, for example from Detroit to Connecticut Avenue. Capitalism was shamed. The wonder was that no Marxist revolutionary or Socialist egalitarian marked out a coherent or even incoherent alternative to the path pursued all the way to perdition. But people rioted, broke windows and denounced both their governments and the system whose golden harvests they had enjoyed for so long.

Although there was every reason of precedent to assume that what had gone precipitately down would go up again one day after a shorter or longer interlude of economic discomfort and even pain, there were those who suggested that nothing would be the same again; they were often the same people who had predicted that we could continue to make whoopee so long as whoopee was what we wished to make. As Britain's wise octogenarian monarch implied, with the question quoted at the head of this chapter, these had not been good days for those whose claimed economic prescience had frequently earned them their livings.

There were several causes of the crash. First, greed, madness and fraudulence are invariably parties to the creation of bubbles. Second, in America in particular, there were longer-term social and economic causes of the hunt for easy pickings. Third, it turns out – as had been true at the time of the crash in 1929 – that there were aspects of the modern economy that we did not really understand. Fourth, what we did not understand we certainly did not regulate. Fifth, the globalization of banking and shadow banking meant that financial contagion spread like pandemic disease. Sixth, behind the growth of earlier years, whose results we have noted, lay a fundamental instability which it will be difficult to remedy. Some suggested in the early stages of the recession that parts of the world would survive unscathed from its effects. Their economies were said to be decoupled from the rest. But in the modern global economy no one was decoupled save perhaps North Korea; we all went up together, and came crashing down together as well.

The sub-prime mortgage crisis is widely seen as the dislodged boulder that began the avalanche. Put simply, people had been encouraged to buy homes which they were frequently ill-placed to afford; these mortgages were packaged as securities to be traded on the world's financial markets; growing demand for housing pushed up prices; the value of these assets soared, people borrowed more against them, and all jostled for a piece of the action. Home ownership is part of the American dream – the British dream, too. But in America, even at the time that the original colonies broke away from the imperial master, home ownership was more widespread than back in Britain. It had been promoted for some time by bundling the loans – principally for housing but for other purchases too – made by banks and others into vehicles for investment by institutions such as hedge and pension funds and even foreign governments. Since the American housing market was worth trillions of dollars, the securitisation of mortgages seemed an attractive business, and two government sponsored organizations – the Federal National Mortgage Association, known as Fannie Mae, and the Federal Home Loan Mortgage Corporation, Freddie Mac – themselves bought up mortgages advanced by banks, thus enabling the banks to offer even more finance for house purchase. The practice picked up speed from the late 1970s onward as investment banks first began to package these loans like conventional bonds and then to slice them, with the riskiest investments carrying the biggest potential returns. These became the toxic waste which brought down the whole system, along with a form of purported insurance against the toxicity involving immensely complicated derivatives. This type of insurance, packaged as credit default swaps, was instrumental in bringing the giant insurance company AIG to its knees. What this process did was to push much American credit into an unregulated shadow banking system. By 2006, eight dollars out of every ten that were lent were provided by unregulated operators. Did the regulators and indeed those involved in the trade really understand what they were doing? I remember a young banker trying, rather impatiently, to explain to me how the mortgage of an unemployed single parent in St Louis could be morphed into a reliable financial investment in London, New York or Paris. Improverishment was magically transformed by clever financial manipulators into a Special Investment Vehicle. The poor got the house; the rich got the bonus. Try as hard as the banker did to get me to comprehend the beautiful simplicities of the whole process, I remained baffled. How stupid of me not to understand what I was being told by this young man, who worked for the Lehman Brothers Bank, RIP. Some journalists suggested that this bank never recovered from the curse of Gordon Brown's comments when he opened its new London office in 2004. 'Lehman Brothers' he said, 'is a great company today; they can both look backwards with pride and look forward with hope.'

Perhaps the hubris of bankers on Wall Street, Canary Wharf and in the other marbled halls of this business had been laminated by the

successes that had apparently survived past disasters. What was supposed to be respectable and a bit boring had become spivvy and
reckless. There had been scandals about outrageous bonuses and
modest returns to shareholders, the internet bubble had burst, Long
Term Capital Management – the invention of Nobel Laureates – had
collapsed, but still the universe had acknowledged its masters. One
of the smartest of them, former Treasury Secretary Robert Rubin,
appeared as godfather of several of those appointed by President
Obama to try to clear up the stinking mess, which another of these
bubble barons, Hank Paulson, had tried in vain himself to contain as
Treasury Secretary in the dying days of the Bush administration. Until
disaster struck, troughs had been regularly refilled and snouts sunk
into them. One analyst of the sub-prime market noted, 'What I learned
. . . was that Wall Street didn't give a shit what it sold.' Another
admitted that, 'I was the only guy I know covering companies that
were all going to go bust. I saw how the sausage was made in the
economy, and it was really freaky.'[18] Historically the ratio of median
home price to income in the US ran at about 3 to 1; by late 2004 it
had gone up to 4 to 1. But in Los Angeles it was 10 to 1, and in Miami
8.5 to 1. In 2000, sub-prime mortgage lending had totalled 130 billion
dollars, of which 55 billion dollars was repackaged as mortgage
bonds; by 2005 the first figure had grown almost five fold to 625
billion dollars, of which 507 billion dollars was in mortgage bonds.
Speculation soared, and rubbish spewed into the financial markets.
Some companies specialized in loans for homeowners with bad credit
and no proof of income who were not required to put anything down
as a payment and were encouraged to defer capital payments in favour
of interest only as long as they could get away with it. A Mexican
strawberry picker in California who spoke no English and had an
income of 14,000 dollars was lent all he required to buy a house for
720,000 dollars.[19] The wonder is that it took so long for the palace
of cards to come tumbling down. Triple B loans continued to be
transformed into triple A bonds; risk accumulated because that was
the way that people made more money. Perhaps some of the bank
bosses did not know the difference, as one former Citigroup executive
put it, between a collateralised debt obligation (jargon for a bundle
of debt) and a laundry list; but they understood the simple truth in a

remark attributed to Robert Rubin (who after a successful banking career had served in President Clinton's cabinet), 'You have to take more risk if you want to earn more.'[20] The management and rating of risk were engulfed by avarice. Toxic wastes out: bonuses in. The band got louder; the party rocked on; and then one day the music stopped.

Banks and their shadows began to fall like trees in a gale. One of the first to be hit was Northern Rock, a British demutualised building society. Hungry for a bigger market share, this once prudent and respectable North-East England building society grew rapidly partly because of risky lending but above all because it shifted from lending mainly what was deposited in its accounts by savers to lending much larger amounts which it borrowed short-term from the international financial markets. When they dried up and the Bank of England twisted and turned indecisively over what to do, worried depositors settled the matter themselves by queuing to withdraw their savings. Britain suffered the first big bank failure since the collapse of Overend Gurney in 1866. The British government eventually nationalized the bank. Other banks around the world were broken or were bailed out by taxpayers. Bear Stearns was taken over by J. P. Morgan and Merrill Lynch by the Bank of America; Lehman Brothers and Washington Mutual went bankrupt; Fannie Mae and Freddy Mac, which though public sector institutions had behaved like the greedy private sector, were bailed out; AIG was also saved by the taxpayer after its London office gambled wildly on collateralised debt obligations. Banks elsewhere – for example Fortis in Belgium – were dismembered, taken over, nationalized in part or in whole, or kept on life support by taxpayers as their stock plummeted. The failure of the banks in Iceland brought down the government and lost foreign depositors their money. Banks' losses ballooned into what seemed largely incalculable billions, and the value of their assets fell like a stone. The size of government bail-outs grew exponentially as governments and central banks sought to stop the haemorrhaging of money, to recapitalize the private banks and to get them to lend again. Where they had once lent, so it appeared, to anyone for anything, they were now scared to lend for everything to anyone, particularly to one another. The financial crash produced a credit crunch and the victim was what we call the real economy – jobs, homes, pensions, shops, investments, businesses small, medium-sized and large. Bank losses were increasingly compared to the earlier rewards made to those who had midwifed the disaster. Sir Win Bischoff, chairman for a time of Citigroup, conceded that he could understand why the public should be critical of what he called 'the asymmetry' between these figures. Fabulous as the rewards had been, 'the asymmetry' became ever more spectacularly pronounced. As the public mood became more bitter, with some voters angry that the banks had to be bailed out because of their central role in every monetary economy, bank chiefs queued up to apologise – well, sort of apologise – and some were even prepared to admit that the bonus culture had gone too far. In America, nevertheless, a few criticised the cap that President Obama set on the rewards that could be earned by those who ran the banks that had been saved by taxpayers. They chided the President for a decision that could, so they said, allow banks from abroad to poach their brightest executive stars.

Should we blame bankers alone for the scale of the disaster? This hardly seems fair. The British government, for example, had sought approbation and re-election for its success in presiding over an unregulated boom. It spent too much money itself during the economic upswing and allowed the public to do the same. Mortgage borrowing rose and house prices rocketed, and the British were encouraged to spend the notional wealth secured against their property in a long-running consumer boom. Mr Blair, the prime minister while all this was happening, escaped from the ensuing economic and political disaster, by demitting office in the nick of time in the summer of 2007 and by the fact that no one believed that during the preceding ten years he had been allowed by the man who succeeded him as premier anywhere near the management of the economy. Mr Blair, who left office to make his fortune and (so he averred) to reconcile the world's great religions, had been on the bridge but not at the wheel. He had 'left it all to Gordon' and Gordon Brown had allowed British consumers to run up half of the total European credit card debt. The indebtedness of British consumers – mostly on mortgages and credit cards – was about the same as a year's GDP, £1.4 trillion. New Labour's legacy was to privatize the gains of a synthetic boom and to socialise the losses of a real bust: 'the Third Way.' But it was not the government that spent all that money on a second foreign holiday, a flat screen television, an iPod for each of the children and other consumer desirables. Nor was it the chairman of this or that bank who did so, though the credit cards that bore those banks' names gave us the wherewithal to purchase all that instant pleasure. At least some of the guilt has to be shared around; after all, a consumer boom requires consumers, some of whom must know deep down that they cannot really afford what they are spending.

The growth in domestic debt in America dwarfed that in Britain or Europe. In the mid-1970s, US domestic debt stood at 680 billion dollars; by 2008 it had risen to 14 trillion dollars, doubling in seven Bush years. American households had on average thirteen credit cards with forty per cent of them carrying debts. What explains this curious manifestation of grasping family values? Sociologists and economists will debate this issue, but there is surely a malign relationship between the way rewards have been distributed in the American economy and one of the core challenges of the American dream, the absence of a concept of reasonable sufficiency. Alexis de Tocqueville had begun his book *Democracy in America* in 1839 with the famous observation, 'Amongst the novel objects that attracted my attention during my stay in the United States, nothing struck me more than the general equality of condition among the people.' No longer. The poor and the middle class have fallen further and further behind the rich (as we noted earlier), and they have bridged the gap from what they earn to what they want by borrowing money. Inequality in America has been growing for years; it is not simply a result of the Bush administration. In 1999 average wages adjusted for inflation had still not reached their 1973 level. Workers were working longer hours but median family income in the 1990s hardly rose at all. Whether one judges the gap by wages, income or wealth, the rich did far better than other groups before and after the turn of the century; at least President Bush achieved this one dubious objective but it is uncomfortable for Democrats to recognize that he built on what had gone before. It was not only stock indexes and private riches that soared under President Bush. The same was true of the government's budget deficit. President Clinton had left behind a balanced budget, but the Republicans, in Vice-President Cheney's words, argued that the Reagan years had shown that deficits did not matter. With tax cuts showering down on the better-off and on corporate America, and with the cost of the Iraq war consuming billions, the deficit rose steeply and the national debt almost doubled to 10.7 trillion dollars. Within weeks of his departure from office, Mr Cheney criticised the cost of President Obama's fiscal stimulus package which would raise the deficit in order to attempt the revival of the economy. The Cheney credentials as a guardian of fiscal rectitude were not obvious to most observers.

Governments had made mistakes, and so too central bankers, especially the former chairman of America's Federal Reserve, Alan Greenspan. Once fêted as the presiding genius of America's long-running boom, he was increasingly seen as a principal architect of the bust. A predecessor at the Federal Reserve during the Nixon presidency, William McChesney Martin, had said, 'The function of the Federal Reserve is to take away the punchbowl just as the party is getting good.' This was not how Mr Greenspan had seen his job: the more riotous the party, so it seemed, the more need to pour another bottle of brandy in the bowl just to keep things swinging. Moreover, he stood accused not only of running too lax a monetary policy but of failing to understand what was going on, or perhaps of thinking he understood it and reaching the wrong conclusion. At the start of the Great Depression, John Maynard Keynes had argued that while most of the economic engine was fine a crucial part of it was not functioning. 'We have a magneto problem,' he said, adding that, 'We have involved ourselves in a colossal muddle having blundered in the control of a delicate machine, the working of which we do not understand.' Mr Greenspan had believed that financial markets, not least the casino of housing finance, would regulate themselves, reining in their own excesses and abuses. With the bust he has admitted that there had been 'a flaw' in his thinking: an expensive flaw for America and therefore the world.

As governments everywhere struggled to recapitalize their banks, deal with toxic debts, melt the permafrost that has frozen lending, allay economic fear, restore confidence and establish a bottom to their free-falling economies on which the foundations of growth could be once more laid, they often referred to the need to redesign what they called the international financial architecture in order to save their own and others' economies. This was often an excuse, an attempt to shift the blame for the failure of national policies on to shadowy international institutions and forces. Indeed, when the Bretton Woods institutions, especially the International Monetary Fund, had criticised the careless management of the boom in some countries like Britain, they had got short shrift. But as in most of the other cases of challenges to our security and wellbeing discussed in this book, tackling the financial and economic fall-out of the crash requires both better domestic policies and sensible international cooperation, and that cooperation may have to go further and deeper than we have hitherto imagined.

One obvious task will be to realign the balance of power within the World Bank and the International Monetary Fund so that it more closely corresponds to the growing economic clout of emerging economies like China, India and Brazil. Historically, the G7 countries – the leading industrialized democracies who have recently added Russia to their meetings – regarded themselves as the unofficial mentors of global economic behaviour. One immediate effect of the crash was that a group of about twenty countries, who represented the strongest economies of the new century, was summoned to a meeting in Washington in late 2008, and this G20 grouping met again in April 2009 in London to establish a new focus for global economic policy making (though the results of the April meeting did not live up to the advance billing).

Once the economies have been stabilized attention will need to turn to the question of how to stop the same thing happening again. This is bound to involve greater surveillance and regulation of both capital flows, which can cause chaos at the click of a few mice, and of banks themselves, since so many of them operate across borders. We redesigned the machinery of financial markets after the Great Depression so that we thought we could understand them and prevent them blowing up. The same principle applies today. Any institution or agency that may have to be bailed out because of its ability to destroy the economy if it collapses will need to be regulated so that it cannot take the risks that could lead to such a catastrophe. You cannot eliminate all risk from economic life, without depressing any prospect of economic growth. But the risk needs to be understood, transparent, calculable and manageable if things go wrong. Shadow banking has to be brought within a regulatory framework, and banks themselves have to remember how to be boring and prudent.

It will not be easy to persuade national governments to accept a greater degree of international supervision of their financial sectors. Even more difficult will be tackling what has enabled the over-consuming countries like the US, Britain, Spain, France, Italy and Australia to binge, namely the huge imbalance between deficit and surplus countries around the world. Throughout the 2000s, high income countries with lax monetary policies have run up huge debts, for example in housing, which have offset large surpluses created elsewhere. The US and China are seen inevitably to be at the heart of this problem; for some years much of the world's growth has come from America's deficit and China's exports. Americans were prepared to buy whatever the rest of world wanted to sell them. They borrowed much of the money to do this from the Chinese and other Asian exporters. There was a sort of implicit bargain. The Americans would keep their markets open and in return the Chinese would buy their Treasury bonds. This arrangement suited both sides. The Americans were able to live beyond their means. For their part, the Chinese linked their own currency (the renminbi) to the dollar to keep it, and therefore the price of their own exports, competitive. Chinese exports to the US increased by 1,600 per cent in fifteen years. To avoid this resulting in monetary expansion and inflation at home, China stacked up vast foreign earnings well in excess of a trillion dollars. Chinese purchases of American debt helped to keep US interest rates down, a policy as we have noted pursued in any event by the US Federal Reserve, anxious to avoid a slow-down, let alone a recession, in the economy. So China's exports soared; American borrowing soared; and the world economy grew. Yet all this fell squarely within the American economist Herb Stein's First Law of Economics, 'Things that can't go on forever, don't.'

China is certainly the biggest surplus country, with a current account surplus in 2007 of over 370 billion dollars, out of a world surplus figure of 1,680 billion dollars. The US deficit absorbed 44 per cent of these surpluses; add the UK, Australia and Spain and the figure is 63 per cent. One inevitable feature of this unbalanced relationship has been that the collapse of growth and markets in the deficit countries has led to a collapse in exports from surplus countries. Consumers cut up their credit cards in America and Britain and factories close in China. The Mayor of Shenzhen announced in late 2008 that almost 700 factories had shut down in his Special Economic Zone that year: so much for decoupling. The danger now is that some countries will see coupling, or integration, as the problem and will seek to decouple their way to salvation, closing their economic borders to others. This is what protectionism really means, and we have already seen and heard the first stirrings of the protectionists around the world. American legislators have sought to insert 'made in America' provisions into a stimulus package. Striking British trade unionists have paraded banners that quote an ill-chosen Gordon Brown party conference slogan from 2007, 'British jobs for British workers.' President Sarkozy has sought to provide state aids for the French motor industry that raised suspicions elsewhere in Europe of protectionism. The European Union as a whole has not always shown the commitment to integration, cooperation and the single market about which it has so regularly boasted. The Chinese have examined new ways of supporting exporters, through tax rebates for example. Protectionism would lead step by step to disaster as it has in the past, restricting trade, slowing growth and stimulating the sort of nationalist sentiment that can easily have dangerous political consequences.

Protectionism is not the answer to the issue of the surplus–deficit imbalance. But it will require coordination of national policies to address it. As they recover from the recession, Americans will need to save more and borrow less. The Chinese will have to spend more at home and save less, encouraged to do so by switching away from investment in capital intensive, exporting manufacturing industry towards service industries and consumption, and establishing safety net social policies covering health care and pensions. That is the real shift required in China. The fact that the Chinese do indeed manipulate their exchange rate, as alleged correctly by President Obama's Treasury Secretary Timothy Geithner, is not really the point; rebalancing China's economy – the mirror to America's – is what has to happen. Getting global agreement to do that is what international meetings should aim for, once governments have halted the slide of their economies, the results of which will mark our politics around the world for years to come.

What all this confirms is that globalization had not replaced the state. To work well and to avoid disaster, it needs effective states, which will in the case of the US and Britain, for example, run a responsible fiscal policy and encourage saving. So we must not let the word globalization get the better of us; if we do, we could easily find ourselves in the same company as Ross Perot, arguing that economic activity is losing its territorial roots. He believed that the first thing the United States would hear when it signed NAFTA would be a 'great sucking sound' as jobs disappeared down the plughole into Mexico and Central America. However, while globalization has expanded the potential opportunities open to any company, the fact remains that all economic activity has to take place somewhere, and a great deal of economic activity remains tied to specific clusters, not because it is a requirement but because it is advantageous. High-technology industries cluster in the Silicon Valley and the London–Oxford–Cambridge triangle; financial services cluster in New York and in London. The result is that the global economy does not comprise a set of uniform global flows. It remains complex, dynamic and uneven. Robert Keohane and Joseph Nye remind us that distance is not quite dead, nor certainly are boundaries. Toronto, they point out, trades ten times as much with Vancouver as it does with Seattle.[21] Globalization has provided businesses with new choices for cutting wage or regulation costs, and new incentives for states to streamline spending and regulation and improve public services. We should not exaggerate the point. The state and its welfare services have not been dismantled in the last quarter-century. The growth of spending as a proportion of GDP may have slowed, but we have not seen the triumph of laissez-faire. The high tax and spend economies of northern Europe have been at the cutting edge of much of the activity in new higher-technology industries. Nor do tax figures suggest that all countries have been obliged to dance to the same tune. What is true is that the overall management of their economies by states, the efficiency of the services they provide, and the stability they offer, have played a significant part in attracting investment and corporate activity. Good governments are good for business.

Moreover, we have to remember that spending and regulation are only some of the matters affecting choices in the global economy. The location of people with the right skills, the location of the right markets, the location of the right kind of infrastructure (for example port facilities), the opportunity costs in making a big move: all these things help to determine choice. Global companies know too that global communications, global media and global organizations like NGOs keep them and the way they work under close scrutiny. A global wheelbarrow-making business might be able to pay its workers in (small) food rations if it moved to Zimbabwe. But state corruption, instability, lack of infrastructure, uncertain opportunities for exporting, not to mention lack of skills and education in the population – and the fact that they might find themselves subject to unpleasant scrutiny if they did cosy up to President Mugabe and pay their workforce in food parcels – ensure that they stay away.

As we have seen, the global market is not capable of managing itself. There are numerous tensions built into the global economy that make it potentially fragile. Some are as old as greed itself. There is nothing particularly new, no distinctive twenty-first-century sentiment that encourages some people to allow avarice to overwhelm common sense.

There is a problem in trying to create multilateral institutions to oversee world markets because when something is everyone's problem, it becomes nobody's problem. Modern global governance in economic and indeed in other affairs cannot be a project driven by a single state. Even if the US had the will to provide the leadership – and the swelling protectionist tide there raises doubts about this – it would have to operate as the biggest but not the only kid on the block. Yet there is plenty for us to build on. As Anne-Marie Slaughter has argued, state governments have responded to economic globalization by working together more than ever before. They have created networks of intergovernmental cooperation – bankers, securities regulators, insurance commissioners and antitrust officials.[22] Consider, for instance, the strengthened working relationship between competition agencies in the US and Europe. Plainly, the creation of these networks has to go further and faster in the wake of the crash. We are not – praise the Lord! – witnessing the death of the state: we know what happens when the state collapses, in China in the 1920s and 30s, in the constituent republics of the Soviet Union as it fell to pieces, in parts of Africa today. The consequences are awful. We require states to work together in ways that preserve a sense of accountability to their citizens. This is necessary in the non-economic as well as the economic sphere. Interdependence does not end the autonomy of states. What holds the system together is not the weakness of states but the choice that many states have made to stick together. Self-interest should be the glue that binds globalization in economic and other matters. This constitutes both the greatest strength and the greatest potential weakness of the global environment, that it is held together by many choices made in beneficial concert. Such an idea suggests not the demise of states, but that they need to exercise their sovereignty in more cooperative ways, pushing and shoving globalization wherever they can in better directions.

4

Skies of Flame

The first, the supreme, the most far-reaching act of judgement
that the statesman and commander must make is to establish
. . . the kind of war on which they are embarking; neither
mistaking it for, nor trying to turn it into something that is
alien to its nature.   Carl von Clausewitz, *On War*

[H]is primary objective is not battle. It is to bring down upon
the community in general a reprisal for his wrongs, in the hope
that the fury and resentment roused by punishment and meted
out to the innocent will gradually swell the ranks of those
forces from whom he will draw further recruits.

                                      Lawrence Durrell, *Bitter Lemons*

When does contemporary history, the modern world, begin? The
study of history is divided into convenient chunks – the Homeric
Age, the Roman Empire, the Medieval World, the Renaissance, the
Enlightenment and so on. The last nugget of the past is followed by
our own times. But when did they start? When did a new shape or
pattern to our lives first emerge? When did events leave the rails and
spin off in a new direction? Which deed roused us from complacently
assuming that we knew what our world was about and surprised
us with the recognition that things had changed, that all was now
different, that nothing would ever be quite the same again?

Britain's fly-fishing foreign minister, Sir Edward Grey, is said to
have observed one evening at the beginning of August 1914, as he
awaited the dispatch of an ultimatum to Germany warning against

the invasion of Belgium, 'The lamps are going out all over Europe. I doubt that we shall see them lit again in our lifetime.' It is a remark that at one level has always puzzled me since Sir Edward (though admittedly a man with poor eyesight) was at the time watching the gas lamps being lit, not extinguished, in the Foreign Office courtyard. Nevertheless, it is not difficult to recognize, as he did, the ending then of one chapter and the beginning of another. The events that were unfolding had been triggered, quite literally, by an act noted in the first chapter – the terrorist murder of Archduke Franz Ferdinand of Austria by the Bosnian Serb Gavrilo Princip. In 1916 Princip told a prison psychiatrist that he was appalled by the consequences of what he had done. He and his fellow conspirators had no very precise objectives. They were excited by the example set by Russian anarchists and resented the poverty and the annexation of their country. Princip himself was bitter about his rejection, on the grounds of his size, for military service in the Serbian army in its war of 1913. Too small to fight himself, he was the proximate cause of millions of others doing so. Though he desired a hero's death, he was denied the chance to risk one, unlike most of his generation in the terrible war that his action helped to bring about. Terrorist acts are invariably most significant because of the outcomes they set in train rather than the enormity of the damage and evil they perpetrate at the time.

September 11 2001 was a Sarajevo moment for many of us, the real beginning of the millennium, the dreadful opening of a new century, the snuffing out of the lamps. We all remember where we were when we saw or heard about the atrocities. I was between meetings in my Brussels office and had just remembered to telephone my wife in London to send my love on our wedding anniversary. Had those nineteen terrorists changed everything with the murder of almost three thousand men and women? There was no shortage of people to tell us that that was indeed the case, that things would never be quite the same again. 'Night fell on a different world,' President Bush said just over a week later, 'a world where freedom itself is under attack.'[1]

This was a world where evil-doers lurked in the shadows, a grim battlefield where only the fittest would survive. It was not enough to think that we in the civilized world would inherit the kingdom of the earth because of the strength and universal validity of our values. We would have to fight tooth and claw for what we believed and take that fight to our enemies. God was, after all, on our side; the God of the Old Testament; the God that smote His enemies. 'Saul hath slain his thousands, and David his ten thousands.' Divine pre-emption would scatter our foes.

The scale of the murderous 9/11 attacks was certainly unprecedented. There were more casualties on American soil than at any time since the Civil War, over five hundred more than at Pearl Harbor in 1941, and they were all civilians. Timothy McVeigh killed 168 people in Oklahoma City in 1994; seven years later almost twenty times as many died. While the body count was horrendous, and the act itself as terrifying as it was meant to be, the world did not become as 'night fell' a much more dangerous place, nor was the murderous activity itself an entirely new manifestation of evil. For forty years after the Second World War we had, after all, lived in what one UN Secretary General, Perez de Cuellar, called 'a world of potentially terminal danger'. Like the Abbé Sieyès in the French Revolution, we could say with relief at the Cold War's end that we had survived, thanks to mutual fear in Washington and Moscow that each side was capable of destroying not just its adversary but our planet. The silos, the bombers and the submarines remained on stand-by to end the world, and there were times – the Cuban missile crisis in 1962, the shooting down of the South Korean airliner in 1983 – when we came close to tumbling over the edge of the geopolitical precipice. Reading books on foreign policy written before the late 1980s, I am struck by how much the fear of miscalculation and the hope for nuclear demobilization dominated their conclusions. That really was a different world, and not a more obviously peaceful or benign one. This is reflected in many ways. John Le Carré has difficulty today in making multinational pharmaceutical companies seem as threatening as the KGB once were in his novels. The debate about the possession of nuclear weapons in Britain does not have quite the edge it once did; holding on to our few bought-in missiles is more a matter of very cautious household insurance than protection against the flattening of London.

So there does not seem to be more original sin about than there was, nor, of course, is its manifestation in acts of terrorism a new phenomenon. Josephus described the panic caused in Palestine by the brutal tactics of the Sicarii or Zealots in their campaign to end Roman rule there in the first century AD. They would move in and out of a crowd to stab their selected victims, targeting in particular those they regarded as Jewish collaborators. Their campaign inspired popular uprisings and the mass suicide at Masada, and contributed to the disasters suffered in the long term by the local Jewish population. The Shiite Assassins also stabbed and slashed their victims, aiming in the twelfth and thirteenth centuries at what they believed to be the purification of Islam. They deliberately courted martyrdom, persuading some by their recklessness that they were drugged (their name comes from the Arabic term for hashish-eater) when committing their attacks. The Hindu Thugi may have murdered half a million people until stamped out by the British in the nineteenth century, strangling most of their victims with a silk cord.

More recent terrorist groups include the Russian anarchists and Irish terrorists of the nineteenth century. Revolutionaries assassinated seven heads of state between 1881 and 1914. Among those leaders who died were President William McKinley of the USA, King Umberto I of Italy and Prime Minister Antonio Cánovas del Castillo of Spain, all three at the hands of anarchists. Irish terrorists killed six civilians in London in 1867, trying to organize a break-out from Clerkenwell prison by bombing its wall. One Fenian was convicted – to Queen Victoria's satisfaction, though she would have preferred a higher count – and became the last person publicly executed in Britain. Irish terrorism continued until almost the present day, achieving considerable notoriety from time to time, for example with the Phoenix Park murders of Lord Frederick Cavendish, the new chief secretary for Ireland, and his undersecretary in 1882; Lord Mountbatten (admiral and viceroy) and Margaret Thatcher's close aide Ian Gow were later victims. Irish terrorism was indulged and even supported by much American opinion until the very end, since it was seen as a patriotic protest against the continuing incorporation of six counties in the north-east of the island of Ireland within the United Kingdom. The fact that there was a strong Protestant majority in these counties in favour of union with Britain, and that most people in the south probably felt that they were lucky to be rid of the truculent Protestants of Ulster, did not have much impact on American attitudes. Osama bin Laden was not the only person to raise an eyebrow at the welcomes to the White House offered to Gerry Adams during the years after he had put away his balaclava.

My first personal experience of terrorism was the assassination of Airey Neave on 30 March 1979. I was then the director of the Conservative Party's Research Department. It was the last day of the parliamentary sitting before campaigning began in the 1979 General Election. Margaret Thatcher was in her North London constituency and I was with some other members of her election team in her Westminster office overlooking the yard next to Big Ben and the exit from the underground car park. We heard an explosion, looked out of the window and saw the smoking wreck of a car on the exit ramp. It was rapidly identified as Airey Neave's car. Neave, an acknowledged war hero (he had escaped from Colditz in 1942) and head of Margaret Thatcher's successful campaign team when she stood for the party leadership, was murdered by a small, militant Irish republican group, the Irish National Liberation Army. Enoch Powell had his own conspiracy theory that Neave had been killed as part of a CIA plot, and others suggested, with no credible evidence to support the claim, that left-wing Westminster insiders had been involved in the assassination.

Four years later I found myself a junior minister in Northern Ireland, with a protection squad of four burly Northern Ireland policemen, at least while I was in the Province. Back home in London and in my constituency, Bath, we had a reinforced front door and a mirror on a stick to look under the car for bombs. We lived in Westminster, just behind the cathedral in a block of flats which also housed Northern Ireland's secretary of state and which was bombed itself in the mid-eighties. We were advised not to park outside in the street, but to leave our car half a mile away in the Westminster parliamentary car park. I had already seen for myself just how safe that was and declined the security-conscious inconvenience. Several people I knew in Northern Ireland were murdered; it was particularly dangerous to be a moderate Catholic who supported the governing authority in the Province. I once saw bits of human flesh being scraped off the road in Newry, and a boot – with or without a foot in it, I am not sure – collected from a nearby rhododendron bush. Somehow no one in my family thought much about the violence, though I was taken aback –

almost as much as my children – when, while watching the TV news one night, it was announced that I was on a death list picked up during a raid on an IRA bomb factory. The police had thought it more important to tell journalists than us; maybe there was money in it.

As I have recorded in another book, even after leaving my job in Northern Ireland I was sent fairly regularly to Washington and other American cities to explain British policy in Ireland and to try to persuade US politicians to stop IRA fundraising in their country. I was usually received politely, but nothing changed. It took 9/11, IRA involvement with Colombian terrorists and the bravery of the McCartney sisters – who refused to allow the sanitization of their brother's murder at the hands of IRA members – to change public and political opinion in the US, obliging politicians to recognize that the IRA was not the militant arm of the St Vincent de Paul society. Northern Ireland re-entered my life in 1998–9 when I chaired the independent commission that made recommendations on the re-organization of the police force in the Province. It was set up in the wake of the Good Friday Agreement, brokered by Senator George Mitchell and made possible by the brave leadership of the prime ministers of the UK and the Republic of Ireland, Tony Blair and Bertie Ahearn. As part of our work we held about forty public meetings around Northern Ireland, some in places where no British politician had ever been before. I was acutely conscious of the fact that my security was in practice in the hands of terrorists, who presumably felt honour-bound not to blow up either me or any members of my commission. To depend on a terrorist's sense of honour – now that was something! It was curious and unpleasant to find myself dealing with people who had once been trying, happily not too hard or successfully, to kill me and who had killed people that I knew. It was a reminder of the chasm between those who simply argued for their political aims and those who have murdered the innocent in the same cause. I have no sympathy for those who treat Gerry Adams, Martin McGuinness and the rest as though they have moved from one hush-hush career as undercover community workers to another rather more public role. Martin McGuinness enjoyed the soubriquet 'the butcher's boy', and like his colleagues he had not earned it simply on account of early experience with the mincer in Dewhurst's. There is a sort of terrorism which requires (as I will argue) some degree of political accommodation if it is to be ended. This was certainly true of violent Irish republicanism, but the sometimes necessary acts of accommodation are not for the squeamish.

My other principal brush with terrorists came in Sri Lanka. Back in 1987 when I was Britain's minister for overseas development, I had taken an interest in the bloody civil war that tore that beautiful island apart. The Indian army had intervened in 1987 and, during a visit to the country to see what help we could provide for peace-building and reconciliation, I was flown into the Tamil city of Jaffna in the north in an Indian helicopter gunship. India's intervention led four years later to the murder by a female Tamil suicide bomber of the Indian prime minister Rajiv Gandhi. The civil war has brought 65,000 deaths and bloodily aborted the prospects for peaceful development in what should be one of the most successful countries in Asia. I went there again in November 2003, while a European Commissioner, to give support to the Norwegian efforts to end the conflict. I agreed to meet Velupillai Prabhakaran, the leader of the terrorist organization the Tamil Tigers (LTTE), to make clear to him that the international community wanted a settlement, would not accept one that undermined the territorial integrity of the island, and wished him to abandon his terror tactics, especially the forced recruitment of children and attacks on Muslims in the east of the island. Only one Western minister had met him before, and it was a controversial visit with Prime Minister Wickremesinghe urging me to go and President Kumaratunga taking a more ambivalent position. She eventually gave her permission and I was flown off in a government helicopter to the LTTE's former headquarters in a ramshackle village called Kilinochchi. It was the rainy season and clusters of children had been marshalled in the drizzle to wave Tamil Tiger flags at us – terrorist ticker tape – as we drove from the helipad to a bungalow where we were to meet Prabhakaran. Given his fearsome reputation as a terrorist killer, he made little impression. Young men in dark glasses surrounded him trying to look like TV 'hoods'. A man with a weak handshake, Prabhakaran left most of the talking to two associates, rarely looking directly at us. He seemed extremely unsure of himself. He is unquestionably ruthless, but lacks even the negative charisma that one might associate with someone who has sanctioned so much killing. One of the Tigers' victims, some time after my meeting, was a friend and fellow Balliol College graduate Lakshman Kadirgamar. A Christian from a Tamil family, an international lawyer of distinction who conducted the first formal investigation of a country (South Vietnam) for Amnesty International, he was twice foreign minister of Sri Lanka, arguing against foreign funding of the Tigers and in favour of democracy and civil liberties. He knew that trying to understand the political context of terrorism was not to condone it. 'Terrorism', he said, 'is a method – a particularly heinous one – rather than a set of adversaries or the causes they pursue. Terrorism is a problem of what people (or groups of people) do, rather than who they are or what they are trying to achieve.' Lakshman was murdered at his home in Colombo in August 2005, shot whilst taking his daily swim. The moderate and the brave have always been the most prominent targets for political savagery.

The scale of the Tamil insurgency in Sri Lanka makes the LTTE rather different from most terrorist groups. While terrorist tactics are used by the Tigers – suicide bombings and assassinations, for example – there are also pitched engagements between the Sri Lankan armed forces and their opponents. Therefore, to use the word 'war' for what is happening on that island would not be wholly inaccurate. (It is a conflict which seems recently to have moved decisively in the government's favour.) But to describe overall what we are presently doing in the Middle East as fighting a 'war on terrorism' is to misunderstand the task at hand and to chart a course where success is less likely. What is more, as we shall see, where America has been strikingly successful, it has been because the complexity and specific nature of the exercise has been recognized. This is evidently not as President Bush or his long-time public relations guru, Karl Rove, saw things. Better a 'war president' – now voters could really understand that – than a president trying to cope with the complexities and the shadows of global terrorism. So President Bush announced on 20 September 2001, 'Our war on terror begins with al-Qaeda, but it does not end there. It will not end until every terrorist group of global reach has been found, stopped and defeated.' Having declared war on terrorism, the president went on to broaden the target for hostilities. In December of that year he characterized the enemy as people who 'hate progress and freedom, and choice, and culture and music, and laughter, and women, and Christians, and Jews, and all Muslims who reject their distorted doctrines'. The war turned into a fight against evil and evil-doers. A war on evil is an ambitious project, and alas even more unwinnable than a war on terrorism.

First, you do not need to be a grammarian to know that you do not fight wars against common nouns but against personal ones. You fight a war against this or that country or enemy. Wars on drugs, wars on poverty, wars on waste – all these things are idle if grandiose ways of describing doomed political ventures. The ambitious, overused cliché gilds the prosaic policy. The additional problem about a war on terrorism is that the mindset that produces the metaphor makes it less easy to implement a successful policy. First, the opponent is unique – uniquely evil, for example – so any normal wartime rules of engagement are discounted. The prisoners of this war are not to be treated like the prisoners of more conventional engagements. Since anything goes for the terrorists, anything goes for the rest of us in combating them, with consequences that can make achieving the primary aim more difficult. In real wars there are battles, advances, retreats, parleys, communiqués, surrenders, victories, spoils, reparations. That is not at all what we are about in dealing with terror. Britain's director of public prosecutions, Sir Ken Macdonald, noted at the beginning of 2007, 'the fight against terrorism on the streets of Britain is not a war. It is the prevention of crime, the enforcement of our laws, and the winning of justice for those damaged by their infringement.' Is it actually possible to 'win' the war on terror, in whose exact name American gallantry medals for brave service in Iraq and Afghanistan are struck? Perhaps the Cold War and its dramatic end encouraged the overuse and abuse of words like 'war', which suppose a conflict of limited duration which we will inevitably win. But the 'war on terror' like those other wars on drugs, poverty and waste, is a process. While we should be able to 'hold the peace of the border line', there can never come a moment, as came at Checkpoint Charlie, when the last guard stands down and the patrols go home. The Cold War, after all, was about a particular ideology, a particular monstrosity. By contrast, terror lives and grows in the heart, beyond the reach of pickets and munitions. So the 'war on terror' is essentially unwinnable; any time you declare victory you can find that your crowing is the precursor to this or that extremist strapping bombs to his or her body and descending into an underground transport system to cause death and maiming. Prime Minister Zapatero discovered this in Spain at the end of 2006 when he boasted about the success of his peace talks with ETA shortly before one of their bombs killed two people at Madrid airport. If it is a war we are fighting – a war on a tactic and a cast of mind – how can we ever win it? Before ripping that statement of the blindingly obvious out of context, the fact that we can never win the 'war on terror' – let alone the 'war on evil' – should not lead us to the conclusion that the battle against terrorists is unwinnable too. Indeed, we made some progress in that battle on President Bush's watch, despite his strategy but because of some of his tactics.

Speaking to the New York Conservative Party in 2005, Karl Rove argued that 'Conservatives saw what happened to us on 9/11 and said: we will defeat our enemies. Liberals saw what happened to us and said: we must understand our enemies.' Now of course there is such a thing as evil that has to be resisted. But it is surely odd to assert that there is a contradiction between understanding and defeating; no one would accuse George Kennan of not understanding the Soviet Union when he designed a policy for defeating its awful ambitions following the Second World War. He understood it even before the Yalta conference, all too well. I suppose we know what Mr Rove was really getting at. In his view, 'understanding' equals 'hand-wringing irresolution': except that with enemies like terrorists, even more than with Soviet communist foes, unless you understand them you are unlikely to know who they are and how to defeat them.

What are the main characteristics of terrorism and terrorists?

We know from history that whether or not we call people terrorists or freedom fighters depends above all on who wins the struggle, who loses it and the nature of the authority which is the target of violence. Victors normally write the authorized version of what has happened, and terrorism – look at the histories of Israel and Ireland, for example – melds into freedom-fighting when the side backed by the terrorists comes out on top. Were those rebels who took part in the Easter Rising in 1916 in Dublin or the partisans of the Resistance in France in the Second World War terrorists? Were the members of the Stern Gang freedom fighters? What would Mr Bush have had to say about the role of evil in these struggles? We adjust our terms according to whether or not we agree with the cause for which terrorist tactics are sometimes used. We gave financial and military support to the mujahideen in Afghanistan as they battled the Afghan government and its Soviet troops. Were the mujahideen terrorists, like the Taleban whom we hunt through the mountains of Afghanistan today? Definitions can be hopelessly tangled; objectivity is not always easy. Like spotting an elephant, we know a terrorist when we see one, although others may see no elephant at all.

What definitions can we agree? First – and it is not unique to them – terrorists have a political agenda. It can be as narrowly focused as freeing the animals from a university laboratory in the name of their rights, or as broad as establishing an Islamic caliphate from the Atlantic to the Indian Ocean. Much of the terrorism that we have witnessed in recent years has been connected to the fight for national independence. The FLN in Algeria, for example, like the Sicarii in Palestine, struggled to free their country from a colonial master in a war of terrible ferocity that cost half a million lives and destroyed the French Fourth Republic. Sometimes it becomes difficult for a political leader to hold the line against the use of violence in a forceful political campaign that involves civil disobedience, for instance. Excessively aggressive reactions by state authorities to non-violent protest can also actually provoke violence, or be taken at least as a justification for it. In the fight for independence in Kenya and against apartheid in South Africa, Kenyatta and Mandela found themselves walking a narrow path between politics and violence. The more effective a moderate leader, the more the authorities will usually try to blacken him or her with the charge of condoning or using violence. But it is not difficult to distinguish between a strong political campaign and savagery. John Hume's values and tactics were always different in Northern Ireland from Gerry Adams's.

The amount of violence employed by terrorists varies and the options available to them have clearly been increased by technology. Semtex is easier to handle and use than the barrow of gunpowder detonated at Clerkenwell in 1867. Terrorists have to decide how much violence, injury and death are required to further their political agenda; murder becomes a part of their manifesto. The aim may be to create a mood of fear through showing the ability to commit acts of random violence at will; it may be to demonstrate the capacity to target an identifiable enemy, a political or security leader for example, or foreigners like the Western tourists targeted by al-Qaeda's affiliate, Jemaah Islamiyah, in Indonesia. The hope will often be to provoke a reaction by the authorities that will appear unreasonable to those who may sympathize with the terrorists' objectives. This was plainly one of the aims of the Pakistani jihadist group which murdered about two hundred people and injured another three hundred in a ferocious assault on Mumbai, and its famous Taj Mahal hotel, in November 2008. It followed previous terrorist atrocities in the city with similarly heavy loss of life in 1993, 2003 and 2006. The Indian government, showing admirable restraint, refused to be provoked into taking tough military action against Pakistan. It has invariably been the reaction to acts of terrorism that has created more political momentum than the terrorist acts themselves. The assessment of appropriate security measures needs to weigh political costs against security gains.

Terrorist groups are not usually state organizations; Libya – for instance in the case of the Lockerbie bombing in December 1988 – is an exception to this generalization. But terrorism as a tactic is sometimes covertly or not so covertly supported by states. During the Cold War both the US and the Soviet Union supported terrorists who were fighting national governments believed to be in the opponent's camp. Proxy wars were a norm even while the armies stayed in their barracks on the central German plain. In Africa, the US was prepared to help nationalist groups like the FNLA in Angola, fighting against Portuguese colonial rule, to try to keep them out of the Soviet camp. The principal covert American activities were closer to home in Cuba, Chile and Nicaragua, whose governments were thought to be on the wrong side of the ideological dividing line. Apartheid South Africa and Iran have both been big sponsors of terrorism elsewhere: South Africa, during the apartheid years, attempted to destabilize its neighbours in order to weaken their support for Nelson Mandela's ANC; Iran has tried to export its fundamentalist Islamic revolution to Saudi Arabia, Iraq, the Gulf, Egypt, Lebanon and Palestine. Iran also regarded its support for terrorism as a useful piece on the regional chess board, though its ability to turn the terrorist tap on and off may have been exaggerated. Engaging Iran would be the most sensible way of confronting this issue, but there has been for some time an influential lobby in Washington that believes that you can best stabilize the region by destabilizing Iran and Syria. This is a dangerous approach guaranteed to make a very bad situation far worse. President Obama's fledgling administration appeared to understand this point very well.

While terrorists are not directly state agents or employees, the tactics they use have sometimes been practised by states set on cowing their own people or those in other countries. In the French Revolution, terror was regarded by one of its main advocates, Robespierre, as 'nothing else than justice, prompt, secure and inflexible'. It was directed at those who were deemed to be enemies of the people and at those who questioned terror as the way of remaking them in a suitable revolutionary mould. Robespierre himself was to die on the guillotine in 1794, devoured by the very terror he had launched.

Occupying powers often use terror tactics to deter armed opposition, for example the German SS massacre of 642 French villagers at Oradour-sur-Glane north-west of Limoges in 1944. Indiscriminate aerial bombing of civilian targets has had the aim of terrorizing an enemy and sapping the will to continue fighting; this is regarded today as neither morally acceptable nor strategically effective. In areas like this, states can and often do accept and stand by international conventions and norms that constrain their use of force. Terrorists do no such thing, intent as they are on maximizing the psychological impact and unpredictable nature of their actions. As Audrey Kurth Cronin has argued, 'Although States can use terrorism, they cannot by definition be terrorists. Their use of force at home is described as law enforcement, its use abroad an act of war.'[2] This description can cover terrible acts of state violence such as the suppression of dissent in Tiananmen Square in 1989.

The victims of terrorist attacks are not on the whole the main targets. When, for example, Islamist terrorists killed fifty-eight tourists and four Egyptians in a particularly barbarous attack in Luxor in 1997, the principal targets were first the tourist industry, Egypt's main source of foreign exchange; second, the Egyptian government, in an effort to provoke a repressive and unpopular response; and third, those Islamic groups within Egypt which had recently made a deal with the government renouncing violence. More widely, the main target of terrorism is invariably public opinion, both where the attack is launched and where the terrorist group has its core support. Another is the government where the attack takes place, in the hope that it will overplay its hand in retaliating and act as an involuntary recruiting sergeant for the terrorists, or alternatively show its incapacity to maintain order. As noted earlier, the terrorists in Mumbai seemed to be partly motivated by this. Terrorists also focus on international opinion which will learn about the terrorists' cause and their ability to strike and do terrible damage. Terrorists – particularly those with a political rather than religious cause – try to calibrate the scale of the atrocity to the public response, especially within their community of natural supporters. Louise Richardson has noted that the IRA bomb that killed six people outside Harrods in December 1983, would have killed hundreds if planted inside the store on what was the first day of the after-Christmas sales. The IRA (unlike al-Qaeda) often gave warnings of bombings in an attempt to make it look as though they had tried to avoid casualties. The terrorists were keen not to alienate Catholic supporters in Northern Ireland.[3] Similarly, the response of IRA and Sinn Fein leaders to the bombing of Omagh by dissident Irish republicans in August 1998 showed their sensitivity to public opinion, especially given that they had only recently signed up to a peace deal in Northern Ireland. When shorn of any other arguments or justifications, Islamist terrorist groups usually describe Israel or its relationship with the USA as a reason for their assault, confident that however vestigial or non-existent their real concern about Palestinians, any reference to the Israel–Palestine struggle will enthuse their supporters, real or potential, in Islamic countries.

Louise Richardson believes that there are three overriding motivations for most terrorists: revenge, renown and reaction. The four young British Muslim terrorists who attacked London on 7 July 2005 cannot have expected that this would bring about the early establishment of the caliphate. They presumably believed that they were revenging wrongs done in the Muslim world by the British government for which its citizens should pay, including Muslims like themselves.

They certainly achieved some renown, not – as Sir Ken Macdonald said – as 'soldiers' but as 'criminals and fantasists'. I am pleased to say that I cannot remember any of their names. Thankfully, partly because of the tolerance and calm of the British public, and partly because of a mostly sensible reaction by the government, the response did not inflame the situation and encourage support for subsequent copycat atrocities on the heels of the July attacks (though other attacks in July were undoubtedly planned and thwarted). The wolfish craving for revenge is not simply a phenomenon of Islamic terrorism, yet it is particularly well described in a novel by Paul Bowles, *The Spider's House*, set in Morocco in the mid-fifties during the insurgency against the French colonial authorities. Bowles describes a young Moroccan's understanding of why the terrorists

were willing to risk dying in order to derail a train or burn a cinema or blow up a post office. It was not independence they wanted, it was a satisfaction much more immediate than that: the pleasure of seeing others undergo the humiliation of suffering and dying, and the knowledge they had at least the small amount of power necessary to bring about the humiliation. If you could not have freedom you could still have vengeance, and that was all anyone really wanted now. Perhaps, he thought, rationalizing, trying to connect the scattered fragments of reality with his image of truth, vengeance was what Allah wished his people to have, and by inflicting punishment on unbelievers the Muslims would merely be imposing divine justice.[4]

Revenge has been a potent force in the conflict in Northern Ireland. Catholic terrorists have responded to what they have seen as Protestant attacks on their community; Protestant terrorists have responded with their own bombs and bullets. One pub is burned out for another; a family bereaved in Belfast's Protestant Shankill Road matches another in Catholic Andersonstown. Other divided communities have experienced similarly emotional charges. Bosnia, which witnessed examples of ethnic cleansing in the 1990s, is, in the words of the Nobel laureate Ivo Andric, 'a country of hatred and fear . . . hatred acting as an independent force: hatred like a cancer consuming everything around it'.[5] Social revolutionary movements in Germany and Italy have targeted security officials and corporate bosses, calculated revenge for their role in fighting terrorism or captaining capitalism and a deliberate attempt to assert the integrity of their quarrel.

The intellectual godfather of modern Islamic terrorism was Sayyid Qutb, an Egyptian writer who was educated partly in the USA. He understood the importance of the third factor, reaction. Convicted of being involved in a plot to overthrow Colonel Nasser's government in Egypt, Qutb expressed gratitude when he received the death sentence at his trial. 'Thank God,' he said, 'I performed jihad for fifteen years until I earned this martyrdom.' Nasser realized the likely impact of hanging him, and offered him mercy and even the post of education minister in his government. But Qutb knew how he would make the greatest impact. 'My words', he told his sister, 'will be stronger if they kill me.'[6] Others, who have had less intellectual influence than Qutb, have been equally clear about the public impact of their activity and their death. I recall visiting homes in Northern Ireland where photographs of Bobby Sands and other republican hunger strikers hung on the walls alongside pictures of the Pope, the Sacred Heart and the Blessed Virgin Mary. Sands's renown was sufficient for him to win a by-election for a seat at Westminster while starving himself to death. The families, friends and confessors of some of those who were committing suicide urged them to break their fast; others encouraged the strikers to continue it, embracing a hero's death.

The reaction to terrorist acts tests any government's political skills, especially in an open democracy. Do too little, and a government may both appear weak and fail to prevent an escalation of violence. Crack down too hard, and the result may be early success on the security front at the cost of longer-term encouragement of the forces that help sustain terrorism. In Algeria the assault by General Massu and French paratroopers on the insurgent terrorists in the FLN, and the Muslim population that might be supporting them, brought a bloody end to what was called the Battle of Algiers in 1958. It seemed as though the French colonial power had won decisively. Within four years the Algerians had secured their independence, and France had to settle for what General de Gaulle somewhat dishonestly called 'an honourable exit'. French security measures had destroyed any middle ground in Algeria and greatly enhanced support for the FLN. It was reported in 2006 that the brilliant history of this colonial conflict by the British historian Alastair Horne, *A Savage War of Peace*, was being widely read in the Pentagon and had even been recommended to President Bush by Henry Kissinger. Who knows whether any lessons were learned in dealing with violence in Iraq? There was admittedly no General Massu, nor an 'honourable exit'. But it was again true that in Iraq, as elsewhere, it was the response to terrorism rather than the initial terrorism itself that caused the biggest problems. So, the argument runs, it was not 9/11 that changed the world so much as the response to 9/11. Perhaps one day a successor to President Bush will be advised to read not only a history of the Algerian conflict but studies of Guantanamo Bay and rendition.

The deeper causes of terrorism are more widely asserted than carefully examined. It is generally assumed that terrorism is seeded and thrives in poor communities where there is a deep sense of social injustice. The development lobby has seized on the argument that spending money on the alleviation of poverty would have a much greater impact on abating terrorism than expenditure on security. Better education is regarded as a powerful weapon against terrorism. Terrorism, it is believed, is less likely to flourish in democratic societies. Pluralism and openness deter the development of a terrorist mentality. Terrorism grows in failed or failing states where the institutions of government are breaking down or are pretty well non-existent. A terrorist mentality is a response to the forces of modernization and globalization, an appeal for not allowing one's sense of traditional identity to be overwhelmed by alien commercial, political or cultural forces. Terrorism is, in particular, fanatical Islam's answer to the humiliations and brazen offensiveness of the modern world, supported and encouraged by Islamic states for their own ends.

How much in fact does poverty explain terrorism? A smart answer discounts deprivation, arguing that if poverty accounted for terrorist activity, most of it would have its roots in sub-Saharan Africa. There has, of course, been terrorism here, in Burundi, the Congo and Liberia, for example. But terrorism has much more frequently come from further north, in Algeria, Egypt, Somalia and the Arab and Muslim countries of west and central Asia. The countries of the Arab League, from Iraq to Morocco, have done almost as badly economically in relation to other regions as sub-Saharan Africa, though they are not as poor in absolute terms. While wealth has been growing elsewhere, Arab countries have proved extraordinarily unproductive despite oil and gas revenues. Taking out of the figures what they make from petroleum, Saudi Arabia and the other states in the Gulf have been exporting less than is achieved by 5 million Finns. They have imported big, dry, prefabricated lumps of materialism. What prosperous industries have these countries created? They have young populations, with too few jobs but no shortage of chances for seeing on television what others enjoy. As Lawrence Wright noted in his book on the background to the Twin Towers atrocities, 'Radicalism usually prospers in the gap between rising expectations and declining opportunities.'[7]

While poverty may undermine the institutions in those states that provide havens for terrorists, and while it may and does depress educational opportunities, poverty itself is perhaps less significant in absolute than in relative terms. Relative poverty feeds grievance and anger. It is interesting that it is not usually the poor who have recently joined the most prominent terrorist groups. A study of Islamist recruits to anti-government organizations in Egypt in the 1970s, cited by Wright, indicated that the majority were the sons of middle-level bureaucrats; they were well qualified academically and not typically alienated or marginalized. Similarly, 'the men who came to Afghanistan in the 1990s were not impoverished social failures ... Most of the prospective al-Qaeda recruits were from the middle or upper class, nearly all of them from intact families. They were largely college-educated, with a strong bias towards the natural sciences and engineering.'[8] Better-educated terrorists, speaking several languages, are more able to carry out acts of international terrorism. They obviously find it far easier than would the impoverished and uneducated to travel, find jobs and accommodation and adapt themselves to foreign environments.

Education may play a role in radicalizing the young. Attention has focused particularly on the Pakistan madrasas – religious schools – typically funded by charities in Saudi Arabia and the Gulf States through local religious parties. Even before the influx of Afghan refugees into the country, literacy rates in the Tribal Areas and around Peshawar were so low as to be difficult to count at all. I visited the area in the mid-eighties, as Britain's development minister, and tried to increase the money available for state schooling and a broad secular curriculum. I was still trying to do the same as a European Commissioner, working with the World Bank and USAID, almost twenty years later. But Pakistan still has a wholly inadequate state school system and, despite the often creditable efforts of its Ministry of Education, the writ of the Islamabad authorities appears to stop well short of the border regions of the country. In the madrasas a rigid Wahhabi doctrine is taught, concentrating on the Quran, Sharia and the heroism of jihad, an Islamic term literally meaning struggle which has come to stand, as far as extremists are concerned, for aggressive warfare against those perceived to be enemies of Islam (although it can also describe the internal struggle of every believer against temptation). These madrasas have always been the most fertile recruiting grounds for the Taleban and other extremist groups. Qurani schools flourish in other countries where poverty inhibits the development of state education. The United Nations Development Programme (UNDP) reckons that only 14 per cent of children in Somalia attend primary school and a mere 17 per cent are literate. Children at these usually religious schools acquire few practical skills but learn the corrupting danger of Western influences. They are vulnerable, at an age when their minds and personalities are being formed, to the activities of those with radical Islamic agendas.

Would democracy smash terrorism? Is the ballot box the answer to the bomb? It is rather a simplistic notion – although I believe it to be true in the longer term and in its totality. But it does start a debate that belongs in the category: rubbish in, rubbish out. Free and fair elections in some countries in the Middle East today would undoubtedly produce governments initially more sympathetic to Islamic fundamentalism and jihad. What would the Sunni Saudi suicide bombers in Iraq have voted for if they had had the chance back home? At the very least, we would probably find ourselves in greater disagreement with elected governments in the Middle East than with authoritarian ones. An elected government in Iraq, originally advertised as a potential model for the region, has, for example, espoused the sort of views on Israel and Palestine that the US and Europe would usually find deeply troubling. The argument against the magic properties of democracy is taken further by some, who note the difference between the number of terrorist incidents in democratic India and the relatively few incidents in authoritarian China. This is a point that ignores the multi-ethnic, multi-religious politics of India in comparison with a more homogeneous China, takes no account of the divisive nature of south Asia's transition from empire to independence, and assumes that we know as much about what is going on in China as in India. We don't. The number of attacks by Uigur separatists in Xinjiang province, for example, is unknown; the Chinese authorities claimed to have foiled a plot of terrorist violence by Uigurs against the Olympics in 2008.

The overall argument about democracy and pluralism stands up if you define terms accurately and if you look at the connections between politics and economics. First, Fareed Zakaria has argued that democracy is not just about the electoral process, which can simply produce majoritarian and illiberal results.[9] It should encompass the creation of all those institutions and values that go to provide both the hardware and the software of a plural, open state: independent courts and the rule of law, freedom of speech, assembly and worship, the right to own property, accountable public services, civil society. As we know to our cost from Russia to the Balkans, it takes more time and effort to create a functioning plural society under the law than simply to give people the vote, though this should not be regarded as a sophisticated reason for postponing indefinitely the introduction of the ballot box. Secondly, we have already noted the economic backwardness of Middle East Arab League countries despite their energy resources. There is clearly a connection, as the UNDP has regularly asserted, between authoritarian governance in the region, attitudes to gender and education, and economic performance. The combination of the curtailment of political and other civil liberties, and low rates of economic growth, produces unemployment and hopelessness. The population in the Arab world has increased from 187 million in 1985 to over 280 million today. It is forecast to rise to well over 360 million by 2020; 33 per cent of Arabs are below the age of 14. There are today 20 million jobless in Arab League countries with 32 million seeking jobs in the coming decade. The region would need an annual growth rate of 7 per cent or more to cut the jobless figures. A large number of young unemployed combined with political and civil repression nurtures violence and extremism. So better, more account-able, more open governments, pursuing more liberal and successful economic policies, provide the best long-term answer to political jihadism.

The frustration engendered by economic hardship in a world of apparent and televised affluence has undoubtedly created hostility to what is perceived to be American-led globalization. This is given sharper focus in those Muslim countries where the sentiment has a religious edge to it. What for most of us, including many Muslims, looks like greater opportunity and more individual choice and freedom can be and is portrayed as brash and amoral in tone and imperialist in intention. This is not a new sentiment. This was the rage felt by Sayyid Qutb when he returned at the beginning of the 1950s from studying in the America of anti-communism and the Kinsey Report. 'The white man in Europe or America is our number-one enemy,' he declared.

The white man crushes us underfoot while we teach our children about his civilization, his universal principles and noble objectives . . . We are endowing our children with amazement and respect for the master who tramples our honour and enslaves us. Let us instead plant the seeds of hatred, disgust and revenge in the souls of these children. Let us teach these children from the time their nails are soft that the white man is the enemy of humanity, and that they should destroy him at the first opportunity.[10]

Osama bin Laden, many of whose lieutenants were strongly influ-enced by Sayyid Qutb, has expressed similar bigotry. This was rather different from the emotions that inspired Arab nationalist opposition to the colonial powers of the 1950s and 60s. The point is well described by the young Muslim potential terrorist in that Paul Bowles novel, written fifty years ago. 'If the word "independence" was uttered, they saw platoons of Muslim soldiers marching through streets where all the signs were written in Arabic script, they saw factories and power plants rising from the fields; he saw skies of flame, the wings of avenging angels, and total destruction.'[11]

Most Muslims have very different sentiments. A number of com-parative surveys suggest that citizens in Arab countries have much the same ambitions, fears, likes and dislikes as people elsewhere, though they have stronger views than others about Israel and Palestine. Moreover, three-quarters of Muslims live outside the Middle East in Asian countries that have suffered from terrorism. In many cases they have established effective functioning democracies (as in India, Malaysia and Indonesia) where support for jihadism is limited. There is a terrible tendency to describe the whole of the Muslim world as though, embittered by the grievances of the colonial and post-colonial era, it is inherently hostile to Western pluralism and has a tendency to mindless violence and social repression wired into its genetic base. Islamo-fascism is said to be rampant among Muslims. This is as ludicrous a proposition as it would have been to demonize all Catholics because most Irish terrorists were members of what (as a Catholic myself) I used to be taught at school to describe as the 'One True Faith'.

But the response to terrorism committed by Muslims, in many cases directed by or in imitation of al-Qaeda (operating in Colin Powell's phrase as a holding company for terrorism), is not helped when it is couched in the crude and illiberal terms of identity politics. Whether or not terror is a response to 'globalization', principally an assertion of identity by those who feel threatened or left behind by predominantly Western cultural and economic homogeneity, it certainly seems to be the case that terror based on religion is closely linked to asserting a particular *kind* of identity. It does not seem to embrace any legitimate or negotiable political goal. Some commentators talk of al-Qaeda's aims being 'limited' politically and territorially to the eradication of Israel, the expulsion of the US from Saudi Arabia and the erection of a new caliphate stretching from Morocco to Indonesia. These objectives surely stretch the word 'limited' well beyond breaking point. The pursuit of, say, regional autonomy may be defined as a 'limited' one, because it possesses certain characteristics: the objective itself is viable; the objective has a degree of political legitimacy; the objective may be negotiated; various parties to that objective are willing to negotiate it, and so on. Chechen terrorists, who have used ruthlessly wicked tactics, could be said to fall into this category; they want an independent Chechnya. But al-Qaeda's aims, with respect to Saudi Arabia, are the only ones that come close to satisfying some of the criteria just enumerated.

Here, then, are the ends of many of the new terrorists in the twenty-first century: to make us acknowledge the legitimacy of a division of the world along religious lines; to compel us to acknowledge *them* as the spokespeople of the Muslim community; and, finally, to make Muslims acknowledge *them* as their natural leaders by the will of God.

We may defeat this or that group of terrorists, but we will not overcome what Louise Richardson calls 'transformational' terrorism if we accept the legitimacy of identity as the basis for international society, and argue that identity should be the basis for a transcendental worldwide view. The point has been well made by Amartya Sen in *Identity and Violence: The Illusion of Destiny.*[12] He argues,

While religious categories have received much airing in recent years, they cannot be presumed to obliterate other distinctions, and even less can they be seen as the only relevant system of classifying people across the globe . . . The difficulty with the thesis of the clash of civilizations begins well before we come to the issue of an inevitable clash; it begins with the presumption of the unique relevance of an inevitable clash.

Sen goes on to warn against those who

present a superficially nobler vision to woo Muslim activists away from opposition through the apparently benign strategy of defining Islam appropriately. They try to wrench Islamic terrorists from violence by insisting that Islam is a religion of peace, and that a 'true Muslim' must be a tolerant individual (so come off it and be peaceful).

The rejection of a confrontational view of Islam is certainly appropriate and extremely important at this time. We must also ask whether it is at all necessary or useful, or even possible, to try to define in largely political terms what a true Muslim must be like. Substitute for Muslim the term Christian, Buddhist, Confucian, Hindu, agnostic, atheist or consumerist and the point is even more obvious.

Why do we behave as Professor Sen has described? Because we forget that the only way to 'win' the war on terror is to remember our humanism, the foundation of any global civil society. The first goal of terrorists may not be to force us to give up our civil liberties, but to lose our civic ideals. In open, liberal and tolerant societies we need to beware binding the expressiveness of an individual to the expression of a single, given community. Our proper desire to recognize and respect the identity which people choose may easily become the very means by which we deprive individuals of rights in favour of artificial collectives, in which a variety of self-appointed leaders are deemed to speak for their communities. Stressing identity, which is where their power lies, these 'leaders' (in Northern Ireland, for example) control the debate, the airtime, the resources and the individuals; they seek to trap members of ethnic groups within those with which they identify themselves at the expense of a sense of broader community. This twisted reading of politics has converted some murderous thugs into community leaders – in the Balkans for instance. Who knows? Perhaps one day we will be asked to sit down with the Janjaweed from Sudan and respectfully ask them for their views of their community and its needs. Before you know where you are you can find yourself talking to and legitimizing groups representing nothing more than thirty armed young men with a jeep and a lot of attitude.

The main breeding grounds for terrorists have not been failed states. Strong, authoritarian Arab states – Saudi Arabia, Algeria, Egypt – have been the most productive recruiting areas for terrorists. The Syrians say that two of the biggest terrorist groups they have interdicted on the way to Iraq have been Kuwaitis and Tunisians. Moreover, strong – or strongish – states often support terrorism themselves. Russia supports terrorists in Georgia; Pakistan supports them in Kashmir; Iran has supported militants in Iraq and elsewhere in the Middle East. Yet globalization has made state support less necessary to terrorist networks. Cell phones, satellite phones and email may keep networks in close contact; couriers can move rapidly around the world with large sums of cash; aeroplane tickets and passports are readily available. Terrorist groups, which often operate with or as transnational criminal organizations, benefit from the same technology and openness which make international crime such a threat to sovereignty.

Failed states themselves do bring other advantages for terrorist groups. Such states, or 'no-go' areas in states, provide territory for arms depots and training. Bosnian terrorists took over a number of districts in their country. Al-Qaeda ran businesses in Sudan and trained in Afghanistan. Failed states also lack the law-enforcement capacity to prevent the smuggling and drug trafficking that often fund terrorist operations. Terrorists in Colombia protect coca fields and cocaine processing facilities in return for a cut of the profits from the drug trade. Some of the central Asian republics provide safe havens for terrorist groups, for example in the Fergana Valley. Because failed states retain the symbols of sovereignty, they can legitimize terrorist activity. Osama bin Laden is said to have held Sudanese, Bosnian and Albanian passports. Failed states provide the sort of network for terrorists that would be recognized in the business world. From Bosnia to Afghanistan there is an ancient, poorly controlled highway of goods and people running the length of central Asia, with links along the way to Chechnya, Abkhazia (in Georgia), the 'tribal regions' of Pakistan and Kashmir. Another ancient route, which extends from the Horn of Africa and Yemen in an arc across south Asia, Malaysia and Indonesia, is today connected to the vast hinterlands of central and southern Africa from Angola to Rwanda. Globalization may have made the world somewhat flatter, but there are hills and valleys enough to hide bin Laden, the most wanted man in the world, and to provide shelter for terrorist cells and transport routes.

The nature of the states – weak, rogue, failed – that help terrorism wilfully or inadvertently is not a straightforward issue. When al-Qaeda chose to shelter in Sudan, it opted for Khartoum where the government was firmly in control, not parts of the country beyond the government's writ. It took up residence in Afghanistan after 1996 when the Taleban were firmly in charge, not in the years of civil war before. With this sort of qualification, we can categorize states into four groups. First, there are those that have failed or are failing, and which provide terrorists with ample opportunities for fundraising, arms purchasing and trans-shipment. Secondly, there are states which are relatively permissive, or willing to strike bargains with terrorist organizations on one basis or another, and where training, recruitment, stockpiling and supply may take place with a minimum of intervention. Thirdly, in some states deal-making and more 'legitimate' fundraising may occur under the banner of charitable, business or religious-interest groups and also recruitment and propaganda may be pursued. Fourthly, there are target states where surveillance, intelligence, safe houses and sympathizers are required.

One state that was fingered as belonging to the first three of these groups was Iraq after 2001. There is no point in labouring the arguments now. In the ultimatum that he presented to Saddam Hussein on 17 March 2003, President Bush said that Iraq had 'aided, trained and harboured terrorists including operatives of al-Qaeda'. In December 2001 Vice-President Dick Cheney argued, with his usual regard for the truth, that it was pretty well confirmed 'that one of bin Laden's operatives had met an Iraqi intelligence officer'. Just after 9/11, only 3 per cent of Americans believed that there had been an Iraqi link to it; thanks to the Bush administration's winks and nudges, by 2003 44 per cent thought that the 9/11 hijackers had been Iraqis. Saddam Hussein himself was believed to have been behind the attacks. Maybe this is not surprising, given the size of the audience for Rupert Murdoch's Fox TV and the readiness of the Bush administration, as one senior CIA analyst put it, to allow their wishes to be the father of the facts. While Saddam had certainly given money to the families of Palestinian suicide bombers, and had provided a safe haven for secular Palestinian terror-groups like the Abu Nidal organization, there is no evidence that he collaborated with al-Qaeda or assisted the 9/11 attacks. It would have been odd had it been otherwise. So far as bin Laden was concerned, Saddam was an apostate. He was a non-Islamic ruler and had betrayed true Islam. Saddam and bin Laden had diametrically opposed political goals and ideologies. Professor Paul Wilkinson of the University of St Andrews and BBC journalist Jane Corbin have both demolished the arguments that Iraqi agents met the leader of the 9/11 hijackers and that al-Qaeda had a base in northern Iraq and ran a network in Baghdad.[13]

The Iraq war is a terrible example of how terrorism can provoke a government into taking actions which do much more damage to it and its country than the original terrorist assault. As was predictable and predicted, not least by intelligence agencies in Washington, London and elsewhere, the Iraq invasion has in many respects increased rather than diminished the terrorist threat. The conflagration, in part a civil war, predominantly between Sunnis and Shiites, and in part a fight to expel US and allied forces, has provided a magnet for jihadist terrorists; as happened in Bosnia, Chechnya and Afghanistan in the eighties, this conflict will almost certainly generate a wide range of professional guns for hire. It sadly confirmed the unfair caricature of America as hostile to the Arab world, mainly because it is a friend of Israel, but also because of America's alleged wish to steal Muslim resources, mainly oil. Bin Laden had hoped to provoke the US into an expensive, and militarily and morally draining, invasion and occupation of Afghanistan. He cannot have believed his luck when Iraq became the scene of the neo-conservatives' grievous and foolish error, taking attention away from Afghanistan and the adjoining Pakistan border regions where al-Qaeda continues to find refuge. There are other factors as well as the encouragement of terrorism that make up the price paid for Iraq. There has been the money itself, the costs of the invasion pushing America's federal deficit through the roof. There was the discrediting of American hard power, with troops tied down in a confrontation they cannot win and unable to be deployed to the more important front in Afghanistan, where victory for the recharged Taleban and their supporters would spread disorder in Pakistan, the region and beyond. The satellite surveillance that should have been telling the US what was happening around the world was largely trained on the fight against insurgents in Iraq. There was the draining away of America's moral authority in Abu Ghraib and Fallujah, in some respects the gravest and most costly consequence of all, and a heavy dilution of America's previously emphatic soft power. We got rid of a brutal dictator in Iraq, but further brutalized the country and brutalized the region and the world. The Iraq war has made the world less safe and the effort to contain terrorism more onerous. With this recent history, President Obama saw the need to reach out from the beginning of his mandate to Muslims around the world. He gave his first television interview in the White House to an Arab TV satellite station, Al Arabiya, arguing that his administration wanted to listen not dictate, that America was not an enemy, and that he hoped for a restoration 'of the same respect and partnership that America had with the Muslim world as recently as twenty or thirty years ago.'

The suicide attacks that Saddam Hussein undoubtedly supported financially in Israel and Palestine are not, as we noted in relation to the Sicarii and the Assassins, a new phenomenon, but they have been more frequently deployed in recent years and cause particular horror both because of their effectiveness and because the fanaticism that inspires them is so incomprehensible. Irish terrorism in the UK never deployed suicide bombers although the IRA claimed their own martyrs with the hunger strikers in the 1980s. So the public transport attacks of July 2005 in London when four young men – one a respected teacher, another a young student sportsman – blew up themselves and fifty-six other people and injured 700 more, caused shock and horror. It was not only the first suicide attack in Britain but the first in Europe. Between 1981 and 1999 there were similar attacks in seven countries. Since the beginning of this century there have been suicide attacks in twenty. The perpetrators have included Europeans, a husband-and-wife team and a growing number of women, whose families in the Palestinian territories receive half the monthly stipend paid to the families of men, $200 a month in comparison with $400.

What terrorists and others in the Middle East describe as martyrdom operations, rather than suicide attacks, often result from a sense of weakness on the part of the terrorist group as well as a deep fanaticism. Until Iraq, the LTTE in Sri Lanka had carried out more of these attacks than any other terrorist group. Between 1987 and 2001 there were about 150 suicide attacks by the Tamil Tigers, perhaps more, killing over 900 people. Use of this lethal tactic took off in the Middle East with the attacks in Beirut in 1983 on the American embassy (planned by a present supporter and adviser of the 2008 Iraqi Prime Minister Maliki), on the US Marine barracks and on the headquarters of the French paratroopers. Almost 400 people were killed in the first three attacks and more died in attacks in Lebanon and Kuwait later in the year. From the Lebanese civil war, suicide bombings spread to Israel, Palestine and elsewhere in the region and were the weapons of secular as well as religious groups. Kurdish and Chechen terrorists launched these attacks, with the Chechen terrorists recruiting a special unit called the 'Black Widows', who became terrorists after the death of their husbands. The number of suicide attacks in Iraq has exceeded the figures anywhere else. Some have been carried out by Iraqis, others by Saudis, Syrians and Algerians. Al-Qaeda has been one of several groups that have organized these massacres.

The chilling proficiency of these attacks is one of the reasons for public anxiety about terrorism. You can attempt, while acknowledging the truly appalling nature of the attacks on 9/11, to put the figure of fatalities on that day – 3,000 – in a broader context in order to avoid hysterical over-reaction to the problem. Louise Richardson herself cites the 16,000 homicides and the 18,000 Americans killed by drunken drivers each year in the USA. On the other hand the sheer randomness of the horror, from New York to Beslan, and the ability and willingness of terrorists to cause so much death and destruction inevitably generate forebodings. These are aggravated by fear of the results if terrorist groups ever get hold of chemical, biological or nuclear weapons, or are able to build a dirty bomb. Some experts think that sooner or later this will happen. One of the greatest experts on terrorism, Walter Laqueur, for example, has argued that 'it is only a question of time until radiological, chemical or biological weapons will be used more or less systematically by terrorist groups; the first steps in this direction have been made'.[14] But who is it who has actually taken these steps, and how do we think the efforts to pursue this aim would fare?

We do have one clear example of a terrorist group that sought to develop this terrible capacity to kill in very large numbers.[15] The fanatical Japanese religious group Aum Shinrikyo (or Supreme Truth) had upwards of 60,000 members, and assets of about $1 billion. It specifically recruited members with scientific and engineering backgrounds (especially from Japan). It possessed a large research-and-development budget dedicated to developing weapons including sarin (they had enough sarin to kill 4.2 million people) and other powerful nerve agents like VX, tabun and soman. They were developing pathogens such as anthrax, Q-fever and possibly even Ebola. They also had a nuclear programme; they had bought a 500,000-acre sheep station in Western Australia where they hoped to mine uranium and practised gassing sheep. Their conventional capabilities included an Mi-117 helicopter (with chemical spray dispersal devices) and they were in the market for robotic manufacturing plant, tanks, jet fighters, rocket launchers and a tactical nuclear weapon. Despite this vast array of kit, cash and expertise, the group failed utterly in its efforts to weaponize and disseminate biological contaminants. Even the infamous sarin attack on the Tokyo subway was undertaken by the laughable if horrific means of storing the agent in plastic bags and poking the bags with sharpened umbrella tips. While it is true that twelve people died in that attack, roughly three-quarters of the 5,000 'affected' in some way were found to be suffering from shock, mental trauma or psychosomatic symptoms (as well they might have been). Aum Shinrikyo would have enjoyed greater success, if we can call it that, had the organization placed its faith in old-fashioned incendiary or fragmentation devices.

This is not to discount the worry felt about the use of these new weapons; the fears that followed the delivery of the anthrax letters in the US after 9/11 (they killed five people) were wholly understandable. Nor can we argue from the relative failure of Aum Shinrikyo that there is no threat from chemical, biological or radiological weapons. However, the fact that organizations might include them in their overall strategy does not mean that they have surmounted the considerable operational obstacles to acquiring the relevant material or the necessary expertise to weaponize it; avoided the extraordinary hazards associated with radiological weapons and detection in the pursuit of fairly high-profile activities; or have the capacity to deploy any weapons which may result. These obstacles may remind us that, while the twentieth century was an era of superweapons, most of them (from dreadnoughts to chemical weapons to nuclear bombs) have been exceptionally expensive exercises in deterrence or privilege. It might be more appropriate, though a lot less romantic, to call the 'Nuclear Age' the 'Kalashnikov Age'. We turn to the serious question of nuclear terrorism in the next chapter.

The bloody and blundering effects of the strategic response to al-Qaeda and 9/11 by America and its allies have been noted. They have been costly – financially, politically and morally. Commentators very often refer to the alleged resemblance between Vietnam and Iraq, a comparison initially resisted by the Bush administration and its supporters since it implied that the US was up to its eyebrows in a quagmire from which escape would prove immensely difficult. I have always worried that the comparison failed on another count. Vietnam was clearly the end of a process, even if we could not see it at the time. Communism as a system and an ideology was about to crumble away. Technology and the opening of markets were set to transform the global economy and the living standards of tens of millions in

Asia. Capitalism in a variety of forms – from Leninist party control of the process to market gangsterism – would dig the graves of Marxism and Maoism. The troubling aspect of the Iraq war is that it reflects what Audrey Kurth Cronin has called 'the coincidence between the evolving changes of globalization, the inherent weaknesses of the Arab region, and the inadequate American response to both . . .'[16] It is unfair to refer solely to the US here; Europe is culpable, too. What we have managed to do is to give credence to Huntington's thesis of 'the clash of civilizations' by aggravating the Muslim sense of grievance in a part – admittedly the smaller part – of the Islamic world. Unless we make some strategic adjustments, we shall discover that we have started something that we cannot easily finish. That is why Vietnam is irrelevant.

Yet tactically, despite political and strategic blunders, some argue that the containment of terrorism has been moderately successful – a point that political leaders should try to avoid making without a satchel full of qualifications and the crossing of every finger and toe. If you do not regard us all as being in a good-versus-evil war on terrorism – with Iraq the Omaha Beach of the campaign – but reckon instead and more realistically that we are trying to cope with this or that group of terrorists at this moment in history, then the record is not all bad. After surveying much of the available evidence, James Fallows is of the opinion that 'what is controllable has been controlled; al-Qaeda Central has been broken up'. He believes that America should now move on to the three-fold job of 'domestic protection, worldwide harassment and pursuit of al-Qaeda and an all-fronts diplomatic campaign'.[17] An important focus for the campaign should be Afghanistan and Pakistan – especially border regions like North Waziristan, where al-Qaeda has been trying to build an operational hub. Other experts argue that al-Qaeda has been doing better, hidden but regrouping in this border wilderness, than Mr Fallows suggests. A former chief of the CIA's Osama bin Laden unit claimed on the sixth anniversary of 9/11 that under the protection of some of President Musharraf's security services al-Qaeda was 'on balance' even more threatening today than then, a worry supported by classified intelligence leaks at about the same time. The most honest response is – who really knows? At the very least, what we do know is that for the moment bin Laden is holed up somewhere in a mountain cave; there is greater international cooperation in pursuing terrorists; and in par- ticular the practical cooperation in tackling terrorist financing – while still very far from perfect – has been enhanced. Moreover, whatever has happened in Europe, there appears to have been no Muslim backlash in the US. Despite some of his early gaffes – the launching of 'a crusade', for example – President Bush was solicitous of Muslim groups and opinion at home, and Muslims appear to be well integrated into American society.

This might encourage us to recall that counter-terrorism can and does succeed. It worked in Malaya and the Philippines in the 1950s; it worked against the Red Brigades in Germany and Italy in the 1970s; and it had some success against the IRA in Northern Ireland. Terrorist campaigns do end, as Professor Sir Adam Roberts has noted,[18] though claiming victory is an unwise provoker of any terrorist who may be left, as well as of the gods. In any campaign, the keys are good intelligence and police work in which the public should have confi- dence; it is a particularly bad mistake in a democracy, where public faith in the basic integrity of government is vital for the defence of freedom, to abuse intelligence as happened after 9/11 and in the run-up to the Iraq war. To conclude a terrorist campaign, you need (despite Mr Rove's animadversions on the subject) to know whom you are fighting, and you also require achievable goals in your operations – closing down cells, winding up networks, drying up sources of financing.

It is also wise to remove any underlying sense of grievance where you can. Terrorism associated with the struggle for national indepen- dence is usually only concluded by the granting of independence by the sovereign power, though that does not happen (the Basque country, Northern Ireland) when the sovereign emphatically embraces the dissi- dent region culturally, politically and within its own value system. Even in cases like this, devolving some political power is invariably part of any conclusive agreement that ends terrorism. It is not comfort- able to own up to this, let alone sometimes to do it. Dealing with terrorists is an offensive business for democratic politicians, and it is almost as distasteful to have to work with those who, while not terrorists themselves, are content to ride on the tiger's back. There are other cases where there is no real political gesture that a counter-terrorism campaign can embrace. Do we really believe that we can give ground on the establishment of Osama bin Laden's caliphate? Yet even here our policy on regional issues in the Middle East and in west and central Asia, can help to aggravate or diminish that sense of Muslim grievance that terrorists play like a musical instrument. The US and (on the whole) Europe are believed to be biased against Palestinians and unqualified supporters of Israel, whatever that country does. The suggestion in 2006 by US Secretary of State Condoleezza Rice that the bombing of Beirut and the unsuccessful Israeli response to Hezbollah's provocations represented the birth pangs of a new Middle East; the perception of the application of double standards by Western countries throughout the region; the sense that for all Washington's verbal commitment to a Palestinian state, it will never push Israel to give up parts of the West Bank in order to make such a state a negotiated and viable reality; the devastating Israeli response in late 2008 to rocket attacks from Gaza – all these are issues that, certainly cynically in many cases, are used to justify terrorism or at least to gain sympathy for it. Israel finds the proposition unpalatable, but a settlement of the long-standing dispute with Palestine would do more to hack through the roots of terrorism in the Middle East than anything else.

It is always possible to create more causes of grievance by the way that governments respond to terrorism. Sir Robert Thompson, one of the architects of success in Malaya in the 1950s, wrote of the crucial importance of the government functioning within the law (which it did for most of the time in dealing with that insurgency). International legal standards matter as much as national ones. In his account of overcoming the communist insurgency he noted:

There is a very strong temptation in dealing both with terrorism and with guerrilla actions for government forces to act outside the law, the excuses being that the processes of law are too cumbersome, that the normal safeguards in the law for the individual are not designed for an insurgency and that a terrorist deserves to be treated as an outlaw anyway. Not only is this morally wrong, but, over a period, it will create more practical difficulties for a government than it solves.[19]

When Donald Rumsfeld in 2002 said of the prisoners in Guantanamo that he did not have even the slightest concern over their treatment, and when it became apparent that American forces had not only used torture but that their commander-in-chief had debated with his advisers just how much torture was legitimate, the anti-terrorism cause was heavily discredited. In Nasser's Egypt, terrorists were tortured and became jihadist fanatics. In Putin's Russia, the human rights of Chechens were massively abused, driving more of the diminishing population into the terrorists' arms. Massive brutality can probably scotch terrorism for a time. Crassus put down the revolt of the slaves in Rome by lining the Appian Way for a hundred miles with their crucified bodies. Spartacus was defeated. But on the whole, history does not suggest that you eliminate grievance by creating more of it – the sort of grievance that is passed on down the generations in grandmothers' and mothers' milk. When terrorists can be made to look like martyrs, their blood irrigating the seeds of a new and horrible church, they make bad enemies.

Democracies should live by their principles in fighting terrorism. It is those principles and the values they incorporate that distinguish the leaders of free societies from terrorist fanatics and psychopaths. Holding on patiently to that precept, and having the sense of prudence and perspective advocated by Louise Richardson, there is no reason to conclude that the main threat to us all in future decades will be posed by terrorists. But a knowledge of history should inform us how best to deal with them, encourage us not to be dispirited in our campaigns, and remind us (without plunging us into pessimism) that terrorism itself is something that is very unlikely to be expunged from our lives.

5

Mushroom Clouds

> I will leave the city's rush,
> Leave the fancy and the plush,
> Leave the snow and leave the slush
> And the crowds.
> I will seek the desert's hush,
> Where the scenery is lush
> How I long to see the mush-
> room clouds.
>
> Tom Lehrer,
> 'The Wild West Is Where I Wanna Be'

> We have gone on piling weapon upon weapon, missile upon
> missile, new levels of destruction upon old ones. We have done
> this helplessly, almost involuntarily, like the victims of some
> sort of hypnotism, like men in a dream, like lemmings headed
> for the seas.   George Kennan, 1981

> We must abandon the unworkable notion that it is morally
> reprehensible for some countries to pursue weapons of mass
> destruction yet morally acceptable for others to rely on them
> for security – and indeed to refine their capacities and postulate
> plans for their use.   Mohammed ElBaradei, Director General
> of the International Atomic Energy Agency

The last century did not unveil for the first time the phenomenon of
terrorism that we have just considered. But in those years we could

certainly point to one ferocious debut. Scientific enquiry showed us how to unlock the gates of hell, and we did so twice at Hiroshima and Nagasaki in 1945. The pilot of the B-29 bomber that dropped the first atomic bomb told *Newsweek*, 'A bright light filled the plane. We turned back to look at Hiroshima. The city was hidden by that awful cloud . . . boiling up, mushrooming.' The nuclear age had left its calling card.

I was born in 1944 with work on the Manhattan Project that constructed the atomic bomb well into its second year. I am therefore one of the generation – the *real* baby boomers – that grew up in the age of the nuclear peace, when East and West survived because the alternative was to destroy our planet. It was a crazy world, and looking back I cannot fully comprehend how so many of us managed to be so indifferent to the balance of terror, so remiss about worrying ourselves witless. It is true that at home in our London suburb, one of the few novels in our glass-fronted bookcase was Nevil Shute's *On the Beach*, written in 1957 and describing the last months on the Australian shores of the survivors of a global thermonuclear war. Beyond that, all I can remember is my parents' disapproval of those who marched every Easter to Aldermaston, the Atomic Weapons Research Establishment in Berkshire, to protest against Britain's possession of what was called, somewhat erroneously, our independent nuclear deterrent. Certainly these intrepid marchers included a few who wanted the West disarmed, but were more ambivalent about the position of the Soviet Union, where their ideological sympathies lay. But the majority were surely motivated, like a modern Children's Crusade, by simpler hopes – naïve, perhaps, though hardly irrational or insane. How could it be mad to want a sane world? It was better perhaps to protest, one of the touchstones of a vigorously plural society, than to pretend that there was nothing to protest about.

Sometimes gallows humour helped to laugh the nightmare away. I was introduced in my mid-teens, by the same English teacher who recommended Donne, Isherwood and Auden (he was a one-legged war veteran and Cambridge pupil of F. R. Leavis), to the caustic satire of Tom Lehrer. There was a time when I knew the words of all his songs, from 'Poisoning Pigeons in the Park' to 'Oedipus Rex' ('Whose name appears in Freud's Index, 'cos he loved His mother'). Alongside his song about the Wild West quoted above, Lehrer had a jolly revival-ist hymn for these nuclear years, or rather a *sur*vivalist hymn:

> We'll all go together when we go,
> Every Hottentot and every Eskimo,
> When the air becomes uranious,
> We will all go simultaneous,
> Yes, we'll all go together when we go.

As Lehrer noted, it would be a brisk, no-nonsense business:

> You will all go directly to your respective Valhallas,
> Go directly, do not pass 'Go', do not collect 200 dollars.

So I listened to Lehrer, and laughed at Stanley Kubrick's *Dr Strange-love*, but I did not march. Indeed, I convinced myself that we really did need a British finger on the nuclear button (one day, as things turned out, it could have been my finger) in order to survive the threats from Moscow and the East. My conviction was strengthened by the Cuban missile crisis of 1962, when the world came close to nuclear catastrophe and when some of my Oxford friends demonstrated against President Kennedy and what they oddly regarded as American provocation. To most of the rest of us, who accepted the case for Western nuclear deterrence, it seemed that Mr Khrushchev had made most of our point for us. How could we have withstood Soviet bullying had we not been locked in a mutual suicide pact with Moscow's bureaucratic tyrants?

As a politician, I often debated the nuclear issue with priests and nuns, radicals and pacifists, fellow-travellers and holy innocents, in Catholic church halls and Methodist chapels. The audience usually knew what it believed already. But it wanted to see how I could possibly justify the unjustifiable – 'And him, saying he's a practising Christian.' I remember once being locked in a fierce debate with one of the most articulate of the nuclear disarmers, then not just a Catholic priest but a Monsignor to boot, Bruce Kent. Another of the panellists was a scholarly nun, who was asked a leading question clearly intended to embarrass me. How should a Christian deal with the nuclear issue in a way that could be reconciled with his or her beliefs? She replied that there was a very old Russian nun in her convent,

Sister Michael, and every night for years she had prayed to the arch-angel whose name she bore to bring peace and freedom to the land of her birth. Now Mr Gorbachev had become Russia's leader – Mikhail Gorbachev – and the old nun thought that her prayers had been answered. The threat of war – nuclear war – had miraculously receded. 'So you should pray,' concluded my fellow panellist to the confusion of the large audience crammed on the pews in our Bath church. Now there was a thought – perhaps it was the power of prayer that got us through, that enabled us to avoid all going together 'when we go, all suffused with an incandescent glow'. Prayer and humour were probably the best antidotes to exculpable anguish.

Looking back on our survival through the second half of the twen-tieth century, it is difficult to believe that today's world is more dangerous. In 1959, the year that the film of Shute's novel appeared, the United States had over 7,000 nuclear bombs to 360 deployed by the then Soviet Union. In the next two decades the Soviet Union played catch-up, though its military strength was invariably exaggerated (as it still is), a reason for Moscow's reluctance for so long to accept inspection and surveillance of nuclear weapons as a basis for disarma-ment. By the time that Jonathan Schell wrote *The Fate of the Earth* in 1982, there were 50,000 nuclear weapons in the world, with over a million times the power of the Hiroshima bomb. These weapons, as Schell wrote, 'grew out of history, yet they threaten to end history'.[1]

Since then, the number of weapons has fallen dramatically. The Cold War has ended, though not without occasional scares. In 1995, for example, the Russians feared that they were under attack from a US submarine-launched missile. The alarm had in fact been triggered by a Norwegian weather rocket. Disaster was avoided, but not before President Yeltsin sat for some time, his hand that day steady, wonder-ing whether to press the button to launch a counter-strike. Yet overall the world today is a safer place, with US and Soviet treaties to reduce the size of their nuclear arsenals leading to substantial cuts in the number of these doomsday weapons: a safer world but still a very, very dangerous one.

The dangers are invariably described in terms much broader than nuclear threats. We became accustomed, particularly in the run-up to the Iraq war, to the Bush administration's denunciation of weapons of mass destruction. As has been argued in *Deadly Arsenals*, a Brookings Institution Report, this is not a very helpful catch-all phrase.[2] It was doubtless deployed in order to magnify the dangers that would abound from allowing Saddam Hussein to remain in power. Administration spokesmen were relentlessly one hundred per cent certain not just that Iraq had once had a programme to make nuclear weapons but that it had one still. Yet as Hans Blix's UN monitoring team observed, surprisingly they had nil per cent knowledge of where these manufacturing facilities were. For Condoleezza Rice, Saddam's smoking gun looked like a mushroom cloud. But just in case that did not frighten us into acquiescence in the Iraq invasion, then America could point to Baghdad's possession of chemical and biological weapons. There was no argument at all about them. Indeed, chemical weapons had been used by Saddam in Iraq against his own Kurdish people and during the country's long war with Iran. In the latter case, we had looked the other way; after all, when that war started Saddam was the West's man, all that stood between us and – so it was suggested – a bunch of bearded psychopaths. No wonder Iranians are more than a little hesitant these days about taking Western advice on how they should best protect their future security.

The truth is that some countries have weapons of mass destruction but are not themselves nuclear powers. The Egyptians probably have an offensive biological warfare research programme. The Syrians are thought to have chemical weapons, and Sudan and Taiwan are suspected of conducting chemical weapons research. Moreover, while all these weapons – chemical, biological, radiological (dirty bombs) and nuclear – do terrible damage and kill substantial numbers of people in grisly ways, the threats are different, as are the consequences and the lethality of their use and the best ways of protecting against them. Chemical weapons can be manufactured easily, but in comparison to nuclear weapons they do relatively little damage over a limited area.

Thucydides records the use of arsenic smoke by the Spartans against the defenders of the Athenian city of Delium during the Peloponnesian war in the fifth century BC. Chinese forces used similar smoke during the Sung dynasty 1,500 years later. In 1863 President Abraham Lincoln banned the use of poisons in warfare. It was 'out of the pale of the law and uses of war'. The Hague Declaration of 1899 prohibited 'the use of projectiles the sole object of which is the diffusion of asphyxiating or deleterious gases'. But the German army used chlorine gas – described by the code name 'disinfectant' – at the second battle of Ypres in 1915, killing 5,000 French and Algerian soldiers and seriously injuring thousands more, many of whom died of the after-effects, drowning in their own mucus. The British and French retaliated with horrific gases and by the end of the war both sides were using mustard gas; Adolf Hitler was one of the victims, suffering from skin burns and temporary blindness. The fact that chemical weapons were not used in Europe during the Second World War may be taken as an early example of the effectiveness of mutual deterrence. But the Italians used gas in Abyssinia and the Japanese in Manchuria and China. In most wars since then, for instance between Israel and its Arab neighbours, gas has not been used. But it is believed to have been deployed by the Egyptians in the Yemen in the 1960s, by and against the US and its allies in Vietnam and Laos, by Soviet forces in Afghanistan and by Iraq as already mentioned, both in its war against Iran and against rebellious Kurds. Between 3,200 and 5,000 Kurds were killed in Halabja in 1988 and 10,000 were injured.

Biological warfare of a sort has been used in the past. The Assyrians poisoned wells; others tossed the bodies of plague victims into besieged cities; the British army in the mid-eighteenth century in America provided blankets infected with smallpox to Indian supporters of the French. But while many countries have researched the use of biological weapons, the Geneva Protocol of 1925 banning bacteriological agents in war has been widely observed, with the exception of Japanese forces before and during the Second World War, who employed these weapons against China and the Soviet Union. Chinese, Russian, Mongolian and Korean prisoners were certainly used by them as guinea pigs, as probably were up to 3,000 American, British, French and Australian POWs.

Diplomacy has helped to get rid of the arsenals and the production facilities of chemical weapons. By 2005 168 countries had signed up to the provisions of the 1996 Chemical Weapons Convention, undertaking to destroy any chemical weapons in their possession in a safe and environmentally friendly way by 2007, and to destroy the facilities that enabled them to make these weapons. The United States,

Russia, India and South Korea have declared stockpiles totalling more than 70,000 metric tons, of which the Russian stockpile represents more than half. Several countries – including China, Egypt, Iran, Israel, North Korea and Syria – are suspected, whatever they assert, of retaining significant chemical weapons programmes. Of course, many more countries have in the past been manufacturers of chemical than of nuclear weapons. It is far easier to weaponize gas than to make a nuclear bomb. Nevertheless, deterrence and moral disapproval appear to have discouraged proliferation and encouraged disarmament in this area. Moreover, whatever the awful effects of a chemical agent like the nerve gas sarin, they are not equivalent to the consequences of the detonation of a nuclear device.

Robert Hutchinson is probably correct to argue in *Weapons of Mass Destruction* that biological weapons are 'the most terrifying of all the weapons of mass destruction' and that anyone who used them would have to 'verge on the insane'.[3] The main reason for these judgements is that you can predict neither the outcome of the release of bacteria or a virus, nor the longevity of any epidemic that might result. You do not know whether medical science could deal with mutation nor how widely disease would spread and what effects it would have on the planet's ecology. This may explain why these weapons have been used so rarely, though not why several countries are suspected of retaining biological weapons or programmes to make them. The countries mentioned in the previous paragraph as suspects for having chemical weapons programmes are on the list, as is Russia. There are also worries about Taiwan and Sudan.

The principal impetus for banning biological weapons came from President Nixon, who announced in 1969 that the USA would unilaterally and unconditionally renounce their use. The American biological weapons stockpile was destroyed and all production facilities were converted to peaceful purposes. The 1925 Geneva Protocol was also ratified, and Nixon successfully negotiated the Biological and Toxic Weapons Convention in 1972. President Yeltsin disclosed in 1992 that Russia, which was one of the signatories, continued to produce and stockpile weapon agents.

Despite these transgressions, all states more or less agree that chemical and biological weapons should be eliminated, which distinguishes these weapons from nuclear ones. The Nuclear Non-Proliferation Treaty (which entered into force in 1970) has from the outset been the subject of rival interpretations.[4] Some have agreed that it is primarily a disarmament agreement which obliges those of its signatories who possess nuclear weapons to work towards their elimination. The nuclear powers themselves, on the contrary, have tended to assert – albeit usually rather coyly – that they are only obliged to negotiate 'in good faith' for an early end to the nuclear arms race, and that the treaty is concerned above all with non-proliferation rather than disarmament. One reason why nuclear powers are reluctant to surrender their weapons is that they have become the sole guarantor against cheating by states over chemical and biological weapons. So while the chemical and biological non-proliferation regimes move from strength to strength, the nuclear non-proliferation regime is in serious danger, and only survives despite growing clamour about its fairness and purposes. The current threat of an arms race is once again a threat of a *nuclear* arms race. Existing nuclear states want to hold on to their weapons, though mostly in reduced numbers, because they regard them as the ultimate shield or hedge against cheating by others. Potential nuclear states worry about cheating too.

In the Cold War, deterrence operated on fairly clean lines. 'We' had the bomb, so that 'they' would not use it against 'us'. Deterrence was achieved not by the power to inflict terrible damage on an opponent but by a balance of terror. For deterrence to work there has to be a subtle agreement that A can destroy B and B can destroy A. This state of affairs was called 'mutually assured destruction'; the appropriate acronym was MAD. As defensive weapons, nuclear weapons represented not just a will to power but a will to suicide. These terrible certainties have been replaced by vague premonitions and muddled fears, so that a (potentially growing) number of actors feels the necessity of holding out, just in case, against a commitment to non-proliferation. States edge or lurch into taking decisions that they believe best serve their security. It is at best naïve and at worst dangerous to think that they will act against their perception of their interests in the service of an abstract morality. To take an example, to which I will return later, it is foolish to think that one can prevent states in the Middle East or in east Asia eventually reaching a collective tipping point on nuclear proliferation unless there are regional settlements guaranteeing their individual security.

I am not a physicist; I have no technical skills beyond the rudimentary capacity to change a plug and type emails with one finger. But nothing I have seen, heard or read suggests that it is easy to manufacture a nuclear weapon. Some experts disagree. Ambassador Thomas Graham, for example, who was President Clinton's special ambassador for nuclear disarmament issues, argues in his book *Commonsense on Weapons of Mass Destruction* that when he toured the South African nuclear weapons programme infrastructure, which had been closed down in the early 1990s, he was shown the room where the weapons had been assembled.[5] 'There was nothing in that room that would not be found in a high school machine shop.' Well, maybe he was right: assembling finished components is a relatively simple job. All a person needs, for instance, to assemble a computer is a screwdriver. It does not follow that where there are screwdrivers, computers appear, hey presto! The real question is, where do those finished components come from? The answer in relation to nuclear weapons is complicated.

In order to produce a nuclear explosion, you need to split an atom's nucleus and so release a huge amount of energy. The essential ingredient for this is called fissile material, most commonly uranium or plutonium, which can sustain an explosive chain reaction. This is essential in all nuclear explosions. Part of the challenge of preventing the spread of nuclear weapons is that the materials required to make them can also be used for legitimate peaceful means. Making these materials suitable for weapons is lengthy and complex. The first material, uranium, requires enrichment; the second, providing an alternative technology, is plutonium, which comes from reprocessing the spent fuel rods used in a nuclear reactor.

Joseph Cirincione has noted that 'Producing specialized nuclear materials and designing and building a well-engineered explosive device requires the construction of large and thus highly visible facilities (those required for nuclear materials production) making the clandestine acquisition of nuclear weapons extremely difficult.'[6] Perhaps we should distinguish more clearly between production and acquisition. Certainly the production of weapons-grade fissile material or of a nuclear weapon is far more likely to be managed by a state than by a terrorist organization. Converting and enriching uranium or reprocessing spent uranium fuel rods into plutonium are protracted and laborious enterprises. The chief danger posed by terrorist groups would therefore be the result of purchasing or stealing the fissile material or a bomb itself from a state or state agency. This would probably be achieved clandestinely.

From the very beginning of the age of nuclear warfare in 1945, the terrifying destructive force of nuclear bombs (measured in terms of kilotons, each equivalent to a thousand tons of dynamite or TNT) spurred political leaders to find ways of controlling these monsters. President Harry Truman told Congress in October 1945, two months after the flattening and incineration of Hiroshima, that 'the hope of civilization lies in international arrangements looking, if possible, to the renunciation of the use and development of the atomic bomb'. Along with the British and Canadian prime ministers, Clement Attlee and Mackenzie King, he put forward to the UN the first non-proliferation plan under which all nuclear weapons would be eliminated and nuclear technology for peaceful purposes would be shared and overseen by a UN Atomic Energy Commission. In the following year, encouraged by the alarm and anguish of the scientists who had created the abomination, he fleshed out these proposals with plans covering most of the areas affecting non-proliferation that we still debate sixty years later. Truman's initiatives were strongly opposed by Stalin. He would brook no infringement of Soviet sovereignty nor run any risk of leaving the Americans, albeit temporarily, with a strategic advantage. Soviet work on nuclear weapons had begun in 1943, and in 1949 Moscow held its first nuclear test in Kazakhstan, to be followed by over 450 more during the Cold War. The race was on. The United Kingdom joined it in 1952, France in 1960 and China in 1964. The US estimate in 1958 was that sixteen nations could have nuclear weapons within ten years, and in 1960 John F. Kennedy warned that there would be fifteen, twenty or twenty-five nuclear states 'by the end of the presidential office in 1964'.

In the decade in which President Kennedy made those remarks, twenty-three countries either possessed nuclear weapons, were doing research on them or were considering starting research – Argentina,

Australia, Brazil, Canada, China, Egypt, France, India, Israel, Italy, Japan, Norway, Romania, South Africa, Spain, Sweden, Switzerland, Taiwan, the UK, the USA, the USSR, West Germany and Yugoslavia. By the 1980s this figure had fallen to nineteen – Argentina, Brazil, Canada, China, France, India, Iran, Iraq, Israel, Libya, North Korea, Pakistan, South Africa, South Korea, Taiwan, the UK, the USA, the USSR and Yugoslavia. Today, there are eight confirmed nuclear states – China, France, India, Israel, Pakistan, Russia, the UK and the USA. North Korea *may* have weapons. Iran is suspected of having an active programme to manufacture them. These declining figures, given that about forty-four states are reckoned to have the industrial and technological capacity to develop weapons (partly because of their civil nuclear-power programmes), represent the partial success of the efforts to contain proliferation that were promoted particularly vigorously in the aftermath of the Cuban missile crisis of 1962.

Why do some states want these weapons while others are happy without them? There are generally reckoned to be five relevant issues – security, prestige, national politics, technology and economics. These are not discrete motivations; they mingle and merge.

Security is an obvious consideration, though it does not in all circumstances stand up today to rigorous scrutiny. The Soviet Union developed a bomb because the United States already had one. China did not trust the Soviet Union or the United States; and once China had tested a bomb, India wanted one too. Anything India could explode, Pakistan wanted. It was even more directly relevant that India began researching nuclear weapons after her defeat in 1962 at the hands of China, and that Pakistan began research on them ten years later after her defeat by India. Britain did not think it could wholly depend – special relationship or not – on its main ally. From the outset, under the post-war Labour government, there were worries both that an American nuclear monopoly would not be acceptable, and that other countries might develop weapons of their own. Moreover, Britain was at the time – perhaps until Suez in 1956 – still regarded by many as one of the world's superpowers. France was explicit that it could not depend on America. Israel was worried that it was surrounded by hostile Arab states, committed to wiping it out. Its nuclear weapon (whose production South Africa may well have assisted) was the final deterrent against conventional threats. Many of these security considerations have been publicly argued. For example, the former Indian foreign minister Jaswant Singh has said that 'the nuclear age entered India's neighbourhood when China became a nuclear power in October 1964'. David Ben-Gurion, Israel's first prime minister, argued that 'the Jews of Israel will never be like the Jews in the Holocaust. Israel will be able to visit a terrible retribution on those who would attempt its destruction'. France had perhaps some justification for thinking that it required its very own *force de frappe*, or (as it was renamed) its *force de dissuasion*, given the efforts by America and Britain to deny it the missile technology that those two countries shared.

Other European countries, especially members of NATO but also including Sweden and Switzerland, did not believe that they required their own system of nuclear deterrence. West Germany, for example, could have developed nuclear weapons very fast, but was content with having nuclear weapons on its soil at NATO bases and with participating in the Alliance's Nuclear Planning Group. It was content to shelter in America's nuclear bunker.

Elsewhere, countries have decided that their security is no longer threatened or that it can be guaranteed by alliance. South Africa built a small nuclear arsenal with six weapons in the 1970s. It was feeling threatened by African states hostile to apartheid, especially Angola where large numbers of Cuban troops had been deployed. Moreover, South Africa's sense of isolation and beleaguerment was increased by the mandatory arms embargo and a voluntary oil embargo imposed in the late 1970s. Nelson Mandela's post-apartheid government announced in 1993 that it had dismantled its nuclear weapons programme and wanted a nuclear-free continent. In Asia, South Korea was strongly dissuaded by the US from developing nuclear weapons to deter invasion by North Korea. Washington gave security assurances in return.

Prestige has been another reason for joining the nuclear club. In October 1946 Britain's foreign secretary, Ernest Bevin, told a cabinet committee: 'Our prestige in the world as well as our chances of securing American cooperation would both suffer if we did not exploit to the full a discovery in which we played a leading part at the outset.' Those who actually attended the meeting at which the official minute-taker recorded this argument recalled Bevin using earthier language than appeared in the record. 'We've got to have the thing over here, whatever it costs. We've got to have the bloody Union Jack on top of it.'[7] In December 1962, when the British prime minister Harold Macmillan was trying to persuade President Kennedy, at a summit at Nassau in the Bahamas, to provide Britain with Polaris submarine-based nuclear missiles, he reportedly conceded that 'the whole thing is ridiculous', not least since the small British nuclear force added little 'to the existing nuclear strength which is enough to blow up the world'. His chief scientific adviser, Sir William Penney, told him at the time that it would take only seven or eight nuclear missiles to destroy Britain, 'to be on the safe side'. However, 'countries which have played a great role in history must retain their dignity', said Macmillan.[8] In a television interview in February 1958 he also said that 'the independent [nuclear deterrent] puts us where we ought to be, in the position of a great power'. Three years later President de Gaulle made similar comments, noting that 'a great state' that does not have the nuclear weapons that others have 'does not command its own destiny'. Both Britain and France, their empires melted or melting away, harked back to a great-power status recently dissolved. They both thought too that having 'the bomb' guaranteed them a place at the top table of global diplomacy; it was their membership subscription to the club.

Sometimes domestic politics determines the decision to develop or reject nuclear weapons. In India, the arrival of the conservative Bharatiya Janata Party (BJP) in office in 1998 led rapidly to turning a small and more or less covert nuclear capability that had existed since 1974 into a more open programme, with several nuclear weapons tests being conducted in 1998. The horrors of Hiroshima and Nagasaki have helped to sustain public opposition in Japan against a nuclear weapons choice, and there are substantial constitutional hurdles there against their development.

The technical ability to make weapons undoubtedly increases the likelihood that a country will do so, but the cost of the technology can be a barrier. This was evidently a factor in the decisions by Ukraine not to retain its nuclear weapons and by Libya not to seek to join the nuclear club. But economics is plainly not a relevant factor in Pakistan or North Korea, where nuclear aspirations load costly burdens on these poor countries. (The economy of North Korea, for example, is worth $26 billion compared to the $950 billion of the South Korean economy.)

The reduction in the size of nuclear arsenals, and the limited growth in the number of nuclear states, should not make us complacent. There is enough fissile material in the world for at least 300,000 bombs and the nuclear states have about 27,000 in their arsenals. The US has 5,400 warheads and Russia 4,200. Altogether, we have a thousand times enough kilotonnage to destroy our planet. Moreover, the world is more uncertain and unpredictable than it was, which produces a sense of nostalgia for the decades of the Cold War when the red lines seemed clear to all and were understood by all. Where are today's red lines? Are we deterring strong states or weak ones? How does deterrence work in regional hot spots? How can we prevent the hedging and cheating described earlier? How do we legitimize fundamentally unequal international agreements? What sort of red lines are recognized by what are euphemistically described as non-state actors, who are not covered by treaties and international protocols? The danger posited by President Kennedy in 1963 seems as real today, in some ways more so:

I ask you to stop and think for a moment what it would mean to have nuclear weapons in so many hands, in the hands of countries large and small, stable and unstable, responsible and irresponsible, scattered throughout the world. There would be no rest for anyone then, no stability, no real security, and no chance of effective disarmament. There would only be the increased chance of accidental war, and an increased necessity for the great powers to involve themselves in what otherwise would be local conflicts.

To which we would today add the terrorist dimension.

The nuclear dangers that we face are all related. New nuclear states could trigger regional arms races. Iran's possession of nuclear weapons would encourage Saudi Arabia, Egypt, Syria and others to develop their own bombs: a Shiite route to destroying the Middle East would be matched by a Sunni one. North Korea's ambitions could push its southern neighbour and Japan over the edge. The existing stockpiles of nuclear weapons pose an ever-present danger. Do the United States and Russia need thousands of missiles on hair-trigger alert? The more nuclear weapons that exist, and the more fissile material, the greater the chance of terrorists stealing or buying their own way to lunatic acts of devastation. The existing agreements that have been relatively successful in limiting proliferation could themselves break down if we fail to uphold them firmly and realistically. In short, while many of our worries at the beginning of a new century are focused on preventing a carbon summer, we are still menaced by the danger of a nuclear winter.

Proliferation describes an existential threat to states, and non-proliferation denotes a policy with the full weight of modern, techno-cratic statecraft behind it. These subjects (as we saw in the case of Iraq) are smothered in secrecy, conjecture, unnamed sources, unconfirmed leaks, grey literature and a range of ongoing negotiations and initia-tives. Real dangers lurk among the thickets of acronyms – COCOM, CTBT, CTR, DGP, FMCT, IPP, MPC&A, NCI, NPT, NSG, PSI and several copses of others.[9]

There are essentially three layers to the non-proliferation regime: across-the-board undertakings and obligations with universal intent; coalitions of one sort or another; and special initiatives or actions, often aimed at a particular sort of proliferation threat. At the heart of all these efforts is the Nuclear Non-Proliferation Treaty (NPT) administered by the International Atomic Energy Agency (IAEA). Negotiation of the NPT began in the wake of the Cuban missile crisis and was completed by President Kennedy's successor, Lyndon Johnson, in 1968. Under the treaty, 183 nations have now pledged never to acquire nuclear weapons. In addition, the five nuclear powers recognized by the treaty – the USA, Russia, China, France and the UK – are all members of the pact and have committed themselves under Article 6 of the treaty 'to pursue negotiations in good faith on effective measures relating to cessation of the nuclear arms race at an early date and to nuclear disarmament, and on a treaty on general and complete disarmament under strict and effective international control'. The vagueness of this language, and the reservations which hedged it about, left a lot of questions unanswered, as Joachim Krause has pointed out. 'Was nuclear disarmament meant to be complete or was it not? Was there a linkage or conditionality between nuclear disarmament and general disarmament? Would complete nuclear disarmament be envisaged only as part of general and complete disarmament, or should it be pursued independently? Most likely, accepting this vagueness was the only way to strike an agreement.'[10] Certainly the British government did not seem inhibited by the treaty when it announced in 2007 that it had decided to design and build a new generation of submarines to carry its Trident nuclear missiles. The states that possess nuclear technology have promised to sell it to those that do not, provided that the have-not countries commit themselves to use it solely for peaceful purposes. The IAEA seeks to regulate global trade in nuclear commerce, technology and reactors. Alongside this treaty is the Comprehensive Test Ban Treaty, negotiated for years, signed by President Clinton in 1996 but not yet enforced because of resistance in the US Congress and hostility on the American right to what is seen as a barrier to upgrading the country's nuclear weapons. This continues to be one of the most blatant examples of American exceptionalism in foreign and security policy.

In recent years the Bush administration used the UN Security Council to sponsor global 'legislation' (for instance Resolution 1540 passed in April 2004) which calls on states to prevent proliferation and to put in place adequate safeguards of existing nuclear sites and of exports. The IAEA has introduced the Additional Protocol to the NPT treaty which commits states to accept IAEA inspections wherever the agency sees fit. Under the basic NPT, these inspections could be confined to locations which had been 'declared' in line with this treaty. This made cheating easy. While subscription to the Additional Protocol is entirely voluntary, the numbers signing on have been increasing over the years, and this should become a cornerstone of the non-proliferation regime. When I began the negotiation of a basic trade and cooperation regime with Iran after 2001, one of the conditions was that it should sign the Additional Protocol. It was the IAEA's evidence of Iranian cheating over the NPT that first brought these trade talks to a halt in 2003.

Universal non-proliferation regimes aim to control both the supply of and the demand for weapons of mass destruction; coalition-building tends to focus on the supply side, particularly on denying access to states. For example, the Nuclear Suppliers Group (which began meeting in 1975 after the Indian nuclear test) has introduced tough export controls and detailed and precise information on nuclear transfers. More than thirty countries are members. The Proliferation Security Initiative was launched by the Bush administration in 2003 and aims to identify and interdict shipments of missiles, chemical and biological agents and nuclear components.

When it comes to limited, targeted initiatives, the US is the clear leader. For instance, the Nunn–Lugar Cooperative Threat Reduction Initiative (first pioneered by these two senators in 1992), combined with the diplomacy of the Bush (Sr) and Clinton administrations, provided the basis under which Belarus, Ukraine and Kazakhstan gave up their nuclear armaments; it is also accounting for, and down-grading, a large portion of the highly enriched uranium in Russia. The US State Department's International Science and Technology Center is attempting to provide employment to an ageing body of Russian weapons scientists and technicians, to preclude their employment by rogue regimes or organizations. America even offered to fund the construction of new early-warning radar systems in Russia in order to replace its deteriorating detection capabilities, reassuring the Russians and attempting to preclude a panicked or accidental nuclear launch on inaccurate or incomplete information.

Holding the line on proliferation is the best way of preventing terrorist acquisition of nuclear weapons, as well as regional arms races with the potential for deadly conflict. As I have argued already, the most likely way for a terrorist group to acquire nuclear weapons is by theft or gift from a state. The latter possibility seems very unlikely. Nuclear weapons are a prized possession, the ultimate guarantor of state survival. If there were the faintest hint that a state had deliber-ately armed terrorist groups with nuclear weapons, the consequences would be incalculable, perhaps (depending on the political make-up of the American administration at the time) including nuclear retaliation. That is an extremely high risk, and it is worth bearing in mind that even the most brutal, revolutionary and extreme regimes in recent history have nevertheless proved utterly rational when it comes to nuclear deterrence. Theft from one of the more unstable nuclear states like North Korea or Pakistan is a much greater danger. A general collapse is entirely possible in the former, and some kind of radical revolution might take place in the latter. Indeed, this sort of danger is one excellent reason why we must do all we can to prevent Middle Eastern states from acquiring nuclear weapons – because many of them are incompetent, corrupt and unstable, rather than evil.

How do states proliferate? The short answer is that in the past they have done so with the help of other states. American nuclear research emerged out of Anglo-American cooperation. The first Soviet atomic bomb was modelled on stolen American designs. The British bomb was built with the help of Canada and Australia, and Britain's present nuclear weapons missile system, Trident, is, of course, American. The Chinese bomb was developed in conjunction with the Soviets. The Indian bomb was devised from plutonium processed out of a Canadian-built reactor. But today there are essentially three challenges to the non-proliferation regime: that states will maintain a façade of adhering to the NPT while developing weapons; that states will engage in 'first-tier' proliferation, that is stealing or purchasing equipment and material from private companies or state nuclear programmes; and that states will engage in 'second-tier' proliferation, in other words developing states with varying capabilities will trade among themselves to bolster their ability to produce nuclear weapons.[11]

One reason that Pakistan should be of concern to us all is that it falls squarely into both the second and the third of these categories and is a fundamentally unstable state. I have been visiting Pakistan for over twenty years, and remain puzzled by its paradoxes. It has a good domestic civil service and produces international civil servants (particularly economists) of the highest ability. It has a brave and vibrant civil society, with strong professions. It produces some high-quality lawyers. There is a growing middle class who see their prospects threatened by religious fundamentalism and their quality of life outdistanced by that in India. At the same time, the country is wretchedly governed by a turn-and-turn-about succession of corrupt military regimes and corrupt political clans. Poor Pakistan.

The West's recent policy towards Pakistan was determined mainly by the judgement that General Musharraf was all that stood between his country and a fundamentalist deluge. He might be an occasionally mendacious, undemocratic general, but he was *our* general, an ally in the war against terrorism. Unsuccessful assassination attempts against him demonstrated the risks he was prepared to run to cleave to a policy that was by and large on our side. How could we (for instance in Britain) risk antagonizing someone whose security services could be more or less relied on to keep tabs on visiting would-be terrorists from Pakistan's UK diaspora?

This was our approach in the US and Britain until the democratic genie escaped from the military bottle, thanks to growing disorder, protests against the regime, the return to her country of Benazir Bhutto, and her assassination. An elected government of Musharraf's opponents, but with the General himself (shorn eventually of his epaulettes) still in the presidency, coexisted uneasily. For years we had all deluded ourselves. There were indeed links between transnational and home-grown Pakistani terrorists. But you could not eliminate the one without tackling the other, and General Musharraf's government was unwilling to do this. Because his regime had so little domestic legitimacy, it relied on alliances of convenience with the religious right. The secular democratic forces in Pakistan were marginalized with the rigging of elections at the local and national level. The choice, as the International Crisis Group argued, was not 'between the military and the mullahs . . . it [was] between genuine democracy and a military-mullah alliance that is responsible for producing and sustaining religious extremism of many hues'.[12] Despite General Musharraf's promises, banned sectarian and jihadi groups, supported by networks of mosques and madrasas, operated openly in Karachi and elsewhere. The rapid growth in madrasas exploited the young, the alienated and the impoverished in the burgeoning cities, training and dispatching jihadi fighters to Indian-administered Kashmir and to Afghanistan. The Federally Administered Tribal Areas along Pakistan's north-western border with Afghanistan provided a safe haven for Taleban, al-Qaeda and other militants. The Pakistan government did deals with the militants in 2004 and 2006 under which some of their colleagues were released, their weapons returned and security checkpoints disbanded. As President Karzai of Afghanistan has claimed, attacks on his country and on the NATO forces there have been conducted from the mini-Taleban state that has been allowed to establish itself in North and South Waziristan. What has been happening in these border areas is a threat to Pakistan as well as to Afghanistan. Bad and corrupt as have been many of Pakistan's democratic politicians, at least they opposed the sectarian Islamization that has threatened to overwhelm the country if democracy is not given a prolonged chance there.

Musharraf's growing unpopularity – increased by a fight with the judiciary over his position – led to his reluctant acceptance of the return of democratic politics in 2007–8. First, Benazir Bhutto was allowed to come home; then, following her assassination at the end of 2007, her widower Asif Zardari (once known during her premiership as 'Mr 10 per cent' for obvious pecuniary reasons) took over as President when the general was obliged to quit office in order to avoid impeachment in August 2008. The Zardari government's inability to deal with extremism and with the Taleban and al-Qaeda bases in the Pakistan border areas was an early diplomatic and security concern of the new Obama administration, and the president despatched the formidable Richard Holbrooke, who had pushed and shoved the Dayton process to a successful conclusion in the Balkans in the 1990s, as a special envoy to Pakistan and Afghanistan. What always made Pakistan such a source of worry in its own region as well as in western capitals was the cocktail of extremists, terrorism, unstable government and a weak economy in a country that also possessed nuclear weapons.

Pakistan's nuclear ambitions were overlooked by Washington in the 1980s because of Pakistan's value as a front-line state in the Afghan war against the Soviet Union, just as Pakistan's record of proliferation a decade later was initially overlooked because of the country's similar position in the war against the Taleban and terrorism. At the centre of Pakistan's nuclear programme and proliferation was the so-called father of Pakistan's nuclear bomb, A. Q. Khan, a national hero. Khan was a scientist and metallurgical engineer who worked at the European nuclear energy consortium Urenco's enrichment plants in Almelo in the Netherlands and Gronau in Germany. Early and second-generation centrifuges were developed here. He returned to Pakistan in 1975 taking design information and listings of component suppliers with him. Khan was, initially, a first-tier proliferator. He used this information to help speed up Pakistan's nuclear weapons programme, but Pakistan was strapped for cash in the 1990s; it required IMF bail-outs to prevent the economy foundering; there was little money available to purchase the missile technology or system required to deliver its nuclear bombs. So Islamabad concluded a nuclear-for-missile barter deal with Pyongyang – second-tier proliferation. Pakistan got North Korea's Nodong missiles and North Korea got nuclear material and nuclear know-how. While A. Q. Khan was the likely point of contact with North Korea, it seems highly unlikely that his deal was simply another example of the sort of venality and corruption of Khan and his network that was on such prominent display later, when he toured the world touting for nuclear customers. Several sources (most notably Guarav Kampani) suggest that Khan's activities and the missiles-for-enrichment deal must have implicated senior figures in the Pakistan government.[13] While the Pakistan military supervised the nuclear programme, it is difficult to believe that civilian prime ministers knew nothing about what was going on. Was the late Benazir Bhutto, for instance, unaware when as prime minister she visited Pyongyang in December 1993 of the plot being hatched to meet the twin national requirements: Pakistan's desire for medium-range ballistic missiles and North Korea's need for a new route to atomic weapons once its efforts to process plutonium were detected?

Other Khan-centred cases of proliferation are a little more difficult to place. Khan was definitely supplying P-2 centrifuges to Libya (a large shipment was seized in Taranto harbour in October 2003) via a network positively Byzantine in scope. Scomi Precision Engineering in Malaysia manufactured centrifuge components. A Turkish company, Elektronik Kontrol Aletleri, was used as a front to purchase other components, such as motors and frequency converters. A Sri Lankan businessman, Buhary Syed Abu Tahir, helped to move components (and launder the money) by trans-shipment through Dubai. Other companies involved former associates of Khan's and former engineers at Urenco. A further link in this chain is Iran, which used Khan's P-2, and which apparently provided technical assistance to further North Korea's uranium-enrichment programme, while North Korea supplied Iran with motors and other assistance for its medium-range ballistic missiles.[14] It was odd to target Iraq as a potential nuclear weapons proliferator on the dodgiest of evidence, with results that have made the war on terror so much harder to win, while turning a blind eye to what Pakistan was really doing, because of its allegedly vital role in that same war on terrorism. Anyway, when Khan's activities were finally exposed, to the 'shock-horror' of Pakistan and the US, it was convenient for both of them to draw a line under the affair by publicly agreeing that A. Q. Khan was a bit of a rotter, sending him home with a pardon, and leaving it at that. In February 2009, he was released from house arrest, his wrist duly slapped. It is lucky for him that he was not an Iraqi or an Iranian.

North Korea may have had the capability to test a nuclear device since the 1990s. It was more or less kept in check during this decade by a combination of diplomacy and assistance in meeting its energy requirements, paid for by a consortium of donors including the US, Japan, South Korea and the European Union. North Korea is run by a truly dreadful regime which pursues Neolithic economic policies and is guilty of kidnappings and serial human rights abuses. Making trouble – counterfeiting and selling drugs and weapons – is the main export. Hunger and the lack of economic opportunity drive many North Koreans to flee their 'worker's paradise'. Scores of thousands have fled already but only just over 9,000 have made it to safety, mostly in South Korea. One reason China and South Korea have been reluctant to apply as much pressure through sanctions as they could to the North, because of its nuclear policy, is their worry that tough measures would bring the feeble economy crashing down, triggering a torrential outflow of refugees. During the massive famine in North Korea in the mid-1990s, an estimated 100–300,000 Koreans crossed the porous border with China. The Chinese are anxious about the impact of this scale of migration on their rust-belt industrial provinces of Jilin, Heilongjiang and Liaoning.

No one would claim that the talks conducted by the Clinton administration in North Korea led to a sea change in that country. Indeed, the North Koreans undoubtedly cheated on the promises they had given about nuclear development. But as those who negotiated with them during the Clinton presidency have pointed out, America succeeded in bottling up their nuclear programme for eight years; they did not produce any plutonium – now their favoured fissile material;

and the only way to get them to give up their programme is to talk to them. President Bush (Jr) took the view for the first four years of his presidency that North Korea should be denounced, not addressed. When I went to Pyongyang in 2001 and met Kim Jung-Il, he was clearly obsessed with America, the change of approach from one administration to the next, and Washington's declared policy of regime change.[15] North Korea became increasingly provocative. It withdrew from the Non-Proliferation Treaty in early 2003, launched seven missiles into the East Sea in July 2006 and conducted an underground nuclear test at Punggye, north-east of Pyongyang, on 9 October 2006, using some of the plutonium it had been accumulating despite its explicit denials since the late 1980s. The test, which experts deemed to be a not wholly successful 'fizzle', was conducted on the day that South Korea's foreign minister, Ban Ki-Moon, was approved by the UN Security Council as the organization's next Secretary General.

Fortunately, negotiations with North Korea resumed, with the US in 2006–7 taking a more positive stance. It was about time. These talks (which involve four other countries – China, Japan, Russia and South Korea – as well as the principal participants) have edged towards and have perhaps now secured a successful outcome. This was always going to involve dropping sanctions and talk of sanctions, the provision of substantial economic aid, and security and energy guarantees in return for dismantling North Korea's military nuclear programme with full transparency, inspection and verification. China has played a constructive role in this diplomacy, clearly worried by the behaviour of a state that was once regarded as a client but is now seen even in Beijing as a reckless and unpredictable threat to regional stability. The containment of North Korea's provocative behaviour appears to be working, though it is difficult to read what is happening in the 'Hermit Kingdom', cut off – probably more definitively – from the rest of the world than any other country. Will the present regime survive? Can it change? Would change be possible without turmoil? Is the powerful army a conservative or radical influence on policy? Given the regime's need for foreign currency, can we depend on it refraining from selling or threatening to sell nuclear material to a third country or terrorist group? So far, we have just about dissuaded North

Korea from complete lunacy, but the country needs to be watched with care and engaged with firmness by the international community. The problem would probably only disappear completely with peaceful reunification of the Korean peninsula, maybe in the wake of economic collapse in the North. In the meantime, all those engaged in the six-party talks should try to move on from the nuclear issue to a general understanding on regional security. That will not be easy, given the mutual suspicions, distrust and downright dislike that characterize relations between these countries, reflected perhaps in Japan's growing interest in how quickly it could turn its technical nuclear know-how into an independent deterrent should the regional security environment deteriorate.

If ever there was a truly convulsive example of blowback – the unintended consequences in the long term of security decisions taken some time before – it is the position of Iran, both in its own region and in its relations with the US and the West. The attempt to under-stand why Iran has acted and continues to act as it does in no way excuses that behaviour. Repression at home and murder around the world have made Iran, since the overthrow of the Shah in 1979, a menace for much of the time. Iran's legitimate aspirations to be regarded as a great pre-Islamic civilization, as well as an Islamic centre of culture (go and visit Isfahan and see for yourself), are undermined by acts like the assassination of the former Iranian prime minister Shapour Bakhtiar, the bombing of the Jewish community centre in Buenos Aires leading to ninety-three deaths in 1994 (believed by Argentinian prosecutors to be the work of Iranian agents), and Iran's involvement in the suicide bombings that killed American Marines in Beirut and Saudi Arabia. How could so much go wrong, not least with the growth of such virulent anti-Americanism, in a country which had enjoyed from the nineteenth to the mid-twentieth century a close friendship with the United States?

The primary cause was the coup (called Operation Ajax) launched by the CIA with British encouragement against the elected Prime Minister Mossadegh in 1953. Mossadegh wanted a bigger take for his country from the oil that was being drilled in Iran. He proposed to nationalize the Anglo-Iranian Oil Company (later to become British Petroleum) that had originally been set up when Churchill in the First

World War decided that the British fleet should run on oil not coal. The 'idiots' (as they were later called) who ran the oil company, cosseted by London officials, regarded this as an intolerable attack on Britain's national interest. The British persuaded the US administration of Dwight Eisenhower that there was a danger of Iran falling into the hands of the Soviet Union. Eisenhower's predecessor, Harry Truman, had believed that mishandling the crisis in Iran would produce a 'disaster to the free world'. He was right. While the veteran American diplomat Dean Acheson noted that 'never had so few lost so much so stupidly and so fast', Vice-President Nixon and other Washington hawks reckoned that Iran was where America could show the world (in Nixon's own words) that his country was no longer part of 'Dean Acheson's college of cowardly Communist containment'. For all his vaunted sophistication about foreign affairs, Richard Nixon's years in the vice-presidency did not coincide with a glorious period of US diplomacy. America followed this calamitous start with equally disastrous coups, assassinations and attempted assassinations in Guatemala, Cuba, Chile, the Congo and Vietnam.

Nations develop grievances when old scores need to be settled, and this certainly happened in Iran. The United States, with British connivance, toppled Mossadegh. Shah Mohammed Reza Pahlavi was made boss and installed the brutal General Zahedi as his prime minister. The oil profits were parcelled out more generously for British and American companies. The Shah spent $10 billion on US weapons from 1972 to 1976. He cracked down on dissent through his security police, Savak, and drove opponents (including the cleric Ruhollah Khomeini) into exile. The Shah was sufficiently favoured to be helped in starting Iran's civil nuclear programme. Thrown out in a popular uprising in 1979, he was given refuge in the US, provoking Iranian fears of another coup and the subsequent hostage crisis (fifty-two American diplomats were held for fourteen months) which destroyed the Carter presidency and poisoned relations with the US. American and European support for Iraq in its war with Iran (1980–88) strengthened the militants in the fundamentalist regime that now ran the country.

Ayatollah Khamenei, who was to succeed Khomeini as Iran's supreme leader, argued, 'We are not liberals like Allende and Mossadegh, whom the CIA can snuff out.' The West condemned repression in Iran, but it seemed to many Iranians that the US and Europe were prepared to tolerate repression and even promote it elsewhere provided that Western oil interests were preserved. When a more moderate Iranian leader, Mohammed Khatami (an intellectual and philosopher), was president (1997–2005), he was still frozen out by America despite Iranian attempts to begin a dialogue with Washington. Almost inevitably, Khatami was replaced by the hard-line mayor of Tehran, Mahmoud Ahmadinejad. Neo-conservatives in Washington have regularly called for regime change in Tehran, perhaps not realizing how much this sort of external interference damages the cause of Iranian moderates. Engagement is a better way of promoting a change of regime in a country where there is a young population and an educated middle class. Iranians who have studied in the West are more likely to support reform than those whose nationalist fervour has been increased by Western hostility to their country. Western policy on Iran began by being stupid and remained pretty stupid until the Obama administration indicated that it was prepared to open a dialogue with Tehran.

This history has made it far more tricky to deal with Iran's threats to the non-proliferation regime. As noted earlier, Iran's nuclear research began after the fall of Mossadegh with American support. In 1976 the Ford administration (with Dick Cheney, the president's chief of staff, and defence secretary Donald Rumsfeld) offered Iran the chance to buy and operate an American reprocessing facility for extracting plutonium from nuclear fuel. The Iranian government has continued to assert in recent years that its aims have not changed from that time and that it only seeks civil use so that it can export more of its oil instead of burning it at home. Iran's own actions – supporting terrorism in the Middle East and cheating on its promises to the IAEA – have raised doubts about its intentions, even with those who (like me) might otherwise give it the benefit of the doubt because of the history I have recorded. Today we know that the Iranian nuclear programme is broad-based, with its gas centrifuges distributed widely; only about 10 per cent of them (about 360 of 3,000 or so) can be located on a map, though they are known to exist. In February 2009, UN officials claimed that Iran had reached what is called 'breakout capacity', the stage where it could produce – if it was able to further enrich the uranium – enough fissile material to produce a bomb. We should not forget, nevertheless, that as late as September 2008, the CIA reported that Iran had no nuclear weapons programme. Iran certainly possesses a broad enough technological base potentially to switch from highly enriched uranium to plutonium production. However, its supply chain is still vulnerable – a cessation of Russian support could put a serious dent in the programme. Moreover, while Iran has broadly radical, revisionist goals, many of these concern its place in the international system. Iran, in other words, desires not merely strength but legitimacy. For instance in 2003 Iran signed the Additional Protocol of the NPT to which I referred earlier. Much of Iran's nuclear activity has been reported to the IAEA, though it has also been secretive and at times extremely uncooperative as the IAEA recorded in 2003–4. Iran has signed the Chemical Weapons and Biological Weapons Conventions. It may be that its goal is not nuclear weaponry as such, but the sort of 'basement capability' which Japan is thought to possess.

The scope of the Iranian 'problem' is much greater than that of North Korea. A successful Iranian nuclear test could potentially spark a nuclear arms race across North Africa, the Middle East and central Asia. So how can we best hold back Iran and keep an admittedly frayed NPT more or less intact? Most countries accept, some more explicitly than others, that Iran has the right under the treaty to acquire the ability to produce civil nuclear power. This increases their reluctance to support such tough measures through the UN that would force Iran to stay in line and forgo its ambitions to develop full nuclear fuel cycle capability. There is no question that the best outcome to this worrying row would be to persuade Iran to surrender indefinitely its right to enrich uranium in return for guaranteed supply from an offshore source. Russia has more or less proposed this already. It would require many more incentives from the US and Europe to get this solution to fly.

A fallback approach, less attractive but incomparably better than either a continuing stand-off or military action, would be to accept that Iran has the right to produce nuclear energy and to enrich domestically (perhaps under the auspices of an international consortium), with Iran in return agreeing to a several-year delay in beginning its enrichment programme, substantial limitations on its initial size and scope, and a highly intrusive inspection regime. It would be a lot easier to secure international support, especially from China and Russia, for tough sanctions to prevent Iran moving from civil to nuclear use than for similar measures to prevent any civil deployment on the grounds that we do not trust Iran to stop there. Allowing the present row to continue indefinitely, with Iran simply pushing ahead with an unsupervised programme, risks a much worse outcome than we have seen in North Korea.

Iranian ambitions are, of course, augmented by its understandable sense of insecurity, not only in dealing with its Arab and Israeli neighbours but also with those neighbouring countries – Iraq and Afghanistan – that it sees as offering bases for mainly American armed forces. All the security issues in the Middle East and west Asia are interlinked. Iraq, Iran, Saudi Arabia, Syria, Lebanon, Israel, Palestine, Turkey, Hezbollah, Hamas – if wands were available, they would be waved energetically across the region. In the Bush years, all that we had was American reluctance to exert leadership and UN Security Council hesitation in supporting the sort of interventions that might produce peace, stability and disarmament. To avoid drifting, as we did in the early years of the last century, into a terrible conflict – a 2014 to match its predecessor one hundred years before – we should explore through the UN Security Council a regional security pact, with the US, Russia, China and the rest of the Security Council guaranteeing the territorial integrity of the countries in the region and their right to live beside one another in peace. The lynchpin of such an agreement would have to be a comprehensive deal between Israel, Palestine and their neighbours. It is an understatement to say that such a settlement would be a very tall order. But tall orders save lives, and this one would have hugely beneficial consequences in and beyond the region.

International agreements, which seek to incorporate the prerogatives of power in a system of juridical order, have been the route for dealing with global problems preferred by all modern American presidents since the war – until, that is, the latest Bush administration. While President Bush did not completely abandon treaties and agreements, he and his advisers much preferred to work with other countries to cut deals that furthered their view of America's immediate interest, and to get rid of those regimes that decline to play this game. Thus John Bolton, a neo-conservative former American ambassador to the UN, argued that a 'fascination with arms control agreements' was seen by the Clinton administration 'as a substitute for real non-proliferation of weapons of mass destruction'. Better by far, to invade Iraq . . . and do what exactly with Syria, Iran, North Korea and the rest?

This dangerous approach risks not only repeating elsewhere all that we have seen already in Iraq, but the destruction of the international regime that has just about prevented a race to nuclear weaponry since the 1960s. We are coming close to a nuclear 'tipping point', with the grave danger that North Africa, the Middle East and much of east Asia may throw restraint overboard and rush to join the nuclear club. While we do not lack examples of how to restrain or roll back the threat of proliferation, we should bear in mind that big issues like non-proliferation do not slowly fizzle and die the way unwanted trade talks do; if a collapse comes, it is likely to be unexpectedly sudden, wide-ranging, extremely loud and potentially catastrophic.

The two great tasks in non-proliferation are to hold down the number of nuclear states and to toughen inspection, verification and the control of nuclear material in the non-nuclear states. This is where the prerogative of power creates the greatest problem. By what right do the five nuclear powers that are signatories of the NPT lay claim to the doomsday weaponry they deny to others? By the right of realism and common sense, I suppose. What if the 'Big Five' had never exerted their power and had denied themselves these weapons? Would the world be safer? If the choice was between today's chronic insecurity and security, we should naturally choose security. But what if the choice was between chronic insecurity and the absolute insecurity which would result from a single state cheating on a global regime which had sought to ban nuclear weapons? The bad is bad: no doubt about it. Yet it is better than the worst. A lack of trust in the under-takings given by others has bedevilled disarmament negotiations ever since Stalin turned down the proposals of President Truman in 1945.

To earn the right to be trusted to police this insecurity, the five signatory nuclear states have agreed with all the parties to the treaty to 'act in good faith' in the pursuit of nuclear disarmament. This promise, with all the ambiguities and qualifications I noted earlier, to reduce and eventually eliminate nuclear arsenals has been accompanied by other treaty proposals, for example the Comprehensive Test Ban Treaty. The non-nuclear states, who have promised not to go nuclear in weaponry in return for help with civil nuclear power, have fretted increasingly at the lack of serious commitment to achieving the Article 6 pledges or thirteen related measures. This frustration at the very limited progress in disarmament was increased by an advisory opinion of the International Court of Justice in The Hague in 1996, that the nuclear powers should implement their side of the treaty. Some modest steps have been taken by Russia, the UK and France. The US has cut back the size of its stockpile but has taken other measures that cause mounting concern. The US withdrew from the 1972 Anti-Ballistic Missile (ABM) Treaty in order to allow for the establishment of the (unproven) 'Star Wars' anti-missile defence technology, and the CTBT remains unratified. Indeed, the Bush administration spoke about new battlefield uses for nuclear weapons and argued for a programme to replace all existing nuclear warheads. These approaches could lead to more nuclear tests and perhaps to lowering the nuclear threshold. The administration was oblivious to real worries that its declared interest in smaller nuclear weapons (for example, so-called bunker busters for use against well-defended underground targets) risked blurring the vital distinction between nuclear and conventional weapons. Unfortunately, it is easy to see why Washington carries far less credibility as the global gendarme on nuclear issues than it should. This matters because no one else has the clout to give a really strong lead on proliferation.

At the beginning of 2007 four giants of America's recent foreign policy and security establishment surprised the world with a call for 'a bold initiative, consistent with America's moral heritage'. They wanted to reassert the 'vision of a world free of nuclear weapons' for which President Reagan and General Secretary Gorbachev had argued at the Reykjavik Summit in 1986. The four spoke from a wealth of experience: Henry Kissinger was secretary of state from 1973 to 1977; George Shultz held the same post from 1982 to 1989; William Perry was secretary of defence from 1994 to 1997; and Sam Nunn was chairman of the Senate Armed Services Committee. They urged the world not to enter a new nuclear era and to move on from security strategies based on the 'mutually assured destruction' of the Cold War years. They wanted US leadership to create 'a solid consensus for reversing reliance on nuclear weapons globally as a vital contribution to preventing their proliferation into potentially dangerous hands, and ultimately ending them as a threat to the world'. The steps they advocated included getting the nuclear states to change their deployment of weapons to increase warning times, to reduce substantially their nuclear arsenals, to get rid of short-range weapons, to stop production of fissile material for weapons globally, and for America to work on a bipartisan basis for Senate ratification of the Comprehensive Test Ban Treaty. Unfortunately, this bold and imaginative initiative died on the breeze at the time, and appeared then to make little impact on policy makers in the US or elsewhere. We must hope that its good sense is not lost for ever. In 2010, there is a Review Conference of the Non-Proliferation Treaty. Given the Bush/Cheney/Bolton attitudes to disarmament, the previous Review Conference five years ago was a non-event. This time we should focus on and attempt to deliver the recommendations of these four wise men, and perhaps add to their agenda the proposal from the director general of the IAEA, Mohammed ElBaradei. He wants to restrict the ability of countries to produce plutonium and enriched uranium which can be used for fuel in civilian nuclear programmes but are also essential for nuclear weapons. He has called for the establishment of a reserve fuel bank under IAEA control to ensure that countries have alternative supplies of this fuel.

During his election campaign and in the first weeks of his presidency, Barack Obama appeared to be prepared to respond positively to the ideas of Dr Kissinger and his colleagues. As early as October 2007, he made a campaign speech on arms control, favouring a further strategic arms reduction agreement with Russia. This objective was confirmed by his Secretary of State, Hillary Clinton, during her confirmation hearings in the Senate. Obama had also pledged during the campaign to oppose building a new nuclear warhead, and once in the White House pledged to campaign for Senate ratification of the Comprehensive Test Ban Treaty and for a ban on production of fissile material. He was clearly sceptical of the money spent on missile defence technology, which suggested that there could be a reversal of the planned siting of missile defence bases in Poland and the Czech Republic. So the new Democratic administration seemed ready to breathe new life into the prospects for serious reduction in nuclear weapons, and in a major speech in Prague in 2009 on his first European visit President Obama pledged to work for a world without nuclear weapons. He said that he would reduce the US nuclear arsenal, negotiate a new Strategic Arms Reduction with Russia, seek to ratify the Comprehensive Test Ban Treaty, and work for an end to the production of fissile material.

We know that from an early stage in his terrorist career bin Laden tried to acquire nuclear material. In 1993, in Sudan, he thought he was purchasing uranium from a Sudanese general, but it turned out to be a substance called red mercury which resembles uranium oxide but is quite different. Lawrence Wright records the later discussions that bin Laden had with his leading al-Qaeda lieutenants in Afghanistan about the use of chemical, biological and nuclear weapons. Bin Laden appeared to prefer nuclear weapons, and was encouraged to put aside any moral considerations by the argument that the US had itself used nuclear weapons twice, was using depleted uranium in Iraq and needed to be deterred from its assaults on the Muslim world. The ambitions of transformational terrorists may, therefore, be clear but it is also pretty plain that they could only get the weapons from states. For this reason Graham Allison, a former US assistant secretary of defence and expert on nuclear issues, argues that to prevent a nuclear terrorist catastrophe there are three requirements. Since without fissile material there can be no nuclear explosion and hence no nuclear terrorism, we require a new international order based on a doctrine of 'Three No's – No Loose Nukes; No New Nascent Nukes; No New Nuclear Weapons States.' To this he adds measures to deal with a 'dirty' (i.e. a radiological) bomb. A dirty bomb would typically scatter radioactive material across a wide area, using, say, dynamite to detonate material like cesium or cobalt. The best protection against this happening is tougher accounting and control of the radioactive isotopes most likely to produce a weapon. These stringent standards should become part of globally agreed rules.

The way to implement the three main 'no's' will naturally include more financial assistance to Russia to secure its nuclear stockpiles. Allison argues convincingly for 'the establishment of a new gold standard' for protecting the arsenals of all countries with nuclear weapons to render them safe from theft or purchase by terrorist groups. But the biggest task is to toughen up the provisions of the Non-Proliferation Treaty. As the International Atomic Agency's director, Mohammed ElBaradei has argued, this should include making it impossible for countries to withdraw from the treaty (as North Korea did), turning the tougher inspection arrangements in the Additional Protocol into a mandatory requirement on everyone, transforming the existing agreements in the Nuclear Suppliers Group into a treaty in order to prevent the export of peaceful technology to countries that might seek to develop weapons, ending the production of fissile material for weapons and restricting enrichment technology as well as setting up an IAEA enriched-uranium fuel bank.

ElBaradei, whose reappointment in 2005 Washington tried to prevent, won the Nobel Peace Prize in the same year. In a speech that year he pointed out the great difficulty in tightening up the agreements in the way he had suggested, and introducing sanctions against proliferation, if the big nuclear powers did not face up to their own responsibilities. 'Unless we have created the environment in which nuclear weapons are seen as an historical accident from which we are trying to extricate ourselves,' he said, 'we will continue to have this cynical environment that all the guys in the minor leagues will try to join the major leagues. That is a reality. It has nothing to do with ideology . . . They will say, "I would like to emulate the big boys if I have a security problem. If the big boys continue to rely on nuclear weapons, why shouldn't I?"'

'Do as I say, not as I do' will not get us very far in strengthening the Non-Proliferation Treaty. At the very least, the nuclear states need to show they are serious about their nuclear commitments. This will also clearly be necessary in order to reconfigure the treaty so that India (and Pakistan) will sign up to it. India's sense of injustice about the present arrangements was strongly expressed by Jaswant Singh, India's former foreign and finance minister, in his autobiography *A Call to Honour*.[16]

The 1995 indefinite extension of the NPT, essentially a Cold War arms control treaty . . . legitimized in perpetuity the existing nuclear arsenals and, in effect, an unequal nuclear regime . . . Chinese and Pakistani proliferation was no secret but neither was America's docile acquiescence. India, the only country in the world sandwiched between two nuclear weapons powers, faced a permanent legitimization of nuclear weapons by the 'haves', a global nuclear security paradigm from which it was excluded, trends towards disequilibrium in the Asian balance of power, and a neighbourhood in which two nuclear weapons countries acted in concert. Clearly, this was not acceptable. India had to protect its destiny, and exercise its nuclear option.

It fell o Strobe Talbott, deputy secretary of state in the Clinton years and more recently president of the Brookings Institution, to try to persuade the Indian government in the 1990s to become (with Pakistan) what Talbott calls 'NPT outliers rather than outlaws'. This would not involve expanding the nuclear five club to a membership of seven, but 'a "5 + 2" arrangement, whereby India and Pakistan would earn a degree of leniency in exchange for their yielding to international arms control measures and non-proliferation safeguards'.[17] Talbott is a strong believer in updating and improving the NPT, not scrapping it or allowing it to fall to pieces. He would like, sensible man, 'to engage India as a constructive force in global non-proliferation efforts'. He supports India's case for a permanent seat in the UN Security Council in these circumstances.

This was not the path followed by the previous Bush administration. It chose, instead, to circumvent the existing basic NPT provision, that only those states that renounce nuclear weapons should benefit from civilian nuclear trade and assistance, in a bilateral deal with India on civilian nuclear cooperation. This drove a coach and horses through the treaty, while at the same time angering some Indian nationalists and atomic scientists by insisting on a not very demanding inspection regime for its civilian reactors. Washington was intent on shoring up its relations with India, partly (it seems clear) to balance the ascent of China.

For over forty years there has been a strong consensus that proliferation is a threat to the entire international community. The threat remains; indeed, the danger of nuclear weapons falling into terrorist hands has increased it. There has always been a contradiction in the consensus. On the one hand it is clear that somebody has to have power if we are to deter proliferation. On the other hand there is a presumption that nobody ought to have nuclear weapons now or ever again. It is possible to fudge a way around this huge inconsistency, even at a time when we expect more commitments (for example the acceptance of intrusive inspections) from non-nuclear states, provided that under American leadership the existing nuclear weapons powers do more to meet their own treaty undertakings. Multilateralism does not work when big countries make it abundantly plain that the rules do not apply to them but only to others. Realism tells us that we are unlikely to live in a world free of nuclear weapons; realism also argues strongly for the nuclear 'haves' reducing the number of weapons they possess, making their arsenals safer, ending testing and research for good, and eschewing a new generation of weapons, big or small. International cooperation has worked pretty well in this potentially cataclysmic domain. It would be tragic if this cooperation were now to fall apart. This is not an area where we need to take seriously at present sandwich boards that tell us that 'the end of the world is nigh'. But we are perfectly capable through our acts of commission and omission of creating a world where such warnings become frighteningly more credible.

6

A Hundred Million Rifles

*Every gun that is made, every warship launched, every rocket
fired signifies, in the final sense, a theft for those who hunger
and are not fed, those who are cold and are not clothed. The
world in arms is not spending money alone. It is spending the
sweat of its labourers, the genius of its scientists, the hopes of
its children . . . This is not a way of life at all, in any true sense.
Under the cloud of threatening war, it is humanity hanging
from a cross of iron.*

Former U.S. President Dwight D. Eisenhower,
16 April, 1953

*I've got the motive which is money, and the body, which is
dead.* Rod Steiger, from the film
In the Heat of the Night (Stirling Silliphant)

*I've always wanted to improve and expand on the good name
of my weapon by doing good things.*

Lieutenant-General Mikhail Kalashnikov, explaining to
Reuters TV in 2004 why he had begun selling
his own brand of vodka

The world is quite dangerous enough already, without any need to
exaggerate. That conclusion, reached by the Human Security Centre
at the University of British Columbia, is welcome if counter-intuitive.
The Centre has attempted with scholarly verve to scratch away behind
the assumptions and the headlines to find out exactly how dreadfully

members of the human race are behaving towards one another. Myth after myth has been subjected to a barrage of statistical evidence. So is it really true that the number of armed conflicts is increasing; that wars are getting deadlier; that genocide is on the increase; that all the horrors of warfare – rape, refugees, the deaths of the innocent – are on the up? Are we the witnesses to a descent into that Hobbesian world where, as that author wrote in *Leviathan*, 'the condition of man . . . is a condition of war of everyone against everyone'. Actually, no. In their *Human Security Report* for 2005, the Centre noted that while the wars that hit the headlines in the 1990s were bloody and brutal, about 100 conflicts have ended since 1988, a period during which more wars stopped than started. Armed conflicts around the world are down by more than 40 per cent since the early 1990s and more armed struggles for self-determination have been contained or ended than started (forty-three against twenty-eight). In 2004 twenty-five armed secessionist conflicts were under way, the lowest number since 1976. Despite the horrors of Rwanda and Srebrenica, genocides and politicides fell by 80 per cent between the 1988 high point and 2001, and from 1992 to 2003 the number of refugees fell by 45 per cent (though conflict in Iraq and Afghanistan appears to have increased in the last three years). Global military expenditure and troop numbers also declined sharply in the 1990s (though the number of mercenary outfits and guns for hire remained worryingly high).[1] The reason for these figures is partly the end of the Cold War and of the proxy wars that accompanied it, in which the free world was locked in deadly combat with communism far away in someone else's jungle or urban squalor – usually distant countries of which we knew too little. But we can also afford a little self-congratulation. We have got better at resolving and preventing conflicts, not least as the UN Security Council has escaped the confines of almost automatic Cold War vetoes from the great powers. This is reflected in the increase in the number of UN peacekeeping operations. In 2008, the UN was involved in seven such operations in Africa including Sudan and Congo.

Given the evidence that wars really can be stopped, it is disappointing that we have not made more progress in dealing with the issue that makes today's remaining pitiless conflicts possible, namely the trade in arms, both licit and illicit. Here is an international business which demonstrates, as well as any other, the disjuncture between economic globalization and political globalization. The first thrives (though it has not disposed of economic cycles or financial folly), the second only occasionally splutters into life. Meanwhile, people die; their states rot; and their already moribund economies flatline.

Today's conflicts are above all a curse on what the economist Paul Collier calls 'the bottom billion' – one curse to add to all the others. He calculates that 73 per cent of the poorest people in the world have recently been through a civil war or are still involved in one.[2] This is the main type of conflict that we have witnessed since the Cold War's end. There are few examples nowadays of the traditional warfare fought between states in the eighteenth and nineteenth centuries, or in the twentieth century's two world wars. Iraq is an exception, though even here most of the killing and maiming has resulted from the internal conflicts – including, of course, attacks on the occupying powers – that followed the brief and militarily successful invasion in 2003. Iraq has been through a civil war. Intrastate conflicts reflect the weakness of governing institutions in the countries involved, ethnic and sectarian hatreds, demography and greed. They encompass many actors – governments, armed political militias, rebel movements, tribal clans, ethnic and religious groups, diaspora and expatriate groups, child soldiers, mercenaries and criminal gangs. The sort of weaponry used both reflects and sustains the conflicts being fought.[3] Of course, there were genocides and atrocities before the invention of gunpowder, and even today – in Rwanda and Kenya, for example – we can see the human butchery achieved with machetes and other agricultural implements. But small arms and light weapons have been responsible for most of the 4 million deaths in forty-nine major ethnic and sectarian conflicts in the 1990s. Forty-seven were fought exclusively with small arms. Despite its poverty, the conflict belt in sub-Saharan Africa from Liberia, Sierra Leone, Nigeria and Côte d'Ivoire in the west to Sudan, Somalia and Uganda in the east, taking in the Congo, Rwanda and Burundi on the way, has been the market for many of the arms purchases of recent years. After the Cold War, arms transfers within the industrialized north and much of the developing world declined, but imports have been on the rise in sub-Saharan Africa.

The Cold War saw an inevitable and understandable political focus on the sort of weapons of mass destruction with which we have just dealt. But the New World Order, as George Bush Sr optimistically dubbed it at the time, that followed the fall of the Berlin Wall proved to be remarkably disorderly, with the arms trade – particularly its illicit side – benefiting from the stockpiles of weapons in the former Soviet Union and the plethora of arms production facilities in Russia's former empire. Munitions dumps in Ukraine were reckoned to contain 2.5 million tons of ammunition and equipment. The Czech Republic, when it joined NATO in 1999, had a military inventory of 500,000 small arms and weapons for armed forces that totalled less than 50,000 men and women. Others too played their part in creating this deadly cornucopia. Between $6 and $8 billion worth of weapons were provided by China and the US to the Afghan mujahideen in the 1980s; almost 60 per cent of these armaments have found their way subsequently to Pakistan and the surrounding regions. The resistance to Soviet forces in Afghanistan led, after their withdrawal, to the establishment of a Kalashnikov culture elsewhere in south Asia; and this ubiquitous weapon is easy to replicate and produce in bulk since it requires little lowish-grade steel to manufacture.

Rebel groups, gangsters and armed militias in most of these intra-state conflicts (while sometimes having military budgets and capacity which rival those of governments) are not in the market for tanks, aeroplanes and heavy artillery. The gangs of young thugs used by the warlord and Liberian president Charles Taylor, for example, in Liberia and Sierra Leone would have had some difficulty mastering the geometry required by trained gunners. In any event, their mode of slash-and-burn, rape-and-pillage warfare demanded flexibility and rapid movement. Small arms and light weapons were their armaments of choice. The *Small Arms Survey* of 2006 defined 'small arms' as revolvers and self-loading pistols, rifles and carbines, assault rifles, sub-machine guns and light machine guns. It listed the following as 'light weapons': heavy machine guns, hand-held and mounted grenade launchers, portable anti-tank and anti-aircraft guns, recoilless rifles, portable launchers of anti-tank and anti-aircraft missile systems, and mortars of less than 100mm calibre.[4] The very characteristics that give these weapons their appeal to the combatants in internal conflicts also make it difficult to control their trafficking.

Given their size, these weapons are easily transported but hard to track down. They last a long time, take little maintenance and can therefore remain in circulation for many years. Authoritative sources estimate the total small arms and light weapons in circulation to be at least 875 million. There are a large number of producers and producer countries – an estimated 1,249 companies in more than ninety countries – which hampers supply-side restrictions. The multiplicity of their legitimate use by the military, police and civilians makes it easier to move them both legally and illicitly across what are often porous borders. Their small size and ease of mobility reduce the success rate when demobilizing ex-combatants at the apparent end of conflicts. In addition there are many different national regulations for manufacturing them, for buying and selling them, and for owning them. On top of all these advantages for the irregular fighter, the weapons are not difficult to use, requiring little training, and are increasingly lethal and sophisticated. Weapons have also become cheaper. The tens of millions of arms on the market have driven down their price. In 1986, in the rural Kenyan town of Kolowa, it took fifteen cows to buy an AK-47. In 2005 it cost just five.[5]

It is estimated that the average annual production of legal small arms ranges from 700,000 to 900,000 weapons. Altogether the world's militaries procure annually around a million, with the poorer states more likely to buy weapons from stockpiles often created when wealthier states launch new procurement programmes. The largest exporters of small arms and light weapons are the Russian Federation, the United States, Italy, Germany, Brazil and China. The value of recorded exports is about $2 billion. Each of these countries sells over $100 million worth, including parts and ammunition. The most transparent of the exporters are the United States and Germany; the least transparent are Bulgaria, Iran, Israel and North Korea.

The wealthiest states will continue to upgrade their arsenals and are planning major procurement initiatives over the next twenty-five years. It is estimated that up to a million new weapons are likely to be bought in this period, creating a peak in procurement and a cascade of surplus weapons. Procurement on this scale is likely to spur additional competitive buying by states like China that seek to modernize their infantry capability. Unless the states undertaking these big procurement programmes systematically destroy surplus stocks, there will probably be very large transfers to secondary markets, as happened after the meltdown of the Soviet bloc. The global rise in procurement could mean, according to the *Small Arms Survey*, a market for surplus stock of about 280,000 units a year, or 14 million units over a fifty-year period. Despite the adoption by the UN in 2005 of an International Tracing Instrument (to which we will return), the lack of transparency on the part of the leading suppliers and recipients will make it difficult to control these flows.

Stockpiles around the world of military and law-enforcement weapons are already large. Given the likelihood of increased production, the importance of stockpile management and security is critical. At the worst, hundreds of thousands or millions of weapons can be looted from government facilities. In 1991 several hundred thousand small arms were pillaged in Somalia. In 1997, 640,000 small arms were stolen from the arsenals of the Albanian government. After the fall of Baghdad in 2003, an estimated 4.2 million were looted in Iraq, and weapons supplied to the recreated army there repeatedly disappear. On a smaller scale, reports of the loss of military weapons come from Russia, Uganda, China and elsewhere. Law-enforcement arsenals are also pilfered, mainly through break-ins and corruption. This haemorrhage of weapons helps to keep the marketplace full and the prices down.

The trade in small arms is said to be worth $4–6 billion a year, and there is estimated to be a further $1 billion of illegal trade. But the distinctions between legal trade (involving governments in an active or passive role and in accordance with both national law and international law) and the grey and black markets are pretty fuzzy. In the illicit grey market, governments or their agents either get around national or international laws and policies or exploit loopholes in the rules. The grey market fuels crime, civil conflict and corruption, often allowing weapons sales to countries with no identifiable government or authority and to non-state actors, for example rebel groups. The black market is, of course, part of the illicit market. It simply goes further, operating well outside the law and in clear violation of national and international laws and policies. These definitions are frequently contested, which makes it difficult sometimes to demonstrate beyond doubt at any given time that a deal is illegal.

One reason for overlap is the survival of Cold War networks and habits. Several of the so-called 'merchants of death', to whose activities we will shortly turn, were set up or kept in business by states that wanted to support at one remove what they regarded as their own preferred side in distant wars. Making trouble for your enemies, declared or undeclared, by helping those fighting against them, is as old as warfare itself. The French government ran arms, for instance, to Britain's rebellious colonial subjects in America in the 1770s: Louis XVI employed a French arms broker, operating under a fictitious company name, to ship military supplies clandestinely, some of which came direct from the king's arsenal. In more recent times, the USA has trafficked weapons in the name of freedom in Central America (involving some creative diplomacy with the 'pariahs' of Iran), in Afghanistan and in Africa. American support, including weapons, for Fatah in Palestine has been given a veneer of legitimacy by labelling it assistance for the Palestinian president's guard and security force; it has probably looked rather different to Hamas. France has sold weapons to Africa, for example to Burundi and Rwanda, in order to try to preserve her influence in and beyond the Great Lakes region. China has become a big arms trader in Africa, for example in Sudan. The Russian Federation has sold 100,000 new AK-103 assault rifles and ammunition to Venezuela. They will replace the older Belgian FAL rifle, which is already being given to insurgent groups in Colombia by the Venezuelan armed forces. Venezuela will now have a large surplus of these weapons. It will be surprising if many more of them do not find their way to rebel groups in Colombia and other countries in the region. The UK allegedly pursues an ethical arms sales policy (prohibiting arms exports to countries where they might be used for internal repression or external aggression). Maybe this now controls the flow of small arms more successfully than it did the sale of Hawk jet spares to Zimbabwe and sales to Israel, both countries plainly in breach of end-user assurances. Pakistan provides weapons to Muslim separatists in Kashmir; the weapons presumably include large numbers of the pretty basic Kalashnikov AK-47, which make up a substantial part of the 100 million modern rifles believed to be in current use worldwide. Iran has supplied weapons to Kurdish insurgents in Turkey; Sudan has done the same for anti-government forces in Uganda – the list goes on and on.

There is increasing evidence that the main way in which their purchasers and users obtain arms for international conflicts is through diversion from legal to illicit channels. Most of the diversion depends on the complicity of governments and their agents. Through corruption and wilful neglect, government actors allow millions of weapons to enter the black market.[6] First, as the UN Sanctions Panels on Angola and Liberia noted, there is widespread flouting of national, regional and international sanctions and embargoes, including governments allowing their own countries to be used for transshipment. During the Angolan civil war, for example, one faction – UNITA – was armed in part through Congo, whose then president Mobutu Sese Seko put UNITA's boss Jonas Savimbi in direct touch with his arms broker and was paid for his go-between services in diamonds and cash. There has been an arms embargo on Somalia for sixteen years, but the quantity and diversity of arms available there is greater today than at any time since the beginning of the 1990s. Second, corrupt government officials issue false export licences or simply avert their gaze when weapons are shipped through the ports they were supposed to control. The use of containers facilitates this. Low and delayed salaries make the criminal purchase of officials more likely. Experienced arms brokers have no trouble buying certification which alters the shipment of weapons from illegal to sanctioned purchases. Third, weapons leak or are stolen (as we noted earlier) from government stockpiles. The *Small Arms Survey* in 2004 reckoned that each year a million light weapons were lost or stolen around the world. UN peacekeepers have been known to sell their weapons to insurgent groups and, according to newspaper reports, some Israeli soldiers have sold their own weapons to Palestinians. Fourth, lax domestic gun laws can assist illegal trade across borders. This clearly happens between the US and Mexico, though relatively small-scale trafficking by individuals on what are called 'ant runs' does not compare with the large illegal shipment found in a cargo hold at a Mexican border crossing in 1997. The shipment of thousands of unassembled grenade launchers and parts for M-2 machine guns originated in Vietnam, where the US military had left behind large quantities of weapons after the war. The crates had been shipped from Ho Chi Minh City to Singapore, and had travelled on via Germany, the Panama Canal and Long Beach, California. The final example of diversion bears the rather quaint name of 'craft production'; weapons are copied and the parts assembled in garages, private workshops and backyards. Colombia's craft firearms industry produces non-automatic firearms for petty criminals, but is also capable of producing – under the control of insurgent groups – sub-machine guns, mortars and grenades.

There is no problem in defining or describing the arms black market. It is the stuff of thrillers; its principal characters come straight off the pages of books by John Le Carré, Gerald Seymour or Frederick Forsyth. Their trade may lack the technological sophistication of A. Q. Khan, but the merchandise in which they specialize is also deadly and their commercial networks – like Khan's – are a reflection of the impact of globalization on every form of business activity.

The poster boy of the arms dealers was a Russian, Victor Bout (pronounced 'butt'), who was born in 1967. A demobilized military pilot in the Soviet Union, in his twenties he began to buy elderly Soviet cargo aircraft – Ilyushins and Antonovs – building up a fleet of about sixty. They enjoyed the cover of a network of front and shell companies and were registered in a variety of permissive jurisdictions from Liberia to Equatorial Guinea. He began by buying and selling cut flowers (gladioli) and frozen chickens but moved on to more lethal and lucrative products. From a series of smaller, second-grade airports he shipped small arms into Sierra Leone, Rwanda, Angola and other conflict zones. His companies and other associated operations were even used to fly UN peacekeepers to their destinations and to ferry logistics to the American military and occupation authorities in Iraq. Bout, who is said to speak eight languages, controlled his widespread business interests – mostly sending arms in and bringing loot (like diamonds) out – from Moscow. He worked from there with apparent impunity despite Interpol's interest in him and an indictment by the Belgian authorities on money-laundering charges. American interest in Bout increased when it was discovered that he had switched sides in Afghanistan. He began by supplying the government's forces there, but after one of his planes was detained by the Taleban in 1995–6, he negotiated its release with Mullah Omar and was believed to have profited by $50 million from doing business with Omar's men in the late nineties. The Afghan permanent representative to the UN claimed that some of his planes flying from Sharjah in the Gulf to Afghanistan had transported chemical poisons to Kandahar, bought in Germany, the Czech Republic and Ukraine and intended not for the Taleban but for al-Qaeda. Mr Bout remained beyond the reach of national and international law enforcement agencies, another (though slightly less orthodox) Russian tycoon, until in March 2008 he was arrested in Bangkok on a tip from the US, where he had been indicted for providing arms to the terrorist group FARC in Colombia. Nevertheless, he stayed ahead of the law for longer than some of his 1990s peer group. Leonid Minim had tried his hand at a wide range of fraudulent and other illegal activities, including identity theft and drug smuggling, before turning to arms deals. He shipped grenade launchers, rockets and missiles purchased in the Ukraine from Bulgaria to the rebel group (the Revolutionary United Front) in Sierra Leone. Minim was eventually caught by chance in 2000, snorting cocaine in a suburban Milan hotel with a group of young ladies. The Italian police charged him with smuggling offences. His career of crime had caught up with him. The Belgian arms dealer Jacques Monsieur was arrested in 2001 in Iran; at the time he was under investigation by both the Belgian and the French police for illegal arms deals. He had moved from supplying weapons to Iran to re-cycling Iranian weapons into embargoed conflicts in Africa. Dealing with one of the Congo's short-lived post-Mobutu regimes had got him tangled up with the French state-owned oil company Elf, which also helped the Congolese to purchase helicopters from Russia along with the services of forty Russian technicians.

Others have been more fortunate, covering their black-market activities by the performance of a few services for national security authorities. Washington refused to cooperate with the UN when it tried to investigate the activities of the American arms broker Fred Keller in the African Great Lakes region. Keller's networks were also looking after US allies like the Sudanese People's Liberation Army in the south of that country. The South African arms broker Wilhelm 'Ters' Ehlers supplied arms, bought from a stockpile of weapons impounded by the Seychelles government, to Hutu soldiers implicated in the genocidal attacks on the Tutsi in Rwanda. This flouted a UN embargo to stop the mass killings in that country. For whatever reason, Ehlers has avoided indictment for aiding and abetting genocide.[7] The biggest American arms broker is said to be Sarkis Soghanalian, who works with a Miami-based financier, Charles Acelor. Their arms deals have included the purchase of 10,000 Kalashnikov rifles from Jordan for delivery to the Revolutionary Armed Forces of Colombia (FARC) in 1999. They were air-dropped in crates on the jungle in FARC-controlled areas. Meanwhile Washington was, of course, providing a huge amount of military assistance to the Colombian government to fight FARC and other rebel groups. Soghanalian's arms dealing has served both Saddam Hussein's Iraq and Anastasio Somoza's Nicaragua. Soghanalian and Acelor have managed to avoid a complete shut-down of their arms-trafficking network through services rendered to the US authorities, like renting out planes to the CIA and helping to wind up an operation in the Lebanon to print counterfeit US dollars.[8] Arms dealers have many uses, a shabby example (I suppose) of realpolitik and another example of the sort of case where any short-term gain engendered by the use of illicit means is outweighed by the long-term damage to the rule of law and the security of the state.

Globalization has been the most important patron of the dealers. They operate with and through modern technology, taking advantage of compliant jurisdictions. Even when dealing with hostile authorities they enjoy greater flexibility than governments and operate in smaller and tighter turning circles than the agencies that come lumbering after them. They have been helped by deregulation, migration and improvements in transport technology. The development of the traffickers' networks is helped by falling costs of sea, freight and air transport, the anonymity served by containerization, improvements in overland transport routes, and the availability of decommissioned aircraft from the Soviet military fleet, able to fly into rudimentary airfields in remote conflict zones. The growth in global financial markets has made it easier to pay for and profit from arms deals with even the shadiest customers.

Arms traffickers selling into Africa use front companies sometimes masquerading as aid organizations. An arms dealer who formally supplied Renamo forces in Mozambique went on to sell weapons into Burundi, disguising the operation as a Christian aid charity. Weapons are sometimes camouflaged as humanitarian relief supplies. A shipment of weapons from China to Burundi was listed as farm implements. Pilots file false flight plans. They take circuitous routes to their destinations. They operate from different bases using differing company names. In south Asia, the weapons originally supplied to the warring parties in Afghanistan have cascaded through the subcontinent. New smuggling operations and transit routes have been developed in the north and east, in Nepal and Bangladesh, for instance. The banking systems of these countries have been compromised by illegal financial movements. Local rebel groups have been armed, and criminal networks – trading drugs, endangered species and prostitutes as well as guns – have flourished. Kalashnikovs and other automatic weapons have been found and used in a growing number of Indian states. The sophistication of the weapons used has increased. There are shoulder-fired missiles in Sri Lanka and rocket-propelled grenades in Pakistan. In Latin America, porous borders and corrupt officials help the trafficking networks to expand. There are said to be twenty-one known arms-trafficking routes into Colombia from Venezuela, twenty-six from Ecuador, thirty-seven from Panama and fourteen from Brazil.[9] Armed groups fight regularly for control of favoured traffic routes into Colombia, for example in the jungle along the Pacific coast.

To give some examples of the organization and impact of arms trafficking, we can look at one area in some detail – the Mano basin (Liberia, Sierra Leone and Guinea) and neighbouring Côte d'Ivoire – and, more briefly, at northern Uganda and a benighted European backwater which is also a leading facilitator in the business.

Liberia lies at the heart of a region rich in natural resources but torn apart by conflicts for over two decades. The killings have been funded by the plundering of valuable resources – diamonds, alluvial gold, timber, cocoa and coffee. These commodities have helped pay for the 8–10 million small arms now circulating in West Africa. Liberia was founded as an independent republic in 1847 by 300 black settler families from the United States. It was an odd place, governed for a century by the same party, the True Whig Party, and controlled by the same small group of families. They behaved like white colonialists, keeping the indigenous population under their thumb, some in effect as slaves. The end of colonialism elsewhere started to put pressure on a system under which 1 per cent of the 2 million population controlled the whole of Liberia. The last of the Americo-Liberian presidents was the grandson of freed South Carolina slaves, William Tolbert. He and his family creamed off a fortune from an economy based on rubber, iron ore and the registration of foreign ships. Modest reforms were insufficient to save the regime from a coup led by a master sergeant called Samuel Doe in 1980. Then the descent into violence began. Doe survived thirty-eight coups in his ten years of tyranny, perhaps helped by his juju men but sustained principally by American support. Washington's financial aid topped $500 million in ten years. The US used Liberia as a military and intelligence hub in Africa. Violence and rigged elections did not shake America's resolve, and Doe repaid President Reagan's administration by giving strong support over international issues like Libya and Iran.

Charles Taylor, who was to become the most notorious warlord in West Africa, was educated in the United States and trained by Colonel Qaddafi, an unusual double entry in anyone's curriculum vitae. He put together a gang of young illiterate men and boys and, with the support of the leaders of Côte d'Ivoire and Burkina Faso, who had their own grudges against Doe, invaded Liberia in 1989, marauding across the country. His young thugs quickly established a deserved reputation as psychopathic killers. The civil war that Taylor launched was to claim more than 250,000 lives and displace half the country's population. With the support of another rebel group, Doe was rapidly overthrown by Taylor and murdered; one of his ears was eaten by the leader of his captors for the benefit of a film camera. Taylor himself established control over most of the country, did a series of deals with foreign companies for timber, rubber, and iron ore concessions, and used some of the $200 million he raised in a year to finance dissident forces in Sierra Leone, the Revolutionary United Front (RUF), under an army corporal called Foday Sankoh whom Taylor had met in a Libyan training camp. The warfare that raged across Sierra Leone was particularly bitter, with child soldiers drawn into the fighting on both sides. Ishmael Beah describes in terrible detail some of his own experiences as a boy in Sierra Leone, press-ganged at thirteen into the government's own army.[10] Taylor's main motive in invading Sierra Leone had been to control the diamond mines there, and Sankoh himself soon seized many of the diamond fields in the east of the country with a traffic of $300 million. His forces also overran the areas containing the bauxite and titanium mines.

Through the twists and bloody turns of a decade of fighting in Liberia and Sierra Leone, Taylor dominated the smuggled diamond trade, with his capital Monrovia acting as a major centre for diamond laundering. Meanwhile, Sierra Leone hit the bottom of the UN's league table for human development; 50,000 people died there, 30,000 were mutilated and more than three-quarters of the population were dispersed. Having caused chaos in Sierra Leone, Taylor then turned to destabilizing Côte d'Ivoire, organizing, arming and deploying two rebel groups in the west of the country. After military interventions by mercenaries and by Nigerian, British and UN forces, after tough UN sanctions, and after a failed attempt to unseat the president of Guinea backfired with the invasion of Liberia itself by a Guinea-backed rebel group, Taylor fell as Sankoh had already done. Peace of a sort was restored and Charles Taylor was put on trial in The Hague for crimes against humanity in 2007.

Why had these terrible events happened and how had the horror been sustained? In Liberia and Sierra Leone poverty, corruption, the looting for private gain of national resources, weak institutions and human wickedness all took their heavy toll. The issue of resources – and the relationship between greed and conflict – is one that we will examine in the next chapter. But Taylor and Sankoh and the other warlords would not have been able to cause such mayhem if they had been dependent on machetes and other farm implements for their weaponry. What turned them into such a terrible menace was the easy availability of firearms and the ability to pay for them with the resources of the areas and countries they overran.

Conflict-commodity sales are managed in several ways. One of the usual methods of payment in Liberia was to meet half the price in weapons and the other half in cash. Much of the money made from timber sales was channelled through the state timber company, Oriental Timber Corporation, to one of Taylor's business managers who acted as paymaster of the rebels in Sierra Leone. Money from diamonds and logging was also paid into Zurich and Burkina Faso bank accounts. The Swiss National Bank publishes figures for the total amounts of foreign funds held in Swiss banks. In 2002 Africa as a whole had a total of $14.3 billion; Liberia had $3.8 billion, more than Nigeria ($900 million) and South Africa ($2.4 billion). Taylor's Swiss account was opened in 1993. One of the two Burkina Faso accounts, the Banque Internationale du Burkina, was first opened in 1990 and used as a channel for Libyan funds to pay for Taylor's original insurgency.

While in late 2002 there appeared to be an increase in the import of heavy weaponry into Liberia (believed to be for deployment in Côte d'Ivoire, where it was easier to use), most of the weapons were small arms and light weapons, for example Chinese-made AK-47s, machine guns, rocket-propelled grenades and armour-piercing incendiary rounds. The NGO Global Witness (an excellent example of the beneficial effects of globalization) has detailed some of the regular delivery of weapons, despite a UN embargo, in 2002 and 2003. Imports by ship happened two or three times a month (depending on the availability of timber exports) and there were regular movements by plane into the former American airbase at Robertsfield. For example, on 6 February 2002 a consignment of weapons was flown in on board an Antonov from Ouagadougou in Burkina Faso and on 16 February a Boeing 707 from Kinshasa delivered crates of arms. Ship movements were also tabulated. In May 2002 a 30-ton weapons shipment was sent to the Liberian port of Harper from Bulgaria via Nice on a logging ship. The broker had been involved in shipping weapons from Bulgaria to Liberia for a decade. In July a 15-ton shipment, mostly of ammunition packed in navy blue and grey containers, arrived courtesy of the same dealer. In September of that year a consignment of food aid – rice – from Libya to Buchanan port was accompanied by weapons. Further shipments were recorded in October and December. Just before Christmas the MV *Posen* unloaded nineteen camouflaged trucks with sealed containers on board packed with arms and ammunition.[11]

Many of the shipments of weapons to Liberia have involved planes chartered in one country but registered in another, arms consignments originally purchased for another country that finished up in Liberia, shell companies and doctored end-user certificates, and the supervision and involvement of diamond and timber dealers. It may be entirely coincidental that China has recently been the biggest importer of Liberia's timber (though its purchases have been understated in official statistics) and has also been a major source of Liberia's arms imports. China's two largest arms factories, Norinco and PolyTechnology, have been significant suppliers of weapons to underground arms brokers.

Arming insurgents in northern Uganda has been a less sophisticated exercise than that in the Mano basin, and much less substantial in scale. Nevertheless, it has helped to keep the conflict between the Lord's Resistance Army (LRA) and the Ugandan government going for over twenty years. This bitter fighting is partly the legacy of two decades of coup and counter-coup, massacre and pitched battle as Milton Obote and Idi Amin fought for supremacy in the 1970s and 80s. It culminated in Obote's overthrow by the initially rather Cromwellian figure of Yoweri Museveni in 1986. I met Museveni soon after he had defeated Obote. He seemed to have several pluses in comparison with his predecessors. First, he was clearly not a murderous madman. Second, he set his hand – at least at first – to the implementation of some sensible economic reforms. Third, he had an admirably bluff, no-nonsense way of speaking his mind, not least in talking about AIDS. Where other African leaders were often in denial about this pandemic, behaving as though any mention of it by Western governments and the WHO was simply a reflection of neocolonialist racism, Museveni launched a sensible national campaign against a disease that affected probably rather more than a fifth of the population of his country.

Museveni's candour was on display when he first visited London in 1986. My development ministry had put together an early package of support, a grant of about £35 million to buy imports like medicines and cement. The idea was that Prime Minister Margaret Thatcher would announce this gift at her first meeting with Museveni in Downing Street to encourage him, as it were, to keep up the good work. She led up to the announcement with a good deal of diplomatic flattery eventually giving him the figure. 'Thirty-five million pounds?' he shot back. 'That's not very much.' The PM was put off her stroke only momentarily. After a brief pause she advanced on the net, flashing volleys. 'Thirty-five million pounds that you don't have to pay back seems rather a lot to me,' she responded. I never saw her lost for words for very long.

Western aid donors understandably began to fall out with Museveni after his army got involved in the fighting and looting in the Congo, and as he short-circuited democratic arrangements in Uganda, for example locking up some of his political opponents. Like many other African leaders – a declining number, to be sure – he was reluctant to accept electoral and institutional arrangements under which he might lose power. Yet it was probably the military diversions in the Congo that were more important in weakening Museveni's hand in the north of the country.

When he took power in 1986, Museveni overthrew a government dominated by the Acholi ethnic group. The creation of the LRA has its roots in northern resentment at this. The LRA is led by Joseph Kony, a man described by one historian of Africa, Martin Meredith, as 'a messianic psychopath'.[12] Kony's rebels attack government forces from time to time, but their main targets have been civilians in districts dominated by the Acholi. They attack and destroy civilian camps and settlements, loot whatever they find there, rape and abduct people, including children, to act as slaves or to be dragooned into their military force. They use mutilation to create fear, cutting off noses, lips and ears to punish those suspected of collaborating with the government. Despite the twenty to one advantage in numbers enjoyed by the Ugandan armed forces, the conflict simmers on, perhaps partly because of corruption, harsh behaviour and incompetence in the army. The results have been devastating, with about 90 per cent of the population in the worst-affected area – 1.4 million people – herded into camps guarded by the army. Mortality rates in these camps are appallingly high, with an estimated 1,000 people a week in 2005–6 dying from treatable illnesses like diarrhoea and malaria. The former

UN undersecretary general for humanitarian affairs and emergency relief coordinator Jan Egeland called it 'the world's most neglected humanitarian catastrophe'. Since Christmas 2006, the LRA has moved into both the Congo and Sudan, driving tens of thousands of terrorised people from their homes.

What has enabled the conflict to last for so long? The answer is pretty simple. In the civil war between the Muslim north of Sudan and the Christian south, the Ugandans acted as a main source and supply route for weapons for the southern forces under John Garang. Like others, the Ugandans were alarmed by the regional jihad which President Bashir was calling for in Khartoum. As the Sudanese civil war stumbled towards a temporary peace – temporary because north–south violence is likely to explode again if the south (where 80 per cent of the country's oil is located) votes for independence in a refer-endum to be held by agreement in 2011 – Bashir retaliated against Uganda's support for Garang by providing weapons to the LRA and other northern Ugandan dissidents. Even after the creation of a Muslim–Christian government of national unity in Khartoum, elements of Sudanese military intelligence are still thought to be aiding the LRA. So here national governments have been directly responsible for throwing lit matches into one another's political petrol dumps.

In the case of the Mano basin, governments and insurgent groups were able to go into the global arms bazaar, with a commodity-based chequebook. Failed or failing states bought in the causes of further calamitous failure. With Uganda and Sudan, neighbouring states themselves have acted as conduits of arms to rebels. There are other examples where states or statelets are themselves a primary source for the arms business – with no questions asked about the end use of the weapons. North Korea has been one example; another suspect in Europe is the rebellious province of Transdniestria in Moldova.

Moldova is the poorest ex-communist country in Europe. It was a principality that found itself trapped on the borderlands between three empires: Turkish, Russian and Austro-Hungarian. Moldova today stretches from the Romanian border to the Ukraine. In the west, Moldovans identify with Romania, across the River Dnieper its prov-ince of Transdniestria lines up with Russia. There are 3.4 million people living in Moldova (the overwhelming majority are ethnically

Romanian, of whom 800,000 hold Romanian passports); just over half a million live in Transdniestria.

Moldova is pitifully impoverished, with a per-capita GDP of roughly $2,000. It is dependent on Russia, which squeezes its economy with natural-gas price hikes and supply interruptions and with bans on wine and agricultural exports. Moldova has to fall back on dribbles of European and American assistance, remittance income and the grey/black economy. When Moldova declared independence from the Soviet Union in 1991, the Russian 14th Army tacitly helped the Russophone Transdniestrians fight for their independence, intervening in the conflict between the two sides after several hundred deaths. The Russians have left 2,000 troops in Transdniestria, allegedly to guard the old Soviet Union weapons dumps that were left there and eventually to move these arsenals back to Russia.

There are some things we know for sure about Transdniestria, some things we strongly suspect and some things on which we may have started to exaggerate just a little. First, Transdniestria is one of the so-called frozen conflicts in the old Russian empire, which could be resolved very rapidly if Moscow showed any interest in sorting the problems out rather than keeping them bubbling away on the back burner. The territorial dispute between Azerbaijan and Armenia over Nagorno Karabakh is in a category of its own, but the brawls that are on a par with Transdniestria are those involving two rebellious provinces in Georgia, South Ossetia and Abkhazia. In each case, Russia encourages independence movements (in a way that it would rightly denounce if others were doing the same thing in Chechnya) in order to weaken neighbours and extend Russian influence. Russia has promoted a quasi-military association between these statelets called, with a Soviet-era rhetorical flourish, the Association for Democracy and People's Rights. In Transdniestria itself, it is difficult to distinguish between the local elite and its Russian cousin. The President, Igor Smirnov, is from the Russian east; he led the strikes and demonstrations that created the Pridnestrovian Moldavian Soviet Socialist Republic, a forerunner in old lingo of today's breakaway province. Smirnov's son Vladimir runs the company called Sheriff which organizes the bulk of Transdniestria's trade. He is also, helpfully, in charge of the customs service. The president has two principal sidekicks. The state security minister, Vladimir Antufeyev, was forced to flee Latvia in 1990 after failing to orchestrate a Soviet crackdown there. The third local boss is the pony-tailed Dmitri Soin, who runs a youth movement called Breakthrough, similar to the Kremlin's own band of young fascistic thugs. Just to prove that satire is not dead in eastern Europe, Soin also commands the Che Guevara School of Political Leadership.

While these local bosses seem like a violent, financially slick and ruthless throwback to an earlier age of former Soviet officials, there is at least one way in which they appear very modern. They are clearly media savvy. Google your way on to Transdniestria's websites and you discover a wealth of comment and allegedly factual information about the country where, according to the *Tiraspol Times*, 'the Class of '07 is Dancing in the Streets'. The main problem about the *Tiraspol Times* as a journal of record is that it does not exist. There appears to be only one journalist on its staff, an Irishman called Des Grant, but the paper oddly has no offices.[13] Transdniestria also has the good fortune to be supported by a world-class think tank called the International Council for Democratic Institutions and State Sovereignty, which sprays across the internet major policy essays purportedly the work of a legion of distinguished scholars and international lawyers. The contents page of its professionally designed website includes the question, 'What is your response to claims the Council does not exist?' What indeed?

One argument that infuses most of the Transdniestrian regime's contributions to the internet is that allegations of arms smuggling from the province are fabricated. Obliging witnesses from the EU and the Vienna-based Organization of Security and Cooperation in Europe (OSCE) are called in evidence. This flies in the face of what was for long asserted and the fact that weapons traced back to Transdniestria had been found in civil wars right across Africa. A former Romanian foreign minister – not, of course, an unbiased witness – went so far as to call Transdniestria 'the black hole of transborder organized crime – including drug smuggling, human trafficking and arms smuggling'. Certainly when I was a European Commissioner from 1999 to 2004, we believed in 'the black hole', though we were not always sure about what was in it. What we did know was that when the Soviet Union

1 (*above*) They should have stayed at home – the Archduke Franz Ferdinand and his wife set out for their last drive together, St Vitus's Day, 1914, Sarajevo.

2 (*left*) David Lloyd George, Georges Clemenceau and Woodrow Wilson stepping out at the Versailles Peace Conference.

3 The allies – Churchill, Roosevelt and Stalin – sharing a joke at Yalta, 1945: no laughing matter for Poland and eastern Europe.

4 Planning for a better world – the conference that launched the United Nations, San Francisco, 1945.

5 France's favourite fast food.

6 China's ubiquitous trade partner: the new store in Shanghai.

7 In Delhi too, everyone – rich and poor – loves a Coke.

8 So let's build fortress Australia.

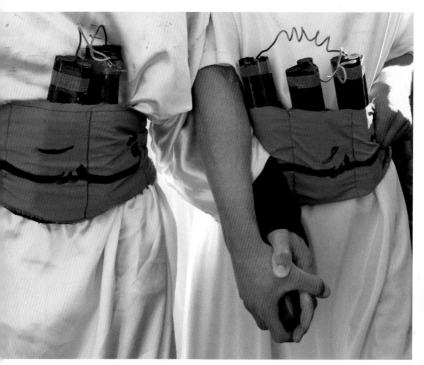

9 Wannabe suicide bombers hand in hand: an Islamic Jihad march in Gaza.

10 A demonstration of solidarity with Spain after the Atocha bombing in 2004; but ETA was not responsible.

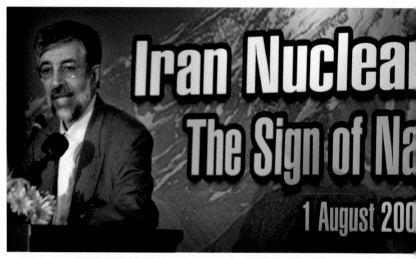

Iran Nuclear
The Sign of Na
1 August 200

11 Do they want nuclear weapons? Iranian Parliament Speaker Haddadadel.

12 How many has he got? Kim Jung-Il inspecting his navy.

13 How many did he sell? Pakistani nuclear retailer Abdul Qadeer (A. Q.) Khan, on a poster at a rally in his support.

14 Bringing up baby: a rally of the Michigan militia.

15 The view in Ethiopia – Africa's 'weapon of mass destruction'.

16 (*above*) The misery of a refugee camp in Rwanda.

17 (*left*) Welcome to Monrovia – we hope you brought your chequebook

WELCOME TO LIBERIA

CHINESE PRESIDENT
HU JINTAO

collapsed, it left behind arms dumps of about 40,000 tons. Some contained heavy equipment like tanks. There were fortified bunkers containing artillery shells, mines, rockets and lighter weapons. At the OSCE Conference in Istanbul in 1999, which I attended, the Russians agreed to dismantle their dumps and take their troops home. At subsequent meetings with Russian government officials, a number of imaginative excuses were put forward for why this had not happened which belonged to the cat-ate-my-homework school of diplomacy. I recall the amiable Igor Ivanov, then Russia's foreign minister (described by President Putin to an interlocutor as 'my tame Georgian'), telling us on one occasion that the Russian 14th Army had to stay in Transdniestria to guard the arms dumps and that when they had tried to transport the weapons back to Russia on freight trains, outraged Russophile Transdniestrians had lain down on the railway lines to prevent the trains moving. Old ladies, babushkas, were mentioned in particular; it was a poignant thought.

The Russians kept half their word, taking home approximately 50 per cent of their weapons but leaving behind about 20,000 tons of ammunition. Did none of this find its way on to the black market? It would be deeply surprising if this were so. The Russian army has a track record of selling off weapons, including to Chechen rebels. Moreover, Transdniestria was at the very heart of a large smuggling ring connecting the Ukrainian ports of Odessa and Illichivisk with markets in the Ukraine itself, Moldova and beyond. Transdniestria has a long, ill-protected perimeter, including a 470-kilometre frontier with Ukraine and a border with Moldova crossed by large numbers of barely checked cars and trucks every day. We in the EU tried to strengthen border controls, not least with Ukraine. We did this partly in order to nudge Transdniestria back towards a negotiated settlement with Moldova, and partly because of what we knew was being smuggled through Transdniestria, including drugs and prostitutes. It may be true that arms smuggling has dropped off in the last few years, though Transdniestria still has the dumps and the capacity in at least six factories to manufacture assault rifles, machine guns and multiple rocket launchers. The *Washington Post* claimed in 2003 that it also made Alazan rockets, which were known to have been fitted in the past with radiological warheads; in other words, dirty bombs. If the arms trade has fallen off, a main reason may be that the price of many weapons has fallen below other products that are smuggled through Transdniestria. The recent most famous smuggled commodity was frozen chicken, of which 40,000 tons arrived in an eight-month period in Transdniestria without paying duty in Ukraine since they were purportedly for consumption by half a million Transdniestrians. A perhaps not enormously palatable Chicken Kiev must have featured regularly in every family's diet during that period.

Transdniestria has been and remains an example of a would-be state run along gangster lines, under the protection of a bigger power, exporting trouble to its region and beyond. Whatever the situation today, weapons have plainly been part of the province's trade alongside other profitable black-market and illegal goods. The only way to deal with this particular sore in Europe's side is for the EU to swallow hard and embrace Moldova more warmly – lowering the boundaries to Moldova's exports of wine, farm products, textiles and steel – and to develop a firmer and more coherent policy towards Russia, a point to which I shall return later in this book.

Serious efforts to control the proliferation of small arms really took off in the mid- to late 1990s. The terrible conflicts in the Great Lakes region of Africa were one of the reasons. In a single week 50,000 Burundians were killed following the abortive military coup in the country in 1993. After the Rwandan civil war from 1990 to 1994, a million people died in a three-month period. There was ethnic killing in the eastern Congo by both Hutu and Tutsi forces in subsequent years. The UN Secretary General called for a 'micro-disarmament' regime and the creation of a UN panel of government experts on small arms in 1996. In addition to global initiatives, a number of countries in Africa started to join together to prevent porous borders and transnational networks fostering 'bad neighbourhoods' flooded by arms and torn apart by spillover conflicts. Mali pioneered a regional initiative covering the import and manufacture of small arms in West Africa, and South Africa tried much the same in its own region.

All these activities paved the way for a UN Conference on the Illicit Trade in Small Arms and Light Weapons in 2001. The objective was international agreement to a programme of action committing states to defined measures to prevent and control black-market arms transfers and brokering. The high hopes for the conference were punctured by the Bush administration and by the US gun lobby, which has been so successful that there are today ninety guns for every hundred Americans. The United States is the most heavily armed nation in the world. The American Second Amendment Foundation had already denounced those NGOs working for restrictions on light weapons as 'fronting for an army of ultra-wealthy foundations that want to make the world safe for big money – which means taking guns away from everybody'. Gun Owners of America (GOA) characterized the United Nations as a 'tourniquet that is slowly being drawn around gun owners' necks'. It is not clear whether that is better or worse for the UN than being called the Antichrist, a charge made on the conspiratorial right in America from time to time. At the conference itself, where America was represented by the then US undersecretary of state John Bolton, any progress was rapidly stopped in its tracks. Bolton said that his country would not accept a document contrary to the United States' 'constitutional right to keep and bear arms'. This must have been a reassuring lesson in strict constitutionalism for Charles Taylor. It certainly pleased the US National Rifle Association (NRA) whose CEO, Wayne La Pierre, had denounced the conference for trying to place a 'global standard ahead of an individual country's freedom'.

The resulting very weak programme of action (POA), in 2001, largely defined the issue as an illicit trade problem, diverting attention away from regulation and reform of the profitable legal trade. The main provisions of the POA set a series of minimum global standards, norms and practices related to small-arms proliferation that could be used to combat the illicit trade. It called for the marking of guns at the point of manufacture for later identification and tracing and the issuing of end-user certificates for exports and transit. It – admirably – urged greater information exchange and transparency, better management and security of stockpiles and the identification and destruction of surplus weapons, better arms control at the end of conflicts with the collection and destruction of ex-combatants' weapons, and better enforcement of arms embargoes. But overall it was a hodgepodge of compromises. It was not legally binding, though there was said to be a strong political agreement to take appropriate domestic action in line with its terms. Highly popular measures like a ban on small arms transfers to non-state actors (for example insurgent groups and warlords) were excluded. Moreover, parts of the programme were rendered largely useless because of the vagueness of the export criteria that countries are supposed to take into account when considering arms transfers. There was no clear agreement that would prevent the sale of arms that could be used to violate human rights, threaten civilians or violate international law.

There was some pretty threadbare optimism that a Review Conference in 2006 would strengthen the POA. The reverse seems to have happened. A group of unlikely bedfellows prevented any agreement on an outcome document. In bed alongside the US were Cuba, Venezuela, Iran, Egypt, India and Pakistan. American negotiators were understandably keen to get agreement to prevent the sale of man-portable air defence systems, or MANPADS, which can be and are used to shoot down low-flying aircraft. Two were fired unsuccessfully at an Israeli passenger aircraft taking off from Mombasa in 2002. The *Small Arms Survey* calculates that there are 500,000 to 750,000 in the world, 100,000 of which are unaccounted for. It was a pity that American concern about this weapon did not extend a little further, but at least on MANPADS there has been some agreement to control supply, for instance by the G8 countries. According to NGOs that covered the conference, the USA appeared to be opposed to any global/UN follow-up, contending that any future discussions should be limited to regional and national action. There were several other deal breakers at the conference. They included an outright refusal to include provisions on the issue of regulating civilian possession, ammunition (a crucial question), transfer controls (specifically to non-state actors), and the relationship of greater gun control to development assistance. Indonesia and India led the expression of concern about any aid conditionality in relation to weapons' purchase. Given the domestic problems and insurgency faced by both these countries, observers might have expected more enthusiastic support from them for a tougher anti-proliferation regime. A few useful shreds and tatters remained of the early hopes – on stockpile management and security, surplus destruction, end-user certification and the implementation of the International Tracing Instrument, which allows checking on weapons from manufacture to use. But that was about it; there was no cause or justification for even a crouching ovation.

Since the failure of the 2006 review conference, there has been some modest progress. First, the Secretary General of the UN has issued several reports, calling for measures to establish international standards for the arms trade and for ways of calculating progress towards curbing the business and making it more transparent. In 2008, 147 States voted at the UN to move forward with work on the main elements of an Arms Trade Treaty. The large 'yes' vote was particularly strong in Africa, South and Central America and Europe, in other words covering both countries severely affected by armed violence and some of the major exporters. Twelve states from the Middle East abstained. The U.S. and Zimbabwe were the only two countries to vote against the initiative. It is, therefore, especially important and hopeful that as a senator Barack Obama took up the issue of 'small arms' working with the Republican, Senator Lugar, to pass legislation to prohibit cluster bombs and to make secure, conventional weapons like shoulder-fired missiles. During his campaign he called for international initiatives to limit the harm done to civilians by conventional weapons. After eight years of the Bolton–Bush blockade we may therefore now see positive US engagement on the issue.

There are several issues which EU member states and other like-minded countries could push even as attempts to forge a global agreement progress. First, we know that UN embargoes do not at present work; Liberia is a good example. How can we strengthen the monitoring of international sanctions and embargoes? The EU could begin by creating a monitoring unit itself. When I was a European Commissioner, I got used to foreign ministers expressing their strong disapproval for the bad behaviour of other states by announcing sanctions against them. They were usually more interested in form than substance. One of my officials – a Dutch lawyer of impeccable integrity – had the job of trying to ensure that the member states were actually doing what they had voted for. It was a Sisyphean task. This suggests strongly that, second, the EU should put its code of conduct on arms sales on a statutory basis. Third, it should give more support in its development programmes for post-conflict disarmament, demobilization and reintegration programmes, including weapons buy-back schemes. As part of these programmes, more effort should also be made to trace the origins of the weapons bought up, and to publicize the result of these surveys. Where did the purchasers get them from? There is a close connection between promoting security in this sort of way and economic development. Fourth, the Nunn–Lugar scheme for buying up stockpiled nuclear weapons from Russia creates a model for conventional weapons stockpiles as well. Europe could start with Ukraine, and indeed with some of its own member states which escaped from the Warsaw Pact at the end of the 1980s. How much of this will happen, and how much political will is available for this issue, are presumably questions which failed for years to disturb Mr Bout's sleep. Maybe there are just too many issues on governments' lists of international priorities for them to give this the attention it deserves, or perhaps there is a more cynical reason for the lack of progress. 'The weakness of the global regulation', argues Neil Cooper, 'stems in part from the fact that the most influential states in the international system – those with the power to effect change in the global governance of armaments – are the same states that have the largest defence sectors and benefit most from global arms sales.'[14] OECD states account today for 78 per cent of global military expenditure.

In many of the states where civil wars have been sustained by the easy and relatively cheap availability of light weapons, it has not only been the guns for sale that have been at the heart of combat. There have also often been guns for hire, mercenaries who train, support and fight for the combatants. Mercenaries have always been with us – soldiers who fight principally for money, ready to kill and be killed for states with which their main connection is pecuniary. In Chapter 2 I noted the attempt in Florence to give one of the bloodiest of the soldiers of fortune, Sir John Hawkwood, a veneer of respectability. His life and death took him from massacres and extortion to Uccello's painting on the gospel side of the Duomo. But vesting mercenaries with upright virtues has never been easy. The barons at Runnymede, pressing their Great Charter on King John, insisted that he should give up his mercenaries. Machiavelli regarded mercenaries as dangerous to leaders because all that kept them in the field was money and they had no comprehension of the common good for which patriots were prepared to die. The Americans who fought against King George III for the independence of their colonies believed in a citizens' army; the king's use of mercenaries was one of the grievances they set out in the Declaration of Independence. After the French Revolution, states began to fight wars using their own citizens exclusively. The British in the nineteenth century even managed to overcome their historic dislike of standing armies, rejecting mercenaries as they denounced slavery, another example of the trade in human flesh. They were clear that Britain could not be a great country based on Christian principles and the values of a higher civilization if it required foreigners to fight for it. There may be many Indian names inscribed on the First World War memorials like the Menin Gate in Ypres, but even they were thought to be fighting for an empire of which they were – even if not willingly – part. In later years Britain has been happy about allowing Gurkhas to fight for it, though less happy about allowing them subsequently to settle in the country for which they have risked their lives.

The arrival of self-determination in Africa and the departure of the white imperialists saw the return of the mercenaries to conflict. The fact that most of them were white made the moral disapproval in African countries all the more intense. They were not only fighting against Africans but against the UN and its forces, notably in the struggle to secure Katanga's secession from the Congo. On the whole, the mercenary record in Africa has been one of squalid incompetence. Under the command of a court-martialled Cypriot-British ex-paratrooper they put in a bloody but bungled appearance in 1996 in the Angolan civil war. They proved to be just as incompetent in Biafra, Benin and the Comoro Islands. Under the infamous Mike Hoare, an attempted coup by mercenaries in the Seychelles in 1981 turned into pantomime as the soldiers of fortune, disguised as a rugby team called the Ancient Order of Frothblowers, tried to smuggle their weapons through airport customs as Christmas gifts for local children. Unfortunately one of the mercenaries went by accident through the red channel at customs, where his gun was discovered: military intelligence of a sort.

In later years, mercenaries – now called Private Military Companies

(PMCs) – did a rather more effective job in Angola and Sierra Leone, though in the latter one of the companies involved (Sandline) caused much embarrassment to the British government by being caught trying to smuggle weapons into the country despite a UN embargo but with the knowledge of British diplomats. The use of PMCs was in part an inevitable consequence of the shrinking of the world's armies by 6 million after the Cold War. These supposedly redundant soldiers often moved after being demobilized into the private sector which (serving the public sector at a much higher price) had a voracious appetite for their services. In some cases – for example South Africa and Russia – entire cashiered units became private companies overnight. The American 'Army of the Future' will require a legion of civilian employees, the British too. PMCs have not avoided the moral opprobrium that attaches to mercenary activity, not least because they are thought to have been closely associated with some of the resource-extraction companies whose relations with combatants in African civil wars have frequently fed suspicions of collusion. As the market for organizations that take a front-line combatant role has recently diminished, so the demand for Private Security Companies (PSCs as opposed to PMCs) has grown. These organizations, as Sarah Percy has argued, '. . . provide four main types of services: logistical support, operational or tactical support, military advice and training, and policing or security. Logistical support entails tasks such as the preparation and delivery of food, laundry, and maintenance at military bases.'[15] How far away this is from military combat, or at least traditional military responsibilities, is sometimes difficult to fathom. Having seen the armed-to-the-teeth bodyguards who surrounded Paul Bremer in Iraq and President Karzai in Afghanistan, supplied by two American PSCs – Blackwater and DynCorp – I would have some difficulty in not describing them as combatants. PSCs look after the computers for unmanned aerial vehicles, operate missile guidance systems on ships and undertake military interrogations. Are they subject to the same military command structures, the same domestic and international laws, the same international conventions as regular uniformed combatants? The picture is blurred. A good example of what might happen too often in practice is given in Rajiv Chandrasekaran's account of the Green Zone world at the heart of Baghdad, which was the fortified seat of America's governing occupation of Iraq.[16] Chandrasekaran tells the story of an ex-American soldier, recruited by a firm called Custer Battles for various security duties, who armed himself with soft-point bullets, banned on the battlefield by the 1899 Hague Declaration 3. The Pentagon has long kept to its provisions, despite the fact that the US government has never signed this treaty. These soft-point bullets are more likely to deform and mushroom when they enter flesh, leading to catastrophic injury. The contract worker used these bullets during an attempted ambush of his vehicle to devastating effect. Chandrasekaran notes that 'when military commanders heard about the bullets used in the shooting they issued a memo to security firms warning against the use of non-standard ammunition. But there was no effective way to enforce the rule – or any of the other regulations the military wanted to impose on security contractors. They were above the laws of war.' The outcome of the story was an increase in demand for the bullets in the private security community. Blackwater has been involved in a number of similar incidents in Iraq, where it has been widely employed. In September 2007, for example, the firm was involved in the death of seventeen or more civilians in a firefight protecting one of the VIPs they describe as 'packages'. Blackwater, a new firm closely connected with the Republican Party, has received $1 billion worth of contracts from the US government since 2001, many without open, competitive bidding. Its private military operatives are paid about six times as much as an equivalent soldier. In February 2009, Blackwater announced that it was changing its name to 'Xe' as part of a rebranding and reorganization strategy. The Iraqi government had declined in January to renew its licence to operate in the country, and the State Department decided not to renew its contract to protect diplomats.

Maybe the haziness about which laws apply to private contractors would not matter too much if they were used only in small numbers at the margins of engagements. That is far from the case. When the United States led the coalition into the 1991 Gulf War, about one in fifty of its military host were employees or private contractors. In Iraq in 2003 the equivalent figure was one in ten. In 2006 it was estimated that there were at least 20,000 PSC employees assisting US and British troops in Iraq. To say that these men and women do not engage in active combat, that they are not therefore mercenaries, is to go to the very extremes of linguistic flexibility. Partly because it has a volunteer citizen army, and is fighting a very unpopular war in Iraq, partly because it has probably underestimated the need still for boots on the ground in an era of high-technology warfare, it would be extremely difficult for America to go to war today without a large recruitment from PSCs (as is clear, for example, from its use of Blackwater). There is an additional political factor. There are probably, in the US and elsewhere, fewer objections to sending more PSC employees to foreign military theatres than to dispatching more troops. When the employees of PSCs are captured in, say, Colombia, they simply disappear; they are deniable; no one will know about them or care, apart from their families. There are strong reasons in democratic societies, in the interest of understanding the full nature of security commitments, for greater transparency regarding the use of PSCs and its scale. The controls over their engagement, and the relevance of national law, international law, and international treaties to what they do, also need to be clarified.

The peacekeeping role of the UN – confronting brutal civil wars, policing unstable peace settlements, trying to buy time for the rebuilding of collapsed states – has sometimes been compared by critics to mercenary activity, albeit with avowedly humanitarian purposes. This is deeply unfair. UN peacekeeping certainly expanded dramatically in the mid- to late 1990s. By January 2009 there were over 110,000 UN peacekeepers and personnel, with an additional 20,000 authorised for deployment in the course of the year. This is the highest figure ever, well above the millennium low of 12,000. Additional deployments by regional organizations – NATO, the EU and the African Union – increased by over a quarter in 2005–6. There has also been a dramatic diversification of states contributing to peacekeeping: 117 were doing so in 2007. Peacekeeping has been bankrolled, ever since the financial crisis engendered by the UN's Congo intervention in the 1960s (first through Irish troops carrying Enfield rifles), on a separate budget amounting to about $5.5 billion into which the five permanent members of the UN Security Council pay a surcharge. The budget is a source of endless squabbling. It allows for a contribution to be made to governments contributing troops of $1,028 per soldier per month, which some critics argue allows the operations to become profit-making exercises for some countries whose armed forces are badly equipped. There are probably occasions when this is true; the past deployment of Zimbabwean troops in Angola, the resource-rich cockpit in a long civil war, is sometimes cited. On the other hand, the delay in payment of frequently uncertain reimbursement does not suggest that any countries can have made a fraction of the money out of peacekeeping that has accrued to PSC contractors in Iraq. A far bigger problem is the growing concern on the part of developing countries that they do a disproportionate part of peacekeeping's heavy lifting. With less effective equipment and training, they provide bodies and blood, while the rich countries give the money (often reluctantly) and set most of the terms of the debate on this UN role. The latest large-scale UN deployment in Sudan was mostly paid for by the West, which also provided a core of staff officers, but the force itself was overwhelmingly African.

This raises a related point that needs to be discussed more openly in relation to conflict and development – or rather the lack of it in impoverished countries. While it is today politically acceptable to talk in aid-donor countries about governance (though certainly not acceptable in many others, as countries like China, Argentina and Russia made clear to the World Bank in 2007), discussing the relationship between security and governance is largely forbidden territory. To talk about law enforcement, internal security and effective, democratically accountable military capacity in poor countries is thought to taint real development concerns. On parts of the political left it is even worse to talk about security and development than about growth or open markets and development. One result has been that for years the OECD has rigorously policed declarations of development assistance to ensure that they do not cover security. We are all of us in favour of peace, stability and turning swords into ploughshares, but this OECD approach ignores reality. If we want to help states, which are trying to run themselves openly and well, to avoid the conflict trap and the sort of breakdown that eventually requires the deployment of UN peacekeepers, then building up capacity to protect democratic states from insurgency seems wholly defensible. This is a subject on which the OECD and the NATO countries should take a lead, helping countries that are democratic and are attempting to live under the rule of law to do so by training, advising and equipping their military and their law-enforcement agencies. Democracies should be prepared to extend the benefits of collective security to like-minded aspiring liberal democratic states. If the equatorial state of Coupophobia after a conflict establishes a constitutional and democratic government, and makes a genuine effort to set up pluralist institutions, then NATO and preferably the African Union should contract with it to give it the basic capacity it needs to defend its own sovereignty without challenging that of its neighbours. Should the elected president of Coupophobia renege on his contractual commitments, then all bets would be off and support would be withdrawn. Should there be nervousness about helping individual states in this way? OECD countries could begin by working with the African Union and regional African organizations like the South African Development Conference to increase the capacity of African organizations to support legitimate governments menaced by insurgency. This is not an impossibly open-ended commitment. We have seen how few men it takes to tear apart a weak and poor state and we have noted the role of mercenaries. I would prefer governments to do what Sandline and others have done in the past; to have NATO officers rather than Mike Hoare giving military advice to poor countries. All this should be part of a sensible development policy in the poorest parts of the world.

7

Greed, Conflict and the 'Bottom Billion'

Time and chance happeneth to them all.   Ecclesiastes 9: 11

The stranger has big eyes but he doesn't see.
                                     West African Proverb

No new light has been thrown on the reason why poor countries are poor and rich countries are rich.
              Paul Samuelson, *Illogic of Neo-Marxian Doctrine of*
                                      Unequal Exchange, 1976

So how does the world look to the average citizen of – say – Lubumbashi, the second largest city in Congo? The concept of citizenship may for a start be alien to him or her. Where is the network of reciprocal individual duties and communal responsibilities which lies at the heart of most notions of what it means to be a citizen? What service or protection does governing authority provide to those in this city whom it can command and tyrannize?

Lubumbashi was founded in 1910 by the Belgian colonial power and named Elizabethville after King Albert's queen. With a population of around 1.2 million (which rises and falls according to the regional security situation), it is near the Zambian border, close by one of the main tributaries of the Zambezi river. It was the jumping-off point for Tim Butcher's remarkable journey through the Congo as it was for many travellers in safer times in the past.[1] A city of cobbled boulevards, art-deco buildings and a large red-brick cathedral, it is on a once-busy railway crossing. It should still be thriving and prosperous. After all, it is in the heart of the copper and cobalt belt of Congo, with other deposits of zinc, silver, uranium, lead and germanium mined in the area. In or near Lubumbashi, for example, are the Big Hill copper-cobalt tailings and smelter project, the copper-cobalt mine at Etoile, the Kipushi copper-zinc mine and the EXACO cobalt carbonate plant. But most of the wealth from these minerals is pocketed elsewhere, beginning with corrupt customs officials on the Zambian border who nod through tax-free truckloads of cobalt rock for export to South Africa or faraway China. The rock is converted in other countries into concentrated cobalt salts, increasing its value between fifty- and a hundred-fold. So Lubumbashi remains dirt poor, with inadequate or non-existent public services. It is safer than much of the province of Katanga of which it is the capital, though it has not escaped brushes with Congo's brutal history. It was a focal point of hostilities during Katanga's secessionist war after independence, and it appeared again on the political scene when Laurent Kabila declared himself president of the whole country in Lubumbashi after the flight of his predecessor Mobutu Sese Seko, probably the richest of all the African tyrants.

I return to the Congo because it seems such fertile ground for starting an examination of some of the most difficult, overlapping questions of the twenty-first century. Does Congo offer some sort of fearful paradigm of Africa as a whole? Are some countries simply trapped by their geography, pinioned to poverty and violence by climate and topography? Does their history fit some of them with lead-filled boots? What are the main sources of conflict today and does the competition for natural resources in a more populated, faster growing world spell inevitable turmoil? How can we best confront the moral outrage of grinding poverty amongst plenty? How do we best help that 'bottom billion' defined by Paul Collier, 8 million of whom die each year simply because they are too poor to stay alive?[2] Can we in the West make poverty history with one sustained high-minded heave?

Geography, as David Landes argues, is not necessarily destiny.[3] You can abate some of its consequences by technology, by science, by personal and collective effort and by making better choices. Extremes of climate admittedly constrain economic development, which is one reason the poorest countries in the world mostly lie in the tropics and semi-tropics. Heat is more debilitating than cold, especially when the damp of a tropical climate reduces the cooling effect of perspiration. The journalist Alistair Cooke used to argue that it was the discovery and installation of air-conditioning in the southern and south-western states of America after the Second World War which helped to promote their economic take-off. Year-round heat and damp together encourage the proliferation of insects and parasites. The snails that reproduce in African and some Asian waters spread bilharzia. The tsetse fly's bite disseminates sleeping sickness, making it difficult for humans or cattle to live in some parts of Africa. In tropical heat mosquitoes live longer; the African variety prefers to bite humans than cattle. So malaria is more difficult to control in Africa than elsewhere, which is why about 90 per cent of the 3 million people (mostly young children) who die of the disease each year live in this continent's tropical and sub-tropical regions. Jeffrey Sachs has shown that throughout the last half-century the poor regions of the world were largely coterminous with those where malaria was widespread.[4] The hostile climate in tropical areas produces irregular but torrential rain, making cultivation of crops difficult as agriculture competes with jungle. Cutting down forests leads to soil erosion as heavy rainfall scours earth from the rock. Most of the severe existing consequences of the climate in poor countries will be exacerbated in the future by global warming. How much easier life has been in western Europe, lapped by the Gulf Stream, or in China where, in the words of a local adage, 'the land is scarce and the people are many'. But rainfall and temperature are not the only reasons for Europe's and China's ascendancy over the centuries. Individual men and women, the spread of knowledge, science, technology, culture, institutions and good luck have played their part as well. Climate and environment are part of the picture; they are not the whole explanation for everything else.

Nor is history. The story of Africa's relationship with the West (and indeed with the Arab world) has largely been one of its exploitation. Seeking a sea route to the East Indies in the 1480s, the Portuguese mariner Diogo Cão discovered as he sailed south that beyond Africa's western bulge the water suddenly turned brown and was drinkable miles out to sea. It was the Congo river, pouring its fresh water with huge force into the Atlantic Ocean, gouging a deep channel in the sea bed. There is an obvious metaphor: that ever since then Africa has been pouring its wealth into the lap of greedy plunderers. To be fair to the Portuguese, the story did not begin too badly. There were peaceful exchanges of gifts and ambassadors. The local king was converted to Christianity and joined forces with the Portuguese to rout his enemies. But soon the discovery of the Americas created a huge demand for labour on plantations in the New World. It was met by the slave trade, already conducted by Arabs in the east of the continent and by African tribes themselves. Slavery was the most indefensible of the West's assaults on Africa.

The freebooting of previous centuries turned into the wholesale ransacking of the continent in the 1870s as the European scramble for Africa began. By the time it finished, many thousands of tribal African polities and several empires had been cobbled together into forty colonies and protectorates. David Livingstone had bade others to follow in his adventurous footsteps and 'make an open path for commerce and Christianity'. With the encouragement of the journalist and explorer Henry Morton Stanley, the Europeans did exactly this, crowding after King Leopold II of the recently created country of Belgium, a man who espoused philanthropy and practised pillage. In a gloomy, hidden-away corner of the Cinquantenaire Park in the centre of Brussels, laid out with King Leopold's loot from the oppression of the Congo to mark the fiftieth anniversary of his country's creation (once described by General de Gaulle as Britain's revenge on France), there stands a monument to Belgium's colonial rule in central Africa. It is about as politically incorrect as it is possible to be in modern times, as a shamefaced little notice to one side more or less admits. A grateful Negro lies beneath the sculpted reliefs of brave Belgian soldiers, missionaries and explorers spreading their own brands of commerce and Christianity across the dark heart of Africa. Doubtless there were good men who taught the young, and good women who healed the sick, but the colonial story in Congo around the turn of the twentieth century is above all one of depredation – forced labour, amputations as a means of discipline, the cropping of rubber and the mining of minerals and gems at whatever murderous cost to local tribes. There is not much to brag about.

The story elsewhere in Africa is sometimes as bad, sometimes a lot better. Few today seek to justify colonial exploitation. After all, during the imperial age the economic gap between Europe and its colonies grew. But there were territories where under colonial administrations health was improved, education introduced, infrastructure built, new crops brought in, governing institutions established. Any visitor today is surprised at the extent to which the built environment in Africa still bears a colonial stamp and the institutions still seem shaped by Western administrators, even where in practice they mock the ideas of governance that they were established to exemplify.

When the colonial era ended, when independence came to African countries in the late 1950s and 60s (beginning with Ghana in 1957), self-determination rapidly captured the continent. It was an unstoppable process. Even legitimate anxieties about the readiness of many countries to embrace their own destinies were swept aside. The hour did not allow for a second's hesitation in doubting whether colonial administrations had done all that they could to prepare recently subject people for assuming sovereignty in autonomous countries.

The withdrawal of the colonial powers did not leave Africa penniless. The economic future looked bright. The world price for commodities had soared in the post-war years. Groundnut and tea production had doubled in a decade, and coffee production trebled. The price of oil was low and the same was true of public debt in the new Africa; foreign currency reserves were high. From 1945 to 1960 the economies of colonial Africa had grown annually by between 4 and 6 per cent. Even the rains came, boosting agriculture. Perhaps in these largely propitious circumstances some of the extravagant promises made by nationalist politicians in their independence election campaigns would be redeemable.[5] But the imperial powers also bequeathed the continent a litany of problems. For a start, what exactly were all these countries that now flew their own flags and claimed sovereignty within their own borders? The borders themselves often reflected little more than an arbitrarily drawn line on a map, a bargain haggled over by statesmen under Europe's chandeliers decades before, trading one place they did not know for another they had hardly heard of; or borders could mark impermeably a geographer's assumption about natural frontiers or the prejudice of bureaucrats. This was, for example, how Sudan, which has spent much of the last two decades in a vicious war between north and south, came improbably to be created. In the 1940s the Arabists among British bureaucrats (known in the Foreign Office as 'the camel corps'), who were influenced by educated northerners, overcame the Africanists, who looked after the south of the country, the inhabitants of which were regarded by the north as little better than slaves. So in full knowledge of what they were doing, British colonial officials hammered together the Muslim north and the Christian south. Today Sudan has 6 million internal refugees and it will be a surprise (as I suggested in the previous chapter) if there is not yet another north–south conflict to add to the one now raging between Khartoum and Darfur in the west. As well as creating some countries in which religious, ethnic and tribal differences made problematic whether any sort of state could survive at all, the colonialists also established too many countries; almost twenty-two countries south of the Sahara have populations fewer than 10 million. Transport links between them were and remain weak and markets were and still are small. Borders are often meaningless in terms of the payment of duties and tax, since much of what regional trade there is is in the hands of smugglers.

It was not only in Africa that colonialism ended in the 1960s and 70s. New, independent states came into existence in Asia, escaping at war's end from Japanese colonialism (like Korea) as well as breaking free of Europe (Malaysia and Singapore) and the United States (the Philippines). In addition, China had emerged from a terrible century of Western exploitation, Japanese invasion and rampant warlordism, into the patriotic excitements of the communist revolution of 1949. Singapore had no assets save its naval base. Malaya was riven by a struggle between the British colonialists and communist insurgents. Korea – a country with virtually no natural resources – was torn apart by civil war between north and south. History did not seem to be on the side of Asia; nor could most Asian countries boast the resources of, say, Congo. Comparisons of subsequent progress in both continents are salutary, and raise plausible questions about whether history always slams the brakes on progress.

The economy of the African continent today is about the same size as that of Argentina. Exclude South Africa and Nigeria and the economy is worth roughly the same as Belgium ($200 billion). Africa has 10 per cent of the world's population and 1 per cent of its international trade. Since 1980 world poverty has fallen overall, with hundreds of millions of men and women in India, China and elsewhere escaping indigence. But in too much of Africa the figures have moved in the opposite direction, with the incomes of the poorest actually dropping. Approximately one billion of the world's population of six billion people are falling further and further behind; 70 per cent of them live in Africa. In the last twenty-five years, the number of the poorest – those living on less than a dollar a day – has risen in sub-Saharan Africa but fallen in east and south Asia. The proportion of extremely poor in east Asia dropped from 58 per cent to 15 per cent from 1981 to 2005, in south Asia from 52 per cent to 31 per cent in the same period. In Latin America it stuck at about 10 per cent. The proportion in Africa has risen slightly, to almost half.

Per-capita and overall GDP in Congo and three Asian countries, 1960 and 2007 (constant 2000 US$)

Country	Per-capita GDP ($)		Country GDP ($ billion)	
	1960	1960	2007	2007
China	105.5	1,791.3	70.3	2,364.4
Japan	7,137.7	40,655.7	671.1	5,194.6
South Korea	1,109.9	14,540.3	27.7	705.6
Congo	323.6	94.0	5.0	5.9

Source: World Bank Data.

The table shows what has happened in our principal African example. Between 1960 and 2007 Congo's per-capita income fell by well over 200 per cent while those of China, Japan and South Korea increased by between 570 and over 1,700 per cent. The overall GDP figures confirm this comparison.

These figures tell their own tale. Anecdote adds its footnotes. I have a Korean friend who became a provincial governor and an influential economic adviser to President Kim Dae Jung. He grew up in the most backward part of South Korea during and after the devastating war on the peninsula. Clever at school, he won a place just after that war at the National University in Seoul, and working hard there earned a scholarship to Rutgers University in the USA. Waiting at the airport for his flight to New York, he suddenly thought he should buy something that had been manufactured in South Korea to show his American hosts that it was not just a backwoods economy, its cities flattened by war. The only thing he could find in the airport shop that was made in his own country was a pair of nail scissors. They broke the first time he used them. That was in 1960. South Korea has virtually no natural resources – no copper, diamonds or timber. But today it is a sophisticated high value-added economy, one of the foremost exporting countries in the world with a formidably numerate population. Yet the Almighty was hardly as kind to South Korea as He was to the Congo and other African countries, denying it any resources and giving it a war-ravaged economy to build on and a glowering, unfathomable and dangerous neighbour.

Africa, on the other hand, contains very large reserves of some of the world's most significant minerals – bauxite, cobalt, copper, chromium, manganese, gold, platinum, titanium, uranium and phosphate rock. Foreign mining companies invest heavily. Gems and other minerals are exported by – among others – Congo, Angola, Guinea, Botswana, South Africa, Zambia and Namibia. Africa has valuable timber resources and hydrocarbon reserves. In 2008, it was estimated that Africa had 9 per cent of the world's proven supply of oil and 8 per cent of its natural gas reserves.[6] Is all this potential wealth one of the reasons African countries should have done better; or a reason they have done so badly? Moreover, in a world where Asia with its growing manufacturing and service sectors will be looking further afield and searching harder for the resources to fuel continuing growth, will Africa fall victim to a more successful continent's appetite for what Africans can dig, mine or pump from their own soil?

Perhaps we are faced once again with a counter-intuitive proposition. Even in the age of al-Qaeda, is greed more important than creed in triggering impoverishing conflict? Is civilizational clash a less potent reason for violence than the desire for a pocketful of diamonds? Are need, poverty and starvation the consequences rather more often than the causes of greed?

Motivations for conflict vary; there is no open-and-shut explanation. Some argue that the real reasons for the 9/11 atrocities was America's relationship with Saudi Arabia and the presence of American bases in the Kingdom. Ever since President Roosevelt's secret meeting with the founder of the modern Saudi dynasty, King Abdul Aziz ibn Saud, on the way home from Yalta in 1945, US policy in the region – it is argued – has been driven principally by the determination to safeguard oil reserves with unshakeable pledges to stand by the Saudi government. America has fought two oil wars in just over a decade; the internal-combustion engine drives American foreign policy. Yet if Washington's policy in the Middle East was based solely on protecting oil supplies, how do we explain the historic links on grounds of identity – that is, creed – with Israel, links that have embittered many Arab oil-producing states? Moreover, can we really argue that the al-Qaeda terrorists were simply driven by hostility to America's economic imperialism? Was there *no* ideological reason for their behaviour, nothing that reflects creed?

Nevertheless, resources have always played a significant role in starting conflicts. The Old Testament reminds us of this, as Moses is pointed by God in the direction of 'a land flowing with milk and honey'. The Normans who invaded England in the eleventh century were principally after land and loot. General Gordon was killed trying to hold the confluence of the White and Blue Niles at Khartoum. The Germans invaded Russia partly to get their hands on Baku and the oil from the Caspian. The Egyptians have come close to trading blows with their upstream neighbours over the waters of the Nile. Israel has fought its own neighbours over the River Jordan and the Baniyas at its headwaters.

In addition, transit routes for the exploitation and transport of resources have often been causes of tension and conflict. The historian Captain A. T. Mahan argued in the late 1800s that America required a large and powerful fleet in order to protect its international trade, a point that had been axiomatic for some centuries for British strategists. Today, American fleets keep the peace at the choke points of global commerce, the Straits of Hormuz for example, the Panama Canal and the Malacca Straits. On land, Russian policy aims for a monopoly over the transit of oil from central Asia, while the US and Europe seek to construct pipelines that do not cross Russian territory. China has invested heavily in its navy as interest has quickened in the oil reserves of the South China Sea. Beijing has bought naval vessels from Russia, with whom it used to have a tense relationship over its northern frontiers and the resources in that part of Asia.

Perhaps the extent to which the last century was dominated by America's and western Europe's struggles first against German and Japanese fascism, and then against Russian and Asian communism, has distracted our attention from the centrality of resources as the reason for conflict. Yet resources themselves were not irrelevant as Germany and Japan sought living space at the expense of their neighbours, and as Russia sought to extend its empire from the Baltic to the Caucasus, and westward into the very centre of Europe.

At school, I had an Ancient History teacher who divided every issue in the classical world from the rise of Athens to the fall of Rome into tripartite lists – causes, pretexts and results. It was not a bad way of preparing for exams but not a particularly good approach to understanding history. So I am not minded to take sides in the greed versus identity versus need analysis. Very often motivation is a scrambled mix of all three. I am prepared, however, to go along with those who argue that, whatever the undoubted influence of other motivations, the major reason for the sort of conflicts that we endure today is greed. In the aftermath of the Cold War, events in the Balkans, Rwanda and elsewhere meant that we concentrated heavily on ethnic nationalism and tribalism. Why did Hutus kill Tutsis? Why did Serbs kill Bosniacs? The sorts of conflicts that predominate today oblige us to look elsewhere for motivation.

Most of the wars that we have seen since the end of the Cold War have been civil wars – civil wars in failed, failing or shadow states, or in places like Somalia, where there is really no identifiable state to speak of at all. Using a statistical analysis of the seventy-nine major civil wars between 1960 and 1999, Professor Paul Collier, former director of the World Bank's Development Research Group and now at Oxford University, and his colleague Anke Hoeffler, have shown that a range of economic variables, including the level of per-capita income and the relative dependency on primary commodity exports, were more salient to the risk of civil war in a country such as Angola than ethnic fractures or the traditional gamut of grievances such as clan or religious hatred, political repression, political exclusion and economic inequality. The lower the income per head, and the greater the dependency on primary commodity exports, the greater the risk of today's customary war of choice, *civil* war. Poor countries with lootable resources are four times as likely to be sucked in to civil war as countries without Sierra Leone's diamonds, Angola's oil, Liberia's timber, Congo's copper and so on. In addition, countries with a past history of conflict such as Uganda are more likely to experience renewed unrest, with a more than 40 per cent risk of this happening during the first five years following the initial fighting.

There are three interpretations of the proposition that there is a strong correlation between a high ratio of primary commodity exports to overall national wealth and a susceptibility to conflict. First, the commodity helps to finance the fighting. Diasporas, foreign governments sympathetic to the rebels, irresponsible corporations or organized crime networks provide the funds to initiate and sustain rebellion, including arms and troop recruitment. In return for this they get their hands on the commodity, or at least a principal role in trading it.

Just as more orthodox markets manage trade, not only in what you can handle today but what you might have tomorrow (from pigs to pesos), so insurgents and their financial backers also trade in what are described as 'war booty futures'. These occur when aspiring rebels have no money to finance a rebellion, but stand a good chance of capturing valuable resources in any putative conflict. In such situations, rebels will often sell off the future right to mine, drill for or harvest the resources they hope to capture to companies who will offer in return immediate finance for the prospective bloody adventure. It is like investing in bank robbery. The company puts its money into sustaining fighting in the hope of setting up business in whatever territory the rebels capture, or at least acting as a trade broker there. 'War booty futures' are particularly dangerous because they often fund civil wars that might not otherwise have started, or help support weak rebel groups who would be defeated or wither away without external financial support. They can also lead to stalemates – once soldiers have captured the mortgaged resources they have little incentive to press on to victory (for example in Congo). War booty has a long history of financing conflict; the Northern Alliance in

Afghanistan in the 1990s sold lapis lazuli, for instance. But the market for 'war booty' seems specific to the African continent, including Katanga's rebellion in the 1960s (bankrolled by Belgian mining interests) and the Algerian war of independence when the Italian oil company ENI reportedly supplied money and arms to the National Liberation Front (FLN) in exchange for future 'consideration'.

Sometimes armed factions monopolize different commodities from the same country. The Angolan civil war began in 1975 with the end of Portuguese colonial rule, when the three egotistical Angolan leaders – the MPLA's Agostino Neto, UNITA's Jonas Savimbi and the FNLA's Holden Roberto – failed to reach a power-sharing deal. The Soviet Union backed the MPLA, who controlled the capital, Luanda, so the Americans backed Savimbi. The FNLA was supported by China, North Korea and Romania and (such are the complexities of covert ideological politics) by the CIA. But the FNLA did not last beyond the immediate fighting and most of its members then (confusingly for the agents from Foggy Bottom) joined the MPLA. In what Professor Collier has called 'the ultimate natural resources war', the fighting was protracted because the resources funding it were both valuable and plentiful. The rebel group, Neto's MPLA, was funded by diamonds; the government side, UNITA, depended on oil. The resources were of far more consequence than the original meaning of all these initials. By and large the course of the conflict mirrored the world price for diamonds and oil. When oil prices fell and the income from diamonds was high, Neto was on the march. When the price levels reversed, Neto was in retreat. Eventually, oil trumped diamonds. Neto got his comeuppance when the price of oil rocketed and international action severed his access to the diamond market.

Not only does this looting of exports provide the means for fighting a civil war, but – and this is the second interpretation of the relationship between resources and conflict – it is often the prospect of the loot that triggers the fighting in the first place. Charles Taylor in Liberia and Foday Sankoh in Sierra Leone were plainly keen on the cash that violence and power brought them. The *New York Times* published documents showing that Sankoh personally supervised the sale of diamonds to Europe from parts of Sierra Leone held by his rebels. His lieutenants handed to him over 2,000 stones in the last six months of 1999. When Sankoh discovered that UN peacekeepers were preparing to deploy in the Kono diamond region of the country, he ordered his insurgents to take the offensive against them.

A third element of the Collier thesis is the widely accepted finding that economies rich in natural resources have specific and usually intertwined characteristics that make them more susceptible to civil war. There appears to be a 'resource curse' which saddles these countries with lower growth rates and weaker institutions. They suffer from what is called the 'Dutch disease', named after the economic consequences of the discovery and exploitation of North Sea oil by the Netherlands in the 1970s. The resource bonanza drives up the value of their currency, making non-resource manufacturing and service industries less competitive, so these commercial activities are under-developed. While manufacturing and exporting have been the foundations of sustained growth in Asia, resource-rich African countries have on the whole missed out on this approach. Yet the volatility of international commodity prices requires good governance, which is exactly what too many African countries lack. If you spend all the proceeds of the good years on conspicuous consumption (often abroad), and on the military, there is nothing left to see you through the years when prices fall. Good governance is less likely in these countries, first because leaders do not need to tax the local population. There is therefore little public accountability for what they do and scant electoral scrutiny of their actions. Leaders often become in effect owners of the assets of their countries as well as heads of state or government. Their countries become personal fiefdoms; like medieval feudal monarchs they operate a system of bandit patronage in which they purchase loyalty through sharing some of the spoils with their supporters, who are bound to them by these ties of patronage. By 1992 President Mobutu's fortune was reportedly worth $6 billion, more than the GDP of his country. President Banda of Malawi (leader of his country from 1961 to 1994) managed a large part of national commercial activity through family trusts. Liberia's President Doe amassed in a decade a fortune more or less equivalent to half Liberia's annual domestic income.[7]

The comparison with medieval European governance is not far-fetched. A thirteenth-century English chronicler compared a monarch to 'a robber permanently on the prowl, always probing . . . always searching for something . . . to steal'. England's Edward II stole the gold and plate from the vaults of the Knights Templar to pay for his campaigns. Typically he regarded whatever his kingdom and its inhabitants possessed as potential booty to invest in warfare that promised subsequent dividends from the investment in the military enterprise. The exchequer in the Middle Ages travelled around with the king as part of his household. No distinction was made between what was public and what was the king's own account, his privy purse. As late as the seventeenth century in England, Charles I seized the gold from the Tower of London where it had been placed for safe-keeping. It was relatively late in the day, as we noted in Chapter 2, that monarchs understood that instead of plundering wealth they had to help create it. President Mobutu (and others) took the earlier view of public revenue and private spending power. What was Congo's was his.

Despots who regard public resources as their private wealth, and who create systems of managing and retaining power through violence and patronage, inevitably risk being replaced themselves by brute force. The successor despot comes with a caravan of his own supporters to feed and water. Africa predictably propagates coups. Sixty per cent of Africa's rulers from 1960 to 1992 left office for exile, prison or an early grave. Nor did the security of Africa's rulers improve during the 1990s. There were coups (in some cases more than once) in Nigeria, Burundi, Gambia, Comoros, Niger, Sierra Leone, Congo Brazzaville, Chad, Guinea Bissau, Ivory Coast, Lesotho and Mali. It was only the assistance of French paratroopers that saved the president of the Central African Republic from three military rebellions. Congo is the focus of an ongoing conflict in which, over the past decade, there have been 5.4 million deaths: an average monthly death toll of 45,000, nearly half of whom were children under five years of age. Eleven other African states have been dragged into this, the deadliest conflict since the Second World War.

Congo, which is as large territorially as western Europe, has been wrecked by the lure of its resource wealth. This has not happened in secret. The UN and NGOs have carefully documented what has happened. Yet the despoliation has continued. After independence and the initial fighting, mainly over Katanga's attempted secession, Mobutu Sese Seko with his trademark leopard skin hat was installed in a military coup backed by the US and Belgium. In 1965 he followed King Leopold's example in regarding Congo's wealth as his own private property; but the more Mobutu and his feudatory gangsters tried to control everything themselves, the more the informal economy and smuggling developed. Economic collapse and corruption in the 1990s were accompanied by the breakdown of public services and the non-payment of state employees including (fatally) soldiers. Mobutu was eventually brought down by an armed rebellion partly organized and strongly supported by Rwanda, Uganda and Burundi. Rwanda's new Tutsi government wanted to deal decisively with the Intera-hamwe, Hutu militias who had carried out the genocide of hundreds of thousands of Tutsis in 1994 and whose exodus to the eastern Congo threatened local Tutsi tribes. The leader of the rebellion against Mobutu was his long-time foe Laurent Kabila, who had been at university in Dar-es-Salaam with President Museveni of Uganda. Museveni gave Kabila his support. The subsequent fighting from 1998 to 2001 was hugely complicated because it was both a civil and an international conflict, with troops from several nearby countries drawn in. When Kabila, who was every bit as corrupt as his prede-cessor, requested Rwanda's President Kagame and President Museveni to withdraw their forces, they at first complied but sent their troops back in to Congo within weeks. Kabila's request for help from members of the Southern African Development Community (SADC) brought troops from Zimbabwe, Namibia and Angola into the country. Rebel groups with a bewildering series of titles fought as proxies of the invading African states, which (like Rwanda and Uganda in 1999) themselves fell out, largely over local pickings.

Since 2000, the UN Security Council has produced a series of reports documenting how different groups and their allies have looted the country. The pillage is often centrally organized. For example a group of Ugandan army officers and businessmen, including the president's brother and a former head of the Ugandan army, have built up (partly through military intimidation) a business exporting Congo's coltan, diamonds, timber and gold. This is a fairly typical operation, not particularly covert but extremely lucrative. Collating

UN reports and other evidence, the NGO Global Witness has shown, looking at one resource after another, how Congo has been robbed.[8]

Begin with coltan (in full, columbite-tantalite, a metallic ore used in the making of laptops and mobile phones), which enjoyed a price boom in the early 2000s. Congo has the world's largest resources. Coltan is mined in the east of the country, in a process similar to the panhandling of gold in California in the 1880s. The value of coltan makes this sort of artisanal mining attractive: workers earn from $10 to $50 a week in comparison to the average Congolese wage of $10 a month. Coltan is flown out of the otherwise inaccessible mining districts in Antonov planes to Kigali in Rwanda and Kampala in Uganda, where the price is fixed, before it is sold on to Europe, the US and China (recently the main buyer of officially listed Congolese coltan, though much of what is described as a Rwandan export to China has probably originated in Congo). Several companies have been set up to exploit Congo's coltan in Uganda and Rwanda; these firms are owned by the government or by people close to the government. The role of the Congolese is to mine the coltan; Rwandans and Ugandans act as brokers. The military benefit substantially. In late 1999–2000 the Rwandan army was making about $20 million a month from this trade. When a member of the Congolese rebel group (and political party) established by Uganda and Rwanda to overthrow Mobutu became mining minister he used money from coltan to pay for a 40,000-strong army. The mining and sale of the tin mineral cassiterite has been similar to that of coltan.

The copper belt, which stretches along Congo's border with Zambia and Angola, contains other minerals too, including zinc, silver, uranium and lead. Copper and cobalt, which is extracted from copper, should be a major export earner for Congo, but mismanagement, corruption, political interference and conflict led to a sharp fall in production. Moreover, Zimbabwe has gained a big stake in this industry. After Zimbabwe sent in troops to assist the government, it benefited from preferential treatment when mining concessions were handed out in Katanga. The UN Panel of Experts also claimed that some of the cash passing through a joint-venture copper-mining company was used to buy equipment for the Zimbabwean armed forces. Uranium is also mined in Katanga; it is claimed that the uranium used in the Hiroshima and Nagasaki bombs came from here. Reports that Laurent Kabila's government granted a uranium mining concession to North Korea in return for the North Koreans training Kabila's troops were denied by Pyongyang. Belief in North Korea's word is a fragile commodity.

Throughout central Africa diamonds are a rebel's best friend, the best conflict resource, and they have received the full Hollywood treatment. They are small, valuable and until recently very marketable. Publicity has encouraged some questioning about provenance among potential customers. Congo has particularly rich deposits of alluvial diamonds, which can be mined at little cost and with next to no equipment even in war zones. As Laurent Kabila advanced on Kinshasa in 1996 he handed out diamond-mining concessions and export contracts to raise money and gain support. Rebel groups, and their outside sponsors, have battled for control of the main diamond-mining areas and been active in smuggling conflict diamonds out of the country to the main trading centres like Antwerp (by far the biggest), Tel Aviv and Mumbai. The US is the largest retailer of cut and polished diamonds. In 2000, it is reckoned that about 85 per cent of Congo's diamond production was smuggled out of the country.

Uganda has been heavily involved in mining and selling Congolese gold from the north-east of the country. Angola has a joint venture with Congo in the oil sector. Uganda and Zimbabwe have been prominent in the logging and sale of conflict timber. Plundering Congo fathered a whole new commercial industry, air transport to get the loot out and, as we saw in the previous chapter, to get weapons in. After 1998 several air companies were set up in central Africa which were owned by the families and friends of political leaders. President Museveni's sister-in-law (the wife of a general and former deputy prime minister) owned Air Alexander, flying between Entebbe and Kisangani, a major north-eastern Congolese trading centre on the Congo river, once known as Stanleyville and the scene of a terrible series of brutal massacres over the years since independence.

Nowhere provides a better example than Congo of the effects of greed, conflict, lootable resources, poverty, appalling governance and corruption, a list to which one should, of course, add, without trespassing on the territory of psychiatrists and priests, sheer human wickedness. How else can one come close to an adequate explanation of, for example, the appallingly savage treatment of women in the Congo? In one province alone, South Kivu in the east of the country on the Rwanda border, 27,000 sexual assaults were reported in 2006. A hospital in the city of Bukavu has opened a new ward to deal with victims of rape by government troops and Hutu militias in the surrounding countryside with its beautiful national parks. A doctor at the hospital said, 'There used to be a lot of gorillas in there. But now they've been replaced by much more savage beasts.'

The tragedy is that what is true of Congo is not unique, as we have seen in West Africa. There are things that can be done to rescue countries, specific actions like the brittle internationally brokered peace deal in 2002 which led to the establishment of a coalition government under Laurent Kabila's son Joseph, a good-looking, shy young man. When I met him in 2001 in his gloomy palace under leaden skies in run-down Kinshasa he seemed a political innocent, albeit expensively dressed and surrounded by intimidating heavies festooned with weapons. He has survived so far among the older crocodiles of Congolese politics, a tribute perhaps to his far from obvious political acumen and the tough guys around him; and also thanks, perhaps, to the 18,000-strong UN peacekeeping forces in the country. But the militias still fight to share out the spoils, and the Congolese still suffer and die of poverty and disease in a land rich in resources. There is an old Kiswahili proverb – 'You never finish eating the meat of an elephant.'

There is one rather prosaic thing we can do to help the Congolese and others who live in the conflict-and-greed trap. It is not the imposition of sanctions on exports of resources. First, sanctions require political will and enforcement mechanisms. The absence of those requirements usually makes this commercial weapon impotent from the moment it is adopted. Second, sanctions can have an adverse effect: they can raise the value of the targeted commodities, perversely increasing the incentives for trading them. Third, there is widespread concern about the detrimental effect that sanctions can have on civilians who depend on the export of resources for their livelihood, and who may simply be labourers rather than armed belligerents. So if sanctions are flawed, what else can be done?

A better response to the looting of resources like diamonds is international certification of the products concerned. The Kimberley Process Certification Scheme for example, launched originally by South Africa, is supported by seventy-four countries and covers approximately 99.8 per cent of the global production of rough diamonds. The scheme is a joint government, international diamond industry and civil society initiative to stem the flow of conflict diamonds. It imposes extensive requirements on participants to certify that shipments of rough diamonds do not include any that are being traded to fund fighting. In effect the Kimberley Scheme creates a 'chain of warranties' which provide an audit trail linking each diamond to its mine of origin. This idea can be replicated in other areas, and is indeed already being partially copied by the timber industry.

Transparency and accountability are crucial for exposing and countering the networks and structures underpinning the business involved in the processing and marketing of conflict resources. The movement started with the Publish What You Pay campaign, which urged oil and mining companies to disclose their payments to governments. The British government responded by launching in 2002 the Extractive Industries Transparency Initiative (EITI), laying out standards of transparency, accountability and proper management of resources for participating countries and companies. EITI has had some notable successes, including Nigeria's large-scale reorganization and reform of its state oil company. This initiative has been a significant step in ensuring that revenues from natural resources are used fairly through strengthened and legitimate institutions.

But EITI has not had things all its own way. It still requires the agreement and participation of the governments that sell the rights to mine, drill for and trade the resources, the companies that undertake the operations, and the importing countries where these companies are often domiciled. There are problems on both sides of the commercial relationship. Angola's oil production has soared since the early 1980s, but much of the wealth generated has been filched by President Dos Santos and his family, friends and close supporters, called (after the name of his headquarters) the 'futungos'. While it is difficult to get hold of any reliable or recent figures, it is estimated that from 1997 to 2002 oil generated $17.8 billion in revenues in Angola. The IMF and Human Rights Watch (HRW) have both produced figures that suggest that more than a fifth of government expenditure cannot be traced. HRW calculated that between 1997 and 2002 $4.2 billion were 'unaccounted for'. Attempts to get more information on Angola's oil accounts and on a debt-rescheduling deal with Russia have been resisted on grounds of national sovereignty and the need for commercial confidentiality. When BP tried to introduce greater transparency into its operations in Angola, the Dos Santos government threatened to cancel its contracts and for good measure to do the same to any of the other thirty-three oil companies working in the country who followed BP's admirable example.

This behaviour could be influenced, even conceivably changed, if other governments were determined to uphold the EITI. Unfortunately this is not the case, and the problem is particularly significant because China has become such a big economic and political player in Africa and operates a strict 'no questions asked' approach to its commercial deals on the continent. China's stunning growth has created a huge appetite for commodities – minerals, oil and timber especially. At its most bizarre, this demand led to what one Scottish newspaper in 2004 called 'the Great Drain Robbery' as manhole covers around the world were stolen for export to China, where they were melted down for use in other metal products. In one month alone that year Chicago reported the loss of more than 150 manhole covers. The more acceptable if often more damaging aspect to China's commodity needs is the commodity deals that Beijing has signed all around the world from Burma to Venezuela. It is in Africa that the most damage could be done. Americans and Europeans should not be too sanctimonious about this. We have made in the past exactly the same mistakes as we think China is now making – bigger mistakes very often. Yet we all have an interest in promoting policies in Africa that make conflicts less likely and growth more probable, and that does not include buying favours and ignoring good governance. China's shielding of Sudan for so long from criticism at the UN, even over Darfur, was the most blatant example of the policy, in that case involving a country from which China has purchased up to 10 per cent of its oil.

The African Summit in Beijing in 2006 and the African Development Bank meeting in Shanghai in 2007 were examples of Beijing's growing clout on the continent. I was in Beijing just after the summit and recall one African diplomat who had attended it saying how wonderful it had been to get the Chinese to build some of his country's infrastructure, because they had not asked first for an environmental impact assessment. China has invested about $12 billion in Africa and buys over a tenth of sub-Saharan Africa's exports. China–Africa trade has increased by an average 30 per cent a year this decade, soaring to nearly $107 billion in 2008. Its official Export-Import Bank made loans to Africa from 2004 to 2006 of more than $7 billion. China builds dams, roads and power lines. It buys oil, copper and timber. It asks no questions about governance. It is just the sort of country that President Dos Santos and other leaders like him enjoy doing business with. But oil or no oil, it is bad government that helps keep Africa so poor; this is one of the main reasons why 'the bottom billion' is held down. We are not talking here about anything as sophisticated as environmental impact assessments, nor about a system that requires the filling in of thousands of forms in triplicate, routing them through two dozen overlapping ministries, where graduates are gradually converted into clerks. What is wanted is the rule of law, no corruption or fighting, and some basic can-do competence.

I began visiting Africa in the mid-1980s as Britain's development minister. Our national aid programme was largely targeted on the south Asian subcontinent and those parts of Africa that had once been British colonies. I fell in love with both the look of and the idea of Africa. The light and the relationships between topography and the sky are more thrilling than anywhere else I have been, except perhaps Rajasthan. I was impressed by the quiet striving dignity of so many people that I met and by their optimism even in countries like Uganda that had just gone through the meat grinder with Obote and Amin. I believe I also had the sense that I was doing something useful, something with a partly moral purpose, something that atoned for what colonial powers like Britain had done in the past: not all bad, of course, and in many respects defensible, but not as good as it should have been. Then in the 1990s I went off to Asia. As has frequently been said, where Africa impresses with the scale of its empty landscapes, Asia impresses with its teeming millions, so many of whom seemed to be making their countries' poverty history through their own efforts. They believed that they could make the future better for themselves by work, sacrifice, education and the creation of institutions that encouraged those things. Going back to Africa as a European Commissioner from 1999 to 2004 was a nasty shock. Where had the promise gone? Where was the development? It looked as though many of the countries I visited had regressed. Perhaps the statistics suggested some modest improvement – life expectancy increased, child mortality reduced – but visiting Harare, Kinshasa and Lagos was a deeply depressing experience. Poverty here was clearly far from being history, indeed too often it seemed to be not something that could be escaped but an irremediable condition for the future.

Is this too gloomy? There are certainly African countries that have done well. Botswana has been democratic throughout its history since independence; it runs a balance-of-payments surplus, exporting beef and kimberlite diamonds through a well-run industry. South Africa has thrown off apartheid with scarcely any of the violence that might have been anticipated in Europe in similar circumstances. Rwanda has begun to grow, leaving behind its terrible legacy of tribal massacres. Others too are showing a sustained commitment to economic reform. Many Africans actually think they are better off. In a poll conducted for the *New York Times* and the Pew Global Attitudes project in ten countries in sub-Saharan Africa in 2007 a plurality thought they were better off than five years before and were optimistic about their future and that of the next generation. While all the countries in the survey were nominally democratic, which represents some progress on the continent, there were widespread anxieties about the quality of political leadership (particularly the prevalence of corruption) and about the modest economic gains that appeared to have been made under allegedly democratic systems. Again, this is evidence that the prospects in Africa are not irredeemably bleak. Even the well-disposed have to be careful not to allow post-colonial guilt to morph into post-guilt hopelessness or contempt. Yet experience of Africa on the ground – the smell, feel, look of it – has not always dispersed a sense of desolation about the continent. Keith Richburg, a black American, was the Asian editor of the *Washington Post* when I was in Hong Kong. I got to know him well. He is charming, intelligent and perceptive. Before coming to Asia, he had had the African beat for the paper. Scarred by what he saw in Rwanda, Ethiopia, Liberia, Somalia, he wrote a book about his experiences. 'Excuse me if I sound cynical, jaded,' he wrote. 'I'm beaten down and I'll admit it. And it is Africa that has made me this way. I feel for her suffering. I empathize with her pain, and now, from afar, I still recoil in horror whenever I see yet another television picture of another tribal slaughter, another refugee crisis. But most of all I think: Thank God my ancestors got out, because, now, I am not one of them.'[9] The black actress Whoopi Goldberg put it very simply: 'I've been to Africa, and let me tell you, I'm an American.'

For me one of the recent reasons for pessimism was the failure of other African governments to do anything about President Robert Mugabe's destruction of Zimbabwe, a country in free fall. In 2001 fifteen African governments led by South Africa's President Mbeki had launched the New Partnership for African Development (NEPAD). They signed up to the political and economic equivalent of motherhood and apple pie – democracy, good governance, sound economic management. They also established an African peer review mechanism to monitor performance and punish backsliders. In return for all this they asked for increased Western aid. Where was the diplomacy of the peer reviewers when it came to Zimbabwe? By and large they averted their gaze. It was none of their business. Anyway, how could they criticize a hero of the African independence movement? I heard Mugabe speak in the early 2000s at the UN General Assembly. He denounced the colonialists in familiar terms, particularly Tony Blair's British government (which played an immensely positive, generous and – in Sierra Leone – brave role in Africa). He stopped short of using the language which I heard when I met him in Harare in 2001 about 'Blair's homosexual cabal'. Every ranting sentence in that UN speech was loudly applauded by the African delegations present, who rewarded the president at the end of his diatribe with a standing ovation: NEPAD, indeed.

Is what has happened in Africa – for example in Zimbabwe, Sudan and Congo – 'our' fault, 'the West's' fault, the fault of the 'whites'? Have we lacked any moral compass in dealing with and helping Africa? Do we discount the premature death of an African baby, or of 10,000 African babies? Have we put our own consumption ahead of Africa's survival? Have we made promises that we have failed to keep, not only to Africa but to the very poor throughout the world?

The figures make miserable reading: 10 million children die every year from easily preventable diseases; a billion people lack access to clean water; a billion adults are illiterate; 840 million do not have enough to eat; 70 per cent of the very poorest live in Africa. According to Paul Collier, 73 per cent have been through civil war; 29 per cent live in countries where politics is dominated by the money from natural resources; 30 per cent are in a bad neighbourhood (fancy living next door to Somalia?), have few resources and are land-locked; and 76 per cent have been through a prolonged period of bad governance and poor economic policies.[10] Seven out of the top ten countries in the list of the world's weakest states at greatest risk of failure, prepared by the periodical *Foreign Policy* and the Fund for Peace, are in Africa: Sudan, Somalia, Zimbabwe, Chad, Ivory Coast, Congo, and Central African Republic. In the world as a whole we have made spectacular medical advances, people live much longer, fewer mothers and babies die, their gender no longer imposes a life of drudgery on millions of women in developed and successful developing countries, totalitarianism does not threaten any more to capture continents: all that achieved, so how come we have not made more progress in eliminating the direst poverty?

For many, perhaps these days most, in developed countries the answer is clear. It is a no-brainer. The rich West has given first priority to protecting its own comforts and has forgotten about those cursed by poverty. It has kept its hands and its money in its pockets. Like W. C. Fields when asked for a donation, we say perhaps that unfortunately our money is all tied up in currency. Maybe it is true that more than $500 billion of aid has been spent in Africa since independence; it cannot have been enough. We need to be more generous and more thoroughly organized in our generosity. At the very least we should know that it is not our interest to behave like the priest or the Levite before the Good Samaritan came to the rescue of the beaten traveller on the road to Jericho. Can we afford to do it? Of course, we can. In rich countries we spent $103.7 billion on aid in 2007. In Europe we spent over $7 billion on perfume. Americans spent $40.8 billion on their pets. We in the developed West are not expected to make substantial sacrifices in order to help. But we should do more. A billion human beings are increasingly left behind as other countries grow and develop; the gap between them and the other five billion yawns ever wider. 'Something Must Be Done', as the charismatic and highly intelligent Bob Geldof has argued. He went on to say, though I doubt he really meant it, 'anything must be done, whether it works or not'. Here lies the trouble – what is that 'anything'? Is it just 'more' of the same? Even though the thought trembles on the verge of sin for those who have been so deeply committed to it, aid has not worked as well as we had hoped, and frankly no one really knows quite what makes development happen. Some have always thought that they knew what did *not* make it happen. Almost thirty years ago the economist P. T. Bauer put the case against aid with blistering and unpopular directness. 'The argument that aid is indispensable for development runs into an inescapable dilemma. If the conditions for development other than capital are present, the capital required will either be generated locally or be available commercially from abroad to governments or to businesses. If the required conditions are not present, the aid will be ineffective and wasted.'[11] This is not an argument that can simply be shrugged off, denounced as right-wing, mean-spirited, beneath serious discussion. Between those who simply demand more, and those who want less, where does the truth lie? Certainly, like others, I am sure, my heart is in the 'more' camp, but my head teaches me that my assent should not be unconditional. There must surely be a sensible intellectual route down the middle. We should at least give it a go.

The current foreign-aid debate pits supporters of a 'big push' to fight global poverty with gently increased aid, against sceptics who criticize any worldwide scheme like this for mega-reform. Advocates of the former approach, drawing heavily on the work of the economist Jeffrey Sachs, have been making headway.[12] They helped persuade political leaders across the continents to sign up to the eight Millennium Development Goals (MDGs). The aim is, by 2015, to

1. eradicate extreme poverty and hunger,
2. achieve universal primary school enrolment,

3. promote gender equality and empower women,
4. reduce child mortality,
5. improve maternal health,
6. combat HIV/AIDS, malaria and other diseases,
7. ensure environmental sustainability, and
8. put together a global partnership for development.

Hands up anyone who disagrees with any of the above.

Rich countries agreed at Monterey in 2002 to increase official development assistance to 0.7 per cent of GNP to meet these goals. The Bush administration joined the consensus and in 2005 increased aid spending to 0.22 per cent, well short of the long-term target but higher than at any time since 1986 and a very welcome move, to which America's political leaders invite us to add the huge philanthropic benefactions of some of America's billionaires like Bill Gates. Increasingly meetings of aid donor countries, G8 outings for instance, discuss how the developed world should recommit itself to these targets. They also consider discreetly how much backsliding is going on. It is not a very pretty picture.

The financial crash is unlikely to make it look any more attractive. Rich countries will be sorely tempted to reduce their assistance to the developing world as they wrestle to contain ballooning budget deficits. Yet the impact of the crash on the poor will be severe, reversing gains made in recent years in poverty alleviation and development. The president of the World Bank has argued that 'poor people in Africa should not pay the price for a crisis that originated in America.' The financial contagion has hit stock markets in emerging economies like China, Russia and India, currencies have been devalued and there has been a precipitous drop in foreign direct investment from rich countries to poorer ones. The fall in world growth will reduce income from remittances (which in 2008 was three times the level of development aid to the poor countries from which the migrant workers came), cut exports and halt the growth experienced in many poorer countries from the commodities boom. More people will fall below the poverty line; more children will go to bed hungry; fewer will go to school; more elderly will go out to work; health standards will fall. All this argues strongly for keeping our promises in development spending (focusing on social priorities), resisting protectionism and staying on course to combat global warming.

These immediate concerns may push to one side for the time being the debate between the 'Something Truly Huge Must Be Done' camp and the cautious (as they would see themselves), more hard-headed and realistic proponents of incremental reform. It is a debate that reflects a long-standing philosophical dispute starting with Edmund Burke's criticism of revolutionary change and going on to Karl Popper's critique of 'utopian social engineering'. The 'big push', argue the cautious, is just another attempt at top-down planning. It is doomed to fail as surely as the structural adjustment programmes imposed on poor countries in the 1980s and 1990s failed, and also the shock-therapy transition efforts from communism to capitalism which engendered klepto-capitalism in Russia and other countries.

Sachs argues that ending extreme poverty 'is the great opportunity of our times'.[13] To accomplish this rich countries should double their financial assistance to poor nations by roughly $100 billion a year, which would fill the financing gap between what poor countries need and what they can afford on their own. It would enable them to break out of the poverty trap, providing basic infrastructure and human capital, in other words better healthcare and education. Without helping the poor to get a foot on the ladder, markets will bypass large parts of the world, leaving them in permanent poverty. Sachs argues for a holistic approach to development that would involve 449 interconnected interventions to end world poverty 'applied systematically, diligently and jointly since they strongly reinforce one another'. This is not unambitious.

William Easterly is one of the most forthright critics of this approach, which is not to say that he feels any less moral outrage about the coexistence of poverty and riches than Sachs, Nicholas Stern, Joseph Stiglitz or other advocates of fuelling take-off in poor countries with much more aid. He divides the debate on aid into two camps – the Planners, who argue for the 'big push', and the Searchers, who are the heroes of his latest very readable work.[14] 'In foreign aid', he argues, planners announce good intentions but don't motivate anyone to carry them out; Searchers find things that work and get some reward. Planners raise expectations but take no responsibility for meeting them; Searchers accept responsibility for their actions. Planners determine what to supply; Searchers find out what is in demand. Planners apply global blueprints; Searchers adapt to local conditions. Planners never hear whether the planned got what they needed; Searchers find out whether the customer is satisfied.

The past failures of foreign aid should humble the Planners and certainly make them hesitate before embarking on their 449 interventions.

Easterly wants bottom-up aid, not a grand plan. He wants to take more account of what those allegedly being helped actually want and can make work. He thinks we – from Washington to London to Brussels – should stop telling people in Africa and other poor countries what to do. He wants more accountability to the poor for aid, independent evaluation of its effectiveness, and greater specialization by aid agencies so that they provide what they do best. He wants to support what works and stop bogging down developing-country bureaucracies in donors' requirements for planning meetings and reports; it is not unusual for a developing country to find itself organizing more than 2,000 such meetings a year. There should be far more donor coordination, not competition. We should end our fixation with how much we intend to spend and look instead at how we spend it and whether it works. Easterly believes that aid to Africa has already been large enough to constitute the sort of 'big push' that might be expected to launch a take-off in growth. In fact, as aid has accelerated, growth has fallen. National growth is normally a question of a slow acceleration punctuated by periods of negative growth, rather than a one-off event; there is no starting pistol that begins the ineluctable process, and Easterly argues that there is no statistical correlation between aid and growth.

How has it looked to a practitioner? My memories of three years as a development minister are littered with examples that could be paraded by Professor Easterly as evidence for his arguments. I defy any foreign-aid official to deny possession of a similar memory bank. Perhaps I should begin with what became for me the symbol of failed development in Africa, the cemeteries of Land Rovers, the cavalry of development rusting away because there was no one who could repair the vehicles, no one who could keep them on the road. I recall the prestige projects that raised hopes, satisfied those who judged aid by volume, wasted money and probably reversed any modest progress made hitherto.

On a visit to Tanzania in the mid-1980s we flew down to a hospital near Lake Tanganyika and the Malawi border. It was a pretty frightening trip because, as the purple storm clouds rolled up over the narrow valley where we were landing, our pilot discovered that he could not tell whether the landing gear had worked. With prayers going up, we came safely down to inspect a hospital commissioned by the Tanzanian government and Britain, in a late splurge of generosity at the end of the seventies by Jim Callaghan's outgoing government. His minister, Judith Hart, had wanted to increase the scale of assistance in the sure knowledge that the successor Conservative government would sooner or later cut it back. The objective was at least partly to commit the money fast and hope that the projects worked. The hospital we visited at Mbeya was a wonderful building; it had all the latest equipment. The trouble was that it did not have the means to make the equipment work. There was insufficient revenue to buy drugs, or even to feed patients. The Tanzanian staff – doctors and nurses who had been trained in Britain as part of the project – had stayed in the UK to work for far higher pay in the NHS.

Next I recall the project in Sudan, much pushed by the British company GEC, to get the country's trains back on the rails in working condition. We discussed the economics of Sudan's railway system with Sudanese officials in Khartoum. They had no budget to pay, for example, the bill for the diesel oil, but tens of thousands of employees on the payroll. I suggested to the minister that the answer was either to reduce the staff and run the trains or to get the staff, who otherwise had nothing to do, to push the engines and carriages themselves. I recall other projects that seemed as much designed (maybe more so) to assist ailing British companies as to assist the poor. There was a power station in Khartoum whose purpose was largely to help stave off the collapse of a power engineering company in the north-east of England. Naturally the company collapsed anyway – in my experience, any company whose main entrepreneurial endeavour appeared to be finding imaginative ways to milk the taxpayer went under sooner rather than later. I recall another power station – a joint commercial development this – in central India, which had become, because of the difficulty of the project, a permanent source of out-relief for consultants. And then there was Kenya: poor, beautiful Kenya. Daniel arap Moi was president of the country from 1978 to 2002 and was at the heart of a spider's web of corruption, which was kept secret partly through the murder of one of his ministers (Robert Ouko) who had wanted to expose it. One of Moi's deals had involved grain imports. Local Kenyan businessmen had stocked warehouses with food and grain, anticipating higher prices. But food imports from Uganda kept prices low. So Moi banned imports from Uganda, poor Kenyans paid more for their food, Ugandans lost an export market and President Moi's local friends in the business community doubtless showed him how grateful they were for his decision.

Moi came into my life more regularly than was wholly agreeable during my time as a development minister. Big, crafty, Savile Row suited, charmless, Moi traded on Britain's wish to retain its historic links with Kenya and on Margaret Thatcher's surprising esteem for him. I think she was probably carried away by the sense he liked to convey that he was an African bastion against rebellion and communism. She once told me that she thought he was a sort of African Willie Whitelaw. This was not an observation flattering to Whitelaw, whose differences from Moi were legion going well beyond the fact that Moi was not a Wykehamist. Whatever the reason, every visit Moi made to London always led to requests from No. 10 that he should not depart Downing Street or Chequers without some present – a little balance of payments support here or a favoured project there. The main issue time and again on Moi's agenda was a road connecting his home and farm to the main road system in the country. It had no other real purpose. Again and again I had to produce arguments against putting it in our Kenyan aid programme; again and again the project was put forward by the Kenyans. We managed to hold off the pressure while I was in the job; I hope my successors were equally successful. Kenya's tragedy was that when Moi was eventually eased into retirement, the next president, Mwai Kibaki, and his team were pretty much as bad, provoking the British high commissioner in 2004 to complain about ministers and officials being 'gluttonous' about corruption and 'vomiting' on the shores of donors. The history of development assistance is full of stories like these which too many in what has been called the aid business are unwilling to acknowledge or learn from.

Yet as a development minister and European Commissioner I also saw many examples of where aid really did work. There were rural primary-education projects in India, training programmes for women in Bangladesh, rural water and electrification schemes in Africa, a project to refurbish a hospital in Kampala overwhelmed by AIDS patients, agricultural research stations in Africa and Nepal, refugee projects in Ethiopia for Sudanese children, private-sector schemes in Africa launched with the assistance of the Commonwealth Development Corporation, and – though they are not as above criticism as some of them think – excellent NGO schemes, for example in direct poverty alleviation and child health. Visiting one village in Bangladesh devastated by floods, I spotted by accident a skeletal dehydrated baby; the NGO I was with took care of the little girl. Six months later I was sent a photograph of a plump, beaming child – the same girl. That is what aid can and should be about – dealing with suffering, in this case saving a baby from premature death. That was not achieved by the $20 billion that Mobutu received during his tenure, nor by the 50 per cent increase in aid to Rwanda even while the Hutus were beginning their genocide.

We should all want to see better development assistance, and preferably (as it is more efficiently used) more of it too, though that may still not be enough to help economies take off. It was obviously not acceptable when surveys in Chad tracking money intended for rural health clinics found that less than 1 per cent of the cash actually reached the clinics. In Uganda, greater openness turned around a similar situation. At first only 20 per cent of the funds for primary schools reached them; when the press and the community were kept informed about what was happening and were able to track the money, the figure went up to 90 per cent. We should not abandon the pressure to be more generous to the poorest countries, but we should be equally vigorous in examining outputs and not just inputs. Greater openness about the use of aid, and the ability to hold governments to account for what they do with it, hugely improve performance.

We must stop aid money leaking into military budgets; about 40 per cent of Africa's military spending is thought to be inadvertently financed by aid.[15] Where we want to assist with security, the programmes should be properly ring-fenced. In countries sodden with corruption where governments are pursuing the wrong policies, we should try to work more with civil society, especially in areas like health and education. We cannot impose democracy and the rule of law on other countries, yet good governance does matter very much to development. Poverty may well make bad governance more likely; the opposite is certainly true. Robert Calderisi argues bluntly that the 'simplest way to explain Africa's problems is that it has never known good governance'.[16] There are three obvious conclusions: first, it makes sense to offer technical assistance to governments that have difficulty managing their own affairs; second, bottom-up development and working with civil society makes sense too; third, post-conditionality is sometimes the best approach – reaching a contract with a developing country and after an initial grant relating future payment to actual performance.

Comparisons with Asia suggest that in Africa and other 'bottom billion' countries we should concentrate our institutional efforts on supporting the creation of structures that make it rational for people to form capital and to use capital in their own countries. The Asians on the whole developed such structures on their own. Capital flight – in terms of both financial and human capital – is a major feature of poor developing countries. The middle classes want to get their money out to safe havens, and people with skills want to have them adequately rewarded in richer countries. The citizens of developing countries must be made to feel that even with meagre incomes it is worth saving and investing, worth sacrificing present consumption for future gain. But in too many countries it is often easier to ascertain the rewards of starting a rebellion rather than a business. Capital can also be in the form not of cash but of a skill or educational achievement. Growth comes in those countries where people have the confidence that what they do today, beyond simple survival, can give them a better future.

They will not have a better future if the whole emphasis is on aid. The poor have to be helped to trade as well, and this is not just a question of removing barriers in richer countries to the export of poor countries' products like cotton, grains or fruit. The surge in Asia was based on the development of manufacturing and service industries. Manufacturing produces more wealth than labour-intensive agriculture. How can we enable African and the other poorest countries to catch up with successful countries in Asia? We will only do it by removing tariffs on things made in Africa that compete with Asian products. Paul Collier and Joseph Stiglitz are right to argue not for raising tariffs against successful developing countries in Asia, but for cutting tariffs on what is made in the presently unsuccessful countries in Africa.[17] This means building more imaginatively on the existing schemes like the US African Growth and Opportunities Act and Europe's 'Everything But Arms' initiative, retaining protection against abuse through rules of origin (which stop third countries simply moving their goods through tariff-free countries into their rich-country markets) but making it as easy as possible for Africans to start manufacturing activity. The suggestion made by many NGOs that Africans should be encouraged for their part to retain trade barriers is economically illiterate. They do too little trade with one another already. Poor countries are far more likely to be helped by free trade, shorn of gimmicks and market-rigging, than by protectionism.

There is an African saying, 'The hand that receives is always under the one that gives.' Foreign aid can help the poorest, but they have to be helped to escape hardship themselves, not made to feel that it is only the rich, white world rather than their own efforts that can empower them. There is not, as David Landes argues, a simple lesson or dogmatic solution. 'No miracles. No protection. No millennium. No apocalypse.'[18] Yes, 'Something Must Be Done', above all by the poorest themselves, liberated by how we help, liberated to work, to save, to be honest, to be brave, to resist the temptations of apparently easy pickings, liberated but not beaten over the head with our never sufficiently open chequebooks into resentful and permanent dependency.

8

Blood and Water

> *But the mountain falls and crumbles away, and the rock is
> removed from its place; the water wears away the stones; the
> torrents wash away the soil of the earth; so you destroy the
> hopes of mortals.*   Job 14: 18–19

> *When the well's dry, we know the value of water.*
>   Benjamin Franklin

> *The next war in our region will be over the waters of the Nile,
> not politics.*
>   Boutros Boutros-Ghali, former UN Secretary General,
>   speaking as Egypt's foreign minister in 1988

The price and supply of food have always been potent factors in
provoking civil conflict – like the Madrid riots and the French 'flour
war' (*guerre des farines*) in the eighteenth century – as well as triggering wars between states, for example under the Roman Empire. The
Egyptian Arabic word for bread is *aish*, which means 'life': no bread,
or scarce and expensive bread, and the threat to life causes violence.
In 2008 there were food riots, protests and demonstrations in Bangladesh, Haiti, Indonesia, Uzbekistan, Bolivia, Yemen, Ivory Coast,
Senegal, Mozambique, Mauritania and Cameroon. The world was
taken by surprise by the political consequences of the end of an era
of cheap food. For three decades from the mid-1970s prices fell in
real terms by up to three-quarters. More recently food prices rose
steeply (until the economic crash moderated the increase probably

temporarily), with a doubling in the cost of staple foods like wheat, soya and rice; the *Economist*'s food price index rose to its highest level since it was started in 1845. The price of wheat beat all records. The crisis was sufficiently serious to lead to the holding of a 'food summit' in Rome in May 2008 attended not only by the UN Secretary General and a bevy of ministers, but by President Mugabe of Zimbabwe, presumably in recognition of the role he has played in the starvation of his own people.

There were three principal reasons for this surge which came about despite bumper crops in many parts of the world. First, the success of globalization was partly to blame. As Chinese, Indians and other Asians escaped poverty in their hundreds of millions, their diet fortunately improved and their consumption of meat in particular increased. In China, over a twenty-year period, consumers more than doubled the amount of meat they ate. It takes three kilos of cereals to produce one kilo of pork; for beef the figures are eight to one. Second, demand for ethanol supported by big subsidies for farmers growing corn in American states like Iowa, led to a big switch from growing for food to harvesting for biofuels. In 2008, about 85 million tonnes of maize were produced for ethanol, up from 15 million tonnes in 2000. Fill the tank of one SUV with biofuel and you use up about the same amount of grain as it would take to feed an African family for a year. Third, droughts and floods – thought by many to be possible consequences of climate change – ruined wheat harvests in Australia and vegetable oil production in Indonesia and Malaysia.

As ever, too many governments reacted to food protests by trying to dampen the effects of rising prices for urban consumers (since riots happen on city streets) at the cost of farmers and rural areas. Instead of subsidizing poor consumers, they held down the prices paid to poor farmers. Autarky and tariffs were proposed as solutions to the surge in prices rather than more open markets, bigger rewards for producers and investment in GM drought-resistant crops. The French agriculture minister even went so far as to suggest that what every part of the world needed was a version of Europe's Common Agricultural Policy: a policy which has in practice so damaged the interests of poor farmers and poor countries. But at least history has led us to expect that food can lead to political trouble. We may not be accustomed to the idea that water can do the same thing.

At home in London, we buy about six litres of (imported) bottled water a week. I am resolved in future to depend rather more on London tap water despite the lack of bubbles. Right around the world from Mexico (18 billion litres consumed a year) to Italy (over 10 billion litres), the global consumption of bottled water has been increasing, not least in countries where it is no healthier than tap water. Indeed, the French Senate has invited those who drink the bottled stuff to change brands regularly, since the added minerals which help in small doses may do harm in larger ones. Bottled water, which often costs more per litre than petrol for the car, can cost up to 10,000 times more than what comes out of the tap. Moreover, the fossil fuel costs in transport and packaging – much of the plastic is made from crude oil – and the disposal of the bottles themselves add an adverse environmental impact. To meet the target set by the United Nations in the Millennium Development Goal, of halving the number of people who lack sustainable access to safe drinking water by 2015 (see Chapter 7), would require a doubling of the amount – $15 billion – that is spent at present on water supply and sanitation. Compare that with the approximately $100 billion a year spent on bottled water.[1]

This salutary comparison underlines the central fact about the world's water resources. There is not an overall shortage; this is no time to re-run a watery version of Thomas Malthus, who argued in the nineteenth century that the world's population was growing faster than the earth's ability to produce the food to sustain it. 'Premature death', he believed, would be the inevitable result. We are not faced with Malthusian arithmetic on water, despite some gloomy predictions to the contrary. The problem is different. The rich can buy Perrier, Buxton, San Pellegrino; the very poor are lucky to have a dribbling tap. The world has enough water, but it is unevenly distributed and in many cases its use is very badly managed. The result is increased poverty, worse health and particularly high infant mortality, the risk of internal conflict, the further weakening of already weak governments and the possibility of wars between states.

The supply of water is finite but, unlike oil, it is infinitely renewable through the natural cycle of rainwater from the clouds, the return of fresh water through underground aquifers and down rivers to the world's oceans, and evaporation of water back to the clouds where the whole process starts again. There is no direct substitute for water. It is essential to all forms of life on earth. Only 1 per cent of the world's water is directly available for human needs: 97 per cent is salt water in our oceans and a little more than two-thirds of the remainder is locked up in deep aquifers or in Antarctic ice caps.

The huge rise in the world's population during the last century, from 1.6 billion at its start to 6 billion at its close, has everywhere strained the relationship between resources and demands. Water is no exception. While the population has almost quadrupled, water use has gone up by a factor of seven. As has been the case since the earliest great river-based civilizations – Egypt, Mesopotamia, China – the main uses of water are for irrigation and agriculture. While in the twentieth century industrial and municipal demands for water have grown sharply, agriculture still has the greatest thirst. The reason is simple. Each of us has a bare minimum requirement of 20 to 50 litres a day for direct consumption, cooking and basic hygiene. The food required to give us a daily minimum of 3,000 calories needs 3,500 litres of water to produce it. As the United Nations Development Programme (UNDP) has pointed out, people use about one seventieth of the water for domestic purposes that they require to feed themselves.[2] To produce a kilo of potatoes takes 1,000 litres, of wheat 1,450 litres, of chicken 4,600 litres. The production of a hamburger takes about 11,000 litres. The water required to produce this food is frequently being used for irrigation a long way from where the food is eventually consumed. By the middle of the century the world will have to feed about 2.4 billion more people – on potatoes, wheat, chicken and even hamburgers. So we can expect steadily growing demand for a resource unevenly distributed, and this variability will be increased by the consequences of global warming and climate change.

How should we define maldistribution? At its simplest, some countries and even areas within them have a lot more water than others. Siberia, with its small population, has a quarter of all the world's fresh water in Lake Baikal. This does not help the Yemen or Somalia. Latin America has almost a third of all global fresh water, twelve times as much per person as is available in south Asia. There are regional disparities (for example the Congo has far more water than South Africa), and differences within countries (southern China has historically had more water than the north). Annual figures of availability can also mislead. Any serious gardener would like to see rainfall spread through the year. So would a minister of water or agriculture. But Asia's monsoons mean that in much of the continent 90 per cent of the rain each year falls within 100 hours, leading to floods at some times of the year and drought at others.

There are, naturally, scientific assessments of water sufficiency. Security is usually calculated by examining the relationship between the size of a country's or a region's population and the amount of water available within it. The general view of hydrologists is that the minimum annual threshold per person to cover the growing of food, support for industry, energy needs and environmental sustainability is 1,700 cubic metres. There are forty-three countries with a total population of roughly 700 million that are below this water-stress threshold. Where availability falls below 1,000 cubic metres, water is said to be scarce; where a country has less than 500 cubic metres per person there is said to be 'absolute scarcity'. The most stressed region is the Middle East, and in sub-Saharan Africa one quarter of the population lives in water-stressed countries. The population is growing fast in many of the countries with inadequate water supplies. This could increase to 3 billion by 2025 the number of people living in water-stressed countries. It is by and large true that rich countries that have enough water will continue to be so blessed because their populations are either not increasing at all or are increasing only slowly. Poor countries that do not have enough water today will have even less tomorrow as their populations climb.

That is far from a summary of the worst statistics for water poverty. Many people live in countries where national water figures may seem sufficient but where particular regions do not have enough. This means that there are reckoned to be about 1.1 billion people – over one sixth of the world's population – who have below the 20–50 litres a day believed necessary for domestic needs. On average they have access to about 5 litres a day in comparison to over 550 in the USA and between 150 and 400 in most European countries.

The number of people who lack access to enough safe water for their use at home is surpassed by the 2.6 billion who do not benefit from adequate sanitation. This has major impacts on people's well-being. Millions die each year from preventable diseases. Diarrhoeal diseases kill over 2 million annually, the majority of them children. All told, 1.8 million children die each year from causes related to unclean water and poor sanitation. In economic terms, the shortage of water in poor countries and its bad distribution result in the stunting of industrial as well as human growth. Educational opportunities are lost, labour is switched from more to less profitable activities and health spending is diverted to deal with preventable problems. The World Health Organization estimates that the overall cost of lack of water and sanitation is $170 billion a year, the brunt of which is borne by the world's poor. Not only do they lack enough clean water, but they often pay surprisingly disproportionate prices for what they do get. In many countries pricing policy is skewed against the poor, benefiting the biggest and least responsible users and the better-off. The poor living in the slums of Manila, Jakarta and Nairobi pay between five and ten times as much for each unit of water as those who live in the high-income areas in their own cities. They even pay more than I do in London or than consumers would pay in New York. So poor people often pay more for their water, they get less of it and what they receive is less safe.

Lack of water and bad water management have been among the main factors in triggering the movement of people both within and between countries. India provides examples of both these phenomena which can increase ethnic and other tensions. The 1998–2000 drought in northern India led to a migration from northern Gujarat of about 50 per cent of its farmers. Poor farmers in rural areas could not afford to replace dry wells; increasingly it was only the richer farmers who could pay for the deep drilling required to tap into the depleted aquifers. Arguments about water have also led to riots and inter-communal conflict in Tamil Nadu. In Rajasthan, basic data about groundwater is deemed to be so sensitive that the state authorities refuse to make it available to developmental economists.[3] In Bangladesh, the degradation of good agricultural land, overcrowding, poverty and domestic conflict have all been exacerbated by the disputed management of water regionally, which has allegedly led to the salination of good agricultural land and to the terrible flooding, which some believe results from deforestation in the Himalayas. Over the past forty years the Indian states of Assam, Tripura and West Bengal have become home for millions of migrants from East Pakistan and then Bangladesh. The populations of these states have been increased by between 12 and 17 million. This has, not surprisingly, led to violence, particularly in Assam and Tripura.

These and similar problems which have resulted from the unsustainable way in which water is managed in so many countries will be made even worse by climate change. There is today a hydrological debt crisis; in other words, we have so depleted water resources in some river basins for irrigated agriculture, urbanization and industrial development that it is now increasingly difficult to recover enough water to recharge what has been extracted. It is always worrying and depressing when great rivers no longer reach the sea. This became true in recent years of the Murray river in Australia, which is at the heart of the country's agricultural zone, responsible for about 40 per cent of food output. The heavy irrigation required for cotton, rice, wheat and cattle together with deforestation and evaporation from the region's main reservoir led to losses of cultivatable land and to salination. To support food exports, too little was charged for water, and now taxpayers are having to pay to try to repair the environmental damage that over-farming has caused. As the UNDP argued, the problem here was not 'too little water [but] too much cotton and rice and too many cattle'.[4] The water crisis is not just a problem for developing countries. In this case, bad water management and drought were factors in the defeat suffered by John Howard's right-wing government in the 2007 Australian elections.

China is the home of more serious problems still. The Yellow river has played a central role in the country's long history. 'Do not look down on the Yellow river,' said Chairman Mao, 'because if you do you are looking down on the Chinese people themselves.' The river has been given two names. One of them is 'China's sorrow', for the floods that have spread havoc. The earliest chronicled flood was in 2297 BC, and since proper records were first kept in 602 BC the Yellow river has burst its banks more than 1,500 times and changed course on twenty-six occasions. Between 900,000 and 2 million people died in the floods in 1887; up to 900,000 died when Chiang Kai-shek deliberately breached the dykes in Hunan province in 1938 in an attempt to hold back the advancing Japanese army. Controlling the floods played a key part in the development of Chinese civilization so that the Yellow river deservedly earned its other name, 'China's pride', the great river that brought fertility to the land through which it flowed in such prodigious quantities.[5] But this is history. In most years the Yellow river, like the Yangtze, is now dry in its lower reaches for months on end. In 1997 it was dry for a record 226 days for 600 kilometres inland. A quarter of its flow is needed to sustain the environment. Less than 10 per cent is left after irrigation and industrial and domestic use. Yet only about a third of the water used for agricultural irrigation actually reaches the crops, and inefficient use and water loss are encouraged by low pricing policies for farmers. The Chinese government is trying now to limit up-stream withdrawals. It will be some time into the future – if indeed the time should ever come – before today's dirty trickle returns to yesterday's foaming torrent.

There are other symptoms and consequences of overuse. Water tables are falling by more than one metre a year in China and northern India. There are also huge problems because of over-exploitation of aquifers in parts of Spain – La Mancha, Valencia and Murcia, for example. The Aral Sea (landlocked between Kazakhstan and Uzbekistan), was once the size of Belgium but is now heavily salinated and about a quarter of its former size. Lake Chad in Africa contains today only a tenth of its previous volume.

Quality as well as quantity has suffered because of large discharges of effluent and industrial pollution. As development minister I visited India to inspect projects that we were funding to clean up the rivers. In retrospect, I guess it was mission well-nigh impossible. The residents of Delhi dump every day into the Yamuna river which runs through their city about 200 million litres of raw sewage and 20 million litres of waste. Pollution can affect not only the countries in which it takes place but their neighbours too. In 2000 a dam failure in Romania contaminated more than 2,000 kilometres of the Danube with cyanide and toxic metals. Public water supplies were severely disrupted in several countries downstream. In late December 2005 an explosion at a petrochemical plant in China discharged benzene, a carcinogenic chemical, into the Songhua river in the north-east of the country. The 3.8 million residents in Harbin, the capital of Heilongjiang province, endured five days without running water. The water from China then flowed into the Amur river in Russia.

Few developing countries have coherent national strategies for preventing overuse and pollution, and for accounting sensibly for the deterioration and depletion of such a valuable national asset as water. Nor are developed countries immune from criticism. Large subsidies towards the price of favoured water-intensive crops, like rice in the US, distort global export markets. Spain grows crops in the south with the help of large water subsidies that put stress on the ecological system. The same food, grown without quite such huge subsidies in Morocco, for instance, is then shut out of Europe by the Common Agricultural Policy. Ironically, harvesting in southern Spain of winter crops of fruit and vegetables for export to northern Europe is heavily dependent on North African immigrant labour, legal and illegal. The cost of irrigation in Spain represents up to half the value of agricultural exports.

Pricing policy is invariably a principal factor in depleting and wasting water supplies. Where governments subsidize the irrigation of water-intensive crops (in North Africa, for instance), this raises the cost of the investment in food production and it also puts a further strain on the limited water stocks available. Why use a resource efficiently when you get subsidies for using it inefficiently? Even in some parts of the world where people might be expected to adapt their behaviour to the scarcity of water, subsidies frequently prevent this happening, and the result inevitably is doubly perverse: less water and more demand for what there is. Low prices fill aeroplane seats; low water costs drain supplies. It is the same principle. In Algeria, the price of water is between 1 and 7 per cent of providing it. In North Africa and the Middle East as a whole, with the cost of scarce water set well below the cost of recovering it, only 30 per cent of the flood water used in irrigation ever reaches the crop. Have governments failed to join up the dots in this picture, failed to see the obvious connections? Or are they too unsure of their own ability to sustain politically more realistic pricing policies? It would, of course, be possible to design subsidies that gave greater protection to smaller, poorer farmers while ensuring that the better-off commercial farmers paid a more realistic price. Invariably it is the richer farmers – in Europe and the US as well as in the developing world – who get the lion's share of taxpayers' generous subsidies. Universal suffrage, where it exists (for example in India), does not appear to have been very successful in giving governments the political weight to withstand pressure from lobbies of the better off.

The pricing of water itself is not the only reason for exploitation. Free or heavily subsidized electricity for pumping groundwater aquifers depletes them more rapidly. This requires the drilling of ever deeper wells and the use of more electricity to extract water from them. Inevitably, poorer farmers are simply priced out of ever-deeper drilling. They come to depend in parts of India like Gujarat on their richer neighbours, who have in effect developed monopolies in water markets by exhausting the aquifers that villagers have traditionally used. Similar problems occur elsewhere in the subcontinent. Flying once down the Indus river in a small plane from Lahore to Hyderabad and Karachi, it was astonishing to see how much soil salinity had been caused in part by groundwater depletion. Thousands of hectares of good land had been lost to agriculture on either bank of the river.

I doubt whether it really makes all that much difference to these issues whether the provision and distribution of water is managed by the public or the private sector. What counts is how effective and well managed the operation is. I was environment secretary when Margaret Thatcher's government privatized the water industry. It was a very tricky enterprise since many people thought of water as a public resource out of which no one should make a profit. The rains fell on our green island home. They were part of our birthright and heritage. 'Fat cats' from the City of London should not be allowed to get their hands on God's gift to the nation, nor make money out of selling it to the rest of us.

Most people overlooked the fact that they were already paying a pretty unfair local tax for their water. For me, the real reason for privatizing the industry was not ideological. Consumers were not paying enough to clean up our rivers, streams and coastal waters, and the Treasury was never likely to make up the shortfall with larger disbursements of public spending requiring higher individual or corporate taxes. Schools, hospitals and social-security benefits would always take priority over cleaner water. So we privatized the industry; saw a large increase in investment in cleaning up water and the first sizeable commitments of expenditure to modernizing the water infrastructure. We then suffered as what should have been the political benefits from the whole enterprise rapidly drained away when the directors of the new water companies awarded themselves spanking increases in remuneration. Unfortunately, part of the price that those of us who believe in capitalism have to pay is that from time to time capitalists behave as outrageously as their cartoon caricatures; their noses sink deep into the trough.

While today two-thirds of global water and sanitation systems remain under public control, privatization has been increasing. Excluding revenues from bottled water, the booming business opportunities in the global water industry now total about $300 billion. From Argentina to South Africa, the recent record on privatization and effective water management has been mixed. There have been limited successes in some areas – in Britain, for instance, water management improved once responsibility for providing the water was separated from monitoring its quality. There have been disastrous setbacks elsewhere, for instance in parts of Latin America. Private control and ownership do not perform miracles. The market cannot operate on its own without a strong steer from governments that enforces pollution emission controls on sewage works and ensures public accountability and openness. There needs to be a regulatory regime that ensures at the least that water is priced fairly, that subsidies are economically, environmentally and socially sound, that the basic needs of consumers are met, and that water quality is enhanced and protected. The snag here is that good regulation requires strong governments and effective public agencies and those often do not exist in the regions where privatization efforts are increasing. But without these sort of safeguards, we are likely to see more violent protests against privatization, like those experienced in Bolivia, Paraguay, the Philippines and South Africa.

There is inevitably a tendency to ignore prosaic issues like pricing policy and regulation and look almost exclusively for technological and engineering fixes – however grandiose and ambitious they may be – to the problems of water availability. An aspect of the last century's hubris, the sense that man could always dominate and control nature, was the huge investment to move water from one place to another, or to store water for irrigation and hydroelectric schemes. Water infrastructure development was often a better part of the legacy of empires. From 1859, in the early years of the Raj, the British built an elaborate network of canals across the Punjab to try quite successfully to harness the Indus and its tributaries for irrigation and to prevent flooding. Engineering ambition today goes well beyond that. China has plans that exceed the spending on the famous Three Gorges Dam, the largest project attempted in that country since the building of the Great Wall and the Grand Canal. It diverts waters from the Yangtze to the dry plains of northern China. But the Yangtze itself is increasingly affected by the impact of global warming on glacial melt in the mountains of Tibet where the river rises. Plans to divert the Ebro river in the north of Spain in order to irrigate agricultural production in the south had to be dropped because of the costs and the likely effect on the environment (including the carbon emissions associated with pumping large amounts of water over long distances). Dams have been an increasingly controversial source of controlling and storing water. Without them, it would not have been possible to build Los Angeles in the middle of the desert. Similar developmental justifications would be given for the Savoy Mountains scheme in Australia, the Cahora Bassa dam in Mozambique, the Three Gorges Dam on the Yangtze and the Aswan dam, begun by President Nasser as the most important task facing Egypt and completed in 1970 (with political consequences that will be considered later in this chapter). But dams are criticized first, for displacing communities – including many indigenous people. Over the last fifty years, it is reckoned that 40–80 million people have been driven from their homes without adequate compensation by badly designed dam projects. In China, over 10 million people were moved because of dam construction between 1950 and 1990. The Sanmenxia dam in China alone displaced 870,000 people. Second, there is ecological damage upstream and downstream from siltation and deforestation to damaged wetlands. Moreover, there is evidence of some exaggeration of the economic benefits of dams. All this has led to a plainly misconceived blanket condemnation of all large-scale water infrastructure projects. So great have been the pressures from non-governmental organizations on global and regional development banks – the World Bank and the Asian Development Bank, for instance – that funding of these big projects has shifted to private multinationals like Bechtel, Vivendi and Ondeo. The availability of private capital for big projects has helped circumvent public rows with taxpayers as well as local residents in Turkey, India and China.

Lack of proper infrastructure creates greater vulnerability to floods and drought. This is principally though not exclusively (as we saw with the terrible consequences of Hurricane Katrina in the United States and with the costly drought in California) a problem in poor countries. In 2005 drought in the Horn of Africa affected more than 20 million people. The mid-1990s drought in Morocco cut agricultural output by almost half. Kenya has suffered from droughts in the northeast and from floods elsewhere. In 2000 in Mozambique, floods cost 700 people their lives and half a million their homes; economic growth was cut from 8 per cent in one year to 2 per cent the next. The floods in Britain in the summer of 2007 were damaging and disruptive but the consequence for lives and livelihoods were fortunately minimal by comparison. The capacity to store water as well as to prevent floods gives a clear idea of the differences between rich and poor countries. The US stores 6,000 cubic metres of water per person, Australia 5,000. In Ethiopia, which covers twelve river basins, the figure is 43.

Recycling waste water offers a dependable way of expanding the supply of water. In some countries like Morocco this has been done for years without health problems, but high standards are necessary to avoid considerable health risks. Much more technical and political interest has been shown in desalination, where Israel has been a world leader in pioneering the technology at a reasonable cost. But desalination at present contributes only about 0.2 per cent to global water supply, and the development of the technology is unlikely to bridge the overall gap between supply and demand. The energy costs involved are high (with increased carbon emissions) and it is difficult to see this technology as a likely way of helping either urban dwellers in poor countries or their agriculture.

Even if we lived in a climatically stable world (which is not the case today, nor ever has been), the continuation of water misuse combined with inequitable distribution among an ever-expanding global population would present fundamental problems for future generations. The threat of climate change will worsen what is already a precarious future. There will need to be better strategic planning, nationally and regionally, and the development of infrastructure if we are to mitigate or preferably prevent what appears to be an unfolding disaster.

The UNDP notes that the unparalleled threat to human development posed by climate change – and even prompt action to stabilize or cut emissions of greenhouse gases would not deal with the delayed effect of past emissions – 'will be transmitted through shifts in hydrological cycles and rainfall patterns and the impact of higher surface temperature on water evaporation'.[6] The scale and exact regional location of changes in rainfall are uncertain, but the evidence strongly suggests that the most water-stressed areas will get less, and that flows will become both less predictable and subject to extreme events. Flood followed by drought followed by flood will become more common. Moreover, poverty will increase as the disparity in water availability between the developed and the developing world deepens.

For most of the world's poorest people – about three-quarters of them living on less than a dollar a day – rain-fed agriculture is the source of their livelihood. It is difficult to be precise about the impact of climate change on crop yields and output but the increasing likelihood of drought will reduce yields of cereals in African countries already suffering from food shortages. The serious food emergencies that have already hit Malawi, Mozambique, Zambia and Zimbabwe (sometimes for reasons other than or in addition to the climate) will become more frequent. In some countries – Kenya is a good example – rainfall is predicted to increase in some areas but decline in other semi-arid regions. The yields of coffee, tea and basic foods will suffer. In West Africa the Niger river, which provides the water for ten poor and arid countries, may lose about a third of its flow.

Extreme poverty and malnutrition will increase as water scarcity and the insecurities associated with it grow. According to a study undertaken for the World Summit on Sustainable Development in

2002, 'modelling exercises indicate that climate change could increase global malnutrition by 15% to 26%, increasing the absolute number of malnourished people by 75–125 million by 2080'.[7] Later estimates have suggested that this figure could be very substantially higher. This will not, of course, simply be a rural phenomenon. Agricultural losses will affect whole national economies. Poverty and malnutrition will spread from the country to the town with combustible political consequences.

More extreme weather patterns will raise the risk of both drought and flood and will also increase vulnerability to them. During the 1990s about 200 million people a year in developing countries were hit by climate-related disasters. As continental temperatures and the temperature of the sea rise, the Asian monsoon will become more violent because of the ability of the air to carry more readily available vapour. The floods in Mumbai in 2005 led to 500 deaths. Parts of India where there is already heavy monsoon rain will see even more; but more arid areas will get less. El Niño (the climate-changing warming of the eastern Pacific) is likely to have even less predictable effects on rainfall patterns. Irrespective of rainfall, temperature increases will raise water demands and increase evaporation, so that a 2 to 3 per cent rise in average temperatures will cut water availability by 10 per cent.

Shrinking glaciers and rising sea levels will pose new risks for human security. Global warming means that glaciers melt more rapidly. This will produce springtime flooding and summer water shortages in Asia, Latin America and part of East Africa. Seven of the world's greatest rivers are fed by the glaciers of the Himalayas and Tibet, which have been melting faster than ever in recent decades. The Brahmaputra, the Ganges, the Indus, the Yangtze, the Salween, the Mekong and the Irrawaddy supply water to more than 2 billion people. These families depend for their living on water from glaciers. At the same time rising sea levels will reduce the amount of fresh water in low-lying countries and river deltas. Bangladesh, Egypt, Nigeria and Thailand all have large populations living in delta areas threatened by saline intrusion. The threat is particularly grave in Bangladesh, where low-lying regions support more than 110 million people.

International efforts to curb the growth of greenhouse gas emissions have been feeble and so have attempts to adapt to current and future realities by building the appropriate infrastructure. As noted, there is an inverse relationship between the global distribution of water scarcity with all its attendant economic, social and political problems and the distribution around the world of the infrastructure to mitigate these difficulties. Instead of doing more to help poor countries in this area, we have been doing less. Between 1990 and 2002 global development assistance for large water infrastructure was halved from $3 billion to $1.5 billion. In addition to these projects there is additional spending on matters like supply and sanitation. This total has been rising year on year by less than the overall increase in development assistance. In 2004 commitments for water projects stood at $4.5 billion. In countries receiving this aid, help for clean water and sanitation amounted to 62 cents per head a year. Returning to my kitchen, this is just over half what I spend on a bottle of San Pellegrino. It would help a great deal if rich countries spent more on aid and less on bottled water, and if poorer countries spent less on armaments and more on access to clean water.

Whatever the worries about future conflict over water between states, it is civil conflict within states that has been the most usual example of violence caused by water shortage. Water and conflict have been linked through poverty, migration and food security, especially among rural populations, for instance in Yemen. Where water availability and reliability have an effect on the ability to scratch a living from the land, there is often large-scale migration as has happened in northern Pakistan and Afghanistan. Since migrating groups are usually poorly equipped to develop livelihoods outside agriculture, they are more likely to turn to illicit ways of making a living.[8] Drifting into urban slums – or migrating to them more rapidly because of sudden droughts or floods – they add to the simmering social unrest there. Migration can even produce tensions between local rural communities that are unaccustomed to coming into contact with one another, or are competing for the same scarce resources. These problems are exacerbated when the migrants cross borders, as happens in Bangladesh and neighbouring Indian states. The population of Bangladesh is predicted to double to 235 million by 2025. The authority and legitimacy of governments and state institutions, often weak in any event in water-stressed countries, will be further diminished where climate change makes it ever more difficult to provide water. These governments will need to divert scarce resources to mitigate the effects of drought and flood; they will also need to provide more support to marginal groups and will find themselves under pressure to misallocate capital, subsidize lobbies (frequently of the better off) and hold prices down. At the same time, the impact of water shortage on agriculture will lower economic growth, resulting in reduced tax revenues.

The possibility of water becoming a cause of strife between states is increasingly debated.[9] It is argued that where water resources are shared – with countries drawing from the same river or aquifer, for example – future shortages will raise tensions and may trigger conflict. Naturally, it could equally well be argued that so far there is little evidence of disputes over water being the sole rather than a contributory cause of conflict, and that while the sharing of water resources could lead to conflict, it could equally lead to greater international cooperation. Nevertheless, there is a long list of countries which depend for a large amount of their total water supply on water that originates outside their borders and is under the control of other states. Egypt depends on the Nile for its water, and 97 per cent of the water in this river originates in other countries. Thirty other nations depend on neighbours for a third or more of their surface river-borne water, including Syria, Iraq and Sudan. Other countries in this group such as Hungary, the Netherlands and Belgium seem exceedingly unlikely to go to war over the issue. In addition to the sharing of surface water, countries also share hydroelectric power and ground-water from aquifers.

Predictions of inevitable conflict, with some national security experts arguing that it is a matter not of whether but of when and where, seem to me extreme. But they are worth examining, not least to see how possible wars can be prevented. An exhaustive chronology of water in conflict suggests that water has often been a military target, though infrequently the only issue that caused the fighting in the first place.[10] The Old Testament records the defeat of Sisera and his 'nine hundred chariots of iron' when the Kishon river flooded the plains of Esdraelon. In the seventh century BC the Assyrians drowned Babylon in the waters from an irrigation canal. More than two thousand years later the Dutch opened their own dykes to hold back the French forces of Louis XIV. Britain's favourite wartime movie shows the Royal Air Force bombing dams on the Mohne, Sorpe and Eder rivers in 1943. Israel bombed the construction works begun by Syria in the mid-1960s to divert the headwaters of the Jordan river. Dams, desalination plants and water conveyance systems were destroyed in the first Gulf War in 1991 and in the invasion of Iraq in 2003. Terrorists have planned or carried out attacks on water supplies, for example those by religious cults in the US in 1984–5, and so have the Sudanese-backed militias in Darfur in 2003–4. Inevitably, al-Qaeda has threatened to poison the drinking water in American and other Western cities. But while it is easy to point to rising tensions because of water disputes between states (for example between Turkey, Iraq and Syria over the Euphrates) and to arguments about water resources as contributing factors in disputes (the Six-Day War between Israel and its Arab neighbours in 1967), water wars are not yet a regular feature of international conflict. That water has been, however, a motive in conflict or planned conflict is clear. It is wholly plausible that one reason for South Africa's decisive support for the coup against Lesotho's tribal government in 1986 was the aim of getting water diverted from Lesotho's mountains to Transvaal in order to deal with serious water shortages there.

We can now look at four regions where tensions over water are high (and are likely to be made worse by climate change) and where conflict is possible – the Jordan valley, the Nile, central Asia and the Punjab.

The three sources of the Jordan river rise on Mount Hermon in Lebanon and join in one stream three miles into Israeli territory. The river flows down to the sea of Galilee (Lake Tiberias), is fed just to the south of the lake by the Yarmuk river from Syria, and continuing south loses water from evaporation and becomes increasingly saline before ending in the Dead Sea, which itself has shrunk dramatically in recent years. It provides some of the water for an arid region whose population is predicted to double between 1990 and 2020 to over 21 million people and to go on rising thereafter. Population growth will therefore increase demand in an already water-stressed area. The availability of water would in any circumstances have created tensions between Israel and her Arab neighbours. In a region which has been torn apart by wars and violence, where political agreement has been at a premium and where neither the parable of the Prodigal Son nor that of the traveller succoured by the Samaritan has gained much contemporary traction, the development of a cooperative approach to the water supply has been minimal. The water from the Jordan itself has to be supplemented by that drawn from shared aquifers and this too has proved to be contentious.

The Old Testament Book of Exodus records the struggle between the Israelites and other tribes for the control of the Jordan river valley and the adjoining regions. God directed Moses to lead his people out of 'the house of bondage' in Egypt 'into the land of the Canaanites, and the Hittites and the Amorites, and the Hivites, and the Jebusites'. For many of the Jews who fled from predominantly urban Europe and the atrocities of the Holocaust, the new Zionist state of Israel was not simply a welcome haven where they could be safe from pogrom and prejudice. It was their historic Zionist homeland with whose soil they wanted to identify. So, many of the new Israelis who had previously provided part of the core of commercial and artistic life in the cities of Europe, now wished to work the land in agricultural settlements in arid terrain. The continuation of settlement farming required water and increasingly the spread of settlements was regarded as strategically valuable. The farmers and the generals found common cause. Despite the fact that the Jordan is a small river and does not contain much water in comparison with other rivers – about 1 per cent of the Congo's flow or 2 per cent of the Nile's – it is vital to the irrigation projects in both water-stressed Israel and Jordan, and the supply of water from it has been a bitterly contentious issue since the state of Israel was founded in 1948.

The Eisenhower administration tried from 1953 to 1955 to broker a deal on water sharing without success, and in 1960 the Arab League produced a plan to divert the headwaters of the Jordan which would have scuppered Israel's National Water Carrier scheme to transport water from the Jordan to irrigate the Negev desert and coastal areas in Israel. The first clash between Israeli and Syrian forces came in 1965 near the spring of the Dan river, one of the Jordan's three sources. Military clashes grew in intensity in the run-up to the 1967

Six-Day War which was at least partly precipitated by this water issue, regarded by all the combatants as a matter of national security. 'Water is a question of life for Israel,' declared Israel's premier Levi Eshkol. After her stunning victory in 1967, Israel occupied much of the land surrounding the headwaters of the Jordan. This denied Jordan a significant amount of its previously available water, while ensuring a more reliable supply for Israel. 'Today,' according to Peter Gleick, 'approximately 40 per cent of the ground water upon which Israel is now dependent – and more than 33 per cent of its total sustainable annual water yield – originates in the territories occupied in the 1967 War. Indeed almost the entire increase in Israeli water use since 1967 derives from the waters of the West Bank and the upper Jordan river.'[11]

Since 1967, arguments over water between Israel and its neighbours have been more or less contained. The most sensitive of them – relating to control of the Golan Heights and the land adjoining Lake Tiberias, which would jeopardize Israeli access to the Baniyas tributary of the Jordan – awaits serious negotiation between Syria and Israel. The crux of the disputes over water has now shifted to the relationship between Israel and the Palestinians. Israel's commitment to the existence of a viable Palestinian state can be questioned on a number of counts, one of which is the present lack of an equitable sharing of water. Jewish settlers in the West Bank, for example, receive a lot more per head than the Palestinians: some estimate the figures at four times as much, others go as high as five or eight times. Present Israeli demand for fresh water, including for settlements in the Golan Heights and in occupied territory, exceeds the estimated supply of about 2 billion cubic metres by 10 per cent. Aquifers are over-pumped in order to make good this shortfall, so water tables in the West Bank and Israel have fallen, leading to the exhaustion of some wells and seawater infiltration from the Mediterranean. According to Thomas Homer-Dixon, 'Israel's population growth in the next thirty years, even without continuing major immigration from Russia and the rest of the former Soviet Union, will probably cause the country's water demand to outstrip supply by at least 40 per cent.'[12]

More than half of Israel's water comes from aquifers and two of the three main ones on which it depends drain into Israel from beneath the West Bank. Homer-Dixon reports in the same study that 'Israel restricts the number of wells Arabs can drill in the territory, the amount of water Arabs are allowed to pump, and the times at which they can draw irrigation water. Since 1967, Arabs have not been permitted to drill new wells for agricultural purposes, although Mekarot (the Israeli Water Company) has drilled more than thirty wells for settlers' irrigation.' The drilling of deeper Israeli wells near to Arab ones has led to the drying up or salination of the Palestinian ones. Taken with all the other restrictions on Palestinian agriculture – the difficulty of moving produce because of military barriers on the roads, the grubbing-up of orchards and olive trees, the separation of land from the homes of those who work it by the Israel Security Fence – it is inevitable that many Palestinians have left farming for unemployment in the cities: another factor in radicalizing Palestinian opinion. In five years on the European Commission for External Affairs I discussed with colleagues the tragedy of the relationship between Israel and Palestine with cheerless regularity. While the Commission itself funded some water projects in Palestine, and while the famous Road Map to Peace in the Middle East contained a passing reference to water, I can barely recall any sustained consideration of the issue. Yet it is perfectly clear that without an equitable agreement on water – which should actually be one of the easiest of a number of brutal issues to resolve – there will be no wider agreement and no Palestinian state. The aquifers and any political hope that remains will continue to be depleted.

Four thousand years ago, in the land of King Menes and King Cheops, the wintering place of Europe's swallows, they sang a hymn to what made life in Egypt possible, the source of their civilization: the river they worshipped. 'Glory be to thee, O Nile! You rise out of the earth and come to nourish Egypt. You water the plains and have the power to feed all cattle. You quench the thirsty desert, far from any water. You bring forth the barley. You create the wheat. You fill the granaries and storehouses, not forgetting the poor. For you we pluck our harps, for you we sing.' The singing should be just as loud today, louder perhaps. The Nile flows through arid North Africa, where despite the inhospitable terrain the population is surging. It provides nearly all of Egypt's water, where the population has increased from about 13 million in 1922 when the country became (at least officially) independent to almost 70 million by the end of the twentieth century. It is forecast to rise to 115 million by the middle of this century. Providing water for this growing population and feeding its citizens will be tough, which is why the Egyptian government is proposing to irrigate land in the Western Desert and settle up to 7 million people on these 'New Lands'. Hydrologists doubt whether this can be done (as the government insists) without taking more water from the Nile.

This is where the potential for conflict lies. Nearly all of the Nile's run-off originates outside Egypt in the other nations of the river basin which covers 10 per cent of the landmass of Africa. About 150 million people actually live within the boundaries of the basin in some of the poorest countries in the world, upstream from Egypt. Their populations are growing too. Ethiopia's population is predicted to rise from 62 million in 1998 to an estimated 212 million people in 2050; Sudan's population will likely increase from 29 million to 60 million in this period. The population is therefore set to increase in those countries alone by substantially more than the predicted Egyptian population at the same date. How will the upstream riparians meet their own needs for food and water without taking more from the Nile?

The two main branches of the river system are the White Nile and the Blue Nile. Ethiopia and Eritrea occupy the upstream reaches of the Blue Nile. The White Nile emerges from Lake Victoria (with Rwanda and Burundi to the west, Tanzania to the south and Kenya to the east) and flows into Lake Kyoga in Uganda and then Lake Albert in the Congo. It joins the Blue Nile north of Khartoum. The Blue Nile provides most of the water to the downstream reaches, when the single stream pours into Lake Nasser (the reservoir created by the Aswan High Dam) before running through the narrow valley in which most Egyptians live and grow their food, and then breaking up into the branches that form the Nile delta on the shores of the Mediterranean. There has been an increase in salination in the delta because the falling river levels have been unable to keep the sea at bay.

Upstream states like Ethiopia, Uganda and Sudan have all proposed their own hydroelectric and irrigation schemes. Building new dams and diverting Nile waters into larger annual withdrawals for agricultural purposes alarms the Egyptians, who have usually managed to bully and bluster their way to a successful defence of their privileged position. This may become a lot more difficult if global climate change leads to higher rainfall in Ethiopia and central Africa, and higher rates of evaporation, for example in Lake Nasser, and in the lower, more arid areas. Add the demographic pressures in all the countries concerned to these factors, and there are all the makings of a conflict. In 1995, when the Sudanese suggested that they might amend the 1929 Nile Waters Agreement that favoured Egypt, President Hosni Mubarak responded by saying, 'Any step taken to this end will force us into confrontation to defend our rights and life. Our response will be beyond anything they can imagine.' The Sudanese backed down forthwith. But will they and the other upstream riparians settle for the status quo when they feel under as much resource pressure as the Egyptians?

To the east, with the Tigris and the Euphrates (which formed the bounds of the first manifestations of civilization) the problem is the other way round. These rivers rise in the mountains of south-eastern Turkey, which wants to increase its withdrawals in order to promote development in southern Anatolia and in the process abate support for Kurdish terrorist separatists. This has led to tense disputes with Syria, which gets 85 per cent of its renewable water supply from the Euphrates, and Iraq, which draws all of its supply from the combined rivers. Arab leaders have intervened from time to time to calm down tempers, and Syria has in the past given support to the PKK (the Kurdish terrorist group). As in the case of the Nile, the populations of the countries involved are rising sharply; together they may treble between 1990 and 2050.[13] But it is still further east, beyond the Caspian Sea in central Asia, that water conflict may be even more likely, as glaciers – accurately described by the UNDP as water banks – melt more rapidly because of global warming.

The post-Soviet states of central Asia – Kazakhstan, Kyrgyzstan, Tajikistan, Turkmenistan and Uzbekistan – cover an area larger than India, Pakistan and Bangladesh combined, with a population of about 60 million. The area is arid or semi-arid. This lack of water has shaped the region's history at the crossroads of continents. Agriculture was difficult; there were few cities save those which provided staging posts for traders on the Silk Road. The land was dominated by nomadic tribes and became the route to the West for some of the great world migrations. Pony-riding hordes of Huns and Mongols, repelled initially by the Great Wall from incursions into China, turned west and south under their war leaders, most infamous of them all Genghis Khan. In later days tsarist expansion towards India turned these lands that run along the northern borders of Afghanistan into parts of the playing field of the British Empire's 'Great Game' with the Russians. With the creation of the Soviet Union, Russia swallowed them all, and was forced to disgorge them only upon the collapse of its unifying ideology, communism.

On these dry plains and mountainsides rainfall gives less water than is lost through evaporation. The glaciers and permanent snowfields in the mountains of Tajikistan and Kyrgyzstan provide most of the fresh water that flows into the Amu Darya and Syr Darya rivers. They irrigate the agriculture in Tajikistan, Turkmenistan and Uzbekistan, and water from the same source generates hydroelectric power in the two upstream countries. Accelerating glacial retreat threatens this delicate balance that has already been tipped alarmingly in the direction of environmental catastrophe and political conflict.

Apart from the hydrocarbons found mainly in Kazakhstan and Turkmenistan, agriculture provides the principal economic activity and means of livelihood in the region, with heavy reliance on thirsty crops, above all cotton and rice. Water use in the region is unsustainable, and the situation has worsened since the collapse of the Soviet Union. Centralized regional planning has been replaced by national struggles and arguments. Moreover, irrigation systems have collapsed and half of the available water (some suggest as much as 90 per cent) never reaches the crops for which it is intended. While regional water and infrastructure planning may be a real loss since the days of Soviet bureaucracy, Moscow's legacy elsewhere is appalling; partly because of the heavy emphasis in Soviet days (even more than under the tsars) on cotton farming in order to reduce the country's reliance on imports. The draining of the Aral Sea is the most potent symbol of the region's water crisis.

Both the Amu Darya and the Syr Darya rivers formerly emptied into the Aral Sea, once the fourth largest inland body of water in the world. The shrinking of this sea, which began in the 1960s, means that the parts of it into which the two rivers flow have now been divided into two separate lakes. The original surface area of the sea has shrunk by 75 per cent and its level has fallen by between 13 and 18 metres. The land around the sea, home to 4 million people, has become a toxic wasteland. The water is eight times more saline than it was in 1960, and salt and poisonous dust from those parts of the sea bed that have been exposed are blown by the wind over large adjoining areas, rendering them unfit for agriculture. The twenty-four native species of Aral fish have all been wiped out.

The cotton monoculture in the region touches most of its worst characteristics – political repression, poverty, social deprivation, failure to carry through economic reforms and environmental calamity. The region produces 6.5 per cent of world cotton output and contributes over 15 per cent of world exports. The situation is probably worst in Uzbekistan, which purports to have liberalized the Soviet-era system but has simply replaced the previous management with members or allies of the governing elite (including some alleged members of the Tashkent criminal underworld) and the successors to the Soviet KGB. The president, Islam Karimov (like most of the regional leaders, a Soviet holdover), is a tough bruiser with whom I once spent an unpleasant two hours in his modern palace in Tashkent discussing human rights, in which he was little interested then and seems even less interested today. It did not come as a surprise when he allowed his armed forces to put down a popular rising in the city of Andijan in the east of Uzbekistan in 2005. It was the culmination of months of protests against the country's ruinous economic policies. As many as 750 mostly unarmed civilians, including many children, were killed. Uzbekistan, like Turkmenistan and Tajikistan, coerces its farmers, exploits women in agriculture and uses forced labour by students and others at harvest time. There is abundant evidence as well of the use of child labour. Public health also suffers from the exposure to chemicals used in cotton growing: there is genetic damage resulting in massive increases in cancer rates. High levels of airborne dust have led to abnormal rates of respiratory infections and asthma, while pesticide contamination of food runs at as much as three times a safe level.

Change in the way the cotton is grown, processed and marketed is necessary for environmental, health and security reasons. This is unlikely to happen, given the prevailing political system in these countries. A combination of repression and poverty is driving moderate Islamists into the arms of extremists. Unemployment, hardship and brutal governments threaten to 'Talebanize' the next generation, which is already affected by the drug production over the border in Afghanistan. President Karimov and his colleagues are brewing trouble and degrading their economies and states.

For them, the main national security issue appears to be access to water, not how it is used. Tensions between neighbouring states are undoubtedly rising. The most bitter arguments have been between Turkmenistan and Uzbekistan over the Amu Darya. There are unsubstantiated rumours of a small-scale secret war over the river between these states with the seizure of water-control installations on the Turkmenistan side of the river by Uzbek troops. Furthermore, in 2001 there were reports of a massacre of Uzbek troops in Turkmenistan. Relations between the countries are unlikely to be improved by the construction in Turkmenistan of a large artificial lake – the 'Golden Lake' – which will lower the levels of the Amu Darya in Uzbekistan. Maybe the price of allowing these tensions to spill over into open conflicts will be sufficiently high to deter them. But it is in the interests of peace in the region, as well as agricultural development, to establish some form of effective regional management of water resources, helping in the process to save the environment from further terrible damage.[14]

In Persian, 'Punjab' means land of the rivers; the region's principal river is the Indus, like the Nile, Euphrates and Tigris the main artery of an ancient civilization. During the years of empire the Raj managed the Indus river basin, building a network of canals to irrigate an area of farmland which before partition was more extensive than that under cultivation in the United States at the same time. The river basin now straddles the India–Pakistan border, with India the main upstream riparian. On the trip to Pakistan in the late 1980s that I mentioned earlier, I flew down the Indus valley to a project that my Overseas Development Ministry was funding to restore parts of the barrage on the river at Sukkur, originally built in the 1920s to help alleviate famine caused by lack of rain. The local political chief who greeted me for lunch under a multicoloured canopy was regarded as semi-divine by his followers and received a lot more attention than the visiting minister who only had a chequebook. Sukkur is on the west bank of the Indus and its barrage – originally called the Lloyd – controlled one of the largest irrigation systems in the world. It was joined to seven canals – some longer than the Suez Canal – and irrigated 10 million acres. The barrage and its irrigation system today have to cope with growing water shortage and falling agricultural production. The Indus, like other river systems, depends on glacial water flows, and will suffer from the same problems as rivers in central and east Asia. There are likely to be more flash floods at some times of the year, but overall there will be a substantial reduction in the amount of water that can be used for irrigation at the same time as the populations of India and Pakistan grow rapidly.

At the time of partition, the canals and irrigation system of the Indus basin were divided by the departing British between Pakistan and India and so far, to the credit of both countries, conflict over water supply has been avoided. Indeed, after years of often bitter negotiations in the 1950s, the two countries signed an agreement on water sharing that has survived to the present day. The focus of hostility between India and Pakistan has been Kashmir. While many regard the Indus Waters Treaty of 1960 as a model for peaceful resolution of water disputes, it does not allow for positive cooperation in developing the Indus basin. It will be tested by an increase in salination, deforestation, silting and soil erosion, a surge in population and a decline in agricultural productivity and water supply.

Clearly, while attempts to share water may lead to conflict in several arid or semi-arid regions, the challenge of managing rival claims to this vital resource could also see the development of new patterns of, and instruments for, international cooperation like the concordat for the Guarani aquifer which straddles substantial areas of Paraguay, Uruguay, Brazil and Argentina. Some have suggested that to promote this we need a new body, under the auspices of the UN on the lines of the International Atomic Energy Agency or the UN Development Programme. Such an authority would help states to devise ways of sharing equitably rivers and aquifers, promote research into desalination and more effective use of water in agriculture (so-called drop-for-crop schemes), help countries facing serious water shortages, create early-warning systems on water stress, and promote good practice in water management.[15] I am by nature averse to institutionalizing a response to every problem. In this case, however, water is so important and the solutions so attainable that establishing a real know-how body internationally seems wise. It would assist states in managing their own water resources better and would also establish a programme of preventative diplomacy on water issues.

Yet the new institutions really required are at the national level – promoting good water governance with the help of more generous assistance from aid donors – and at the regional level – crafting programmes of fair and effective development of shared watercourses. The UN should seek to develop a consensus on the principles that are required to guide this sort of cooperation. There are two models of sovereignty over transboundary water management which have to be rejected. First, there is the Harmon doctrine that governed the United States disputes at the end of the nineteenth century over rivers shared with Mexico. It baldly asserted that states should have the right to use the water within their jurisdiction regardless of any effects outside their national boundaries. This absolutist principle is opposed by the equally firm notion that downstream riparians have a right to receive the natural flow of a river from upstream countries, an issue hugely complicated in any case where transboundary aquifers are concerned when downstream pumping can affect upstream supply. In practice – and to avoid tension and worse – the sensible principles underpinning cooperation are: first, the fair and reasonable use of transboundary water; second, the need to avoid significant harm to co-riparians; and third, the demand for prior notification of works which might affect the water resources of others.

Global warming and climate change make all these issues matter much more than they otherwise would. Wiser worldwide environmental policies, which we will discuss in a later chapter, are the best means of preventing future conflict – and not only over water.

9

Stuff Happens

. . . and if you are sure that you are a guide to the blind, a light to those who are in darkness, a corrector of the foolish, a teacher of children, having in the law the embodiment of knowledge and truth, you, then, that teach others, will you not teach yourself? While you preach against stealing, do you steal? You that forbid adultery, do you commit adultery? You that abhor idols, do you rob temples? You that boast in the law, do you dishonour God by breaking the law? For, as it is written, 'The name of God is blasphemed among the Gentiles because of you.'   Romans 2: 19–24

Freedom's untidy, and free people are free to make mistakes and commit crimes and do bad things . . . stuff happens.
                                        Donald Rumsfeld, 2003

It is difficult to fight the good fight against both original sin and the market. As we have seen from Colombia to the Congo, and everywhere in between, they keep cold-blooded company. Given freedom, as Mr Rumsfeld said, stuff certainly happens. Machiavelli argued that no advantageous opportunity to exploit people would ever be missed. This is not a judgement which any of us would happily welcome, though our personal experience may nudge us into conceding reluctantly that it is all too often true. On my first trip to Hong Kong in 1979 I visited the camps established for Vietnamese boat people and heard some of their horrifying tales. They were refugees who had fled from Vietnam from the mid-1970s onwards after the war in their country. Initially, Thai and Chinese fishermen helped them on their way. Then the fishermen got wise to the fact that these refugees were carrying pretty well everything of value that they owned – jewellery, cash, radios, even farm implements. By the time of my visit it was reckoned that some 300 Thai fishing boats, or 5 per cent of the Thai fishing fleet, were engaged in piracy. By 1981 every boat from Vietnam was being intercepted and robbed an average of 3.3 times while in transit to Hong Kong. The UN High Commission for Refugees (UNHCR) accused the Thai government in 1981 of tacitly allowing the piracy to take place to deter the refugees. Meanwhile, the fishermen were becoming professionals. They were using motherships and swarms of small, fast, heavily armed boats with advanced communications equipment; they became adept at herding the Vietnamese into traps, killing the men, kidnapping the women and taking them to a small island off the coast where they were subjected to the most appalling sexual brutality. By the mid-1980s it was estimated that 20–40 per cent of the prostitutes in Bangkok were captured Vietnamese. Similar brutality continued, albeit on a smaller scale, into the 1990s when I was governor of Hong Kong trying to deal with the problem of returning the boat people under UNHCR auspices safely to their homes. For all the committed volunteers there who worked to help them, Machiavelli was plainly not contradicted by this nasty tale.

Elsewhere in Hong Kong, Adam Smith held sway in every sort of market. Commenting on illicit trade in *The Wealth of Nations* in 1776, he wrote, 'Not many people are scrupulous about smuggling when, without perjury, they can find any easy and safe opportunity of doing so. To pretend to have any scruple about buying smuggled goods . . . would in most countries be regarded as one of those pedantic pieces of hypocrisy.' Substitute 'counterfeiting' for 'smuggling' and you could be describing a part of many visitors' happy retail experiences in Hong Kong. While the colonial government tried, eventually with some success, to close down the arcades in Kowloon which did such a flourishing business in counterfeited (and often smuggled) electronic gadgets, video cassettes and software, shopping for fake designer-label clothing went on unrestricted and undisturbed in Stanley Market and elsewhere. Ralph Lauren's polo player galloped across many a tourist's chest: who was to know whether he was the real chap, the genuine article? And if you didn't know where to find this cut-price fellow, you only had to ask. My favourite (and true) counterfeiting story concerns the European minister sent to Seoul to complain about intellectual property theft in South Korea who went straight from his meeting with Korean officials to the downtown market to search for a fake Rolex.

There is a market for everything – frozen peas, plasma-screen TVs, dodgy mortgages, pig futures, cocaine, human kidneys, ozone-depleting chemicals, sex of every imaginable (and for most of us un-imaginable) variety. Wherever there is demand, sooner or later there is supply, and throughout history attempts to disrupt this equation by cutting off supply have usually been totally unsuccessful. The abolition of the slave trade is one of the few obvious contrary examples. Gener-ally markets are not closed down from the supply side. 'From Prohib-ition to prostitution, from gambling to recreational drugs, the story is the same. Supply-side controls act much like price supports in agriculture, to encourage production and increase profits.'[1] Some of the implications of this observation for our efforts to stamp out the global drug trade, calculated in 2005 by the UN to be worth $13 billion at the production level, $94 billion at the wholesale level, and $322 billion at the retail level, will be discussed in the next chapter. Crime pays, which is why so many individuals, gangs, corpor-ations, banks, government departments and states are involved in it.

International crime is one of the outcrops on the uneven terrain of globalization. It rises in the troubled and violent space between developed or developing countries and stagnating or degenerating ones. It shades into civil wars, civic breakdowns and the decline in the authority and potency of nation-states. The battle between law and crime is invariably a battle between regulation and the market, with criminals more fleet-footed and flexible in their use of ever-more sophisticated market instruments than are the regulators. The victims are not just individuals but the societies they comprise and the states that seek to govern them, rotted by humiliating failure and ubiquitous corruption.

I am bidden (not without some scepticism on my part) to believe that from international relations theory to the sociology of lifestyles, there is something called the postmodern. Maybe it is not just a matter of how old you are, since there is evidently a booming trade in setting up the over fifties like me for blind dates, speed dates and even plain old-fashioned date dates. This is apparently not sad/desperate but simply postmodern. Let me buy into this world for just a moment to concede that there is evidently a sort of crime and criminality which postdates the familiar organized crime of the Mafia, the Chinese Triads, the Japanese Yakuza and other criminal corporations which we will look at shortly. These criminals in organized gangs were essentially 'modern', that is, like modern corporations they pursued administrative efficiency and profit maximization through centralized integrated hierarchies. McKinsey and Bain would have recognized their management structures. They were also a little like a modern state; they established and defended specific territorial claims, frequently won by force of arms of a sort. I recall the FBI briefing me in Washington on the expansion of the grip of Albanian gangs over crime in several American cities. They had wrested control over prostitution in one city, I was told, by shooting the existing pimps and terrorizing their girls into submission by running a car backwards and forwards over the legs of a couple of them, *pour encourager les autres*. Yet sometimes control of territory rests not only on fear but on bonds of consent with the local population. The gang supplants the authority of the real state with its tax collectors, police, planners and courts. The IRA (a criminal as well as a terrorist organization) exercised this sort of control in parts of Northern Ireland – on the Creggan Estate in Newry, in Crossmaglen, in the Bogside in Londonderry. Cosa Nostra ran parts of Sicily in a similar way. Land-use planning on the island, for example, owes much to Mafia views on the relative balance between the environment and money.

By contrast, many criminal enterprises since the Cold War are postmodern. They are transaction-oriented coalitions which form and disband in response to market forces and requirements from smuggled tobacco to pirated DVDs. They do not depend on this or that piece of territory, which substantially reduces the threat of internecine criminal warfare. Turf wars are more likely between national security and police forces these days than between these sorts of criminals. The lack of a 'fixed' relationship with local populations means that the connection between criminal and civilian is more casual and often even more brutal.

The postmodern networked criminal is the shadow of the post-modern man, one more person floating through the 'networked society'. His life, like ours (even, ouch, mine), is just another wired-up, market-driven phenomenon. Like the diamond brokers, arms dealers and smugglers in Victor Bout's spider's web of business partners, these criminals fill a niche here, a niche there. They deal in tax-free cigarettes, fence stolen cargo liners, perhaps, or market fake Viagra, which pays for their hobbies, winter sports at Whistler, surfing on Bondi, or watching *The Sopranos* on DVD to see how things used to be done. Our law-abiding networked citizen looks for the gap in the market; his criminal cousin seeks out a gap in the law. He is a violence entrepreneur best served not by the development of the global econ-omy, which provides the bread and butter for the global knowledge elite, but by its destruction. Hence the connection between war zones, failed states, rogue states, transitional states and crime, and the reason so many civil wars, once started, burn on and on. Violence entrepre-neurship makes conflict self-sustaining – more conflict: more drugs; more conflict: more slaves, prostitutes and mercenaries; more conflict: more illicitly mined minerals.

The end of the Cold War and the break-up of the Soviet Union increased instability and the growth of crime, and crime grew as trade itself burgeoned on the back of simpler, faster and cheaper international communications, easier travel, expanding national economies, looser border controls and the commonplace use of information technology, from cell phones and the internet to encryption. It is easier these days to conduct international business and easier as well to conduct international crime. The rapid increase in the number of air passengers and international flights allows greater mobility to criminals carrying illicit commodities. Our global village is their global village too. They use the internet to gather intelligence; they communicate (as did the 9/11 terrorists) through computer terminals at local business centres or internet cafés to protect their anonymity; they use information technology to make and distribute high-quality forged documents. There are even websites that sell replicas of driving licences and Green Cards as 'novelty items', complete with instructions on how to alter them to make them look more official. In Hong Kong the Triads recruited local technical-school graduates to work as counterfeiters.[2]

States find it difficult to control illicit movements of goods and people across their borders, even with the full and tiresome panoply of controls operated for example by the USA, which has nearly 100,000 miles of shoreline and almost 6,000 miles of borders with its neighbours. Every day more than a million people and more than 400 million tons of goods arrive at 301 ports of entry with 3,700 terminals.[3] They come by road, by commercial and private flights and by ship. The nearly 10 million containers arriving at American ports cannot all be searched; it is said to take five inspectors three hours to do a thorough search of a 40-foot container. But the controls that do exist themselves create profitable opportunities. The nature of state and interstate regulatory regimes, and the efforts of the military, the police and customs officials to interdict illegal goods, create numerous lucrative opportunities to capitalize on the resulting arbitrage. Most criminals are not producers; they are speculators and specialists. Their profits come from controlling the price, access, availability and quality of a given commodity. The more barriers and the higher the opportunity costs, the more entrenched the criminal position can become. So while criminal networks use entrepreneurially the techniques of the global market economy, they themselves operate according to mercantilist rather than market principles: the more borders, the more controls, the more law-enforcement agencies, the more crossings, the higher the cost of the traded goods and the higher the profits to distribute. Lowering the barriers to freer, honest trade can admittedly make it easier to move illicit goods. But that does not necessarily follow. Worst of all is to have apparently strict controls that are porous and do not work. That way you generate economic inefficiencies and higher costs for what is done legally, and bigger profits for what is traded illegally. Making the movement of goods and services more open and efficient can put a lot of bad guys out of business. Criminals have a vested interest, not being particularly innovative, in devising and maintaining a profitable status quo consisting of allegedly tough controls feebly exercised. That is more or less the position today, in part because it is so difficult administratively to make the controls work even in reasonably well-governed countries.

The networked entrepreneurial criminals are not as well known as the organized groups, which have often emerged from the dark history of their countries of origin. Older than Rothschilds or Lazards, they have been in the business of unorthodox money-making for centuries. The Japanese Yakuza's origins go back to the sixteenth century. A very nationalistic organization, they helped the Emperor to destroy political opponents before the Second World War; their patriotic credentials for many years helped to protect them from police harassment. The heavily tattooed Yakuza or Boryokudan ('the violent ones') have infiltrated business through almost a thousand networked gangs in their most important groupings. They run protection rackets, dig deep into the profits from public-sector construction projects and extort funds from Japanese corporations abroad as well as at home. They have invested heavily in real estate and manipulated the stock market. From the 1960s onwards, they sank some of their money into the tourist trade in Asia and the western US.

The Chinese Triads have roots in sixteenth-century history and are particularly strong in the south of the country. Originally a resistance movement against the Manchu invaders of the Qing dynasty, they are reputed to have at least 160,000 members worldwide divided between a number of groups – the 14K, the Sun Yee On and the Wo Shing Wo. We battled them reasonably successfully in Hong Kong; Taiwan, where a gang called the United Bamboo is based, and Macau, with its lucrative casino, had more problems. Triads operate from the world's Chinatowns and make their biggest profits from trafficking heroin from the Golden Triangle (parts of Burma, Laos and Thailand), controlled historically by the armies of drug lords who were originally members of Chiang Kai-shek's army and were covertly supported during the Cold War by the CIA.[4]

The Mafia is most people's idea of what organized crime is like, doubtless in part thanks to Hollywood. The Mafia came from the deepest caves of Sicilian history, developing rapidly in the nineteenth century. They too have attempted to demonstrate their strong nationalist sympathies, in modern Sicily breaking off ties with an Albanian group when told it was terrorist, and in wartime America guarding the waterfront against German sabotage. The Mafia deeply penetrated Italian politics, business, banking and the state, and even the Vatican's

Banco Ambrosiano. The seven-time Italian prime minister Giulio Andreotti was twice stripped of his parliamentary immunity because of charges that he had collaborated with the Mafia. They developed successful international operations, striking a deal for example with the Medellín cartel in Colombia under which heroin was traded for cocaine. They were also involved in the spectacular mushrooming of criminal activity in Russia after the dismemberment of the Soviet Union. The disintegration of the Christian Democrats and much of the rest of the traditional party structure in the early 1990s helped restore to the Italian state the ability to tackle the Mafia. Its efforts were contested by Mafia violence and the brutal slayings of leading figures in the struggle against it. This helped strengthen public support for a campaign against pervasive criminality, which had a number of successes including the arrest and imprisonment of Toto Riina, the vicious *capo di tutti capi*. Other Mafia bosses such as Bernardo Provenzano and Salvatore Lo Piccolo have been captured more recently.

Ferocious and pervasive criminality flourished amidst the wreckage of communism in the late 1980s and early 1990s. Criminal organizations were not new in Russia. The *vorovskoi mir* ('thieves' world') had survived the tsarist and Soviet states, despite Stalin's repression in the 1950s, a shade ironic given his recruitment of gangsters into the secret police in the early days of the revolution. But these traditional bandits were not at the heart of the pillaging of Russia by former members of the Soviet nomenklatura, robber-baron capitalists and ethnic mobs, like the hated Chechens. 'Where does the mafia take its source from?' asked Boris Yeltsin's first press secretary, Pavel Voshchanov. 'This is simple, it begins with the common interests of politicians, business people, and gangsters. All others are hostages of this unholy alliance – all others means us.' Liberalization of the economy between 1987 and 1993, added to privatization, produced a feral capitalist free-for-all in a society without the rule of law or functioning regulatory institutions. Moreover, the splintering of the Soviet Union into its constituent republics provided easy pickings for smugglers and other criminals. Strategic metals were freighted from central Russia in unmarked trucks and military aircraft to the Baltic ports. Once the goods stolen from a Russian factory crossed the border into a new republic they were regarded as legal. Estonia was at one time exporting half a million dollars' worth of finished metals a day, though it had no metal plant. Soviet gold and currency reserves were filched, and the secret foreign accounts of the Communist Party disappeared.[5] It took only a small part of this loot to buy Russia on the cheap, in operations that combined corrupt alliances between the officials of the ancien régime and the new warlords of capitalism. When necessary, violence and murder brokered or sustained some of these spectacularly lucrative deals. The proceeds today are available to buy football clubs, yachts almost the size of aircraft carriers, property from London's Knightsbridge to Montenegro's coast, protection squads and prostitutes. As the British journalist Simon Jenkins has observed, Russians today regard London rather as Americans viewed pre-Castro Havana, though in Britain's case the playground for high rollers is mostly under the rule of law. Banks have been central to many of these criminal conspiracies. In congressional testimony in 1994 it was claimed that about 40 per cent of Russia's banks were controlled by organized crime. Russian capital – often illegally transferred, as happened in one notorious case through the Bank of New York in 1999 – has been at the heart of global crime and spectacular scams, like some of those allegedly operated from safe havens by Marc Rich, infamously pardoned by President Clinton in the dying days of his presidency for who knows what reason. Claire Sterling has meticulously described the biggest scam of all in 1990–92, involving the Sicilian mafia and other criminal groups and the complicity of Russian government contacts and perhaps Western intelligence agencies.[6] The plan triggered the devaluation of the ruble by buying billions of them in Russia with 'dirty' dollars and unloading them at a knockdown price on world markets. With the ruble devalued it was easier to buy up Russian assets and commodities and packages of privatization vouchers from individual citizens. It is difficult to distinguish between the early 'liberalization' of the Russian economy and robbery. Maybe the rise in the price of oil has saved Russia from existing largely as a gangster economy . . . or maybe not.

The entwining of organized crime, nationalist politics and states in turmoil has been on notorious view in the Balkans since Yugoslavia came apart at the ethnic seams. In Kosovo, organized crime and political corruption went hand in hand, with the widespread Albanian diaspora procuring arms and setting up distribution deals for local criminals closely associated with the Kosovo Liberation Army (KLA). The KLA have turned their hand to a variety of enterprises from prostitution to petrol monopolies to high-level kidnappings and extortion. Organized crime has also profited in Kosovo from servicing the international community in the country, including the foreign police forces, with brothels and drugs. Similar connections between organized crime and nationalist politics have been seen in Bosnia and Herzegovina. Smuggling arms, drugs and people has been a mainstay of this relationship. In his role as the international community's high representative in Bosnia and Herzegovina, Lord Ashdown worked strenuously to establish a functioning police and legal system in order to disrupt endemic criminality that holds back the country's economic and political progress. He has observed that it does not require rocket science to see how important it is to connect good investigative community policing with a functioning court system and secure prisons. In the post-conflict state building of the last few years, the international community has been bad at putting in place the infrastructure of the rule of law. But that is invariably required far more urgently than the deployment of more soldiers such as NATO peacekeepers. In Kosovo at one point after its liberation from Serbia, twenty-seven different nations were trying with their military forces to conduct policing operations; unfortunately they were unable to agree on basic questions like the definition of murder. When the Germans handed over control of prisons in Kosovo to the UN police force they took away everything with them except the prisoners and the bare walls of their jails. Even the barbed wire was taken home. During my five years as a European Commissioner, responsible among other things for trying to cajole, encourage, push and threaten the former states of Yugoslavia along the road to membership of the European Union, it was often apparent that the main obstacle was organized crime, from cigarette smuggling in Montenegro to human trafficking in Serbia. Too often in Brussels we pretended to believe the promises that were made by Balkan governments about law enforcement, corruption and organized crime, when in fact we and they knew that the promises were like piecrust. Crime is one of the main impediments to enlargement of the European Union in south-east Europe. Despite Bulgaria's woeful record of crime and corruption, which starred some of the country's steroid-filled former wrestling champions, it gained membership of the EU in 2004, promising that it had cleaned up its act. At least it could be accepted that Bulgarians were not as notoriously tough as, say, Serbians.[7]

The relations between traditional organized criminal groups and more recent networked criminals on the one hand, and certain states on the other, bear an uncanny similarity – for all the modern technology that is used these days – to much earlier times. The robber barons who rampaged in the thirteenth and fourteenth centuries across the area of France where I have a home on the frontiers of Languedoc would have understood what is going on. What we have today is medievalism with a BlackBerry. The sort of states that are accomplices to crime (like Surinam) are really sovereignty shells, unable to exercise much sovereign control at all, unable to use it in parts of their alleged jurisdiction, or prepared to sell aspects of it on the market. Of course, as noted in Chapter 2, the state itself originated as a kind of criminal operation. States were once protection rackets, focused on their survival and on the succession to the existing ruler. Their main activities were organized theft and violence. The road from there to political communities was by no means straight; nor did every road lead to the same place. When the young American republic wanted in the early nineteenth century to put an end to the Barbary Pirates, she did not attack the pirates; she attacked the port and palace of the Bey of Tripoli who exercised authority over them. What differentiates the old Bey of Tripoli from the modern sovereignty shell is the way in which sovereignty is used. A sovereignty shell does not exercise authority over anyone or anything; what it is about is preventing anyone else from doing so. So the small state of Surinam on the northern coast of South America provides a safe trans-shipment haven for drug dealers, exporting cocaine from there to the Netherlands, for example. Tajikistan performs a similar role in the drug trade to Europe. Afghanistan under the Taleban exercised fundamentalist religious authority over people, and was even able to limit poppy cultivation. But its principal manifestation of sovereignty was to give al-Qaeda protection and to deny external circumscription of that organization's activities. Afghanistan became not so much a state that supported terrorism as a terrorist cabal that owned a state. Somalia, the most clearly failed of all failed states – torn apart by warlords and jihadist groups – has provided a haven for a wave of piracy that has threatened merchant shipping far off the Horn and brought in the naval vessels of several countries to patrol this danger zone.

The CIA in its 2004 annual report to Congress identified fifty regions or countries around the world where the central government exerted vestigial control at best, and where there was a welcoming environment for smuggling transnational criminals and terrorists. These are places where sovereignty had been completely or partially hollowed out. There are many examples: the jungles and coca fields of Colombia, where the terrorist FARC organization stays in business; the Niger delta with its oil rigs; the already mentioned coltan-producing areas of Congo. In each of these areas, any attempt to step in and impose order quickly leads to the manufacture or exaggeration of some political grievance or other. The hacking, shooting, looting and burning that result can usually be explained away in parts of the West by apologists citing, if they want to impress and have a social-science degree, some highly developed Rawlsian notion of distributive justice or perhaps a Gramscian concern for proletarian revolt.

In some states sovereignty is withdrawn from one area so that it becomes a legal black hole in the regional and global economy. Take, for example, the city of Ciudad del Este, a Paraguayan city at that country's triple frontier with Brazil and Argentina. It is a market at the crossroads for every sort of illicit trade. In 1997 the city recycled an estimated $45 billion in drugs money. It was assisted by the fifty banks that operate in a city of 300,000 inhabitants. As Moisés Naím has written in his excellent book *Illicit*, 'What makes towns like Ciudad del Este attractive for business is that regulations are weak, governments are passive, and law enforcement is irrelevant or on the take ... They provide either a service ..., a product ..., or a commodity ... that the rest of the world wants in spades.'[8]

There are also 'courtesan states' where sovereignty is up for sale, a valuable commodity which is floated on the open market. Some centuries ago the Swiss pioneered the idea of renting out part of the state as well-drilled, heavily armed mercenaries. The Swiss do not do anything so crude these days, though they have profited mightily in the past from allowing the state to be used as a haven for banking and for the salting away in secret deposit accounts of all sorts of loot. African dictators and retired KGB agents have followed as clandestine depositors in the footsteps of Nazi thugs. Tuvalu, a Pacific island nation, goes further, though it does less harm. It licenses its internet suffix, 'tv', for a fee, as well as its international telephone code, 688, for phone sex. The Cayman Islands happily transform their one possession, sovereignty, into a very marketable asset. With a population of just 48,000 the Caymans host some 600 banks (including most of the world's top 50), 6,000 mutual funds, tens of thousands of offshore businesses and a range of innovative financial services. Under strong international pressure both the Cayman Islands and Switzerland have been a bit more cooperative in recent years with foreign law-enforcement agencies.

In many countries, of course, corruption both liberates criminality and enables it to grow and prosper by infiltrating and weakening the institutions of the state, including law-enforcement agencies. Corruption can take a number of forms. The most obvious inducement to connive at, take part in or ignore criminal behaviour is money, but drugs and prostitutes are also commonly supplied. Threats to use compromising information or violence are also commonplace. Sometimes gangs have penetrated governments and placed their own members in sensitive positions. In order to steal Canadian travel documents, Chinese Triads got a sympathizer recruited into the consular section of the Canadian Consulate in Hong Kong.[9] Western security services have inevitably worried about al-Qaeda's possible recruitment of Pakistani officials who sympathize with their cause.

The relationship between organized crime and politics can lead to the disintegration of democracies, with criminals using bribery, exposure, extortion and violence to weave a web of silence, influence and freedom from prosecution around their activities. Sometimes the relationship surfaces as it has done in Italy and Japan. In 1997, the Japanese minister of defence, who was suspected of involvement in a number of joint business ventures with Yakuza groups, was attacked and injured by two gang members. There had apparently been a row with him about his role in securing a large bank loan for a developer for the Yakuza's benefit; 200 million yen disappeared during this dispute.[10] As well as undermining democracies, crime distorts their economies, tilting the playing field against legitimate business activities.

Beginning in the early and mid-nineteenth century the Mafia successfully corrupted state institutions in Sicily and the south of Italy, where the legal infrastructure was weak and respect for the law was low. Extortion and protection were widely employed as the Mafia expanded out of the southern regions of Italy into the rest of the country in the years before the Second World War. It also moved abroad to North America, Latin America, North Africa and elsewhere in Europe. The Italian government has been engaged in a struggle for over two decades to isolate and stamp out the Mafia, a task made much more difficult because of the hollowing out of state institutions through graft, complicity and violence. The Mafia's commercial activities still range wide, from refuse collection in Naples to the import of counterfeit goods from Asia to the fashion business in Milan. Democratic politics and the rule of law have survived in Italy, thanks to the bravery of a few individuals; but it was a close-run thing and, given the recent stinking shambles over refuse collection in Naples, perhaps remains so.

Colombia had been one of the most stable democracies in Latin America, but it was overwhelmed in the 1970s by the Medellín and Cali drug cartels, who made huge profits from the sale of cocaine. They murdered and bribed their way into controlling some of the institutions that were meant to control them, eroding the foundations of the government's legitimacy. They corrupted democratic politics, as others have done elsewhere, paying for local and national election campaigns and supporting criminal leaders for election to public office. One drug baron, Carlos Lehder, actually organized his own (fortunately unsuccessful) political party, the Latin Nationalist Movement. Colombia's President Alvaro Uribe has tried to regain control of his country from the terrorists of the left, the paramilitaries of the right and the drug barons. It is a pretty thankless task and, in attempting it, Uribe has arguably been too soft on the paramilitaries who, like their left-wing foes, are certainly involved in drugs themselves. But Uribe does not deserve the routine criticisms to which he is subjected by the European left, and was re-elected in 2006 with over 60 per cent of the vote. His party has been tainted by its association with paramilitary groups, but at least the paramilitaries and some of their sympathizers are being pursued by prosecutors and the courts for their alleged criminal activities and associations. Moreover, Uribe has not interfered in the election process which has seen moderate left-wing opponents elected in Bogotá and elsewhere. Elections have successfully taken place in areas where the left-wing guerrillas (the FARC) tried to ban them. Uribe is not a hand-wringing liberal or left-winger. He is a tough fellow, a bit like the former Spanish prime minister, José María Aznar – perhaps more open to discussion than Aznar was. The first time I met him, as a European Commissioner, was in Bogotá, the improbably handsome capital of what should be a prosperous and influential country. Whatever its other problems, Colombia has never reneged on its debts and has a strong intellectual tradition. Uribe talked understandingly about some of the criticisms made of him but put up a stout defence. If I were a Colombian, I think I would see the attractions of having a strong but democratic president like Uribe. Flexibility may be a rather overrated virtue when dealing with the sort of problems he has on his plate. He has done more than might have been predicted to make Colombia a rather safer and more governable country, but it may well be that its most likely salvation is a future preference in American and European drug markets for amphetamines over cocaine.

Corruption can go right to the top. Peru's President Alberto Fujimori had a security chief, Vladimiro Montesinos, who worked hand in hand with the CIA and the US Drug Enforcement Agency. The discovery of swag worth $70 million, linked to Montesinos, helped to precipitate Fujimori's flight from office. In the Philippines, President Joseph Estrada was driven from the presidential palace and imprisoned after he was discovered to have opened a $10-million trust account in the name of 'José Velarde'. The Lithuanian president Rolandas Paksas was impeached in 2004 for taking money from Russian organized crime. The Governor of Illinois, Rod Blagojevich, was impeached in January 2009, charged with several federal offences including attempting to sell Barack Obama's vacant US Senate seat. Days after his removal from office Blagojevich, a former amateur wrestler, was offered the job of chairman of the 'Main Event Mafia' branch of a wrestling company.

Postmodern criminal entrepreneurs meet every market demand from the disposal of hazardous waste to the sale of child pornography. Making, shipping and selling counterfeit goods provides an especially lucrative business. Car parts, watches, software, designer-label clothes, medicines – all those products and more are faked and sold, costing American companies $200–250 billion a year in lost revenue and, according to the European Union, about 100,000 jobs in its member states. The US claims to have lost 750,000 jobs for the same reason. You can watch the video of a new feature film before it has been publicly released, buy a fake Rolex so well made that even the company finds it difficult to spot the difference, and purchase fake Viagra, made in China and distributed through India, on the internet. Counterfeit medicines, the World Health Organization estimates, comprise at least 10 per cent of the world's drug supply. By 2010 the Centre for Medicines in the Public Interest reckons that their global value may be up to $75 billion. These drugs can be extremely dangerous, containing either no active ingredient, the wrong one, or contaminants. Counterfeiting is most prevalent in those regions where the regulatory and legal oversight is weakest. In Africa and parts of Asia and Latin America more than 30 per cent of medicines on sale are counterfeit. In China, one newspaper in 2001 estimated (on what basis is unclear) that fake drugs had caused 192,000 deaths in the country that year. Fake car and even aeroplane parts also carry obvious risks to public safety. The terrorists responsible for the Atocha station bombings in Madrid in 2004 had been operating a counterfeit CD business. Hezbollah, the Basque ETA and the IRA are all believed to have made money out of counterfeit goods.[11]

Apart from a Hermès bag or Gucci sunglasses, what else do you want? After drugs, the sale of ozone-depleting chlorofluorocarbons (CFCs) is thought to be the second biggest illicit import into the United States. You can dump radioactive material in Somalia or mercury-laced ash in Cambodia. You can buy endangered species – dead or alive: tigers, leopards, anteaters. Your boa constrictors may arrive, as happened at Miami airport, stuffed with condoms full of cocaine. Ivory is readily available in China, Singapore, Thailand and Congo, for those not too bothered about a few more elephants being shot by poachers. Stolen art may be more difficult to fence, but probably not antique furniture or antiquities, which have even been known to turn up in New York in the Peruvian diplomatic pouch. And then there are body parts.

George Soros has frequently pointed out that, left to their own devices, markets can promiscuously reduce anything to the state of commodities. So when in the United States, for example, there are said to be over 101,000 people on various organ waiting lists, and when – taking the latest figures – about nineteen people a day, approximately 7,000 in all in a year, die for want of an organ, it is not very surprising that organ cannibalism (much of it illicit) has turned into such a lucrative trade.[12] With organ transplantation now much more common and successful – of kidneys, for example – the international market has grown fast, with most of the supply of living organs coming from the poor south of the globe to meet demand in the north. Japanese Yakuza gangsters – called the 'body mafia' – have been prominent in the kidney trade. There has been growing controversy about the purchase of organs obtained without consent from executed prisoners in Taiwan and Singapore, but most notably in China. Human rights activists claim that the incontinent use of the death penalty there has led to a brisk trade in kidneys, corneas, liver tissue and heart valves, with organs being sold to foreigners at a going rate of between $10,000 and $13,000. Cairo is an established centre for kidney transplants, with many of the donors coming from Sudan, Somalia and Ethiopia. But despite a law banning the trade in organs, India has become the biggest centre of the business; so much so that it is called the kidney belt. There is an underground organ bazaar controlled by gangs moving on from heroin to kidneys and other body parts. Many of the customers come from the Gulf States. Mumbai and Chennai do much of the business, with brokers bringing together patients and impoverished donors for fees of up to $1,000. The donors themselves may make about the same or a bit more, which goes to cancel debts, help a family through an emergency, buy food, or pay for a dowry. One Chennai slum is called Kidney Vakkam because of the large role played by organ sales in the local economy. There have been reports in countries from Brazil to central Asia of forcible organ removals. In Europe, the transplant mafia is based in the former Soviet

Union providing, in particular, illicit organ donors from Moldova to the US and Israel.

The organ trade is everywhere associated with the smuggling and illicit trafficking of whole human beings. These twin criminal endeavours are different but related, and the first can easily merge into the second. People are smuggled because they wish to enter another country but are barred by its border and labour market controls from doing so. They pay to be slipped covertly under and over the fence. A one-way boat ticket from the African coast to the Canary Islands costs 1,000 euros or more. Those who are illicitly trafficked are frequently in effect slaves – women forced into prostitution; men, women and children sold into domestic service or sweatshop employment. Some of the smuggled fetch up as virtual slaves, obliged – in order to pay back the cost of their illegal passage – to work for low wages in hard jobs: washing dishes in a restaurant in one of a hundred affluent Chinatowns, stitching pieces of fabric together in a garment factory, picking cockles by the thousand off a beach at low tide. This flood of migrants responds to the demands of the market – the overall labour market and niche markets for particular services. At the heart of the phenomenon of modern migration is a very simple proposition. If there are too many people in location A, and too few people in location B without the ability to look after all their needs, and if the means also exist by which people know about this state of affairs, are informed of better conditions in location B and can find a way of acting on this information, then it naturally follows that they will attempt to do exactly this. The resulting movement has sometimes produced good results, sometimes bad; it rather depends on your vantage point. The movement of Americans westwards across North America was bad news for Amerindians and Mexicans; the movement of Europeans westwards to the US was good news for Americans.

It should not surprise us that many people today are struggling to gain access to Europe and the US. In their countries of origin, there is likely to be overpopulation (in particular, a youth bulge as in North Africa and the Middle East), high unemployment, political instability or repression, ecological problems and disasters, and a low standard of living. These are problems which, in Africa in particular and in south Asia too, result in population movements between the poor countries of the south. But the main pressures are from south to north, from poor to rich. In North America and Europe we make what are in historical terms unprecedented efforts to limit or even halt this movement. In Europe this happens despite the fact that our population overall is set to decline steeply over the first half of the century. We live longer and have fewer babies. In the poor countries that border the EU, and in the countries of origin for migrants from further away, there are too many young people; in Europe there are too few young people and the problem is becoming more pronounced. Our political institutions seem incapable of dealing rationally with the issue. So, the grim business of the smuggling and illicit trafficking of people expands, and the European economy – the same is true in the US – rests at the bottom on a silent, invisible mass of people with no legal protection. On the one hand, labour market needs in some European countries argue for more immigration and less-tight control; on the other hand, we worry about the dilution of our identity as migration expands the non-native numbers in the European population. We also have genuine concerns about the pressure on public services in some of the most prosperous parts of our continent and about the impact on the employment prospects of existing immigrants of new waves of immigration. These concerns are likely to rise in the current economic downturn.

In the meantime the trade in people grows, with the UN estimating that it is now the third largest moneymaker for criminals, behind drugs and weapons, though no one really knows just how valuable it is. The UN Office on Drugs and Crime estimates the figure at $7 billion annually; the UN Children's Fund puts the figure for the 1.2 million children a year illicitly trafficked much higher at $10 billion. For the EU an annual estimate of $8.5 to $12 billion is put on this low-cost business. The estimates of the International Labour Organization (ILO) are that the annual profits from trafficked forced labour run at over $30 billion. The figures could all be much higher, especially given estimates that human smuggling out of China alone, organized by the so-called 'snakeheads', is worth between $1 and $3 billion annually. While exact figures remain unclear, there is general agreement that the unregulated inveiglement and movement of human capital is a very big and rapidly growing business.

The UN has suggested that up to 200 million people may be in other countries as a result of trafficking. About 3 per cent of the world's population – 175 million people – are documented international migrants. Half as many again are thought to be migrants without documents. Then there are about 11.4 million refugees and 26 million internally displaced persons, and a large number of internal migrants, typically – for instance, in China – peasants moving into the cities. In the USA over 10 per cent of the population is foreign born; the figure is about the same in the EU for non-EU-born residents.[13] Legal movement has become easier with falling costs for more widely available air travel. Illegal movement is usually less orthodox and much less safe, with both the forcibly and the voluntarily moved migrants paying a heavy physical and emotional price. They suffer mental strain and physical violence and frequently run the risk of injury and death. In 2000, to give one tiny example, fifty-eight smuggled Chinese men and women, who had been flown initially from Beijing to Belgrade, and then moved by car or lorry through Hungary, Austria and France to the Netherlands, died in the heat of the sealed container into which they were shoe-horned on arrival in that country. The bodies were found on a hot June day when the truck was searched in Dover. It is reckoned that between 100,000 and 120,000 migrants cross the sea to Europe every year in rusting hulks and open boats. They head to the Canary Islands, southern Spain, Malta, the southern Italian islands of Lampedusa, Pantelleria and Sicily, as well as to the mainland Italian coast itself. In May 2007 twenty-seven migrants whose boat had fallen apart spent three days in the water clinging to the tuna fishing nets behind a Maltese fishing vessel. Two months later fifty died after their boat capsized south of the Canary Islands.

But most illegal entries and human trafficking into Europe (and into the United States) are along land routes. One of the most used lies through the Balkans, crossing this region from Turkey and terminating in Germany. The Albanian mafia is dominant in these countries of passage, combining illicit trafficking with the sale of drugs and exploiting the migrants when they have reached their destination. A second preferred route has gone through the Baltic states since the collapse of the Soviet Union. It connects the Asiatic countries with Russia, Scandinavia, Poland and the heart of Europe. The Russian mafia has been particularly active in this trade, falsifying visas and other documents and corrupting police and immigration services.

The scale of the problem of illicit trafficking can be seen along many of Europe's roads, driving from Rome to Naples or from Prague to the German border, or travelling along highway E55 on northern Bohemia's Czech–German border. Prostitutes line the roadsides, warming themselves on winter nights next to blazing braziers. This is a sharp reminder of the distinction between illicit trafficking and smuggling, because many of these women have been forced into prostitution; they are the victims of what is in effect a slave trade. Two centuries after its abolition by the British Empire (Britain even built a special class of vessels to interdict the trade) there are an estimated 27 million men, women and children who are enslaved – controlled through violence or their indebtedness, forced to work, often physically confined. The UN reckons that 100,000 of them work in the USA as prostitutes, 200,000 in the EU and 50,000 in Japan. Women, children and young men too are trafficked for sex, with about two-thirds of the women working in the sex industry in Germany, for example, coming from eastern Europe and a third from Asia and Africa. But the main reason for trafficking is not sexual exploitation but general demand for low-cost labour. A study in 2005 by the ILO suggested that of the estimated 9.5 million victims of forced labour in Asia, less than 10 per cent were trafficked for commercial sex. Labour trafficking forces people into oppressive domestic work, farming, the fishing industry, the construction and restaurant businesses, mining and manufacturing. In some parts of the world it is difficult to get a real grip on the dimensions of the problem. In Thailand, since men cannot qualify as trafficking victims, they are excluded from the statistics. There is no evidence that tougher border controls stop trafficking, indeed if anything the reverse seems to be true as desperate people turn to criminals to help them get out of their own country. Nor do the few convictions that are secured deter traffickers who make so much money from the grim business. Women or children forced into prostitution earn between $120,000 and $150,000 for the criminal syndicates that control them. This 'meat trade', which is in some respects (as David Feingold has said) 'migration gone terribly wrong', is going to be difficult to stamp out without more and better coordinated action by the countries of origin and the countries of demand.[14] Nothing, however, will ever stamp out the dreams of bright lights and big cities. They are often illusory, but there are also in every generation many migrants who claw a prosperous and successful life for themselves and their families out of the rocky terrain, risking all and gaining much in return.

This brings me back to the hole at the centre of the debate about migration, immigration and the criminal activities associated with the movement of people. Criminality is often meeting demands that we refuse to choke off by more resolute domestic measures or by being more realistic and open about our labour requirements. If demand for labour cannot be met domestically, and an increase in pay fails to meet the demand through the recruitment of locals, then you either have to do without the service or activity, move it offshore where you can, or allow the immigration of the people required to do the job. Where employers seek to undercut the standards of employment or the rates of pay they are legally obliged to provide, they should be hit with far tougher penalties than are usually sanctioned. The use of the illegal service in this case should be as much of a criminal act as its provision, and in the case of prostitution either legalization or focusing prosecution on the client rather than the prostitute appear to offer better ways of reducing illegal trafficking for sex than those presently and inadequately applied.

America's growth rate is partly driven by immigration. Legal immigration runs at about 1.2 million a year; the figure for illegals is slightly lower. Some European countries need more immigrants to sustain their desired standard of living as their population ages and falls. Naturally, the EU states will have to be more effective in the training and education of their existing workforce, and more flexible with regard to retirement. But even success in those areas is not going to abate the need for more migrant labour in some places. In Britain, for example, there has been a need for economic migration from outside the EU to fill certain jobs. Half of all newly registered doctors and nurses in recent years have come from outside Europe. In the decade from 1997 to 2007, 1.5 million new jobs were filled by these migrants – a fifth of them in the public services, and a further fifth in jobs in banking and insurance. However, even a country that has absorbed so many migrants cannot simply leave policy to the labour market. Government should set rules and regulations on employment standards and remuneration. This should go hand in hand with publicly debated ceilings on immigration levels. This is not racist. Britain has become an increasingly multiracial society. To leave everything to the market, with no control, undercuts the worst-paid jobs often done by the last wave of immigrants and does put pressure on some overstretched services which are often themselves staffed by recent immigrants. The focus on employment skills raises an important developmental issue. To limit our intake of migrants to those possessing the skills we want constitutes a kind of unofficial tax on the Third World. We are willing to accept people whom poor countries have spent time and resources training, but do not seem able to offer those opportunities ourselves to people already living in our own countries. While any attempt at central planning of labour is doomed to fail, there is a lot to be said for trying to relate our own development policies a bit more closely to our transient demands for skills. We might consider training more of the unskilled from poor countries (if we cannot train enough of our own citizens) on the contractual understanding that on completion of their training they would work for a limited period in our country before returning to theirs.

The size of a country matters and so does population density. America reminds us that it is not only skilled migrants who help create prosperity. The US has benefited over the centuries from highly skilled migrants – its post-war golden age was fuelled by a mighty host of European intellectuals and scientists – but over the long term, it is poor huddled masses, yearning to breathe free, who have built and shaped the nation. Chaos, movement, clutter and progress are the music of capitalism – the rustling and shuffling of papers in immigration bureaus is no substitute. Community harmony and fairness to the host population mean, alas, that you cannot do without them.

Organized crime casts an interesting light on how we allow markets to operate, and on the values we still practise as well as enunciate, nowhere more so than in this area of illicit trafficking. When we debate immigration and the movement of people around the world are we still confident that liberalism and humanism are the currency of the West? Sometimes it seems that the muddled populism that so frequently dictates the policies we follow demonstrates that liberalism and humanism are just as radical today as they were 250 years ago. It can still appear radical to argue that migrants are not possessed of a fundamental essence different from our own; that Western values are human values that transcend racial or national identities; that individuals, left to their own devices, will usually pursue what is good; that there are no limits on prosperity; that free people and free markets will never cease creating; that human potential acknowledges no bounds. Do we still believe all this? From time to time, perhaps.

The numbers on illicit trafficking, counterfeiting, arms dealing – depressing as they are – explain why crime is such a compelling endeavour. People make a lot of money out of it, even states can make a lot out of it, or benefit from other effects (such as loose regulatory frameworks) to such an extent that they have no real interest in stopping it. Generally, in the battle between politics and the market, the market wins. There are exceptions – the piracy and slaving in the nineteenth century noted earlier, for example – but in general life goes on. People make money doing whatever it is they do; other people make money trying to stop them doing whatever it is they do. It is for clerics and statesmen to set the proper tone for the whole struggle. But we could do better in containing and reducing international crime, starting with more effective measures to deal with its financing and the movement and banking of its profits.

In the aftermath of 9/11 we worried about the transfer of money around the world from one Muslim community to another through the medium of *hawalas*. Like the Chinese *fie chen* (flying money), *hawalas* allow a migrant worker in Abu Dhabi or Bradford to transfer money home, by giving cash to someone he trusts where he is working who in turn gives instructions to a colleague to release a similar sum of money in the worker's country of origin minus commission. The exchanges can be made in cash or kind. *Hawalas* are clearly both useful and difficult to control. They can obviously be used to transfer money for criminals and terrorists. But how effective is it to try to block this particular financing channel? After all, the ending of foreign exchange controls, the liberalizing of financial markets, the introduction of electronic transfers and credit cards have given so many opportunities to terrorists. The men who financed the means to bring down the Twin Towers paid on their Visa cards. The sophisticated financial services once located in those iconic buildings in New York can be exploited by criminals and terrorists as well as by those who spin the wheels of global commerce.

The global daily volume of currency exchanged now exceeds $3 trillion. Competition for investment and complexity of financial operations are hallmarks of global financing, with information technology driving the market forward, allowing money launderers as well as fund managers to make instantaneous transactions from almost anywhere in the world. No wonder even the roughest estimates for the scale of money laundering are so difficult to make: they vary from $800 billion to $2 trillion a year, with some experts suggesting that laundered money could represent as much as 10 per cent of the world's GDP. Nor has it always been necessary to go offshore to some Caribbean or Pacific island to wash through the cash. The USA and the UK – both of which have tightened up their regulations recently – have provided onshore services for money launderers in the past, for example Nigeria's dictator General Abacha in London in the 1990s. In any event, money laundering is exceptionally difficult to stop, with the availability of front companies, cash-intensive and legal commercial operations, the internet, e-commerce, emerging markets and so on.

There has been a relatively high level of international cooperation to deal with money laundering; more still needs to be done. A former special adviser to the US Treasury, William F. Wechsler, suggested in 2001 that money laundering havens all share certain characteristics: lack of transparency, the absence of effective exchange of information, 'ring fencing' regimes which subject foreign investors to very different rules from domestic ones, and negligible or non-existent effective tax rates.[15] Fixing the problem accurately described by Wechsler has been difficult. In 1988 the UN passed the Vienna Convention on drug trafficking, which required participating states to criminalize money laundering and cooperate in investigations and extraditions; in 1989, the G7 devised the Financial Action Task Force (FATF: basically a small secretariat) which acts as a financial 'peer review' body; and there is in addition the Basel Committee on Banking Supervision. In 2000 the FATF declared twenty-nine offshore jurisdictions financially deficient, and labelled the fifteen worst 'non-cooperative countries and territories'. The OECD backed this up with its own list of tax havens, and the G7 threatened sanctions against the worst offenders. The result was that several states – for instance, the Bahamas, Cayman Islands, Cook Islands, Israel, Liechtenstein, the Marshall Islands and Panama – all took steps to comply with emerging standards. (It is worth nothing that not all the OECD or FATF countries were totally compliant with the standards that they themselves promulgated.) Following the attacks of 9/11, the USA made banking one of the front lines in the war on terror, with the Bush administration going back on its earlier lack of enthusiasm for tighter supervision of international financial movement. This resulted in a UN Security Council resolution requiring UN states to criminalize the collection of funds for terrorist purposes and to freeze the assets of suspected terrorists.

There was a great deal of tough talking and states have generally responded sympathetically to sequestration requests. But the results of all this have been thin. Other efforts have included a drive by the IMF to catalogue and assess financial abuses, and the Financial Stability Forum (established by the G7 after the 1997 Asian financial crisis) has placed the issue of laundering high on its agenda. The fact is, however, that freezing terrorist or criminal assets has been a nightmare of competing jurisdictions, different regulatory frameworks and legal, financial and law-enforcement requirements which simply do not join up and through which money can still slip with relative ease.

What do we have? At the universal level there is a Security Council resolution and a vague desire to avoid both the ravages of terrorism and the wrath of America, the OECD, the IMF and so on. Ideally, there ought to be a global consensus and a global organization commanding some degree of autonomy and respect, sustained by a global regime to which all states are signatories, or else sustained by and through the UN. At the present coalition level, the Basel Committee and the FATF are able occasionally to crack the whip over the heads of small players like the Cayman Islands. But even in the West there is little internal consistency on how to regulate and police the global monetary environment. The failure to develop broader like-minded coalitions makes it very difficult to place pressure upon the big regulatory no-go areas like Russia and China, let alone integrate them into a more effective regime. So it remains difficult to stem the tide of money laundering or to target terrorists and organized crime. To be more effective in dealing with international crime, there will have to be more regional and global cooperation in monitoring the movement of capital; this should not be regarded as an impediment to the market or a disincentive for investors. The financial crash will inevitably lead to much greater regulation and control of international capital flows, which should help to limit the financing of organized crime.

Similar pictures could be painted of all the major issues discussed in this chapter, from counterfeiting to people trafficking to arms dealing. They are invariably addressed in an ad hoc way with insufficient political commitment. Where we do create structures to deal with these problems at the world or regional level – like Interpol, Europol and Asianpol – we provide them with too little by way of resources and threadbare authority to require cooperation from their members even in the most important areas of their work. Individual governments are good at moral rhetoric and addicted to adrenaline-pumping task forces. They love creating tsars. They are not so keen on providing resources or facing up to some of the unpalatable choices necessary to contain – we will never eliminate – crime.

Consider, for example, two different aspects of security. After the Boxing Day tsunami in 2004, piracy in the Straits of Malacca – the most dangerous waters on earth – stopped. It began again on 8 February 2005. Was that the day the pirates got their boats fixed or filled up with petrol? Maybe this is what happened. But it is interesting that right up to 7 February the sea lanes here were bristling with naval vessels providing assistance to the tsunami victims. Sometimes the answer to criminality is to buy another cruiser or two, purchase another helicopter or invest taxpayers' money in sophisticated security technology from biometrics and radio frequency identification devices to chemical and biological tags and bigger and better security scanners. Voters have to pay for security; they need to be dissuaded from the view that Oxfam can right all the world's ills – admirable as it and other NGOs may be – for a tax-deductible twenty pounds a month.

Unfortunately recent experience suggests that public expenditure on security and low enforcement is likely to fall during an economic recession, precisely when such spending should increase given the historical rise in crime during times of economic turmoil. Since the 1950s waves of crime (particularly property crime and robbery) in the US have typically followed sharp economic downturns with a time lag of approximately one year. The present recession is already visible on Main Street, and in a different way on the internet, the pseudo-Main Street, too. There has already been a ratcheting up of cyber crime. A recent study by the security firm, McAfee, noted that cyber criminals were cashing in on the anxiety of some consumers to profit from 'get-rich-quick' old-fashioned scams. Sophos, a sister online security company, said it found a new infected website every 4.5 seconds. Governments do not appear to have focused on this problem.

Another example of decisive political action would be to establish or re-establish sovereignty in areas where it has been compromised, that is to do more state building. It is a hard battle, and it is not easy politics. It means putting people on the ground, military and civilian, after the initial conflict is over and after the elections are held. It sometimes means working with existing governments who are already democratic, or 'sort of' democratic. It means engaging in the arduous politics of reconstruction, much tougher than the politics of disaster relief.

An even more uphill battle is the domestic one in democracies. How do we curtail the market for crime? It may mean coming to terms with certain criminal activities, seeking a modus vivendi with others, and focusing more resources on the third group. We can see evidence of a modus vivendi in some areas already. The Apple approach to internet downloading, for instance, has brokered an effective ceasefire between the music industry, usually looking to charge more for music, and the public, which has shown a commendable willingness to switch from illegally downloaded music to legally downloaded music for which they pay a reasonable fee. Perhaps this demonstrates that most people do the right thing when they get the opportunity. Other areas which call for a sensible middle way are migration (where President Bush's proposals for an amnesty and the one actually granted by the Spanish government make excellent sense) and prostitution. Why do most governments still focus punishment on the prostitute and not the client? In an existential conflict between life and the law – over seeking a better life in another country or over sexual desire – either the law makes some accommodation, or it may actually enable or encourage the degradation or destruction of human life. The most important and controversial search for a more balanced and effective approach comes in the area where crime pays most of all: the production, trafficking, sale and use of illegal drugs. We turn to that subject in the next chapter.

However much we summon the political will to conduct a more effective global campaign against crime, stuff will continue to happen. Why? Well, in the words of Walt Kelly's comic strip character Pogo, we have met the enemy and he is us. It is our laws which help put trafficked women in such a terrible and impossible position. It is our cravings which fuel the vicious narcotics wars of South America, and put money into the pockets of terrorists on the Afghan–Pakistan border. It is our squeamishness which drives the organ trade. It is our perverse consumerism which worships and forbids sex at the same time. It is our desires as consumers that the counterfeiters fulfil. It is our shallow sense of retribution which fills prisons to bursting with all the small-time crooks who pursued careers of a sort trying to meet the irresponsible and irrepressible cravings of the law-abiding rest of us. When G. K. Chesterton was once asked who or what was responsible for the world's ills, he replied, 'I am.' What a very old-fashioned fellow Mr Chesterton must have been.

10

Hooked

Any bashful young man [should] take hashish when he wants to offer his heart to any fair lady, for it will give him the courage of a hero, the eloquence of a poet and ardour of an Italian.   Louisa May Alcott, author of *Little Women*

The idea of a drugs-free world, or even of a drugs-free Britain, is almost certainly a chimera.

Report of the Royal Society of Arts Commission on Illegal Drugs, Communities and Public Policy, 'Drugs – Facing Facts', March 2007

I left university at more or less the moment that marijuana arrived. For most of my generation, a joint was something that your mother put in the oven on Sundays. So I have never puffed, snorted or injected my contribution to the destruction of civilization as we know it, save for one rather disagreeable and humiliating sharing of a damp-ended spliff over forty years ago with a friend who is now a judge. I smoked; unlike a famous Oxford alumnus from America I inhaled; and I thought I was going to choke to death. Never again. I have stuck since then to healthier, more manly pursuits. I smoked – Virginia tobacco – quite heavily until I was forced by an ulcer to give up in my mid-thirties. I could never quite fathom why I did not feel better as a result. Oh, and I drink; I do not have a problem, you understand, but I do like both white and red wine – good for the heart, my cardiologist says, in the sort of moderate quantities that I would never dream of telling her I exceed.

We know, of course, that alcohol and tobacco – licit psychoactive substances – do more harm to users and the rest of society than those drugs deemed illicit, whether measured in terms of illness, fatalities or drug-induced violence. That is not a reason for legalizing cannabis, heroin, cocaine and amphetamines. Nor is it an excuse to play down the personal, social and political consequences of drug dependency. Addiction to heroin, for instance, can destroy an individual, torment his or her family, lead to a life of crime and incarceration and provide the market for a substance whose production and distribution thrive on and prolong chaos and criminality. But the figures on alcohol and tobacco do inject some shafts of rationality into a debate often conducted in the language of doom. In the United States, alcohol leads to over 20,000 deaths a year; in England and Wales the figure is about one third of that. Tobacco accounts directly for 445,000 deaths yearly in the US, and 82,000 in Britain. There were 6 million deaths from tobacco in Britain in the second half of the twentieth century, though neither tobacco nor alcohol is discussed in the apocalyptic terms invariably used in the debate on other drugs. We are fighting a war (but what else?) on drugs. They are an evil: public enemy number one. Our countries are being invaded by this moral and chemical pollution. Drug traffickers are as bad as the old slave traders (actually, as we noted in the last chapter, they are often modern-day slave traders too). Since drugs are so wicked, there is rarely any space for examining policy in terms of effectiveness and trade-offs. This is a war of absolutes and as such it is not going as well as the crusaders would like.

The UN has a rather different opinion. Some years ago it set itself the target of ridding the world of drugs by 2008. Although this somewhat fanciful ambition remains unachieved, it none the less claims recent progress in the struggle, not least if the longer view is taken. In the 2006 report of the UN Office on Drugs and Crime (UNODC), whose executive director is the admirable Antonio Maria Costa, it is argued that international drug control is one of the oldest forms of multilateralism, and that as a result the drug problem has been contained and reduced over the last hundred years. In a period during which the world population has quadrupled, opium production has fallen from 30,000 metric tons to about 9,000, of which 400 are for medicinal use. In China, there were 25 million opium users out of a population of 450 million just over a century ago. Today, in the far larger population of the whole of Asia, there are only 9.3 million users in all.

Opiates, cocaine and cannabis have a long history of use for recreational, religious, medical and aphrodisiac purposes. Opium may have been taken in Crete from as early as 2000 BC. Queen Victoria was prescribed cannabis to relieve her period pains. It was only during her reign that a larger-scale drug trade was initiated. Portuguese, Dutch and British opium traders had tried previously, despite a ban imposed in 1729, to sell this product from their colonial monopolies to China. In the following century they fought two wars to open up the China market, succeeding in mid-century by driving through the legalization of opium trading in 1858. Drug dealing on an industrial scale was not the greatest achievement of the British Empire, nor the finest expression of Victorian morality. But something had to be done to safeguard Britain's balance of trade in bullion, which was skewed heavily in China's favour. Britain needed silver to satisfy its own addiction to tea. So China was forced to open up to the sale of Indian opium, a less benign addiction.

Much followed from this 'great Disgrace', as Edmund Burke called it, including the acquisition of the colony at Hong Kong and the fabulous enrichment of British 'hongs' (firms) such as Jardine Matheson, builders of the new colony's first large stone building, an opium godown. God eventually triumphed over Mammon; an anti-opium movement motivated by religious and humanitarian ideals (with the Quakers playing a prominent role) developed in the later years of the nineteenth century. With American missionaries adding their enthusiasm to the cause, Britain agreed to cut its opium exports to China in 1907; the Chinese themselves began reducing their own poppy cultivation and in 1909 the first major international conference was held on drug trafficking in the suitably louche city of Shanghai. That was followed by the 1912 Hague Convention, the first international drug treaty, which committed signatories to prevent the export of raw opium to countries that had prohibited or restricted its importation.

Between the world wars the League of Nations Covenant granted the League supervisory powers over the trafficking of drugs, and subsequent treaties sought tougher means to suppress the growing illicit trade. The UN's first drug-control instrument was the Single Convention of 1961; this was followed by the 1971 Convention on Psychotropic Substances. A further Convention in 1988, the most comprehensive international drug law, focused on the criminalization of the supply of drugs – their production, sale and transportation – and on the laundering of the proceeds from drug-related activities.[1]

Celebrating the multilateral momentum of international drug cooperation over the past century is fair enough, though claiming modern successes by comparing the position at the beginning of this century with that at the outset of the last is a bit extravagant. The vast China market was hooked on drugs to bail out the Queen Empress's India. Attitudes changed dramatically in the twentieth century, though the use of opium in China continued at a high level during the twenties and thirties when the country was torn apart by civil war and the invasion by Japan. It took Mao and the anti-opium campaign of the 1950s to break the Chinese habit (which Mao's communists had not been averse to feeding a little earlier by clandestinely dabbling in opium manufacturing in Yunnan – where it was known as 'special product' – during their backs-to-the-wall fight against the Nationalists).[2]

Most of the world's opium comes from and is distributed centrally through two regions – the so-called 'Golden Triangle' in South-East Asia, with Burma/Myanmar and Laos at its heart, and the 'Golden Crescent' comprising Afghanistan and its neighbours. These are the areas from which most of the poppies come. At harvest time the fattened pods are lanced in the late afternoon and the white gum which oozes out is allowed to dry and blacken overnight before being scraped off by wide knives the following morning. Coca comes mainly from the Andean region: Colombia mainly, followed by Peru and Bolivia. The coca leaves are pounded and boiled with kerosene and lime water to make a paste. This is then mixed with chemical compounds such as potassium permanganate, filtered and dried so as to form a cocaine base. That is dissolved in acetone and finally strained, dried and pressed into bricks ready for shipping and snorting. Coca production provides probably the most graphic example of what is called the balloon effect in attempting to stamp out sources of drug supply. You make a big push in one country and production swells in another. Amphetamine-type stimulants (ATSs) including ecstasy are manufactured all round the world, though most ecstasy is produced in Europe. This is a hallucinogenic drug whose origins lie in German chemical synthesis research. It got its street name in California in the 1980s. Cannabis comes in two forms: the herb – marijuana – and the resin – hashish. It is grown everywhere – conceivably in that house down the street where the curtains are always pulled shut and which has large numbers of bin liners and tubs outside. Morocco still supplies most of Europe's hashish. It is easy to remember that kif, as the cannabis plant is called in Morocco, mostly comes from the Rif, the mountains in the north of the country, to produce the partygoer's spliff, a piece of originally German slang for the cannabis cigarette.

In its 2008 report UNODC saw reasons for encouragement in most markets and production areas. The area under coca cultivation has fallen by nearly a fifth on the figure in 2000 of around 221,000 hectares. In Afghanistan the area cultivated for poppies fell in the 1990s because of drought and a price crash, but has been rising steeply since 2001 and had reached 193,000 hectares by 2007, a 17 per cent increase over the previous year. The use of ATSs, cocaine and opiates, though still unacceptably high, appears to have been contained at about the same figure for three years. The total number of drug users worldwide is put at 200 million, 5 per cent of the global population between the ages of 15 and 64. Cannabis is the most widely used drug – about 165 million people use it.

Drug seizures have been rising. Turning to specific drugs, UNODC was pleased that opium production (about 90 per cent from Afghanistan) appeared to be declining, mainly because of progress made in the Golden Triangle. Global cultivation appears to have stabilized below the peak levels of 2000. Most cocaine is used in the Americas, especially North America, which represents half the global cocaine market with 7 million users. Whether harsher economic times will reduce or increase snorting on Wall Street is unclear. Worryingly, while cocaine use is declining in the USA, it is rising in Europe, especially in Britain and Spain (in 2007 a higher proportion of Spaniards than Americans took cocaine). The markets for ATSs are also stabilizing, though ecstasy use is still high in western Europe and growing in south-east Europe. The report suggested a gloomier picture for the most widely used drug, cannabis. Grown on every continent except Antarctica, this drug is present everywhere, its use is increasing globally, a more powerful form – sinsemilla cannabis, the unfertilized buds of the female plant – is taking a large market share, and recent research indicates that the health risks of using cannabis have been underestimated in the past. Yet overall, UNODC believes that the trends are moving in the right direction and that the main task now is to see that these improvements continue.

Even the UN would accept that some of these figures are unreliable and that estimating, for example, the totals for the global drugs trade is at best an inexact science. Yet criticism of UNODC's 'war' reporting goes well beyond statistical quibbles. The charge – implicit and even explicit – is that the UN exaggerates both the success of the international approach to containing and reducing drug abuse, and the scale of the hazards that drug use represents, in order to justify the present heavy Western reliance of policy on supply reduction abroad and enforcement of criminal sanctions at home. Moreover, it has both to claim progress and to point to remaining dangers in order to retain international support for the global cooperation it espouses. This is not a fair charge, though it does raise issues that are crucial to any successful efforts to cope with the size of the global drugs market, and the tone of UN reporting does sometimes sound a little like whistling past the cemetery. In the marketplace, there are states – we tend to regard them as the ubiquitous failed states – where the product is grown and manufactured, and there are states where most of the consumers live. Perhaps in the failed or failing states they would not unreasonably regard the markets for their illicit exports as failed or failing societies. We need to look at both parts of this commercial equation and at what enables them to live in prosperous and lethal harmony.

Drug trafficking is naturally made easier by economic liberalization. First, some of the legal inputs in drug production have become cheaper. This is true, for example, of the 20 per cent of all chemical precursors that are used in narcotics production. Second, as happens with other illegal products and activities, cheaper and easier transportation assists illicit trafficking. Containerization has produced more opportunities for drug traders. While some movement of drugs is by small plane or fast speedboat, smuggling into Europe and the US is mostly done through normal commercial channels – by road, rail and commercial flight. Third, the higher the trade volumes, the greater the chances for smuggling and – very often – the lower the cost. Cheaper air fares facilitate the use of 'mules', human carriers who often swallow small bags of the drugs in order to get through customs checks. Fourth, even with the help of modern inspection technology, customs officials are overwhelmed by the amount of freight passing through ports of entry. Fifth, as we saw in the last chapter, deregulation, large capital flows and e-commerce have all made it easier to launder the substantial proceeds from the drugs business. Perhaps the UN should be entitled to take a bow on the grounds that, despite so many advantages accruing to the drug traders, the situation is not far worse.

The United States is the largest market for illicit drugs and much the biggest spender on the enforcement of laws against the sale and use of drugs. Some experts reckon that the total enforcement cost could exceed $40 billion annually.[3] One in two Washingtonians over the age of 12 has admitted to having used an illicit drug. There are about half a million drug prisoners in the US, more than fifteen times as many as in 1980. This is far higher, both proportionally and absolutely, than the numbers imprisoned in western Europe, even though, for example, the use of drugs is actually higher in Britain than in America. The usual first experience of drugs comes from being introduced to them by a friend or member of the family. Users are contagious and spread the habit like a communicable disease. The first drug epidemic in the US came with high rates of heroin use, mostly in inner-city minority communities, in the late 1960s. It was associated very often with military service in Vietnam. The second epidemic or surge was the use of cocaine in powdered form in the early 1980s. Third, in the later eighties came crack, a highly addictive, powerful form of cocaine that is smoked. Fourth, methamphetamines followed crack and with heroin and cocaine probably account for 90 per cent of the social costs associated with illicit drugs in the US today. Falls in cocaine and heroin prices have not started new surges and there is little doubt that the number of people dependent on the most dangerous drugs has been falling and addicts have been getting older. Endemic drug use has settled at a lower level than was feared when crack first entered the market, and it seems that young people who started using marijuana in the late 1990s are less likely to move on to hard drugs than an older generation of users in the 1970s did.[4] Yet the costs of all this are high – financially and socially – not least the overall increase in the prison population, the result of a heavily punitive approach that also increases social divisions in the community. The figures for drug use are not as bad as they were or as they perhaps could be. They are bad enough, nevertheless, to raise questions about whether it would not be better in America and elsewhere to look at ways of managing the problem more effectively rather than trying to eliminate it completely. Total eradication is an impossible task absent our own home-grown Taleban or a leadership of ayatollahs.

Drug trends in the UK have arguably stabilized, though they have not shown the same improvement that has occurred in America. The UK level of dependent drug use is higher than elsewhere in Europe and the figures for recreational drug use are also at the top end of the tables. In the UK in 1975 there were reckoned to be 5,000 dependent drug users; the present figures are over 280,000 in England and over 50,000 in Scotland. The percentage of young people who have used cannabis seems to have been falling, though it appears to have stuck at about 45 per cent. The UK has the second highest rate of drug-related deaths in Europe: there were 1,644 such identified deaths in 2005. The socio-economic cost of drug-related crime in England and Wales is put at over £13 billion to deal with an illicit drugs market worth about £5 billion. The number of those incarcerated for drugs offences rose by more than 100 per cent between 1994 and 2005, and the courts imposed sentences that involved three times as much custodial time in 2004 as ten years earlier. So demand for illicit drugs remains high in Britain, as it is in the US, despite very tough prison sentences for drug crimes. The prevalence of drug use is comparable in other rich countries. For example in Australia and New Zealand the official statistics suggest rather higher use of marijuana, ecstasy and amphetamines than in the UK or US.

What of the efforts to stamp out the supply of these drugs whose habitual use we do not seem able to kick?

I first encountered Afghans in 1986 on my first visit to Pakistan. I was taken up to the Khyber pass, which has such a rich and blood-soaked history. Rudyard Kipling described it as 'a sword cut through the mountains'. It was the gateway to India forced open by invaders like Alexander the Great and Babur (the founder in the sixteenth century of the Mughal Empire) and – in the other direction – the jumping-off point for Britain's three colonial Afghan wars, as the 'Great Game' was played against tsarist Russia to secure India's north-west frontier. After viewing the pass, we returned to Peshawar, which is situated geographically like the bird's eye, north of the Pakistan parrot's beak that juts mountainously into Afghanistan in the direction of Kabul. The Tora Bora mountains, in which Osama bin Laden has been sought in vain, rise to the west of Peshawar. The main purpose of my visit was not 'history watch'. I was going to the UNHCR camps outside the city which had been constructed to house Afghan refugees – mainly Pashtuns – from the fighting within the country against the Soviet invasion. These refugees had already been in Pakistan for some time. They had arrived with few possessions beyond pots, pans, copies of the Quran and Kalashnikov rifles, which were carried about openly. My British government department was helping to pay for the camps – rudimentary healthcare, emergency food supplies and so on – and it was suggested that the tribal elders in the camps would like to meet me to thank me in person for this assistance. We were taken to a large marquee, hung about with bright carpets, with a table at one end covered in fabrics bearing, rather incongruously, bowls of Fox's Glacier Mints. The elders were sat behind the table and I joined them, facing a large crowd of bearded men in brightly coloured dress who were wielding their rifles like umbrellas or walking sticks. I was invited to address the gathering, rose to speak and began with an oratorical flourish, circling my hands in front of me. Pandemonium ensued. Rifles were fired. Shouts of devotional joy rose to the heavens. Checking quickly I found that at least I had not myself been winged. The British high commissioner in Pakistan, who spoke Pashto and Dari (the local languages), told me afterwards that my body language had indicated that I was a follower of 'the Book'. I suppose I am, really, a different though still venerated Book in the Islamic world. Anyway, it was all a reminder of the wisdom of those bank advertisements that tell you how different every country and culture is, despite globalization. Don't pat a Thai on the head or show him the sole of your shoe. And in future keep your hands in your pockets when addressing rifle-toting Afghan tribesmen.

I first visited Afghanistan itself in the winter of 2002/3. It was not long after the war and the overthrow of the Taleban. President Karzai was installed in his partially ruined palace in Kabul, guarded by heavies from an American security company. Everywhere beautiful white shrub roses grew over what had been left of the city by years of warfare. The once-handsome mud-brick city had been systematically flattened as splinter groups of splinter groups of militias fought for imagined advantage from street to street, or – driven from the city – shelled whatever still-standing buildings they had left behind. The European Commission had pledged to spend a billion euros over five years on reconstruction. I had gone out on a limb to make this pledge at a donors' conference in Madrid chaired by Colin Powell; the French had tried to block what they clearly at the time regarded as an excessively generous commitment to assist in the post-war reconstruction of Afghanistan under American leadership. There were later criticisms that insufficient money was spent rapidly enough to help this desperately poor country to get off its knees. The then finance minister, Ashraf Ghani (an excellent IMF economist and administrator all-too-briefly in post), pleaded for assistance to move his country from abject to what he called 'dignified' poverty. There was some truth in these charges about tardily deployed aid. Donors are invariably better at making promises than spending money, and the money that they do manage to commit is not always well used. But even shortly after the war it was obvious that the biggest problem was a different one. There were not enough army boots on the ground. There was a small force in Kabul to secure the capital and special forces were searching the caves of Tora Bora for al-Qaeda, but elsewhere the military footprint was all too light. On this visit, I was not allowed to travel south to Kandahar because the security situation was said to be too dangerous. The Pentagon's attention had shifted to the build-up for the invasion of Iraq, and America's NATO allies sighed with relief that they were not asked to do more. Afghanistan was a done deal, finished business, mission accomplished. The Taleban were gone. The caravan was rolling on to new desert triumphs far to the west. So the authority of the Karzai government contracted. The president's writ did not run far beyond the city bounds of Kabul, and in so far as government existed outside the capital it usually depended on political deals between Karzai and local clan leaders and warlords. Government was a patchwork of bargains and understandings, and it was increasingly clear that the local and regional bosses, whom the US military and CIA thought they had bought before the ousting of the Taleban, had only been rented for the season like French gîtes.

From an early stage aid workers, allied military commanders and politicians like Karzai and Ghani feared that Afghanistan without help and progress could simply turn into a narco-state. If this was going to happen, the journey would not be a very long one. More than twenty years of fighting in Afghanistan had created an open war economy in which opium production and arms dealing had become the principal entrepreneurial activities. The Soviet occupation of Afghanistan from 1979 to 1989 and the fighting between Soviet troops and the mujahideen, and indeed internally among Afghans themselves, helped to destroy the pastoral subsistence economy. Foreign supporters of the mujahideen, mainly the Americans and the Pakistanis, spent millions in assistance, monetizing economic and social relations in the country and triggering inflation. In areas where poppies could be easily grown, like the upper Helmand valley in the south of the country, the combination of soil and climate produced ideal conditions for opium production. The fields in the area had the highest yields in the world. Even the mujahideen leaders who were thought by the West to be the good guys were involved in smuggling and drugs, partly, of course, to fund the fighting against Soviet troops. If the strategic choice was between tying down and then expelling the Soviet forces or controlling the drug trade, there would only ever be one outcome. Ahmed Shah Massoud, the Tajik commander in north-east Afghanistan who had developed the largest resistance organization in the country, not only controlled the emerald and lapis-lazuli mines in his native Panjshir valley but also got involved in drugs. When, ten or more years later, the US administration under President Clinton considered providing more aid for Massoud and his Northern Alliance to fight the Taleban and deal with Osama bin

Laden, one of the objections to such a course of action was his reputation as a drug baron, for whom more overt support might pose public-relations problems. There was also nervousness about annoying the Pakistanis and their military intelligence service. They had their own warlords on the payroll (such as Massoud's opponent, the anti-American Hekmatyar) and had long been strong supporters of the Taleban (a word which means '[religious] students').[5]

The fall in 1992 of the Soviet-supported government of Mohammad Najibullah was followed by years of heavy fighting between militia groups; the Taleban emerged as victors in the whole of Afghanistan except the north-east, where Massoud held out. Initially, the drug trade helped finance the Taleban. They levied a 10 to 20 per cent tax on the trade, tipping the proceeds into a war chest controlled by their leader, the one-eyed Mullah Muhammed Omar. In July 2000, just before their fall, they negotiated with the UN a ban on the cultivation of opium as part of their attempt to gain recognition from the international community. Combined with a drought and a price crash resulting from bumper crops in 1999 and 2000, the ban led to a 94 per cent drop in opium production. This proved a humanitarian disaster for the farmers concerned. They had no alternative livelihood; a development programme previously promised by the UN had been cancelled. It was suspected at the time that the Taleban were behaving a bit like OPEC oil producers. With the price of the product falling, cutting production helped to stabilize it, and the Taleban were able to leak opium on to the market from their warehoused stocks whenever they needed the cash.

This was the situation when the Taleban fell in 2001 and the Northern Alliance (without Massoud, who had been assassinated by al-Qaeda) entered Kabul, supported by the US and allied forces. Poppy cultivation picked up almost straightaway. When I visited Kabul on that first occasion, I talked to my interpreter one afternoon about drugs. He said that he had been trying to buy a house for himself and his parents back in his home province. In the past, the province had not been an opium centre. Now, he said, opium was being produced in most of Afghanistan's provinces, and the price of the house that he was trying to purchase had been recalculated by the vendors to take account of the number of hectares adjoining the house where poppies could be grown. Today, not many years since the virtual elimination of opium cultivation in the Taleban regime's final year, Afghanistan produces over 90 per cent of the world's total. It is cultivated on almost 200,000 hectares of land, half a million acres. Production in 2007 hit a world record of 8,800 metric tons.

The surge in opium production has been accompanied by increasing insurgent activity, particularly in Helmand province and some of the districts encircling the capital. This has led to a welcome strengthening of US, NATO and international forces, a reversal of the initial mistaken view that whereas it had required twenty soldiers for every thousand Kosovar Albanians to keep the peace after the confrontation with Serbia, we could make do with one peacekeeper for every five thousand Afghans. With some historical irony, British forces who once battled the Chinese in order to secure the right to sell opium in their country now fight in Afghanistan to stamp out production of the same drug. This is proving to be a formidably uphill task, despite the bravery of those troops on the front line whose governments actually allow them to be involved in real fighting. They need to be substantially reinforced if they are to succeed and those governments and parliaments of NATO countries which appear to be prepared to deploy troops in the country only if they can be kept as far as possible out of harm's way need to think again. Failure in Afghanistan, partly as a result of a less than wholehearted commitment by NATO's European members, would lead to a huge loss of credibility for Europe and for its aspirations to play a security role in the world, and would also lead to a serious questioning of the future role and purpose of NATO.

The pressure on Europe to provide non-military support and development assistance in Afghanistan (as well as more troops) was increased by the election of President Obama, whose wholehearted support for multilateralism demanded more from allies who had routinely denounced his predecessor for not consulting them and for wanting to go his own way. Obama had been the darling of crowds in Europe, for example in Berlin when he had visited as a candidate. Now his administration pointed out that partners have to give as well as receive. More was required of Europeans than rounds of applause. The new President quickly sent another 17,000 troops to Afghanistan (adding to the 65,000 Americans already there) to try to shore up the security position in the south of the country and make possible presidential elections. What would the Europeans be prepared to do in addition to their existing efforts? Would the more nervous among them allow their soldiers to be deployed in the more dangerous parts of the country? Would they be permitted to operate as soldiers, rather than as government employees covered by health and safety regulations and discouraged from going out after dark? Much would rest on Europe's response in Afghanistan, principally its credibility as a partner of the US.

Eradicating the drug industry in Afghanistan is beset with difficulties. First, the IMF calculates that the drug trade represents between 40 and 60 per cent of the country's entire GDP. Even though only about 4 per cent of Afghanistan's farmland is used for opium, up to 14 per cent of the population is involved; the figure may be even higher when the role of extended families and clans in Afghan society is taken into account. For many of these people, harvesting poppies or performing some other tasks in the drugs trade provides the only available livelihood and saves them from destitution. Encouraging the cultivation of other crops – fruit, vegetables, cereals – does not provide an easy or well-remunerated alternative. To grow wheat requires more water than to grow poppies, and the farm-gate price for grains is much lower. In the year after the fall of the Taleban it was reckoned that Afghan farmers could make $13,000 on every hectare of poppies compared with $400 for a hectare of wheat. A comprehensive rural development programme has to involve a lot more than simply the growing of alternative crops. It needs to include infrastructure development and investment in a country devastated by years of war. It would also need to provide credit, seed, fertilizer, marketing help for farmers and off-farm income opportunities in districts well before they start to grow poppies, which they know bring a reasonable and assured income. All this is difficult without much in the way of government or government services in a country that has so many no-go areas for NGOs and other civilians. The attempt to create islands of economic opportunity around embedded military units has enjoyed some limited success. But, like the creation of a workable model for agricultural development across the country, it is work for the long haul.

Another approach brings into sharp relief the tension between the various objectives of the US and its NATO allies in Afghanistan. First, the coalition wished to stamp out a Taleban and al-Qaeda insurgency, and to give the president and his colleagues in Kabul the authority to govern the whole country, albeit through a network of deals with those regional warlords who are not going to harbour and help militants intent on causing trouble in the region – Pakistan, central Asia, Iran – and beyond. Few, I suspect, regard the realistic aim as the establishment of 'Founding Fathers' democracy from the borders of Baluchistan up into the ravines and mountains of the Hindu Kush. Something resembling Afghan stability – rather different from the Connecticut or Surrey varieties – is what is sought, and to be fair Afghanistan had been pretty peaceful during the reign of the last king, Mohammed Zahir Shah, before he was ousted in a palace coup in 1973 (to be precise, while taking a mud bath near Naples for his lumbago). He returned to Kabul briefly, after the Taleban were expelled. He was a courtly old gentleman well into his nineties, revered as father of the nation.

I visited him in his villa, the furnishings a mixture of Derry & Tom's and Afghan heirlooms. A small group of attentive courtiers leaned forward in their chairs to catch his every faint word. He was dressed as for lunch at the better sort of golf club, his shoes bearing that patina that can be attained only after years of polishing by diligent retainers. He seemed too good for this world, or at least for the part of it which he had once ruled, and it was not long before, to great outpourings of grief, he moved on to the next.

The dilemma today is this – how can you win a battle against insurgents if you lose the hearts and minds of the communities within which they fight? Hearts and minds are close to stomachs and are surely lost if you destroy livelihoods and only offer destitution as an alternative. So the second objective of the allies, to stamp out the drugs trade, cuts across the achievement of the first. No one has yet resolved this problem. The fighting goes on; the drug trade goes on; and every night on the streets of London, Antwerp, Paris and Madrid, wasted addicts go on injecting themselves with increasingly potent Afghan heroin while their dealers grow fatter on the proceeds. Meanwhile, the fighting on the ground increases as Kabul and its Western allies are seen to be pitched against the Pashtun tribes of the south. Unless this impression is changed, the battle against Afghanistan's dominant ethnic group – the principal supporters of the Taleban in the past – will prove long, bloody and unwinnable.

One option for dealing with opium production is to eradicate the crop, either through spraying or through other forms of manual control. The UK has favoured the latter approach, offering farmers alternative livelihoods when their crops are destroyed. This is regarded as squeamish and ineffective by American critics. It does, admittedly, take time, require the comprehensive agricultural development mentioned earlier and, if it does work, still carries the risk of abruptly removing income with the result that sooner rather than later more poppies will be grown again to pay off increased debts. The alternative, favoured by many Americans, at least in the Bush years, is aerial spraying (which took place under the leadership of William Wood, the former US ambassador to Colombia, nicknamed 'Chemical Bill'); spraying perhaps requires at the moment more air support than the US can make permanently available. This was the method adopted at a high political price in Colombia and Bolivia with only very limited success. For every sixty-seven acres of coca sprayed when 'Chemical Bill' was in charge in Colombia only one was eradicated. Some argue that the massive spraying programme there has been successful, others that total production has increased by 30 per cent. The law of supply and demand suggests that if spraying were making cocaine much scarcer, its price on the street would go up. Since significant spraying started, however, the price on American streets has fallen.[6] Aerial spraying destroys not only crops but also vegetables, fruit and cereals. It can affect health too, and there is evidence of it causing skin ailments and breathing problems, particularly among children. It alienates the rural population, in Afghanistan probably also reminding villagers of of the days when Soviet helicopters used to strafe their homes. If it continues or is stepped up, every dead Afghan cow and child with an unexplained illness will be blamed on the US and the Karzai government. Ashraf Ghani, now chairman of the Institute of State Effectiveness, has argued: 'Today, many Afghans believe that it is not drugs, but an ill-conceived view on drugs that threatens the economy and nascent democracy.'

There is another, much more sophisticated proposal that has been put forward for dealing with the drug problem – an approach that would not distress farmers since it would involve legalizing their cultivation of poppies. This is what happened in Turkey, which was one of the world's main illegal opium-producing countries in the 1960s. Turkey switched to licensing poppy cultivation, with the support of America and the UN. Legal factories replaced illegal ones. They bought in opium from licensed farmers to produce morphine, codeine and other legal opiates. With demand for effective pain-relief medicines growing, it is suggested that a similar scheme (also tried successfully in India) should be attempted in Afghanistan. The idea sounds so plausible – income for farmers, disruption of income for drug warlords, no more need for NATO to confuse military and drug-reduction objectives – that it is worth examining in more detail.

The first contention is that the world supply of opiate-based medicines is not meeting global demand. In fact the global production of opiate raw materials has considerably exceeded consumption worldwide during the last few years. World demand for licit opiate raw materials is 400 tons; production is running at 500 tons; stocks of opiate raw materials are 850 tons, and are increasing every year; Afghanistan's 2007 opium crop could produce 1,000 tons of morphine (about 7 kilograms of opium produces 1 kilogram of morphine). While it is true that narcotic drugs for medical purposes are not sufficiently available in many countries, stocks of opiate raw materials continue to grow and current producers – like Australia, France, Hungary and Spain as well as India and Turkey – are able and willing to increase production if global demand rises. The main reasons for the low availability of certain drugs worldwide, according to the International Narcotics Control Board, are insufficiently developed healthcare systems in developing countries, negative perceptions about opiate-based drugs among many medical professionals and patients, and excessively strict rules and regulations, for example concerning importation. The existence of medical need does not easily translate into the existence of actual customers and real economic demand for Afghanistan's opium. Afghanistan's comparative advantage in poppy cultivation is its very illegality. It needs large tracts of land well beyond the reach of the present rule of law, such as it is.

As a legal crop, opium would face the same problems as other agricultural products – poor infrastructure, outdated production techniques, a slow and inefficient route to market. The value of drugs is partly a result of their very illegality; there is a big price differential between illicit and licensed opium. If you were to seek to reverse this by raising the licensed over the illicit prices, an inevitable result would be to reduce the amount of opium entering the illicit market and therefore boost its price, potentially attracting new growers. Profits from the illegal economy would be much higher than those from the legal market. Traffickers could always outbid prices paid by the government for legal crops (as happens in India where about a quarter of the crop is diverted to the illicit market). Moreover, what is proposed is in effect a subsidy. Why should only poppy farmers be subsidized? What about all the farmers who have been legally growing wheat, pomegranates and melons over the last few years?

Would a variant of the Turkish scheme remove the main source of Taleban and al-Qaeda funding? To some extent perhaps – yet these insurgents have other sources of income (smuggling, for example) and would presumably draw down their stockpiles of drugs if their income were to be seriously affected by a switch to licit production. They would also be certain to target farmers and land involved in any government scheme and also the bureaucracy necessary to run it. In order to avoid political, ethnic and tribal conflict, licensed production would have to take place on an enormous scale. It would need to embrace farmers from right across the country, otherwise it would be necessary to explain to a Pashtun farmer why he could not grow opium in Helmand in the south, while a Tajik could grow it legally with a government subsidy in the north. Nor does it seem likely that a Turkish-style scheme would reduce corruption in Afghanistan; licensing and policing the boundary between the legal and illegal markets would present rich pickings for dishonest officials.

Sadly, there does not appear to be a quick fix or a silver bullet for dealing effectively with the drug industry in Afghanistan without complicating and exacerbating the security situation. What is required is patience, coherence and a rather unglamorous commitment to the long term. First, there has to be political will from the very top of the government – that includes the president – to stamp out drug trafficking and the corruption associated with it. Secondly, rural development has to be given greater priority by aid donors, and should perhaps focus initially on those areas that are not yet growing poppies and can still be 'inoculated' against the lure of the traffickers. Once there are genuine sustainable alternatives to growing poppies, manual eradication is easier to justify and implement. Comprehensive rural development covers not only the policy areas already raised but also the provision of schools, healthcare and security for citizens. Third, the last point underlines the crucial importance of training and putting in place a well-led and uncorrupt police force, with better monitoring of performance and surveillance of operations. A great deal of money has already been spent – and much of it wasted – on policing; no one seems to know, for instance, what has happened to over 40 per cent of the auxiliary police who received at donors' expense a uniform, a weapon and ten days' training. Where are they now?

There are thought to be around twenty-five or thirty key traffickers running this lethal business in Afghanistan with their own laboratories, warehouses and contacts in Pakistan, central Asia and Iran. They should be targeted along with the infrastructure that they have developed. Their two main delivery routes to the principal market in Europe have lain through central Asia to the north and Iran to the west. There is a long history of opiate use and smuggling in central Asia and the Soviet war in Afghanistan from 1979 to 1989 spread addiction and facilitated cross-border trafficking. The unstable social and political conditions and the weak economies and widespread corruption in the central Asian republics after the break-up of the Soviet Union turned them into a major narcotics corridor running on into Georgia, and to a lesser extent Armenia and Azerbaijan. The Chechens were undoubtedly heavily involved in turning the remote and mountainous Pankisi Gorge in north-eastern Georgia into a re-packing centre for drugs from Afghanistan. The murky world of Georgian politics, the low morale and poor pay of Russian troops, the criminality of Chechen bandits, porous borders and Russian meddling in the Caucasus (encouraging for years before the war of August 2008 the ambitions for autonomy of the Georgian provinces of Abkhazia and South Ossetia) all help to make this region good terrain for drug traffickers.

The route through Iran leads on to Turkey, the Arab world and then into the Balkans. It is one of the many paradoxes of the drug trade that the US in effect condoned drug trafficking by mujahideen to pay for their war against Soviet forces in the 1980s while Iran – beset by sanctions – has actually been in the front line of the war against drugs, playing a dangerous and praiseworthy role. Invariably the drug smugglers have been better armed than the Iranian security forces; the smugglers have sometimes been equipped with the rocket launchers and Stinger missiles handed out by the CIA to those resisting the Soviet occupation of Afghanistan; Iran, blacklisted as a rogue state, has had difficulty getting any of the Western technology that would have made the job easier and safer. About 80 per cent of the heroin used in Europe comes through Turkey, despite the considerable efforts of the Turkish police. The PKK, a Marxist-Leninist Kurdish insurgent group (using terrorist means to press for Kurdish autonomy), has been involved in narcotics trafficking with other Kurdish and ethnic Turkish organizations. The PKK has played an active part in every stage of the narcotics business from setting up the laboratories that make the drugs to pushing them on the streets of Europe. As happened with other sorts of criminality, the old Balkan trade routes were easier for gangs to use after the splitting up of Yugoslavia. Balkan countries enjoyed a status that was both within and outside Europe; they were both off- and onshore. Among other crucial weaknesses, including government corruption, they were often unable, despite rather grudging assistance from the EU, to operate proper border controls. Yet Bosnia, for example, has more than 400 border crossings.

While Afghanistan has in recent years been much the largest source of heroin, the Golden Triangle of eastern Burma/Myanmar, western Laos and (originally) northern Thailand has also produced heroin, increasingly alongside amphetamines called 'shaka' or 'ice', primarily for China, the rest of Asia and Australia. The Chinese triads have dominated this trade, which has led to growing figures for addiction in Yunnan province in western China and in the south of the country, and an epidemic of ATS use in Thailand. The UN believes that opium poppy cultivation has fallen quite sharply in Burma/Myanmar and in Laos, and because of economic development is now insignificant in northern Thailand. The authoritarian Burmese military regime is often accused of deliberately promoting the drug trade. This is probably a little unfair to the Tatmadaw (the Burmese armed forces), though I am not generally disposed to give the generals the benefit of the doubt. They have presided over the economic wrecking of their country, butchered opponents to cling on to office, refused humanitarian assistance for their own citizens after the devastating cyclone in 2008 and put under house arrest or in prison the Nobel Laureate Aung San Suu Kyi for the best part of twenty years. (A member of my office used to take her books and videos to show to the staff in her domestic compound, and I was once able to get a filmed interview with her for a TV documentary I was making, but I have never met her in person. Even while another of my former private secretaries was British ambassador in Yangon (Rangoon) I was unable to use her presence there to visit the country and meet the brave opposition leader.)

For years the West has pursued a rather ineffectual policy of trying to isolate the Burmese regime, applying travel bans and selective sanctions. American and European investment in energy-rich, government-impoverished Burma has been reduced, though Total and Chevron are still active in the gas and oil fields. Nothing has worked to weaken the grip of the military or to secure the release of Aung San Suu Kyi. This is partly the result of the pathetic efforts of Burma's neighbours to encourage a change of policy in the country. Her neighbours in the Association of South-East Asian Nations (ASEAN) used to lecture the rest of the world on the superiority of the 'ASEAN way' in dealing with Burma; they were much like those African countries that mutter in private about Mugabe but are not prepared to do anything that might be effective in shifting him. Meanwhile people die. The 'ASEAN way' seemed to consist of tut-tutting in whispers so inaudible that there was little danger of a disobliging headline appearing in any of the region's newspapers. This changed a tad when the generals gunned down Buddhist monks in 2007, an atrocity sufficient to provoke a few words of protest from the Singaporean government as well as from the more robust Philippine president. But ASEAN's Secretary General, Ong Keng Yong, was against alienating Burma. 'It is part of our family,' he said. Burma's big neighbours, China and India, have been even more pathetic. Both of these countries point to reasons of state as well as to the allegedly inviolable nature of state sovereignty to defend their lack of pressure on the Tatmadaw. For the Chinese, Burmese oil has to be weighed in the balance: for the Indians, there is the possibility of the ethnic insurgency in the north of Burma spilling over into India and further destabilizing Nagaland. Whatever the reasons, China and India are not well served now or in the long term by having such an impoverished and unstable neighbour. Both Burma and Zimbabwe should remind us that there is fat chance of promoting change in failing states with brutal governments without support from their neighbours to make a tougher policy stick.

However, as I have said, I have some hesitation in accusing Burma's military regime – originally known by the unattractive Orwellian acronym SLORC (the State Law and Order Restoration Council) and now called the State Peace and Development Council – of deliberate complicity in the drug trade. Yangon's authority has been challenged by warlords and ethnic insurgents ever since the country became independent in 1948. There has been a long-running confrontation between the government and representatives of some of its 100 identifiable if intermingled minorities that has often boiled over into vicious fighting. This has been partly financed by drug trafficking in some areas of the country. The Burmese military is pretty wary of fighting the drug armies to restore order in the opium-growing frontier and ethnic minority regions. A new and democratic government would not find that all these problems immediately melted away, but it should be able to call on more international support; after all the US, for example, cooperated with Burma over narcotics control until its suppression of Aung San Suu Kyi and its widespread violation of human rights. A more legitimate government might also be able to settle the disputes with some of the more peaceful ethnic groups that divide the country, satisfying their legitimate political aspirations. It should also be in a position to call on greater assistance to save the economy from free fall, and to begin the economic development that would provide the best antidote to poppy growing, amphetamine manufacture and drug trafficking. Finally, while Burma's generals may not be actually running the narcotics business, some of them certainly profit from it. Corruption leads to collusion between the soldiers and the warlords' drug armies. A new government would be better placed to deal with this. Nevertheless, stamping out the drug industry in Burma is going to take a lot of effort and time, whoever has the task. Yangon's neighbours have the largest stake in helping a credible and more widely supported government to do this.[7]

Understandably, the primary focus of American counter-narcotics strategy has been on the countries to its south. The Mexican border is a frequent transit route for drugs and Colombia, Peru and Bolivia are the main source of cocaine. The fighting between the left-wing FARC rebels and the paramilitary so-called (mainly by themselves) 'self-defence' forces has seen Colombia push Peru out of first place as the largest coca-growing country. For the best part of twenty years the United States has spent billions of dollars helping the Colombian army fight the drugs trade which provides huge revenues for both the FARC and their opponents, as well as for less politically minded drug cartels and drug barons. There have been some successes – arrests, extraditions, the spectacular rescue of Ingrid Betancourt, convictions, seizures, the scalping of the Cali and Medellín gangs. But the drugs keep on flowing, with a high political cost paid for crop-fumigation programmes that have also encouraged the drug gangs to develop new strains of coca plants resistant to herbicides.[8]

Spain is the main entry point into Europe for cocaine from Latin America. The Netherlands is another important centre for trafficking cocaine. It is carried there through the Caribbean, and in particular the Dutch Antilles. Cocaine use is increasing in Europe; the drug is not expensive. I am told that even in the heart of the civilized city of Oxford on a Saturday night you can see it traded next to the ATM machines for no more than would be paid for a few drinks in the pub. Snorting cocaine has achieved a dangerous and rather puzzling cachet. The links between terrorist groups and narcotics gangs have been seen in the sale of cocaine as well as heroin in Europe. Both the IRA and the Basque ETA have been involved in trafficking drugs as well as arms. ETA is known to have used the sale of cocaine and heroin to pay for illegal arms shipments. It has had an agreement to do this with the Camorra crime organization which is based in Naples.

A major link in the contacts between terrorists in Colombia (the FARC) and the IRA was established in August 2001 when the Colombian authorities arrested in Bogotá three IRA explosives experts.

These three were part of a larger group of perhaps as many as fifteen who are thought to have moved back and forth between Colombia and Europe as part of a $2 million contract under which IRA terrorists gave the FARC training in arms, explosives and the techniques of urban warfare. While the IRA were 'on ceasefire' after the 1998 Belfast agreement, Russian intelligence suggested that in 2001 they bought twenty highly efficient Russian AN-94 assault rifles (from corrupt Russian dealers), presumably using FARC money for the expensive purchase. The IRA and other terrorist groups have bought weapons in the Balkans, for instance in Bosnia and Herzegovina and in Croatia, using cocaine that was thought to be part of the payments that they received from the FARC. A former Bosnian Serb, wanted for war crimes, was one of the Balkan dealers concerned. Overall, arms and narcotics trafficking in Northern Ireland are closely linked, as I discovered when I was chairing the commission that reorganized the police services in the province after the Belfast agreement. The Police Service of Northern Ireland in 2001 estimated that just over half of the seventy-eight criminal gangs that they identified in their region had current or historical links to republican (Catholic) or loyalist (Protestant) paramilitary organizations including the IRA. More than two-thirds of gang members were involved in drugs dealing. Loyalist groups were particularly involved in narcotics, often granting 'franchises' to drug dealers to operate on what they regarded as their territory rather than actively dealing in drugs themselves.[9]

As we noted earlier in this chapter, the most commonly used illegal drug is cannabis. Historically, Morocco has been the main source of Europe's cannabis. An aerial survey conducted by the Moroccan government and UNODC in 2003 estimated that there were 96,600 households in Morocco's Northern Provinces including the Rif mountains involved in cannabis cultivation. This covers about 800,000 people and two-thirds of rural households in the area. Cannabis cultivation covered over a quarter of the arable land surveyed, with total production just under 50,000 metric tons. Total farmer income from cannabis was over $200 million a year, more than $2,000 per household. Cannabis derivatives are transported from farms and stash places in the Rif mountains to wholesale dealers on the coast, who then arrange shipping to the main markets in Europe. The EU has tried in a rather haphazard way to promote agricultural and general economic development in Morocco as an alternative to cannabis cultivation, but growing cannabis has usually been preferred to herding goats and cultivating fruit trees. Moreover, as I recall from my own days as a European Commissioner, there has always been some doubt about how much the Moroccan authorities actually have their heart in eliminating production of the drug.[10]

The international division of labour in cannabis cultivation and trafficking has been volatile, with the area under cultivation thought to double every ten years. More of the drug is produced today in the Western countries where much of it is consumed – in Canada, for example, where Vietnamese gangs, having lost control of the illegal timber trade, moved into growing cannabis. Most cannabis 'farms' in Britain are also thought to be run by the Vietnamese; 1,500 of these production units – often looked after by illegally trafficked young men in suburban homes – were closed down between 2005 and 2007. Stealing electricity from the national grid makes energy-intensive cultivation much cheaper. Worries about widespread use of cannabis have risen because of the stronger varieties being smoked (White Widow, AK-47, Guerrilla's Gusto) and because of the research that links smoking cannabis with schizophrenia, a charge that has been contested.

At least the use of cannabis does not produce the sort of related problems associated with heroin and its trafficking. There is strong evidence that unsafe injection practices have spread the HIV virus along the trafficking routes from the Golden Triangle and the Golden Crescent. Blood-borne pathogens, including HIV and hepatitis C, are spread by unsafe injection practices in countries like Burma/Myanmar and China (where Yunnan province east of Burma has the highest HIV infection rate in the country). Needle-sharing has also spread disease in countries in or on the edges of the Golden Crescent such as Afghanistan, Tajikistan, Kazakhstan, Russia and Ukraine. The majority of AIDS cases in Africa are attributed to sexual transmission, but in South-East Asia, with the exception perhaps of Cambodia, every significant HIV epidemic is associated with heroin and needle use. On some of the main drug-trafficking routes the easy availability of sexual services increases the risk of transmission – via young male sex workers in the trucking industry in Pakistan, for example. During my time there, Hong Kong was able to avoid the worst of the drug and AIDS problem that raged in most of the rest of Asia. This was achieved through sensible heroin treatment programmes and methadone maintenance therapy which was available on demand to drug users. Methadone is a substitute opiate. Successful needle-exchange programmes have led to a reduction in HIV incidence in parts of the Netherlands, Australia and the UK; long-term methadone maintenance therapy certainly also reduces HIV risks.

The main purpose of needle-exchange programmes is clearly not to eliminate narcotics addiction and use; it is intended to limit the harmful consequences of the use of drugs. Reducing harm is increasingly seen as an aspect of counter-narcotics policy that everywhere deserves greater emphasis. I wrote in the last chapter that society occasionally has to adjust its behaviour and rules to constrain the damage done by things it cannot actually stop. I gave as examples internet downloading, prostitution and migration. Finding a modus vivendi in an imperfect world is not always a signal of pusillanimity; sometimes it reflects good sense. This is also true of the policy on drugs. I do not myself advocate wholesale legalization of drugs – putting marijuana, amphetamines, cocaine and heroin on the same footing as alcohol and tobacco. But there is a case for doing this that deserves to be answered with more than moral outrage.

First, there is a view (which I do not share) that in a free society people should be left with the liberty to decide what to do with their own lives. That is what we do with the consumption of alcohol and tobacco, so why not act the same way over heroin, cocaine and marijuana? Should we not, philosophically, be uneasy when what the state does seems absurd? Crime can be contained, whatever the depressing numbers indicate; but it cannot be eliminated, whatever the Panglossians think. Crime is part of the human condition. Sometimes it reflects the stupidity or injustice of law; sometimes it reflects the raging barbarity of man. Wisdom lies in differentiating between the two and acting accordingly. People want to be allowed to live their lives; barbarians must be suppressed. Nothing will save us if we treat everyone like a barbarian, even when they have the next 'fix' in their pocket.

I find the pragmatic reason for legalization more compelling than this. The present policy is not really working. Well, give the angelic host its due. Maybe there are fewer fields under cultivation in one country; the curtailment of a drugs epidemic in another. But Afghanistan, Burma and Colombia still boil; the gangs still make more loot out of drugs than from any other criminal activity; the prisons still fill with the ageing addicted. In Britain and in other countries 'there is little evidence that drug policy influences either the number of drug users or the share of users who are dependent'.[11] A confidential report to Mr Blair's Labour government in Britain found that, despite efforts to interrupt the supply chain, cocaine and heroin consumption had been rising, prices falling and drugs had continued to reach users.[12] In the US incarceration of drug users has gone up; drug prices have gone down. Prohibition did not work in the US with alcohol. It is plainly not working with today's drugs. Production keeps up with growing demand and prices fall. Organized crime profits, and addicts and users are criminalized. No wonder that there is anger in the countries from which the drugs came that the countries responsible for most of the consumption have been so ineffective in abating demand. We sign up to UN declarations about the concept of shared responsibility for coping with drugs while putting most of the weight of ineffective policies on supply reduction and criminalization of use.

So should the UK legalize drugs? Many of the facts seem to point in that direction. But I cannot myself go that far. There is too much risk involved, especially to those who are addicted. Legalization would not eliminate criminality. It would certainly set the UK against the US, which will at present hear of no alternative to the 'war on drugs' being conducted with the full if threadbare majesty of the law. We are more likely in Britain and Europe to convert the US to a more effective approach by showing ourselves that it works. So I do not favour treating heroin and cannabis as though they were much the same as cigarettes and beer. Yet I would draw a distinction between the use of a drug and its manufacture, transport, distribution or sale. I would impose heavy custodial sentences for growing, making, importing and selling drugs, with the severity of the sentence being determined by the danger of the drug. I would also prosecute possession of more than small quantities. I would not impose custodial sentences on users, but would insist on mandatory registration of users of stronger, more dangerous drugs, with compulsory medical supervision and treatment. We should, of course, be spending more on treatment of drug dependence or abuse – for instance, counselling, methadone treatment and other opiate-maintenance therapies for heroin addicts. Such programmes do not produce perfect results but appear to cut overall drug use and crime rates among the addicts in them. They are also reasonably cost-effective. We should also spend more money on clinics where addicts can have clean needles and counselling. Drug policy should distinguish between the crime and violence associated with the buying, selling and smuggling of drugs on the one hand, and their use on the other. Use of drugs should be treated as a health issue like that of alcohol and tobacco. Criminality caused by drug abuse – for example violence associated with drunkenness or drug addiction – should be punished. The emphasis of domestic law should be on reducing harm. Those who harm others should be punished; those who choose to harm themselves should be helped.

Similar, more comprehensive proposals have been advocated in the UK by the Royal Society of Arts.[13] They point out, among much other sense, that education and prevention policies have had little significant impact on drug use. Present policies in most countries that consume the majority of the drugs satisfy moral outrage without delivering success. Governments should treat the problems arising from addiction as a public health problem rather than a test of dubious public morality. A different approach could put whole armies of bad guys out of work inside the hour; the states-within-states that run chunks of South and Central America would collapse; the bottom would fall out of part of the small-arms trade; the warlords in Afghanistan would have to show more interest in encouraging the growing of fruit and vegetables rather than poppies, and we would put a serious dent in the career prospects of a lot of mercenaries, smugglers, gangsters and terrorists. This would end an unwinnable war. It would stem the flow of young people into prison. We could allocate more government resources to combating more serious problems like gun running, political violence and the modern slave trade.

Here is yet another example where domestic policy is foreign policy, and where bad policies at home produce failure abroad. 'More of the same' is not good advice for the future policy on drugs. It is fantasy to think we are going to live in a drug-free world, even if there is much more of the multilateralism organized pretty well by UNODC. Our approach has been worthy, well meaning, mostly soft headed and sometimes politically gutless. It is time to change it by allowing some reason and evidence to blow through the debate.

II

Filling the Tank

Two problems of our country – energy and malaise.
President Jimmy Carter, 1979

From Playground to Stomping Ground.
Advertisement for the Toyota Sequoia
8-seater Sports Utility Vehicle

*Business is business. We try to separate politics from business
... I think the internal situation in the Sudan is an internal
affair.*
Zhou Wenzhong, Chinese deputy foreign minister, 2005

Fancy a heritage tour to a coalfield? Google 'King Coal' and that is pretty well the first thing you are offered. When once on the throne, coal was of course the fossil fuel that powered the Industrial Revolution and the economic growth of the nineteenth century, beginning with the opening of the first deep mine, Tower Colliery, in the valleys of south Wales in 1805. It still has an important future as an energy source, with China, for example, currently opening two coal-fired power stations a week and planning on building 550 of them. It is estimated that proven coal reserves will last another 147 years, far longer than oil and gas. The kingdom therefore survives and coal can be part of tomorrow, especially if we can learn to capture and store in large quantities its airborne trash – carbon dioxide. It is also an iconic relic of yesterday's economic development. The bus tour to the past is still available, taking us to depleted pits in south Alberta and south-east British Columbia in Canada's energy belt. I wonder whether the coal tourists are bussed in addition to the cemeteries in mining areas and to the hospitals, where retired miners cough up a working lifetime's black filth from their lungs. There is a lot of blood on coal, the extraction of which is hazardous work. The fatal dangers from gas explosions and roof collapses have declined, but China still posted over 23,000 coal-mining related deaths in 2004–2008. The US records 4,000 new sufferers from pneumoconiosis (black lung) each year and in the past ten years over 10,000 American miners have died from it. Besides the carbon dioxide released into the atmosphere when it is burned (on which more later), mining coal interferes with groundwater and water-table levels and leaves potentially dangerous tips of waste behind. One of them slid down Merthyr mountain in Wales in 1966, burying alive 144 people, 116 of them children.

Other industrial-heritage tours are available, but I doubt whether any entrepreneur would cover his costs offering such a day trip to the city of Detroit, unless perhaps Motown music was combined with a whistle-stop visit to the wreckage of what was once the hub of the American automobile industry. I passed through Detroit a couple of years back. It is not a great advertisement for urban capitalism or city planning. There was a time when it was the beating heart of American manufacturing industry, a pulsating reminder of the importance of petroleum and the internal-combustion engine in the twentieth-century history of the US. Henry Ford, Walter Chrysler and the Dodge brothers made their cars there in days when most fortunes in their country were related to fossil fuels. As late as 1982 the *Forbes* magazine list of the richest Americans showed that the wealth of half the top thirty was based on petroleum. Back in the days when the US was still able to produce most of its own oil – the swing producer in the world whenever there was a supply crisis; oil's central banker – the automobiles made there also dominated the car and truck market. Foreign competition (from Japan, Korea, Europe, today even China and India) has driven much of America's car industry off the road: hence the sad decline of Detroit which picked up pace as the financial crash devastated car sales in America. With the meltdown of the industry the city has lost a million residents since 1950 and 126,000 jobs since 2000. These figures got dramatically worse in 2008. By September the job count had fallen by 57,000 since the beginning of the year. Crime rose in an already violent city and MSNBC reported that some prisoners who were without homes were reluctant to leave jail at the end of their sentences. A third of Detroit's residents live at or below the federal poverty level. Few of them could afford to drive what the British call 'Chelsea tractors' and the Norwegians 'bourse tractors', the gas-guzzling sports utility vehicles (SUVs), ownership of which is a middle-class way of giving two fingers to warnings of global environmental catastrophe. No wonder the other name for the euphemistically named SUVs is 'urban assault vehicles'; they are an assault on urban roads, on climate-change anxieties and on any commonsensical notion of proportionality. SUVs, many of which average as little as 15 miles a gallon, had a 2 per cent share of the US market in 1975. That grew to almost 24 per cent in less than thirty years; perhaps the recession will have put paid to their attractions to some motorists.

Big fuel-guzzling cars are a major reason for the energy insecurity of which US politicians complain. In the early 1970s the US imported about a third of the oil it consumed; today the figure has risen to 66 per cent. American domestic oil production peaked at the beginning of this period; the car industry and car drivers continued to motor with a heavy foot on the accelerator. The US consumes about a quarter of the world's daily oil production, more than anyone else; most of this is for transportation. Americans, who make up less than 4 per cent of the world's population, own and drive 250 million of the world's 520 million cars. Keeping the tank filled at as low a price as possible is an American obsession that plays an important part in tax, environment, foreign and security policy. In America, about 18 per cent of the cost of filling a car with petrol goes in tax; in Britain, the comparable figure is 70 per cent (which makes it even stranger that it is cheaper there to travel by car than rail). Oil politics swings elections and bails out, props up, dispatches or empowers foreign governments. No wonder that between 1990 and 2002 oil interests gave $159 million to American politicians of both political parties, and the transportation industries put up $256 million. President Bush was a considerable beneficiary of fossil largesse in his 2004 campaign.

Both the Presidents Bush made fortunes from oil. Vice-President Cheney was the very well-recompensed chairman and CEO of the energy services firm Halliburton; he also got rich on oil. The latest Bush administration was full of oil men. Oil oozed from Washington's every pore.

Drilling for oil, though dangerous in some environments (for example offshore platforms), has never produced the calamities that have bedevilled the coal-mining industry. Yet there has been plenty of bloodshed. Oil has been a regular source of conflict, perhaps because of its central importance to modern economies and because so much of it lies beneath the rocks and sands of unstable countries and regions. Is it the existence of the oil that produces the instability, another resource curse, or is geology having a painful joke at our expense? From the moment in 1912 that Churchill and the Admiralty made the decision to change the British fleet from coal to oil propulsion, giving British naval vessels a speed advantage over their German adversaries, the hunt for oil became a major security obsession for all the bigger powers. Where there was any mobility in the terrible battles of the First World War, it depended on oil-driven vehicles, especially trucks. According to Britain's future foreign secretary Lord Curzon, the Allies 'floated to victory upon a wave of oil'. In the peace-making at Versailles and in the diplomacy and power plays that followed the conference, a priority for London was to expand and strengthen oil interests in the Persian Gulf, in Persia itself and in Iraq (a country made up by Britain out of three Ottoman provinces where history, geography and religion all pulled in different directions). Britain just about managed to hold this new country of Shias, Sunnis, Jews, Christians, Arabs, Kurds, Persians and Assyrians together, partly by introducing it brutally for the first time to aerial bombing and machine gunning.

The Second World War saw Japan and Germany struggling to secure the oil that their armed forces required; the Japanese sought it in the Dutch East Indies, the Germans deep in the Soviet Union in the Caucasus and on the shores of the Caspian. The invasion of Soviet territory and the drive for Russian oil proved to be Hitler's undoing. After the Second World War, the US became the dominant external force in oil politics, a fact that was underlined by the meeting between

King Abdul Aziz ibn Saud, the warrior monarch who had established by conquest the Kingdom of Saudi Arabia across the Arabian peninsula in the first three decades of the twentieth century, and President Roosevelt in 1945 after Yalta. The two wheelchair-bound leaders met on Valentine's Day on the USS *Quincy* on the Great Bitter Lake between the north and south stretches of the Suez Canal. Whether or not oil was discussed, we know that American companies had made the first two significant oil discoveries in Saudi Arabia and that American officials were already advising the president that the centre of gravity for oil production would soon shift from the American-Caribbean region to the Middle East/Persian Gulf area.[1] In any event, the story of America's close alliance with the Kingdom began on the *Quincy*, with an implicit, if not explicit understanding that the Saudis could depend on American protection and the Americans on Saudi oil when it was required.

Oil has continued to play a key role in geostrategy, forcing costly errors and misjudgements, complicating the pursuit of otherwise clear foreign-policy goals, leading to real conflicts, inviting nervous speculation about imagined future conflicts, and driving up defence budgets. The first oil coup was, as we noted in Chapter 5, the overthrow of Prime Minister Mossadegh in Persia, the consequences of which still reverberate. Then came the humiliation of the British and French at Suez in 1956. The Arab–Israeli war in October 1973 brought the Arab oil embargo and a four-fold increase in the price of the oil sold by OPEC, a cartel that had been formed in the 1960s and became more significant as US oil production peaked in 1970. The Iraqi invasion of Kuwait in 1990 led to the first Gulf War; America and her allies were understandably worried that, having seized Kuwait's oilfield, Saddam Hussein would next try to grab the oilfields in the east of Saudi Arabia. Oil was a major though admittedly not the only cause of the war. The second war, which overthrew the Iraqi dictator in 2003, was not fought solely to secure Iraq's huge oil reserve, but that was certainly regarded as an added bonus of taking out Saddam. In his book *The Right Man* President Bush's former speech-writer, David Frum, noted that the war was intended to bring new stability 'to the most vicious and violent quadrant of the Earth – and new prosperity to us all, by securing the world's largest pool of oil'.[2] Alan

Greenspan's memoirs endorsed the point: 'The Iraq war', he wrote, 'is largely about oil.'[3]

Where lie the oil wars of the future? We will examine a little later some of the tensions caused in Asia by China's growing demand for energy which, although slowing, has not ground to a halt. But that is only one part of the Sino-nightmare that clearly disturbs the sleep of some American strategists. They fear a conflict over oil with China, as that growing power seeks to satisfy its future requirements by tying up long-term deals with oil-producing countries. With the oil market tightening again in the years ahead when growth returns, the commercial struggle to secure adequate supplies is regarded by some as yet another cause of apprehension as China and the US – so it is feared – compete for global hegemony in later decades of the century. Another less widely remarked source of potential perturbation is on a larger scale. Will there be a North–South dimension to future conflict over energy resources? There is surely a global equity issue here with a 'persistent and disproportional distribution of energy consumption between the populations of the OECD and the non-OECD world'.[4] A citizen in the developed world uses 8.2 times more oil than a person in the developing world: if you compare the figures for consumption of all energy the factor is 5.5. Demand for oil in the developing world is also growing three times as fast as in the developed world – set to increase from about 43 per cent of total world oil consumption in 2004 to 55 per cent or more by 2020. China regards itself as a leader, and even from time to time a spokesman, of the developing world, and all but three of the nineteen principal oil-producing countries are members of the main UN Third World coalition, the G77. Over the long run, and particularly once the global economy picks up again, energy poverty in developing countries threatens to add heavily to global grievances about inequity. If this issue is not managed carefully, with the restoration of some sense of fairness, it is likely to lead to conflicts.

There is a noisy debate about just how substantial those supply constrictions are likely to be in conditions of resumed growth, and indeed about whether they exist at all. It is not just a statistical discussion about geological methodology between optimists and pessimists. It bears the weight of other considerations, for example the determination of those concerned about climate change to make the world confront a potentially chilling reminder of yet another reason we cannot continue blithely as we are. On the other side, some countries and spokesmen for the oil industry are reluctant to concede any case for a fundamental change in global lifestyles or to accept any evidence that they do not have an indefinite stranglehold on the world's economic and political security. After all, if a country is not going to have the ability forever to choke off our economic development if it chooses to do so, can it still expect us deferentially to ignore the way it runs its affairs and treats its own people? Moreover, will it be able to borrow and attract investment as easily? For their part, will oil companies, which no longer control the supply to our economic arteries, carry so much weight in domestic political arguments if oil is becoming a diminished resource so rapidly that we are pushed headlong into the technological hunt for alternative methods of transportation and power generation?

There are three main fossil fuels, the remains of organisms that lived many millions of years ago. Coal is the most abundant. It comes from the plants that grew in huge tropical swamps 300 million years in the past in the Carboniferous period. It is packed in seams between other layers of sediment that have now become rock. Coal produces terrible killer pollution, most notably greenhouse gases, acid rain and heavy metals. Natural gas is cleaner than oil or coal. Like oil it is derived from tiny organisms that lived in warm seas. It is trapped in underground reservoirs – and is very expensive to transport. Oil did not settle like coal in seams but, since it is liquid, seeped through rock until it was trapped by an impervious layer and formed a deep lake. Since the beginning of the twentieth century, with the discovery of oil on the hill at Spindletop, near Beaumont, Texas, and the invention of the internal-combustion engine, the relative importance of oil as an energy source has overtaken that of coal. In the nineteenth century coal had been the main source of energy in developed countries. Wood and dung were crucial elsewhere, for example in Asia and Africa. But by the twentieth century's end, oil was responsible for about 40 per cent of the world's energy consumption; 26 per cent was provided by coal and 24 per cent by natural gas. One thing which all these energy sources have in common should be clear. While there are a few scientists who believe, for example, that oil has abiogenic origins, lying in abundant deep carbon deposits that have existed since the formation of the earth, most accept that oil is a fossil fuel and that, like other fossils, it is for all practical purposes a non-renewable resource with limited reserves. Drilling for oil is not like growing wheat or milking cows. Every day there is less than there was, and sooner or later – we must all hope much later than sooner – there will be none at all. It is around those points that arguments rage, and on the consequences of those arguments that predictions are inevitably made.

At the heart of the debate is 'peak oil'. That is the moment when the maximum global production rate is reached. Beyond that, the amount of oil produced goes into terminal decline. If the demand for and consumption of oil continue to rise before the peak, then as night follows day its availability for consumers after that point will fall and its price will go up. Both those events could be dramatic. The theory that is used to predict oil peaks was developed by M. King Hubbert, who forecast accurately the US oil production peak between 1965 and 1970.

The years of growth before 2008 inevitably raised doubts about the availability of future supply. The International Energy Agency (IEA) had forecast an increase in global oil demand of an average of 2.2 per cent a year from 2007 to 2012, bigger than earlier forecasts. The rise in oil prices had not deterred consumption; and growth in Asia was steadily raising demand. Demand for oil contracted dramatically in the autumn of 2008 as the global recession bit. For the first time in three decades it was predicted that world consumption of oil was likely to decline for two years in a row. But the long-term factors that caused concern about the margin between supply and demand will re-emerge with economic recovery. Consumerism in Asia – for example, the purchase of cars – will increase demand. So will the popularity of low-cost airlines and growth in the pharmaceuticals sector. In addition, plummeting oil prices discourage investment both in the extraction of existing reserves and the exploration for new ones; this was becoming a problem even before the crash in prices. But by far the biggest effect on supply and demand is the extent to which oil remains vital to so much of what we do. How much will this change? Oil fuels 90 per cent of our transportation by land, sea or air. Ninety-five per cent of all the goods in our shops require the use of oil in some way to get there.[5] In 2007, when we were using 86 million barrels of oil per day (mb/d), the US-based Energy Information Administration forecast that this would rise by more than a third by 2030 to 118mb/d. China and India are becoming ever larger consumers, with China's consumption doubling in ten years from 1996 to 2006, and India's imports set to triple to 5mb/d by 2020. Cars and trucks will account for about three-quarters of the rise in oil consumption by India and China between 2001 and 2025. This simply tracks the position in the US, where almost 70 per cent of oil is used for transportation.

Winston Churchill is regarded as having expressed the cynosure of geostrategic wisdom on oil. 'Safety and certainty in oil', he remarked on the eve of the First World War, 'lie in variety and variety alone.' But what exactly happens when variety is overwhelmed by insufficiency everywhere, by a contraction in the variety of sources or by universal shortage? Where lie safety and certainty when oil production peaks? What does 'peaking', whenever it happens, mean in practice? Is it an easily managed moment when we simply recognize that we have extracted half of what was originally in the ground? A peak is unlikely to be part of a smooth process in which consumption adjusts neatly to production and falls in line with declining extraction figures. Unless consumption begins to moderate before a peak, it is most likely to encourage higher production figures at top peak prices to cash in on the seller's market of the century. With a growing demand for a resource that is in decline, oil companies and oil-exporting countries will raise supply for a time, guaranteeing a still sharper production fall when it eventually and inevitably comes. The peak will turn into a plateau with a steep precipice at the end.[6]

The hard arithmetic of oil production should be proof against political wishful thinking. What we presumably have to do is to compare how much oil we have used with how much oil we think we have left. We then compare what we believe to be the size of our unused resources with our estimates of what oil we are likely to use in the future. From this, all else – including peak prediction – should follow. The emphasis is on 'should', because the figures for reserves are fiercely contested.

We can at least start with one agreed figure. We have apparently used 875 billion barrels since the beginning of the oil age. So far as future supply is concerned, there are proven oil reserves and there are those that are as yet undiscovered but strongly believed by geological surveys to exist. Proven reserves are basically the inventories of oil companies and producing states. They are said to total 1.7 trillion barrels, about twice what we have used so far. Half of this amount is in the Middle East. The figure should be accurate. But it is regularly exaggerated by companies as well as by countries for economic and political gain. Oil companies may inflate their reserves in order to increase their potential worth. In 2004, the Shell oil company was discredited by a scandal that involved the sudden evaporation of 20 per cent of its reserves. Producer countries may simply want to boost their international stature and, in the case of OPEC members, to give themselves greater flexibility under the organization's reserves-related quota system in order to raise their output. Without new discoveries and with no allowance given for depletion through production, a number of OPEC members have posted from time to time suspicious leaps in their stated reserves. (Indeed, the overall stated OPEC reserves almost doubled, to general surprise, in the late 1980s.) Iraq's declared reserves went up almost four-fold from 1980 to 2004 despite the fact that they were at war or embargoed for much of that period.[7] Kuwait, whose reserve figures are allegedly (according to leaked official documents) hugely exaggerated, failed to record the oil burned off by Iraqi soldiers in the first Gulf War.

Undiscovered oil is getting harder to find. The best and biggest fields that are the easiest to access are the ones that have been developed first. The discovery of new oil grew for a century from 1860. It appears to have peaked in 1961, since when, with the exception of big discoveries in the Caspian, offshore in West Africa and in the Gulf of Mexico, oil finds have been declining. Discovery of new oil is running at about 40 per cent of what would be needed to prevent the shrinking of known resources. Pretty extravagant claims have been made for the potential contribution to reserves of what are called 'unconventional' oil resources, principally those extracted from the tar sands in Alberta and elsewhere. It is certainly possible to turn these sands into usable oil. But the refining process creates substantial problems and the figures used for Canada's tar sands' contribution to oil stocks run presently to only about 3mb/d. The environmental cost is so high as to ensure strong political opposition to the process: very large quantities of water have to be used in the conversion (which worries farmers) and heating the water requires the use of dwindling stocks of natural gas. In addition, major greenhouse gas emissions result. A barrel of tar sands oil requires up to five times more energy to produce than a conventional barrel and results in five times the amount of greenhouse gas emissions. Estimated production of up to 4 million barrels a day by 2020 is expected to release a huge quantity of greenhouse gases annually.

The US Geological Survey estimates that undiscovered oil may amount to about 900 billion barrels. Add that to the declared reserves and the figure amounts to 2.6 trillion barrels, which on predicted rates of consumption would mean – comparing reserves with demand – oil production peaking at around 2030. But those figures are on the optimistic side, and within the overall figure two important issues are concealed. First, a declining amount of the oil remaining to be discovered and pumped is outside the region controlled by OPEC. The non-OPEC fields discovered recently have been much smaller than the giant fields of the past like Cantarell in South America. Second, energy companies are better at investing in and extracting oil than are energy states. Global gas and oil supplies used to be controlled by the so-called 'seven sisters', the big energy companies like Shell, BP and Chevron. But states have elbowed them off the stage. Today more than a third of the world's oil and gas reserves and almost a third of total production is controlled by seven state-owned companies: Saudi Arabia's Aramco, Russia's Gazprom, CNPC of China, NIOC of Iran, Venezuela's PDVSA, Brazil's Petrobras and Petronas of Malaysia. The old 'seven sisters' now produce only about 10 per cent of the world's oil and gas and hold a paltry 3 per cent of reserves.

Multinational companies have spent the last thirty years exploiting the most competitive oil reserves. What is left is more difficult and costly to extract, and national, state-controlled oil corporations are not always prepared to make the investments required; they are often not even willing to reinvest much of their windfall profits to secure future supplies from the massive reserves where they are the dominant player (and as was argued earlier – a drop in oil prices leads to a fall in investment). An oil bonanza is wasted on prestige projects, disappears in corruption or is allocated to social ventures that aim to bolster a regime's legitimacy. For example, in Venezuela President Chávez (to whom we will come later in this chapter) spends two-thirds of PDVSA profits – almost $7 billion in 2005 – on social programmes. Mexico is the worst example of what happens when a government uses its national oil company as an open bank account while restricting foreign investment. The decline of Mexico's oil company PEMEX has been expedited by its inability to win sufficient funding for investment from the national Congress. One result, which Congress will not welcome, is that Mexico will lose about 40 per cent of its tax revenue as the rapid ageing of its huge Cantarell field turns it within a decade from being America's third largest supplier into a net importer.[8] This is worrying, given the predicted $20 trillion cost of the requirement for new energy development over the next quarter century. Even before the current global economic downturn the chief economist at the IEA reckoned that producers were falling 20 per cent short of the investment that the industry requires. Future global oil scarcity is thus likely to be a result of failings of government policy on reinvestment as well as of finite global supply. The oil reserves in OPEC countries were mostly discovered and developed by the multinationals, not by today's national oil companies which, with the exception of Saudi Arabia's Aramco, do not have good records of exploration and development.

The Persian Gulf illustrates some of these problems very clearly. American dependence on imported oil has already risen to 66 per cent. At least half of this will be from the Gulf. Profligate domestic usage ties the country ever more tightly into the uncertain politics and dubious future energy capacity of the region, and the US has become increasingly dependent on producers whose spare capacity in times of rapid economic growth is thin: before Iraq's invasion of Kuwait, OPEC as a whole – with Iran, Iraq, Kuwait, Qatar, Saudi Arabia and the United Arab Emirates the biggest group of producers – worked at 80 per cent of total crude oil capacity. Before the 2008 crash it worked at 99 per cent, a figure which affected America's relationship with China and other Gulf oil purchasers as well as with the producers.

Overall, OPEC's ability to meet rising demand should be judged against the fact that its oil-producing capacity has fallen over the past twenty-five years, reflecting inadequate investment in some countries, lack of engineering skills and poor management as well as deliberate policy. So why should we expect OPEC to be able to increase output substantially by between 20 and 25mb/d over the next twenty years when growth returns?

The pressure from within the OPEC countries is not in favour of increasing capacity and holding down prices. The producer countries increasingly define their own interests in similar terms to those of the man in the Arab bazaar. They want to squeeze as much from the international community as they can, and they do not want to run down their national patrimony too fast or on the cheap. There is a good deal of bitterness about the suffering OPEC countries experienced when oil prices fell in the 1990s. This resentment has been given greater expression as the press has become less constrained in many OPEC countries and public debate more open. If OECD countries are so keen on the cheap availability of oil to their own consumers, OPEC politicians argue, they should cut the taxes that they themselves levy on consumption. The revenue from these taxes enables them to subsidize their own social programmes. Why should OPEC countries generously choose instead to reduce their own income from oil and so have less to spend on domestic education, health and other programmes? OPEC's tougher line with its main customers is also infused with growing anti-Americanism. This even affects Saudi Arabia. The regime there has paid a price for its close relationship with the US, which appears – despite all the protestations of fraternity – to ignore Saudi concerns about Israel and Palestine. Internal opposition grows and Saudi Arabia can no longer offer America and the West almost automatic compliance with their requests. The Saudis can hold out against the more extreme OPEC demands (for example the proposal in late 2007 that the oil price should no longer be denominated in dollars). But they have not sought to check the organization's growing assertiveness over such issues as production and price.

Against this background – a finite and perhaps overestimated supply, real capacity constraints resulting from the national control and extraction of oil, increased long-term demand – it is inevitable that

18 Cruising the Aral Sea in Kazakhstan.

9 Child's play – collecting water in Uttar Pradesh, India.

20 The cleanest sports utility vehicle on the block.

21 A scan of a lorry reveals the human cargo.

22 Victor Bout, arms dealer, helping the police with their enquiries in Bangkok.

23 Growing up in Colombia: he's 13; he's killed five people already; and what is that he's smoking?

24 Tending the crop in Afghanistan.

25 Gridlock in Xiamen, China – this didn't happen with bikes.

26 Hugo Chavez of Venezuela and King Abdullah of Saudi Arabia – not so sorry about the price when it was sky high.

27 The M1 motorway in Britain and other ways of pumping carbon into the atmosphere.

28 Quite right – why not tell President Bush?

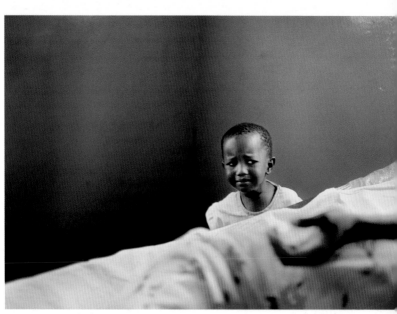

29 A little girl looks at her HIV-positive mother in a Ugandan hospital.

30 Warding off SARS in Beijing.

31 Nepalese police deal with protesting Tibetan monks on their way to the UN Office in Kathmandu, March 2008.

32 As promised by Senator Obama, New Hampshire, 2008.

33, 34, 35, 36, 37, 38 Six who have tried to improve the world – from top left: Robert Zoellick, president of the World Bank; Margaret Chan, director general of the World Health Organization; Pascal Lamy, director general of the World Trade Organization; José Manuel Barroso, president of the European Commission; Mohammed ElBaradei, director general of the International Atomic Energy Agency; and Sérgio Vieira de Mello, senior UN official.

we find ourselves increasingly dependent on unstable countries and regions and on the optimistic assumption that we will manage the sharing of presently essential but limited resources without argument and conflict. Technology is not going to save us from these dilemmas, though it is true that it enables us to explore hitherto inaccessible regions under ice or on the ocean floor, allows for the production of oil from deposits previously regarded as unusable, facilitates higher extraction rates and improves our ability to track down the reserves that are left. But not even all these cheering factors added together can free us from our dependency on OPEC. That is the beginning and the middle of the story; we must hope it is not the end, too.

With two-thirds of the world's untapped oil reserves, the Gulf has inevitably been one of the principal points of balance in global diplomacy and security. The US and its allies have wrapped it in 'doctrines', proclaiming their inviolability and bearing the names of successive presidents – Truman, Eisenhower, Carter. They have sent armies and fleets to protect their interests there. Throughout the twentieth century they have maintained a large and increasing military presence. As the region has more recently become flush in petrodollars, the West has exported vast quantities of modern weapons to it, especially to Saudi Arabia, its largest customer. On his last visit to the Gulf in 2008, President Bush announced a $20 billion arms sale to the Arab countries (after first announcing $30 billion military aid to Israel).

Sometimes, of course, we have discovered that the friends to whom we sold arms in the recent past have turned into today's threats to stability. Iraq and Iran have played leading roles in this bloody burlesque. The main concerns of our diplomacy have been clear: we want the oil to flow and the gas to be sold to us; our fear is another embargo, cutting off our supplies. We want our Gulf friends to be understanding about what seems in the region to be the West's perceived bias towards Israel and against Palestine. We understand that they are Arabs and Muslims and have their own sympathies, but we would like them to be as subdued on the issue as possible. We want them to be on our side when the enemy comes calling – the Soviet Union in the past, then Iraq, then Iran and the night army of terrorists. If they meet those requirements, and if in particular they keep the oil pumping, then we will not make more than the occasional obligatory noise about the way they conduct their affairs. Naturally, we are in favour of democracy, the rule of law, equal treatment of women and so on. But we are men and women of the world; democracy has its limitations, especially in the sands of Arabia or – come to think of it – the slums of Gaza and Cairo. Let us continue on our side to drive our SUVs to our playgrounds, and for their part governments in the Middle East can stomp in their own traditional fashion.

So we depend for much of our well-being on countries with governments that are authoritarian, unstable and undemocratic. The risks we run today are not a rerun of the sort of embargo that hit us in 1973. The present challenge comes from a combination of great oil wealth and repressive government. Governments themselves are vulnerable to extremist and terrorist attack, as are the infrastructures of their energy industries. In some cases there is too little investment in extraction, refining and transportation. These risks are magnified by the long-term increase in demand and competition for oil.[9]

The central player is the Kingdom of Saudi Arabia. It is the dominant and indeed now the swing oil producer, 'the producer of last resort', blessed with the largest reserves in the world and fortunately with a better-run industry than most. It maintains roughly 2mb/d of capacity beyond what it requires. In the event of a significant fall in production on the world market – such as occurred because of problems in Iraq, Nigeria and Venezuela in 2003 – this excess, idle capacity can be brought forward to fill the gap. Saudi Arabia has willingly done this, for example lifting its output of crude oil from 7.3mb/d to 9.4mb/d in the lead-up to the 2003 invasion of Iraq. Saudi Aramco hopes to invest $50 billion over the next fifteen to twenty years to ensure that the Kingdom maintains its pre-eminent position with the aim of producing 15mb/d by 2025. But the country's biggest fields are ageing and some doubt whether these investments will be able to boost capacity much above 11mb/d (even if they are made).[10]

It is a strange land, the Kingdom of Saudi Arabia, so important to our futures as we currently think of them, yet so alien and so incomprehensible. I have visited Riyadh on three occasions, the urban scene like Orange County dropped into the middle of desert, empty streets and shopping malls, burning sun, grand offices where the air-conditioned temperature hovers just above the dew point. Contrasts abound: medievalism and modernity, fierce piety at home and fleshpot extravagance abroad, recruiting ground for terrorists and best friend of Washington and Wall Street, bankroller of missionary Wahhabism and big-spending philanthropist/investor in the West. We know and hear so little about this important country, except when from time to time it explodes in violence. There was the gunning down of King Faisal in 1975, the takeover and subsequent storming of the mosque in Mecca in 1979 and the suppression later that year of Shiite celebrations; and more recently there has been a growing militancy with bombings and the murder of foreigners. Too frequently for comfort al-Qaeda – or those associated with its militant objectives – have put the Kingdom on the world's front page, reminding us of some of the inherent weaknesses of a regime fearful of change and unconvinced that only a careful programme of reform offers the chance of lasting stability.

The roots of Saudi Arabia's current problems lie deep in its history. The al-Saud family had tried for much of the eighteenth and nineteenth centuries to establish control over the Arabian peninsula. The task was accomplished only in the first decade of the twentieth, King Abdul Aziz combining military power and the strict puritanical teachings of an eighteenth-century cleric, Muhammad ibn Abd al-Wahhab. Wahhabism, a creed that advocates a return to the practices of early Islam, is not as unified on matters of dogma and practice as is sometimes suggested in the Western media. But it is fair to associate it with a narrow and unyielding view of the Islamic character of the state, with the clerical establishment controlling education, the judiciary and the policing of public morality. With the first deluge of riches generated by the sale of oil in the 1970s, rulers invested in infrastructure, schools, hospitals and housing; there were handouts for the ruled and jobs for some of them in the growing bureaucracy. There was no reform in a system in which royal power was legitimized by Wahhabi clerics, as popes and bishops legitimized in the name of God the monarchs of medieval Europe. Under the major princes (the sons of King Abdul Aziz) the royal family – its numbers swelled by its many minor members – dominated the political system. Some, like King Abdullah today, have a reputation for integrity; others are deemed corrupt.

Some favour modest reforms; others fear that any reform will open the floodgates and lead to the destruction of the whole system, and them along with it. Who knows which way the debate will go? The day after Saudi security forces killed Khalid al-Hajj, the alleged leader of al-Qaeda in their country, in 2004 the police arrested eleven prominent reformist intellectuals, including several Islamists who had been arguing for the establishment of an independent human rights organization and for wider political reforms. As the International Crisis Group observed shortly afterwards, these two events showed the contemporary faces of Islam in Saudi Arabia: violent Islamists who want to destabilize the regime and throw out its foreign backers and investors, and moderates who seek political and social reform. Which side will shape the future of the Kingdom?[11]

The problem for the regime in finding a way through these dilemmas – bullets, bombs, bigotry on the one hand, and accountability and the long, very slippery slope of social change on the other – is not only that they are virtually irreconcilable, but that the royal family and its supporters have nurtured some of those who are beyond any prospect of such reconciliation. Present-day jihadism was fathered by the official religious establishment which, encouraged by parts of the regime, paid for young Saudis to go and join the mujahideen in the fight against Soviet forces in Afghanistan. Sometimes the experience was relatively innocent – a teenage trip to Pakistan's border; on other occasions, it educated young men in a militaristic and violent world view. In Egypt, jihadists were radicalized at home; in Saudi Arabia they were politicized abroad.[12] At the Afghan war's end in 1989, the Saudi regime had to reintegrate many of these jihadists who were further radicalized by the humiliation some of them felt at their dependence on American and allied forces to protect their security against Iraq in the Gulf War. There were foreign boots in the Holy Places – or at least that is how it was presented.

Fifteen of the nineteen hijackers on 9/11 were Saudis. They had not been sent by Saddam Hussein, as Vice-President Cheney, Karl Rove and others implied. They were young men from America's great Gulf ally, the country whose royal leaders had been fêted in Washington, and who had in return sent their offspring to Ivy League campuses, bought American (and of course British) weapons, written large cheques for charities, invested in their friends' hedge funds, banks and real estate. The Bush administration was restrained in its criticisms. After all, as the assault on Baghdad was planned, Washington had other fish to fry. Some politicians were more outspoken. Senator John Kerry, the Democratic Party's presidential candidate in 2004, spoke for many in and outside his party:

If we are serious about energy independence, then we can finally be serious about confronting the role of Saudi Arabia in financing and providing ideological support for al-Qaeda and other terrorist groups. We cannot continue this administration's kid-glove approach to the supply and laundering of terrorist money. The same goes for Saudi sponsorship of clerics who promote the ideology of Islamic terror. To put it simply, we will not do business as usual with Saudi Arabia.[13]

Terrorists attacked the regime several times after 2003; the Saudis fought back; Iraq went wrong; the price of oil rose; the Iranians got uppity; and the US went straight back to doing 'business as usual' with Saudi Arabia. But the problems for the Saudis have not gone away, though the violent attacks made by the militants have provided a pretext for turning back from necessary reforms.

The problems are exacerbated by social, demographic, religious and ethnic factors. The 1970s oil boom allowed considerable spending on infrastructure and social programmes. Saudi Arabia rapidly became a sort of welfare state with a consumerist mentality and an imported foreign workforce to do skilled and manual jobs. Education had a heavily confessional slant. An increase in riches has been accompanied by a rapid rise in population. In the three decades after the oil boom it tripled to over 27 million, almost 6 million of whom are foreigners. The Saudi American Bank notes that over 45 per cent of the population in 2002 was fourteen years of age or younger. Some predict that the population could reach 40 million by 2025, leaving a substantial unemployment problem in a country where only 2 per cent of the total Saudi labour force is working in the oil sector. Today unemployment is about 30 per cent among young men, and about 12 per cent overall. The standard of public services has been falling as has income per head, which dropped from $18,000 in 1981 to about $8,400 in 2002. With growing social inequity, it will be surprising if there is not more criticism of the lifestyle of some of the princes, more attacks on corruption and more calls for social justice.

The Sunni regime is concerned about how it can placate its growing population and also about the possibility of popular unrest in Shiite areas. The majority of Saudi Shias, who comprise between 10 and 20 per cent of the population, live in the oil-rich Eastern Province, where the vast bulk of Saudi Arabia's oil production is located. About two-thirds of the skilled workers for Saudi Aramco in this province are of Shia origin. Any politically motivated stoppage, protest or strike put down by the regime would spell trouble for the oil industry. It is no wonder that oil revenues are being spent increasingly on domestic security, particularly at the Kingdom's energy facilities.

High oil prices might have encouraged the opponents of reform in Saudi Arabia to reject internal changes or merely to go through the motions. Tumbling oil prices underline the fact that sham reforms are not a credible option. The intransigence of the religious establishment and the fragility of the security situation counsel in favour of cautious change; the changes should not be abandoned and replaced by the caution. Abuses and corruption need to be checked. Civil society should be developed by the establishment of trade unions and other voluntary organizations. Accountability and law-making first by local and regional councils and then at national level (the Shura Council) should be encouraged. The status of women, who constitute about 60 per cent of Saudi university graduates but only 5 per cent of the workforce, needs to be changed, giving them better access to employment, travel and healthcare. The legal system should be changed so that the law applies to everyone, including the royal family and state employees. There should be respect for freedom of expression, assembly and association, and protection for Muslim minorities. With careful reform Saudi Arabia will be a more dependable ally and economic pillar of the world economy. Without it, we are dependent on the ability of a regime run by old men to hold down an increasingly fractious young population in a rough and dangerous neighbourhood. The changes in personnel in the armed forces, the Shura Council, the religious police and the courts, made by eighty-six-year-old King Abdullah in early 2009, and the first appointment of a woman minister for education, may point the way to more substantial future change. One of those removed from his office was the leader of the Kingdom's highest tribunal, the Supreme Court of Justice, who was responsible for a ruling in September 2008 which made it permissible to kill the owners of TV channels broadcasting 'immorality'.

What vision is offered to young – and often unemployed – Saudis today? What future do they see for themselves? Do they listen more enthusiastically to the culturally alien messages of friendship from the West, or to Al-Jazeera's broadcasts of the latest bin Laden tape? We can go on mindlessly putting their fuel in our tanks – but at what political and security price and for how long? Unless we are confident that carefully calibrated reform is likely in the Kingdom, the best bet is to reduce our dependence on what they have to sell us.

Naturally, it is the cash-on-the-barrel price that matters, not just the political cost. The price of oil, like other commodities, principally reflects supply and demand. Built into the supply part of the equation is perception of the certainty and safety of future supply. If, for example, a conflict appears to loom in one producer country, or if a strike is deemed likely to affect oil production in another, the price will change as demand is pushed up by purchasers who wish to insure against future shortages. The oil price peaked in 1980 at a price of $101 (inflation-adjusted to 2007). This was caused by the fall of the Shah in Iran, the interruption in oil supply that followed and continuing production shortages in Iran and Iraq after the outbreak of war between those countries. The succeeding two decades saw wide fluctuations in price (for example, it jumped after the Iraq invasion of Kuwait in 1989), but by and large it fell from the 1980 peak and remained low. It took a further sharp tumble in 1999 when Iraqi oil production increased and the Asian financial crash reduced demand. The price was $25 a barrel in August 2003, after which it climbed steadily to over $100 by the beginning of 2008 and continued to rise thereafter, climbing to over $147 in July 2008. With the crash and the economic recession, it fell to less than a third of this figure – below 40 dollars – in early 2009. Politicians in producer countries who govern in periods of low oil prices count themselves a lot less fortunate than those who take on the responsibilities of government when the price is rising and with it government revenues. That was certainly the feeling of Venezuela's opposition politicians as they watched President Hugo Chávez's oil-revenue-fuelled spending spree. The lower price will test the support for his thuggish populism.

Sadly, the geological benefactions showered on some countries have not always been well used. This is not only because of what economists call the 'Dutch disease', a reference to the problems faced in steering the economy of the Netherlands after the discovery of natural gas there in the 1960s. Oil revenues in a case like this can push up the value of a producer country's exchange rate, increasing the cost of its exports and cutting the price of its imports with potentially damaging effects on the competitiveness of its own domestic industries. The problem seems to go much wider than that. From 1965 to the end of the century annual GNP growth per head in the OPEC countries fell while it rose in the rest of the world. In too many countries oil riches have encouraged the mania for big projects and have fuelled corruption. They have in addition paid the bill for bigger armed forces, allowed governments to override the questioning of experienced bureaucracies and of civil society, and absolved governments of the need to raise taxes (circumventing all the political constraints that are imposed by that process).

Sometimes the wealth is invested in the US and Europe rather than at home. There is constant complaint in the United States about its trade imbalance with China. That is dwarfed by the global imbalance caused by the huge oil windfall made by oil exporters as the price of their main export surged during the boom years. From 2002 to 2006 the countries of the Gulf Cooperation Council – Bahrain, Kuwait, Oman, Qatar, Saudi Arabia and United Emirates – earned a cool $1.5 trillion from oil exports. After paying for all their imports this left them with a surplus of over $540 billion. After the American housing and banking crash in 2007–9 Western banks were grateful for the chance to tap these vast treasures, though the crash itself affected their size.

Venezuela – whose profligacy with oil riches we have already noted – is often given as one of the best examples of how not to use great oil wealth. A trigger for the latest surge in oil prices was the oil strike in the country at the end of 2002. After that the revenues washed in like a tidal wave; but even they have been insufficient to float President

Chávez's project to build twenty-first-century socialism in Latin America off the rocks. Chávez is arguably no fool, though he says a lot of deeply foolish things in his long populist rants, at which I have had the misfortune to be present on more than one occasion.

Fidel Castro was, apparently, even worse. I have never heard or met the Cuban leader, but some of those who have tell me that my experiences of Chávez's rants are as nothing in comparison to a Castro diatribe as a truly and grimly boring experience. I only hope that we do not make the mistake with Chávez that we made with the Comandante, whose isolation and routine vilification by America helped him to survive. (President Obama soon offered an end to this.) Washington is a regular target of the Chávez rhetoric, partly because he suspects the Americans of being behind the failed 2002 coup to unseat him.

The oil-funded Chávez socialist scheme has enabled him to strut Latin America, though even some of his onetime would-be disciples there, such as Ecuador, have started to make their excuses and leave the party. Corruption and incompetent bureaucracy in Venezuela have grown, and neither the future prospects of the oil industry nor the present condition of the poor appear to have been improved much by the high oil price. Oil production is falling partly because investment in the industry was slashed to pay for social programmes. But the gap between rich and poor has nevertheless increased, and from 2000 to 2006 income distribution in Brazil, Mexico and Chile was much fairer than in Venezuela. President Chávez was rebuffed in 2007 in a referendum in which the voters rejected his efforts to increase the executive's powers to carry through a socialist programme and to extend indefinitely his own mandate. President Chavez, however, won a further referendum in 2009, allowing him to seek re-election. With oil revenues down from over $90 bilion to just over $20 billion dollars, he will find his next campaign a lot more difficult. We should keep our fingers crossed. It is not surprising that he has begun a quiet courtship of the same Western oil companies whose fields he nationalized only a few years ago.

President Chávez would hate to hear that another Latin American country mattered much more than his own. Mexico is a bigger oil producer, one of the six largest in the world. But here too corruption, bureaucratic inefficiency, corporatism, inadequate investment, and a long-term tendency to squeeze oil profits for social subsidies have taken a heavy toll. I referred earlier to the importance of the large Cantarell field, which was producing at its peak 2.1mb/d. That figure has fallen steeply. Mexico has not built a new refinery for twenty years; so, despite its oil reserves, it has to import 40 per cent of its petrol from the US. Attempts to privatize the national oil company will be strongly resisted by politicians and the unions, five of whose members sit on the board of PEMEX. The running down of the industry is serious for Mexico as well as for the rest of us. Oil represents 16 per cent of Mexico's exports and produces 40 per cent of the government's revenues.

There have been attacks by rebel groups on fuel pipelines in Mexico, for example in 2007 on both oil and gas, but nothing there has matched the threats posed by militants to Nigeria as a reliable major oil producer. Nigeria has estimated annual oil export revenues of over $45 billion and produces 2.3mb/d, mostly in the southern Niger delta region. The industry's prospects there are bedevilled by corruption, poverty, politics and crime. In the absence of credible state and local government institutions able to use more of the oil revenues to promote job creation and social provision, particularly of health and education programmes, support for the insurgency by well-armed militants has grown. For many years the main export from the Niger delta was slaves; almost a quarter of the West African slaves sent to the Americas in the seventeenth and eighteenth centuries went from its ports. Slaves were followed by palm oil as the biggest export. Today's oil riches should have been sufficient to help develop the region, where resentment at faraway government and at the armed forces runs high. A new group which calls itself MEND – the Movement for the Emancipation of the Niger Delta – has taken oil workers hostage, sabotaged oil installations and carried out car bombings and attacks on government forces. The oil industry itself needs to be transparent about its operations, not least about what it is doing to protect the environment, and to step up its efforts to nurture local development. However, the primary responsibility for resolving what is a serious crisis lies with the government which should begin and sustain a credible dialogue with representative groups in the region about the equitable distribution of oil revenue, act vigorously on the outcome of those talks and promote an arms amnesty with some of the local gangs in Port Harcourt and the surrounding area.

Dependency on the oil from some countries and regions can inhibit and shape the policies of their customers. On the whole, however, energy has rarely been used explicitly as a foreign policy weapon; the oil embargo of 1973 was the exception not the rule. The Gulf States have been frequently unhappy about US policy in their region. This has not led them to make threats about oil supply, partly, it is true, because of the reach and power of the US. President Chávez has talked a big game about Venezuela's oil. This has principally been a sort of Latin anti-gringo tease. Part of that needling of Washington was his public courting of President Putin, who would otherwise not seem to be Chávez's type of fellow at all: hot pepper, cold fish. Perhaps like President Bush, Chávez has looked in to the Putin eyes and soul and seen something rather beautiful there. (Interestingly, President Bush's reported view of President Putin's soul is quite similar to Tsar Nicholas II's opinion of Rasputin's.) One political difference between Chávez and Putin is that the latter has what he regards as a significant energy weapon and is determined to use it, to the discomfort principally of his northern neighbours and to the strategic disadvantage of the European Union. The weapon of choice and necessity is mainly gas rather than oil.

Russia has about a quarter of the world's known gas reserves, about twice the size of the next largest gas producer, Iran. It also has about 6–10 per cent of the world's known oil reserves. Over 60 per cent of the Russian federal budget now comes from oil and gas revenues. Russia has emerged as a major energy player in the world. Europe depends on Russia for over 40 per cent of its gas – the figure is much higher in some EU countries. It is worth adding that Russia depends on long-term contracts with Europe to sell its gas; this is not a one-way relationship. We are, of course, much better off in Europe than we were in the Cold War: better by far to be threatened with a hike in the bill from Gazprom (the Russian state-controlled gas monopoly) or with losing our heating in the middle of a winter cold snap than to be blown into the next world by ballistic missiles. But it would be more comfortable for all of us in Europe if we could avoid placing ourselves quite so firmly as we have in Russia's hands. Paradoxically, President Putin's predecessor Mr Brezhnev seemed to be a more reliable gas man than he; Putin's successor in the presidency, Dmitry Medvedev, is actually a full-time gas man – at least so far as his recent career is concerned: Medvedev was the Putin-appointed boss of Gazprom. While President Medvedev has better manners, few doubt that Vladimir Putin himself will still call the shots.

Anna Politkovskaya – one of a disturbingly large number of murdered journalists who had been critical of the regime, its activities and its main actors – described Putin in a brave book as a secret police snoop, a narrow, vindictive man who had never even made the jump from lieutenant colonel to full colonel.[14] On the basis of several meetings with him, including a bizarre visit with several other European Commissioners to what purported to be his country dacha (I suspect it was a 'show' home, a Russian version of what you might see at the Daily Mail Ideal Home Exhibition at Earls Court), I think that the late Ms Politkovskaya was a little harsh. 'Narrow and vindictive' I accept; but I always thought that Mr Putin was exactly the sort of man who *would* get to the top of a secret police agency. He is clever, articulate, self-disciplined and cool as a cucumber. I pass on his soul. Mr Putin wrote a doctoral thesis (claimed by some to be a plagiarism) on the use of energy as an instrument of foreign and security policy. It is a clear and simple idea and has been pursued with single-minded consistency by him and Medvedev, his loyal presidential proxy. A study of just over 1,000 of his top officials by the Moscow Centre for the Study of Elites found that 26 per cent of them had served in the KGB or its successor agencies. About three times that proportion of Putin's top aides had had some career relationship with the KGB. Russia is not a police state. But the former members of the KGB largely own the state. They are the capital-owning praetorian guard at the heart of what Russian spokesmen call 'sovereign democracy', a concept that is in practice sovereignty-strong and democracy-light.

In some respects it is possible to sympathize with the use of energy and its formerly high price to steady the Russian system. The fall of Gorbachev and the rise of Yeltsin saw the collapse of the Soviet Union and Communist Party dictatorship, though at a price. Mr Yeltsin might have been both hopeless at policy and a drunk, but he was our drunk; he was all that seemed to stand between us and a return to the bad old past. So, since we did not provide enough assistance and pushed him to reform too fast, what Russian people got was the bad old present. The economy collapsed with a 'big-bang' experiment in capitalism in the early 1990s, without the institutions and rule of law necessary to sustain it and to prevent it turning into legalized plunder. The living standards of average Russians were ravaged. The death rate soared by 30 per cent between 1992 and 1994. Infant mortality figures doubled. As we saw in Chapter 9, Russia's assets were looted. Chechen gangs marauded across the Caucasus and Moscow; a journalist – Paul Klebnikov – who detailed the links between Chechen mobsters and the new class of tycoons was murdered. Russian national pride was dragged through the dirt. No wonder Russia looks so much better to so many today. The price of energy came to the rescue of a gas-state run largely by secret policemen. The looting has not been ended; it has been cleaned up and systematized. Mr Putin and his senior colleagues are not going to need to retire on their modest state pensions, that much is for sure. Indeed, brave bloggers have suggested that the secret Putin bank account and his holdings in energy companies would embarrass King Croesus himself. After the dictatorship of the proletariat, Putin promised Russia democracy and capitalism. What it actually got was a sharp-witted kleptocracy.

After he came to power in 1999 Mr Putin methodically consolidated state control over Russia's oil and gas sectors, as well as the pipelines snaking across its territory and that of its neighbours. Foreign energy companies were squeezed out. In 2007, for example, the British–Russian venture TNK-BP sold its 62.9 per cent stake in Russian Petroleum to Gazprom after Rosnedra, the Russian licensing agency, threatened to revoke TNK-BP's licence to develop the Kovykta natural-gas field. Foreign companies have been shut out of other large-scale projects such as the development of the Sakhalin II field. The most flagrant example of the extension of state control over energy was the expropriation and destruction of the Yukos oil giant and the imprisonment of its owner, the tycoon Mikhail Khodorkovsky, who was thought to represent a political as well as a commercial challenge to the Kremlin. His company had risen in the sort of murky circumstances characteristic of the period, had then been run with surprising transparency and regard for good corporate governance, and was finally swept off the board into the Kremlin's lap in even murkier circumstances than those in which it had been born.

Without high-priced gas and oil, the Kremlin's problems look all but insuperable. Most seriously, Russia faces a demographic crisis. The population is rapidly shrinking. In each year for more than a decade after 1993 840,000 more Russians died than were born. Younger men in the 25–55 age range are dying at rates between seven and eleven times those of similarly aged Japanese men. Russian 26-year-olds die at the same rate as Japanese 56-year-olds. One reason for this is rampant alcoholism. Mr Putin himself recognized this public-health challenge and that Russia is a potentially rich country full of poor people (at home, that is: there are some very rich ones with large assets abroad, though the crash has wiped out some of these fortunes to the detriment of those shipyards that manufacture large yachts). His main concerns, however, seem to be how to restore Russia's regional and global status. Russia has had in its history four empires – the first Kieven Rus empire was destroyed in the thirteenth century by the invading Mongols; the second empire of the grand princes of Vladimir Moscow fell in the early 1600s under Ivan IV; the third, Romanov, empire was established in 1613 and lasted until the dynasty's ruling family was murdered in 1918 in a cellar in Yekaterin-burg; the Soviet regime built Russia's fourth empire, which lasted from then until its end under Mikhail Gorbachev and Boris Yeltsin in the early 1990s. I do not believe that Mr Putin and Mr Medvedev are trying to create a fifth empire. They could not do so even if they wanted. What they are certainly attempting is to push back against what they regard as humiliation and bullying by the West and to extend Russia's sphere of influence throughout its neighbourhood by using energy policy. Gazprom is the main weapon that they use but they exploit most of the opportunities that come their way to cause trouble.

Russian grievances about the US and its European allies have accumulated steadily since the collapse of the Soviet Union. There has been the enlargement of NATO (including even discussion of membership for Ukraine), the abrogation of the Anti-Ballistic Missile (ABM) Treaty, the proposal to site part of America's anti-missile defence system in the Czech Republic, the Serbian war, the basing of US forces in central Asia, the Iraq war, the 'colour revolutions' in states neighbouring Russia and recognition of the independence of Kosovo.[15]

The Russians are not by any means right about all these issues, but they are not wholly wrong about them all either. In particular, they have legitimate grouses about the ABM Treaty and the extent of NATO enlargement. Why would we want Ukraine, for example, in NATO? Where is NATO's front line? Where and who is the enemy? EU enlargement makes more sense than NATO enlargement. But one enlargement costs money; the other does not. One is run from Brussels; the other is run from – well, Brussels in theory but really from the Pentagon.

The debate about NATO membership was given greater edge by Russia's military intervention in Georgia in August 2008. Moscow had not been averse to throwing its weight around in its neighbourhood for some time. For example it had surreptitiously launched cyber attacks against Estonia in 2007 (presumably in response to demonstrations about a Soviet war memorial there). Moreover, it had given its seal of approval to the movements for autonomy in Abkhazia and South Ossetia, provinces of Georgia, for several years, in effect providing political and security cover to local separatists to operate quasi-independently of Tbilisi. The Russian military took advantage of a blundering miscalculation by Georgia's President Mikheil Saakashvili, who sought to resolve militarily the problem of governing South Ossetia. They threw the Georgian forces out of the province with humiliating speed and ease and gave cover to ethnic cleansing of Georgians in South Ossetia by Ossetian militias. They then announced that they had recognized the independent statehood of both breakaway Georgian provinces citing Kosovo as a precedent. This bizarre parallel overlooked Serbia's treatment of Kosovo in the run-up to the war there, and brushed under the carpet the recent ethnic cleansing in South Ossetia and the earlier sustained assaults on native Georgians in Abkhazia in the 1990s. In response to this Russian adventure, Washington tut-tutted (having probably done too little to discourage Saakashvili's foolish adventure) and the European Union, through the offices of President Sarkozy, negotiated a ceasefire which ended the fighting but left Georgia divided and Russia with its spoils. Most of the rest of the world was too distracted by the Beijing Olympics to take much notice.

What would have happened had Georgia already been a member of NATO? Would Russia have stayed its hand? Would NATO soldiers have confronted Russians? Fortunately, the issue did not arise. It would have tested the extent to which discussions about NATO enlargement recognized that what was being considered was membership of a military alliance not a tennis club. Europe's early splutterings of outrage at Russian behaviour soon gave way to the feeble acceptance that the EU should go back to doing business more or less on Russia's terms. The issue of NATO enlargement was kicked into the long grass. The biggest sanction on Russia was applied by market forces. Partly in response to Russian adventurism, as well as the collapsing energy price, the Russian stock market and the rouble plummeted – falling further and faster than the indices or currencies in other emerging economies. The Russian economy shrank dramatically; unemployment and the fiscal deficit soared. But that did not discourage Moscow from continuing to buy trouble for its old adversaries whenever it could. So, for example, it helped to bail out the impoverished government of Kyrgyzstan in 2009 with $2.3 billion in return for a threat by this Central Asia Republic to close the American Manas air base, important for the NATO campaign in Afghanistan. Who would benefit from this? So far as the Russians were concerned it appeared that simply causing trouble was the whole point, allied to the assertion of its sphere of influence, an approach redolent of nineteenth century Tsarist policy. 'Spheres of influence' should have no place in Europe in the twenty-first century.

Russia has three principal aims in energy policy. First, it wants reliable transport of its gas and oil to the most lucrative markets in Europe and the West. Most transit states are former Warsaw Pact countries or parts of the Soviet Union. Mr Putin regards them in his own expression as 'parasites'. From Moscow's point of view they benefit from underpriced shipping fees and energy and are notoriously unreliable in their payments. The price and availability of gas have been used against Ukraine (as recently as the mid-winter of 2008–9), Georgia, Belarus and Lithuania in particular as more than a little friendly towel-flicking. The January 2009 Russia–Ukraine gas crisis resulted in eighteen European countries reporting major falls or cut-offs in their gas supplies. Poland and others worry about what could happen to them in the future, given that, according to the Swedish Defence Research Agency, out of fifty-five deliberate gas-supply inter-ruptions, explicit threats or coercive price actions by Russia since 1991, only eleven had nothing to do with politics. Commerce appeared to have been trumped regularly by politics.

In an attempt to circumvent transit states and take complete control over the flow of gas, Russia has set out to construct two pipelines. The first, called the South European Gas Pipeline (SEGP), would extend the Blue Stream pipeline from southern Russia to Turkey, westward through Bulgaria and Romania to Hungary, which would be the designated hub country, with possible termination in Italy. The EU has had an ambitious alternative called the Nabucco pipeline. The aim was to put together a consortium of central and south-east European energy firms to build Europe's own pipeline importing up to 30 billion cubic metres of gas a year from the Middle East and central Asia. Much of the gas would come from Iran (which has the world's second largest gas reserves) and Egypt. The scheme would diversify Europe's supply, meet at least 10 per cent of European demand and help consumers by putting pressure on the dominant Russian supplier. European investment banks pledged to fund 70 per cent of the cost, about 5 billion euros. But Russia – working through Gazprom – has done what it can to scupper the project. The Hun-garian government was persuaded to back Russia's Blue Stream pipe-line and so did Bulgaria, while purporting still to support Nabucco. The EU was understandably accused by the European Council on Foreign Relations of behaving pathetically like a 'naïve bystander'. There are clearly political difficulties in linking Iran's gas fields to a pipeline in Turkey because of the stand-off over nuclear issues. Recent EU efforts on Nabucco have been more encouraging. At a meeting in Budapest in January 2009, the European Investment Bank (EIB) and the European Bank for Reconstruction and Development (EBRD) pledged financial support. Without this pipeline, the EU will be even more dependent on Russian gas, something against which the Reagan administration warned a quarter of a century ago.[16]

Russia's second pipeline is the controversial North European Gas Pipeline (NEGP). This is a joint venture between Gazprom and the German firms Wintershall and Ruhrgas. The NEG pipeline will run under the Baltic Sea from Russia to Germany by 2010 and will supply Germany with 80 per cent of its natural gas imports. When in office, Chancellor Helmut Schroeder was an early supporter of this project; out of office he immediately became chairman of the Russian-led consortium which is building the pipeline. The aim of both the southern and northern projects is to capture European gas markets, locking out competitors and maximizing long-term European dependence on Russian energy. Moreover, in order to maintain its stranglehold on central Asia's energy supply, Russia has opposed the construction of oil and gas pipelines from the Caspian region.

A pipeline with no contracts is money wasted. So Russia – and this is the second element in its strategy – has secured long-term contracts with most individual European countries in order to disrupt what should be Europe's collective bargaining power. Moscow has been overwhelmingly successful in dividing the EU and thwarting efforts to implement a united European policy. In eastern and central Europe, Russia is working to consolidate its presence in Poland (where Gazprom already owns half the Polish gas-supply network and supplies 80 per cent of the gas) and Slovakia (where Gazprom has a 50 per cent stake in Slovrusgaz). In western Europe Gazprom has been aggressive in trying to acquire downstream energy companies and in increasing its market share by targeting key customers. In 2006 Gazprom sent signals that it was interested in placing a bid for Centrica in the UK and began approaching potential customers such as the National Health Service, City Point Tower and York Minster. At the same time that Russia seeks open access to Europe's markets, it denies European access to its own. At the end of the Cold War, initially at the instigation of the then Dutch prime minister Ruud Lubbers, the European Energy Charter was launched. This attempted to build cooperation after the divisive confrontations of the past by integrating the energy sectors of the former Soviet Union, the countries of eastern Europe and the EU. Signed in 1994, the Charter went beyond WTO energy provisions and devised common rules for the whole energy chain from production and generation to trading and transport. Russia has never ratified the treaty, despite occasional public flirtations with its underlying principles, for example at the Russian-hosted G8 summit in St Petersburg in 2006. So the situation is simply this: Russia is freezing Europe out of its own energy market – from production to transit – while gobbling up as much as it can of Europe's.

Russia has been able to get away with the strategy because of the pathetic response of European member states. You do not need to be a crazed Europhile to see the case for a common European energy policy (like a common environmental policy), not least in order to deal from collective strength with Russian energy diplomacy. Some of the countries that squawk most noisily about European visions and commitments – Italy, France and Germany, for example – have been the most nationalistic in cutting their own bilateral deals with Russia and Gazprom. Russia has naturally lambasted efforts to construct a European policy; some may regard this as confirmation that Europe needs one. It should have four elements. First, Europe needs to develop alternative sources of energy, using its substantial loans and grants in the Mediterranean region to finance energy projects. It should also seek partnerships with other producers such as the central Asian and Caspian states. Second, the EU must have a clear common energy framework. It needs to complete the European grid for gas and electricity, so as to facilitate transit from one country to another and to create a working single market for energy that would include real rather than half-hearted unbundling (that is separating generation from transmission) and enforcing competition laws on energy producers and suppliers. It is odd that the EU takes so many plaudits for standing up to Microsoft while being rolled over by Gazprom. Third, the EU should insist on reciprocity, as the EU Commission has long attempted to do. If Russian companies are allowed free entry to the EU market, EU companies should be allowed to enter their market. There has to be an end to Russian bullying of foreign companies like Royal Dutch Shell and BP. Finally, there are important areas for cooperation with Russia – increasing energy efficiency, for instance, where Russia requires twice the energy needed in the EU to produce a single unit of GNP, and raising safety standards in Russia's elderly nuclear power stations.

Europe needs to be tougher minded in its energy relationship with Russia, diversifying sources of supply where it can, for practical as well as security and political reasons. Russia has achieved considerable success in promoting its aims even though its industry is inefficient and domestic demand is on the rise. To use a poker metaphor, Russia has played a low pair like a full house and Europe has folded a royal flush. Moscow's extravagant spending on pipelines and downstream assets has come at the expense of any significant investment in developing new fields for a domestic market which generates little profit, since the Kremlin ensures that prices at home are kept low. Some analysts argue that Russia invests only half as much in its oil and gas sectors as would be needed to sustain expansion of output over the longer term. Moreover, with two-thirds of the domestic production of gas being used to satisfy local demand, Europe is increasingly reliant on the deals that Russia has struck with central Asia and particularly Turkmenistan.

This should ring alarm bells with consumers and investors. Turkmenistan may have signed contracts to supply twice as much after 2009 as it can actually produce. This would come as no surprise in a region where stability is doubtful and transparency largely unknown. The late president of Turkmenistan, Saparmurat Niyazov, a bizarre fellow who disliked gold teeth but liked gold statues of himself, was not an obviously reliable partner. The very real possibility of dwindling production takes place against the backdrop of rising domestic demand. Russian domestic gas consumption is increasing much faster than government forecasts predicted; the figure by 2030 could be as high as two-thirds more than at present. So we could face a situation in which Russia cuts exports of oil and natural gas to foreign markets in order to ensure domestic supplies. In such circumstances it would lose substantial oil and gas revenues, though this would be cold comfort for a cold Europe. With much of the old energy extracted from the less remote Siberian fields, Russia is inevitably in the hunt with Canada and Denmark for the right to exploit Arctic energy reserves as the ice-cap melts more speedily than anticipated. There will be plenty of legal work ahead for the UN Commission on the Limits of the Continental Shelf as rivals stake their claims to sovereignty over, for example, the Lomonosov Ridge, the undersea mountain chain that arcs over the top of the world under the creaking ice.

The third part of Russia's strategy is to reach out to the fastest growing markets outside Europe, notably China, where rapid economic development has produced a huge and fast-growing consumer market for all types of energy. In February 2009, China and Russia signed a $25 billion oil deal over twenty years. In some respects China's growth might be said to be a consequence of not discovering much oil at home. When Deng Xiaoping won his power struggle with Mao Zedong's lacklustre successor Hua Guofeng, he tried to finance the ambitious programmes for the implementation of the Communist Party's Ten-Year Plan by finding oil. Wells were sunk everywhere, but little oil was discovered. The gap in the state's finances was bridged by taking some of the brakes off agricultural development by farmers. Once they had the chance, peasants began to cultivate more for themselves and their families. Capitalism was on the way.[17] Now, to borrow the apocryphal observation of Napoleon, which has become a cliché of Sino-speculation, a sleeping China has not only woken up but wants to own a television and washing machine and drive a car just like you and me. It is salutary to note that if China were to have as many cars per head as Germany today, there would be 500 million on China's roads, most of them made in China, like the cheap Chery, that will doubtless one day devastate the international automobile competition as surely as the Chinese silk-tie industry has blown away its Italian rivals.

China still exports some crude oil to Korea and Japan. But in 1993 it perforce abandoned self-sufficiency and became a net importer of energy. Since then, China's demand for oil has more than doubled, making its market the second largest in the world – 40 per cent bigger than Japan's and second only to that of the United States. While demand has begun to slow, China still imports over 3 million barrels of oil a day. This meets about half of the country's daily total consumption. China's share of the world oil market is only about 5 per cent, yet its share of the total growth in demand since 2000 has been 30 per cent. Of the 7mb/d growth in world demand since 2000, 2 million have gone to China. Future demand will be increased particularly by transport, which is being promoted by the government as one of the keys to lasting economic growth. Cars in China currently consume one-third of its oil. This is projected to grow to 50 per cent by 2020, and China's overall energy consumption is predicted to increase by at least 6 per cent a year up to 2020. Oil imports, especially from the Gulf producers, are expected to rise four-fold between 2003 and 2030. Imports of natural gas should meet 40 per cent of demand by the same year. China has the world's third largest recoverable coal reserves and uses coal heavily to generate electricity. Despite these resources it became a net importer in 2007.

China is well aware of the geostrategic implications of its energy dependency. Securing energy supplies is seen as a lynchpin of the country's ability to sustain economic growth. The Chinese recall the significance of the US denying Japan access to oil in the Second World War. They know that there are limits to how far they can moderate market growth through price liberalization, given the impact of higher fuel prices on the rural poor and on the aspirations of urban citizens. So they have undertaken a modest drive to reduce energy intensity and introduced a more ambitious programme of domestic exploration. This has had some success with, for example, the discovery of a large offshore field in Bohai Bay. Yet China is no more likely in present circumstances to become energy independent than is America: hence what is called the 'go out' strategy (*zou chu qu*). China's four major national oil corporations – the China National Petroleum Corporation (CNPC), the China National Petrochemical Corporation (Sinopec), the China National Offshore Oil Corporation (CNOOC) and Sinochem – have been instructed to purchase equity shares in overseas exploration and production projects, build pipelines and ensure transport routes.

China's relatively late participation in the global scramble to secure energy supplies has meant that the country's overseas investment options are somewhat limited. As a result Chinese companies, supported by their government, have vigorously pursued investments whenever potential energy-rich opportunities arise, wherever they are and irrespective of the reputation of the countries concerned. Wherever there is oil, the Chinese are prepared to go: no questions asked, no strings attached. We in the West should not be too sanctimonious about this. Where they now go, we often ourselves went in the past. We appear to have learned some of the lessons of our ways; that does not entitle us to sermonize.

Chinese government backing for the 'go out' strategy is provided by access to cheap capital and state-directed lending through the China Development Bank and the China Export–Import Bank. The latter is the world's third largest export credit agency mandated to support the state's foreign, economic and trade policies. As well as government backed lending, Beijing uses official visits – President Hu has been a regular visitor to Africa and to Latin America – and increased exports of Chinese manufactured goods, including weapons. The most controversial of Chinese tactics has been the government's willingness to put expensive investment and aid packages on the table to nail down energy (and other) deals. China has been particularly active in Africa where it is now the continent's third most important trading partner behind the US and France and ahead of the UK. In 1999 the value of Chinese trade with Africa was $2 billion; it reached almost $40 billion in 2005 and in 2008 totalled $107 billion, surpassing its $100 billion target two years earlier than predicted. There are said to be 750,000 Chinese living in Africa for extended periods of the year. Since 2002, Chinese energy companies have notched up large deals with, among others, Algeria, Gabon, Angola, Nigeria, Ivory Coast, Kenya, Congo-Brazzaville, Namibia, Ethiopia, Madagascar and Sudan.[18]

In addition to China's statist 'go out' strategy of securing energy resources wherever it can, the government has also embarked on a so-called 'string of pearls' policy of building closer ties with those countries along the sea lanes from the Middle East to the South China Sea in order to ensure the safe transport of what it buys abroad. China is clearly heavily dependent on international sea lanes, in which there are several navigational choke points; 75 per cent of China's oil imports pass through the 1,100-kilometre-long Straits of Malacca. So China views amicable relations with the 'pearls' – particularly Pakistan, Bangladesh, Burma, Thailand and Cambodia – as crucial to maintaining its energy security. China is also building up its navy; this is viewed with concern in Tokyo and Washington.

What impact does China's strategy have on global energy and international affairs? China's investments are more likely in the short term to increase oil flows, not prices. Their investment in exploration and production pushes other oil companies to spend more and to take more risks to extract reserves. A bigger risk stems from the tensions surrounding how China is conducting its strategy and which countries it is partnering. There is a real danger of China undercutting OECD standards for export financing, good governance criteria and efforts to improve the quality of development assistance. Other countries like India, South Korea and Japan feel under pressure to emulate China's strategy. Three particularly damaging consequences of China's present behaviour illustrate the problems.

First, the deeply corrupt Angolan government was seeking an IMF loan in 2003-4 to help its reconstruction programme after the civil war. The Fund insisted on attaching strings intended to curb corruption and improve economic management. China's Exim Bank offered an alternative $2 billion loan with interest rate repayment of 1.5 per cent over seventeen years tied to oil deals and construction contracts. The Angolans accepted the Chinese offer, bragging that with China's help they could get the development money they wanted without political conditions – and without transparency, they might have added.

Transparency and its value in preventing corruption is a second casualty of China's policy, though British ministers have to be a little careful these days when they lecture on corruption, given the Blair government's decision in 2006 to suppress the investigation by the Serious Fraud Office into the alleged payment of bribes by the arms manufacturer BAE to secure a large contract in the 1980s with Saudi Arabia. Nevertheless, four years before this decision, Mr Blair had announced an Extractive Industries Transparency Initiative (EITI) at the Johannesburg World Summit on Sustainable Development. While it may not sound very sexy, it goes right to the heart of many issues that can lead to corruption, conflict and poverty. It seeks to ensure transparency over payments by companies to governments for oil, gas and mining concessions as well as openness in the way the consequent revenues are used by those governments. The initiative has attracted support from twenty-five resource-rich countries. It is precisely the sort of agreement that the Chinese 'go out' strategy undermines, as has already happened in Angola.

Third, to 'go out' for oil – wherever it is, whatever the nature of the regime – can cause short-term political problems and longer-term issues of the sustainability of investments.

Sudan provided the best example of this as it continued to be a major international political embarrassment for China, particularly in the run-up to the Beijing Olympics. China got involved in Sudan when Chevron pulled out, despite big investments there, because of the 1980s civil war. Given the fighting and dreadful human rights record of the Khartoum regime (particularly after the 1989 coup by Colonel Omar Hassan al-Bashir), there was initially no competition for the Chinese from other investors. The Chinese bought a 40 per cent stake in the Greater Nile Petroleum Company (the Canadian-owned successor to Chevron), which aimed to develop Sudan's oilfields in the centre and south of the country and to build a pipeline 1,500 kilometres long to a coastal port facility near Port Sudan. No oil was exported until 1999. However, there are said to be large unexploited reserves and China's investment in terms of money and people has built up fast. Over half China's oil produced through equity purchase comes from Sudan, and two-thirds of Sudan's exports go to China. There are believed to be about 24,000 Chinese workers in Sudan, and as well as running most of Sudan's oil production and owning half the major Khartoum refinery, China has big investments elsewhere – in Khartoum airport, textile plants and hydroelectric schemes, for example. Because of Sudan's desperate poverty when negotiations were conducted, China was granted generous concessionary terms.[19]

China now faces three big problems in Sudan. First, it is heavily identified with the north – with Muslim Arab Khartoum – rather than the Christian African south, where most of the oil is found. It has helped the north to protect its energy infrastructure (and its own political interests) with arms sales including F-7 jets, and even though there is no solid evidence that it has deployed troops in Sudan to protect its pipelines, refinery, drilling and personnel, it is seen to be aligned with northern interests. As part of the deal between the north and south which brought an uneasy peace in 2005, the south will have a vote on secession in 2011. This may bring another war; it will certainly bring the award of oil concessions by the south, which will have to swallow hard before dealing with the Chinese. Second, rogue states are notoriously unreliable partners and now that it has money in the bank and other potential investors (for example from India, Algeria and Romania) turning up in newly glitzy Khartoum waving their chequebooks, the Bashir regime is starting to grumble that the terms given to China were too generous. The soundness of China's investment does not look too good. History has long taught us that when poor oil producers start to see the money rolling in, they want a bigger share of the profits. Third, China has taken an awful hit in the West from appearing to be Khartoum's defender as the Darfur atrocities have continued. It is unfair to regard China's oil interests as the principal sustenance for the Janjaweed, and China has undoubtedly tried to encourage its commercial friends in the Khartoum regime to end the fighting and allow the African Union and the UN to hold the ring. There is also no doubt that the Chinese have used their seat on the UN Security Council to protect Sudan against tougher UN pressure. Sudan has been a dreadful embarrassment to China and its policy of protecting the sovereignty of other countries to do internally whatever they want, especially where China's commercial interests appear to be concerned. In the long run this does not look like a very credible policy for a country aspiring to play a great-power role in the world, and it does not make much commercial sense either. Morality and money are surprisingly often on the same side.

Inevitably, much of the concern about the consequences of the 'go out' strategy has focused on China's neighbourhood. China has spent heavily on its naval forces – buying ready-made warships from Russia and building its own ships which it is keen to equip with Western weapons systems. This has encouraged greater naval investment by other Asian countries, notably Japan, Malaysia, Thailand, Singapore and Indonesia; they are concerned that the reason for this Chinese spending is not only Taiwan, but also the defence of oil exploration claims in the South China Sea. In the recent past there have been disputes between the Chinese and, in particular, Vietnam and the Philippines – about control of the long chain of Spratly Islands. Security provides the first of several obvious ways of establishing cooperation between nation-states in ways that protect their own interests, make sense regionally and globally, and reflect the realities of a new century and the importance of involving Asia more directly – particularly its giants, India and China – in the better management of global issues.

We should, for a start, develop cooperation between air and naval forces to safeguard the transport of energy through existing choke points like the Straits of Hormuz (vital for the transit of Gulf oil) and the Malacca Straits, and to keep the world's sea lanes open and secure. In late 2008, one of the world's largest oil tankers, the *Sirius Star* was captured by Somali pirates 450 nautical miles off the Kenyan coast. In the past, a former US deputy secretary of state, Robert Zoellick – now president of the World Bank – called on China to become a responsible stakeholder in the world. As the *Carnegie Endowment* has argued, if China is to become a stakeholder, 'traditional powers must [actually] offer China a stake'.[20] It is difficult to get China to play by rules we can all accept when we change the rules to suit ourselves, and cut China out of what we still appear to see as our own game, which is not really welcome to interlopers. In 2005 the China National Offshore Oil Corporation tried to take over the old California oil company, UNOCAL, the ninth largest oil company in the world. The American House of Representatives stepped in with a vote asking the president to intervene on grounds of national security. It was happy for the Chinese to buy up its debt – in effect helping to fund its war in Iraq – but not to invest in its energy companies. Chevron took UNOCAL over instead. If China cannot buy its way into respectability, what do we expect it to do?

In order to develop an understanding with China about the relationship between good governance and development assistance, we have to give the Chinese a bigger say in international financial institutions, making them a larger shareholder in the World Bank and the IMF. China should also be brought into the IEA, along with India, Russia and Brazil. The IEA was formed, after the Arab oil embargo of 1973, at the instigation of Henry Kissinger to establish an oil-sharing system between the OECD countries at times of emergency as well as to promote cooperation in other areas like research and development. In a low-key way it has been relatively effective, improving systems for handling supply disruptions, helping to integrate environment and energy policies, developing alternative energy sources and increasing energy efficiency, and operating an information system on the international market. It could be developed further to help deal with the threats that the price and availability of energy are likely to cause in the future. The IEA should be seen as a natural partner to any institutional arrangements that emerge from the negotiations to agree on a follow-up to the Kyoto Protocol to stabilize and cut energy emissions more effectively. The best energy security policy is a good environment policy.

That is the main issue that should drive energy policy in every country. We simply cannot go on as we are. Domestic environment policies should shape our ability to deal better with foreign security problems. 'Emperor Oil' and 'King Coal' have to be dethroned. Without that, we run growing political and economic risks, and face the mounting threat of probably irreversible environmental calamity. To that issue, the most important example yet of the absolute necessity of cooperation between sovereign nation-states – not so sovereign where the weather is concerned – we turn next.

12

Hotting Up

Nature, Mr Allnutt, is what we are put in this world to rise above. Katharine Hepburn to Humphrey Bogart in *The African Queen*, 1951

The work is going very well, but it looks like the end of the world. F. Sherwood Rowland, Nobel Laureate, telling his wife about his research on the hole in the ozone layer

How was the twentieth century for you? Did the earth move, the violins play? Did the triumphs outweigh the disasters? At least you survived it: you certainly had a better chance of doing so if you lived predominantly in the second half. Most of us who had this good fortune have lived longer and healthier lives than previous generations. We are likely to have been better educated than would have been the case a century ago. Technology and changing social attitudes and habits have greatly improved the position of women in society. We eat more (and perhaps better), travel more, have more leisure, and are both better and more immediately informed than our parents were. We have cleaner water to drink. Technology keeps us warm in cold climates and cool in hot ones. There has been nothing like it since the Garden of Eden.

Those scientists who dedicate their lives to the study of the mosquito say that this pest has only two purposes in life, to eat and to copulate. Had a history of our planet been written by a mosquito, say an Asian tiger mosquito taking time out from his day job of spreading West Nile Virus in New York, the insect might have said the same about

Homo sapiens. Uncharitably, he might have added that we fight, too. The figures certainly bear out the point about copulation and consumption. In the last century the world's population increased four-fold, the total urban population by a factor of 13. Industrial output grew by a factor of 40, energy use by 13, carbon dioxide emissions by 17, water use by 9, the catch of marine fish by 35. Meanwhile, the forested area of the world has fallen substantially and we have lost many species of birds and mammals. Some are still just about hanging in there. We have, for instance, brought some species of whales to the very edge of extinction, with the harpoon cannon a particularly lethal weapon.[1] I love whales; no wonder the Old Testament's Book of Genesis tells us 'God created great whales', and that the Vietnamese hold funerals for them when they are beached. Nevertheless, we have been killing these majestic mammals in bloodily prodigious quantities; according to the Worldwide Fund for Nature we killed almost 750,000 fin whales in the Southern Hemisphere between 1904 and 1979. Perhaps we deserve what is coming to us unless we change our ways, although the whales will probably be gone before we are.

Men and women had more impact on our planet in the last century than in all the others put together. Taking advantage of cheap energy, access to clean water and a relatively stable, benign climate, we bred fast and increased the worldwide economy fourteen-fold. 'To get rich is glorious,' remarked Deng Xiaoping. He spoke for the century, not just for China. At the very heart of the success, nowhere more than in the US, was the power given us by coal, oil and gas, the geological result of all those centuries of sunshine captured by ancient plant life. James Watt's business partner, Matthew Boulton, the first salesman for the steam engine, was asked by George III how he made his living. 'I am engaged, Your Majesty,' he replied, 'in the production of a commodity which is the desire of kings.' Asked what he meant, he went on, 'Power, Your Majesty.'[2] Rulers still like both sorts of power, and the ruled like at least what keeps their cars running and their televisions turned on.

Man's relationship with the environment began when hominids learned to make stone tools over 2.5 million years ago and were therefore able to modify their own environment in order to gather and hunt for food. Prehistoric man is believed by archaeologists to have confronted environmental problems like soil erosion and declining fertility, salinization and overgrazing.[3] Agriculture really began with the domestication of plants and animals. By 7000 BC it was the dominant industry in the Middle East and was beginning to take hold in southern Europe and northern Africa. During the Classical Age the Greeks and Romans introduced new crops and farming systems to their conquered territories. Deforestation may have begun as early as the Bronze or Iron Age. It was certainly associated with Athenian naval power and the consequent needs of the shipbuilding industry. After the Roman empire came first the open fields, then the enclosure system and in the eighteenth century the agricultural revolution. The growing labour force in towns, where coal and steam first powered industry, was fed by the food surpluses created by the application of science to agriculture, crop rotations, bigger yields and increased arable land. Though Thomas Malthus deemed it impossible, the population – growing despite epidemics, pollution and poor sanitation – fed itself, partly in Europe thanks to the resources of empire including the humble potato. Colonialism introduced non-indigenous animals, crops and diseases to new continents. Species disappeared and many men and women died. In Granada, visitors to the Royal Chapel, where Los Reyes Católicos, Isabella and Ferdinand, are buried, are invited to celebrate the spread of Iberian culture and the Catholic religion to the Americas. By the middle of the sixteenth century the Mexican population had fallen in fifty years after its first contact with Europeans from between 25 and 30 million to 3 million. It would be seemly for the celebrations to be muted, even on the part of those hard-line Catholics who might comfort themselves with the recollection that at least some of the Amerindians who died were baptized first.

In my lifetime (I was born in 1944) economic growth has pretty steadily accelerated. By the end of the last century, the world's economy was reckoned to be 125 times the size that it was in 1500. Since then it had grown only three-fold by 1820, when the real take-off came with the Industrial Revolution. We have grown more, felled more, mined more, fished more, burned more. There lies the problem. We have behaved as though we could do whatever we wanted regardless of its impact on the world around us. We have gambled with the future of our planet.

Our planet has never, of course, known climate stability. The most recent ice age was at its height only about 20,000 years ago, which is the blink of a geological eye. We emerged from this about 12,000 years ago and for 10,000 years men and women have lived with a temperature that remained much the same, saving a few wobbles – a warm patch perhaps in the eleventh century (though overall the Middle Ages were cooler than today) and a colder one in the seventeenth. We have lived on the bountiful mean, with neither the heat on Venus that would melt lead nor the cold on Mars that would shatter steel. But the way we have sustained our civilization has mocked and attacked what the scientist James Lovelock calls Gaia: the idea that our earth is like a planet-sized organism in which everything is intimately connected including our weather. The ecosystem, like the pollinator and the flower, is a mass of interdependence. Man is not separate from nature, able to do what he wants with it. Our actions affect that interdependence; indeed, they are part of it. The first book of the Bible appears to tell us, as Aristotle did too, that nature is for us to rule as we will. 'So God created man in his own image, in the image of God he created him; male and female He created them. And God blessed them, and God said to them, "Be fruitful and multiply, and fill the earth and subdue it; and have dominion over the fish of the sea and over the birds of the air and over every living thing that moves upon the earth."' It would be insane, criminally insane, to believe that the dominion referred to here meant absolute or untrammelled power. It would be odd anyway for Christians to behave as though God had yielded His sovereignty over either earth or humankind through this grant of dominion. The rest of the Bible is arguably the story of the efforts made by God, His prophets and His son to make clear that men are answerable for what they do, not least to the Most High. So dominion is a clear statement of responsibility as well as a grant of power.

It took Galileo some time to persuade his contemporaries that the planetary system was heliocentric. The Vatican, in particular, long denied that it was the earth that circled the sun in a shifting elliptical orbit, rather than the other way about. So far as Rome was concerned this was an argument that echoed down the centuries, even touching Pope Benedict XVI who was alleged, incorrectly, to be in denial on

Galileo's scientific breakthrough. The science of climate change and global warming has had an almost equally rough ride. But we do not have the time to convert everyone who denies the findings of most scientists (in what is for them surprisingly widespread agreement) that the world's climate is getting warmer and that we – humans – are largely responsible for that. All right, point out if you must the complexities of climate science, the innumerable variables, the cycles within cycles, the feedback loops. Insist on the use of the subjunctive rather than active verbs. Put 'probably', 'possibly' or 'might' into every other sentence. The trouble about this often nit-picking resistance to what is criticized as political correctness about climate change is that too often it turns into an argument for doing nothing. Some would still question the evidence long after the last polar bear had died and rising sea levels had drowned millions of Bangladeshis or driven them from their homes. We cannot wait for reason to storm all the battlements of unreason; it probably never will. We have to start acting now before it is too late. 'Too late' for what exactly? For most of us to live as we have lived; for our children and grandchildren to live nearly as comfortably as most of us have done; for some of them to live at all.

We will turn shortly to some of the details of climate change, though there is little point in labouring every scientific argument, given the extent of the existing literature on the subject. At this stage I simply want to place the importance of this issue in the context of the overall argument of this book. I have looked at most of the global problems faced by nation-states, without hysterical alarm and without suggesting mega-solutions. There is not, as I said at the outset, a catch-all global answer to each messy problem. There are better ways of coping, not least with those problems like nuclear proliferation which have the potential to destroy our planet or to degrade parts of it. In most cases, what we need is a clearer understanding of the importance of nation-states working better together at the regional or global level, accepting the pooling of sovereignty and even agreed external interventions in what some have long regarded as their sovereign right to make policy and wield jurisdiction. They need to accept institutionalized power sharing, the creation of dispute-settlement machinery, regulation of their activities, greater transparency about what they do, the writing of regional and global rule books. None of that is dramatic, though it may take dramas to make it happen, as it took the Second World War to create the impulses that gave us the United Nations and the Bretton Woods institutions.

Climate change is in an altogether different league from the other issues described in this book. It is difficult to find an exact vocabulary for the arguments about it without risking hysteria. There do not seem to me to be any real analogies in the past. Churchill growled his warnings about the coming storm in the thirties, his despair growing when the world refused to listen. Those warnings were about a terrible, conventional military threat to free sovereign states. What we now face is a challenge at least as great as war – but one involving the whole of humanity, its present and its future. It requires literally unprecedented levels of cooperation between nation-states and acceptance that they cannot make their domestic policies on their own with no account taken of the wider consequences. This is not principally a question of environmental policy, nor a matter of economics. It is politics; politics as big as politics gets. It requires political leadership as brave and resourceful as we have ever seen. This cannot be managed by crafty triangulation – finding critics on one side, their opponents on the other, and with the help of a focus group ferreting out a way of scuttling down the middle. Nor is it an issue for partisan confrontation. It requires consensus-building on the grand scale. It must be done. It must be done now. And as I shall argue, it *can* be done. We can reduce the amount of carbon dioxide we pump into our planet's atmosphere, scaling back the greenhouse gases that allow sunlight in but trap some of the warmth going back into space.

One of the arguments used by the US administration for the invasion of Iraq was that no chances could be taken in the fight against terrorism and in Washington's effort to prevent the spread of nuclear weapons. If there was the fraction of a possibility of another attack on America then preventative action was justified. It was a bit like paying an insurance policy. Maybe the worst would not happen. But no chances could be taken. So American, British and above all Iraqi lives had to be sacrificed now in order to prevent worse things happening in the future. In that case, we were paying the insurance premiums partly on the basis of dodgy if not downright fabricated intelligence.

With climate change, the intelligence is plainly not dodgy, even if it may rightly be asserted that not every single scientist in the world accepts it (though *almost* every scientist does). Moreover, the consequences of failing to take action would be more calamitous than another terrorist attack. In 2004 the British government's then chief scientific adviser, Sir David King, argued that climate change was 'the most severe problem we are facing today, more serious even than the threat of terrorism'. There was a row. But it was true. Where are the terrorists who can melt the permafrost, who can shift the weather pattern in the northern Atlantic extending the drought in Darfur as a result, or who can intensify the force of hurricanes like Katrina?

If you decide not to insure your home against fire, flood or theft, you know what the results will be if you turn out to have made the wrong call. We are not so sure about the precise consequences of continuing to pump as much carbon dioxide as we currently do into the atmosphere. Scientists make informed guesses; they make computer models; they speculate; they sometimes make stabs in the dark. It seems to me reasonable to be leery about the precision of some of the predictions. One thing for sure, however, is that the news is not good. The flames are closing in and the house seems highly likely to catch fire. What most alarms me is what the scientists call 'positive feedback', which is not positive at all. It means that cumulative change suddenly brings us to tipping points; you put one book too many on the shelf and the whole lot comes crashing down. Climate change does not appear to operate in a smooth upward continuum. It moves in lurches, each one taking you a bit further in the wrong direction into a world of more regular and more violent lurches. So might not an insurance policy be rather a good idea?

There have been several different sorts of reaction to this. As happened over the initial scientific warnings on the health hazards of smoking and using asbestos in buildings, special interests deny that anything bad is happening. They have helped subsidize a disreputable denial industry to claim, in the words of Senator James Inhofe of Oklahoma, that climate change is 'the greatest hoax ever perpetrated on the American people', or at least that the case is unproven. Environmental policy has always been made against this sort of opposition. The industries attacked over pollution have invariably fought back against any suggestion that the substances they make or employ in manufacturing damage nature. Rachel Carson's denunciation of the use of chemical pesticides (for example, DDT) in her world-changing book *Silent Spring* in 1962 brought the wrath of parts of the agrochemical industry down on her head. She was denounced as unscientific, hysterical, a woman. The Bush administration, which, had it existed fifty years ago, would have been presumably a Carson critic, made a habit of appointing industry advocates as regulators of the very activities for which they had previously lobbied. There were more than 100 such high-level officials in Bush's administration, who made it their business to see that medical drug laws, land use, food policies and regulation of air pollution were not hostile to the interests of the companies and industries they had once served.[4] Special interest pleading affects every sort of environmental regulation. The Japanese argue that there is a scientific case for killing whales. Some mining companies assert the inalienable right to dig up whatever they choose. Developers denounce the market-defiance of land-use planning and green belts. Fossil fuel industries have in the past funded extensive attacks on those who note the consequences of burning their products. Car makers blow their horns about tighter fuel economy and emission standards.

Special pleading blends in to a more general selfishness. Droughts in Africa are not going to hurt us in the north of the globe too much. We will not be swept away by rising sea levels in the Pacific or the Indian Ocean, though we may have to take the Maldives off our list of destinations for winter holidays because they will no longer be there. The problems today, even if we can see their existence, are not nearly as bad as they may be in the future. So leave tomorrow to whoever is around then – like our children and our grandchildren – and we will get on with enjoying today. Inevitably, polling suggests that younger people are more concerned about the environment than their parents.

Selfishness is buttressed by mindlessly optimistic technological determinism. Time, scientists, technology will sort everything out. The future can be trusted to take care of the future. Nuclear fusion will rescue us – or maybe hydrogen. Our ingenuity is not going to let us down now, after all these thousands of years. That may well prove true; but in the absence of conclusive proof that we can produce the energy that we want without the results we fear, it must make sense to take other measures too. Moreover, if we were so convinced that the answer lay out there somewhere, just waiting to be discovered, it would be wise to press for more investment by governments and private corporations in energy research and development.

For some evangelical Christians in the US, inaction before the environmental threat is justified by religious belief. The God who made the world in a week – look, it says so in the Bible – will end it when He wants. It is not for us to interfere with His divine purpose which can be discerned once you unpick the code in the Book of Revelation. The above-mentioned Senator Inhofe believes that God's plan includes the Jews occupying the West Bank of the Jordan, which would help create a short cut to our planet's finale. The future of the Middle East is at the heart of the view that we should just leave everything to the Almighty and stop messing with Him. Once the Jews occupy the Holy Land, there will be a final confrontation in the valley of Armageddon with the legions of the Antichrist; then Jews will convert to Christianity or be burned, and all true believers will ascend to heaven to sit at the right hand of God, from which vantage point they will be able to watch their opponents endure what Shakespeare's King Lear called '. . . such things what they are yet I know not, but they shall be the terrors of the Earth'. What point can there be, therefore, in worrying ourselves silly about carbon dioxide or declining fish stocks or glacier melt? There are, of course, many more Christians who are horrified by this, believing that God made us stewards of our planet, not its reckless masters. Nevertheless, the ones who take the road to Armageddon rather than Kyoto form an important part of the base of support for the right of the Republican Party. Karl Rove certainly knew their importance, even if he may have sniffed at their theology, which presumably accounted for his incessant whistling of 'Onward Christian Soldiers' as he wandered the corridors of the White House in the run-up to the 2004 presidential election.

Another reason for doing nothing is the conviction that anything we do will cost too much, a belief likely to grow stronger as the economic crisis deepens. We will have to sacrifice growth, or a fraction of it at any rate. We will saddle our industries with costs that will blunt their competitiveness. This should worry us particularly since in OECD countries industry already faces tough competition from Asia. But nothing that is done to improve energy efficiency and reduce greenhouse gas emissions is going to affect the advantage that poor countries enjoy because of their labour costs. Higher environmental standards will raise rather than lower future competitiveness. None of the respectable efforts to figure out the costs of dealing with climate change suggest that the burden is insupportable. I do not believe that you need to bury yourself too deep in the economic statistics, and the arguments surrounding them about discount rates and growth assumptions, in order to assert one simple point. As Sir Nicholas Stern, a former chief economist at the World Bank, argued in his own 2007 report, 'The Economics of Climate Change', the issue is not really whether we can afford to abate climate change, but whether we can afford not to do so. The costs of inaction vastly outweigh the costs of doing what is required.

Overall, opposition to action appears to have drifted through three stages. First, it was denied that we needed to do anything at all. The 'hoax' did not warrant a response. At the very least, the case was unproven and we should await more evidence. Then, reluctant acceptance of scientists' findings led to a frantic aggregation of all the things we purportedly needed to do. They looked costly and politically hazardous; they would involve a big change in lifestyle. How on earth could we get agreement to what was required? The third stage brings to mind rabbits in the headlights of an oncoming vehicle. Everything is just too difficult and too awful. Let's hope for the best. The worst might not happen after all. The car might screech to a halt before it hits us. Indeed there may be no car behind the headlights. These sort of calculations are not good for the longevity of rabbits.

The survival of other species has been of growing concern. Admittedly, extinction is not a modern phenomenon. Ninety per cent of all marine species disappeared in a spasm 245 million years ago and dinosaurs made way for mammals about 65 million years in the past. There are thought to have been about 14 million species in existence but most of those that ever lived are now gone.[5] While extinction is not therefore new, its pace appears to be quickening. The current rate of extinction is approximately 1,000 times that in the pre-industrial age.[6] About 1 per cent of the birds and mammals that existed in 1900 were extinct before the end of the century. The erosion of biodiversity has several causes. One of them is deforestation. Forests cover about 6 per cent of the land surface of our planet but they provide a home to between 50 and 80 per cent of all the terrestrial species of animals and plants. When I was Britain's environment secretary I travelled to Brazil to negotiate with the government there a deal under which the UK would provide financial assistance to help protect part of the Amazon forest because of its importance to biodiversity and to climate change. I visited several pharmaceutical laboratories which – taking advantage of biodiversity – were using plants from the Amazon for manufacturing medicines. The world has cleared almost half its forests, and half of the trees felled have been cut down or burned in the twentieth century. At the current rate of clearance a quarter of all the forests that remain will be demolished in the next fifty years. In rather less time than it will have taken you so far to read this paragraph, approximately ten acres of tropical rainforests were felled, at a rate of one football field a second.

The other related reason for the loss of species is climate change. Some have suggested that we could lose between a fifth and a third of all our species by the end of the century; others think that an underestimate and reckon the figure could be as high as a half. Animals and plants are certainly on the move. They are adapted to life in particular climates, and as those change so too do species. Plants, animals and insects were thought in the second half of the twentieth century to be migrating towards the North and South Poles at a speed of about four miles a decade. They need to move faster: temperature zones are reckoned to have been moving at a rate of thirty-five miles every ten years. Most at risk are those species on the slopes of alpine ridges – pushed higher and higher and eventually into extinction by warmer weather – and polar animals.[7] On a more crowded planet biodiversity has less room to manoeuvre, however much species try to track the conditions that best suit them.

Marine diversity is shrinking just as fast as terrestrial, especially in the Atlantic and Indian Oceans. We net fish from the sea faster than they can be replenished. Catches get smaller and so do the fish that are actually caught. Subsidies and technology have destroyed some fisheries and weakened others. The rapacity of our fleets has cut the stocks of North Sea cod to 10 per cent of 1970 levels. By the 1980s fishermen were catching as many fish in two years as their predecessors had in the whole of the nineteenth century. One estimate is that we landed as much fish in the twentieth century as in all the previous centuries together.[8] Aquaculture fills some of the gap that has been created. But fish farming still depends on caught fish for feeding and there are worries about the use made of antibiotics by this industry. Whaling fleets reduced the blue whale almost to extinction and then moved on to decimate the fin whale population. Despite a series of international agreements through the century, whales continued to be destroyed for their oil by their human predators. Pirate whalers included a Soviet fleet believed to have caught 90,000 animals between 1949 and 1980, Norwegians, Icelanders, the Japanese, and Aristotle Onassis, who used helicopters to find the whales and recruited Norwegian former Nazi-collaborators to kill them. The problem in conserving fish and whales is simple. Governments sign up to moratoriums on catching and agreements on stock conservation, which some of them have no intention whatsoever of keeping. Most of our oceans belong to everyone. They are part of the so-called global commons. Since no one owns them, everyone can abuse them. We have yet to develop the sense of common responsibility that is essential to any notion of global stewardship. We fear that it will do no good to stop our fishing fleets overfishing, since our neighbours will not behave in the same way.

There has been some advance in the last few years in implementing conservation measures in certain waters. This has been driven by calamitous falls in stocks. Even so, the Common Fisheries Policy of the European Union, for example, remains only a little less reprehensible than the Common Agricultural Policy. Scientific advice is still passed over; the fishing industry is still counter-productively obliged; subsidies are still proffered. In a report at the end of 2007 the European Court of Auditors noted that member states, which have the responsibility of policing their own compliance with the policy, lie and cheat. The rules are broken by several states, most flagrantly by Italy, Poland and Spain. A survey of the north-east Atlantic showed a large reduction of fish stocks.

As environment minister my toughest tasks were defending inter-nationally the state of Britain's coastal waters and the quality of our drinking water. We had invested too little over the years in water quality and sewage disposal. It took privatization and European regu-lation of environmental standards to raise investment and improve quality. To my great pleasure, we stopped dumping sewage sludge in the North Sea, a practice that had not found favour with our neigh-bours around its coast. Water pollution, driven by urbanization and industrialization, became a widespread rather than a local problem in the twentieth century. It killed tens of millions of people. Soil as well as water was contaminated, particularly in the vicinity of chemical and metallurgical industries. Heavy metal pollution was a serious problem in Japan, rendering about 10 per cent of paddies unsuitable for growing rice. In addition to soil degradation, population growth and agricultural intensification have produced soil erosion leading to the abandonment of almost one third of all arable land in China and to a decline in per-capita food production in Africa since 1960.

Not every tale records deterioration. Air pollution was bad and got worse in some cities; in others there was a marked improvement. Charles Dickens's *Bleak House*, a savage attack on the legal system in nineteenth-century Britain, begins with a description of London. 'Fog. Fog everywhere.' By the time I was growing up in a post-war London suburb fog had become known as smog, a combination of Thames Valley fogs and the air pollution caused in a city of coal-burning homes and industry. There were times in the winter when, walking to school, I could barely see my hand before my face. My older sister used to lead me by the hand down the ghostly residential streets of Greenford until we reached the shopping area, where the lights in the windows gave us an amber glow by which to navigate. In the winter of 1952 12,000 people died from the smog's effects. Legislation on smoke abatement rapidly cleared and cleaned the heavens. There were no more smogs.

Similar dramatic progress was made in Japan, to the great benefit of the citizens of Tokyo and Osaka. Industries were forced to clean up their manufacturing methods and cars were obliged to meet stringent emission standards. Among the results of this were the development of new anti-pollution technology and the Japanese auto industry's success in the American domestic market. Elsewhere, the mega cities of the emerging economies of Asia and Latin America suffered from even worse pollution than Los Angeles, their urban prototype. The citizens of Mexico City, Kolkotta (Calcutta) and Beijing continue to breathe filthy air, with the authorities in the last city on this list struggling to improve air quality in case the athletes who arrived to compete in the Olympics had to pant and gasp their way to renown. Beijing went so far as to close down its industries for a time to improve the air in their lavishly rebuilt city. The forced closure of clapped-out industry in Europe's sulphuric triangle in Poland, the Czech Republic and the former East Germany helped, alongside German reunification and European environmental directives, to reduce air pollution there.

The four layers of the atmosphere that surround the earth were described more than a century ago as a 'great aerial ocean'. They are as interdependent a part of our planet as the real oceans, helping to determine the climate of the whole world and of each region, and within that the weather everywhere every day. Post-industrial human activity has greatly increased our own impact on the atmosphere. Discharges of greenhouse gases cause today's biggest headache. Back in the nineteenth century the French mathematician Joseph Fourier puzzled over why it was that our planet did not simply get hotter and hotter as it was struck by the rays of the sun, and concluded that the answer was what is called 'heat radiation', which carries energy back into space. But since if you left the physics at that, the result should have been an ice-cold earth, he concluded that there was something in the atmosphere that stopped all the heat leaving us. Something must be letting the sunlight in, like a greenhouse roof, but stopping some of the heat going back. The Irishman John Tyndall built on Fourier's insight to discover what really made the greenhouse roof, namely the greenhouse gases carbon dioxide and methane along with water vapour. If you just add a little of these gases to the nitrogen and oxygen in the atmosphere it keeps our climate warm and reasonably equable. So a bit of the greenhouse effect is good. Add too many greenhouse gases, and the climate warms up unpleasantly. That is exactly what we have been doing by burning fossil fuels that pump carbon dioxide into the atmosphere. For a thousand years before 1800, carbon dioxide levels in the atmosphere ranged between 270 and 290 parts per million (ppm). That had gone up to 387ppm by 2008, and it rises by about 2–3ppm a year. Our atmosphere now contains about 40 per cent more carbon dioxide than was there in pre-industrial times. If you add increases in methane (which results partly from more cultivation and from more flatulent livestock) and the artificial chemicals that destroy that world's sunscreen, the ozone layer, then the carbon dioxide equivalent in the atmosphere is 60 per cent above the earlier levels; it has gone up to 430 ppm.[9] (I will come to the moderately encouraging story of how we have halted ozone depletion later in the chapter.)

The first scientific hunches that we were changing our climate by burning fossil fuels led to the UN and the World Meteorological Organization (WMO) establishing the Intergovernmental Panel on Climate Change (IPCC) in 1988. The IPCC, which won the Nobel Peace Prize along with Vice-President Al Gore in 2007, is made up of leading climate scientists and government advisers. It works by consensus, and sometimes this has meant that those who wish to deny or cast doubt on what is happening block the more explicit warnings of climate threat. The Bush administration went so far as to with-draw support in 2002 from a distinguished American scientist who had been an IPCC chairman, presumably on the grounds that his nationality would embarrass the administration that had set up shop as leading sceptic and back marker in the international debate on the issue and on how to tackle it. The work of the IPCC fed into the discussions at the Rio Earth Summit in 1992 and the UN Framework Convention on Climate Change which targeted 2000 as the year by which signatories should reduce their emissions to 1990 levels. This proved much too optimistic, but it was followed by the Kyoto Proto-col, which bound signatories among developed nations to specific targets for emission cuts and also established the arrangements for an emissions trading scheme. The United States and Australia (playing, in the days of the Howard administration, the role of Washington's sidekick) refused to go along with the Protocol for reasons explored later. Overall, Kyoto was a useful first step, no more than that. The IPCC has continued to produce reports of increasing firmness and certainty. Its report in 2007 described the evidence of warming in the past few decades as 'unequivocal', nor could it identify any other factor which would have led to 'such widespread, near universal warming' as the increase in greenhouse gases. The IPCC noted in that year that eleven out of the past thirteen years had been in the hottest top dozen on record: 1998 and 2005 had been the hottest, followed by 1998, 2002 and 2003. The temperature on average is higher today than for a millennium.

The IPCC has noted that there is nothing we can do to prevent our temperature rising to at least 1.4°C above the pre-industrial level. Average global temperatures have risen by 0.75°C since the nineteenth century and, whatever measures we take now to cut the use of fossil fuels, there is 0.6°C of warming in the pipeline while the atmosphere catches up with the carbon dioxide that we have already emitted. If we were able to contain warming at, say, 2°C or below, we would still face some pretty major changes. There would be health problems caused by heatwaves, malnutrition, droughts, floods and infectious diseases. The extent to which we can blame recent extremes of weather on global warming is moot. But those extreme conditions have given us some idea of the consequences that would flow from a marked change of climate. In France during the very hot summer of 2003 (on the day that my daughter was married there the temperature hit about 40°C, more or less the heat at which the body starts to cook) there were reckoned to be almost 15,000 deaths in the first twenty days of August because of the heat. Initial estimates that over 35,000 people (mainly elderly) died in southern Europe that summer of heat-related problems have been revised upwards subsequently by some organizations to a figure above 52,000. In the terrible Hurricane Katrina floods there were 1,300 deaths. In the hot summer of 2007, many more deaths were recorded in Europe as the mercury rose, for example 500 in Hungary.

With a 2°C increase, water scarcity will grow (as we noted in Chapter 8) and there will be more droughts in the semi-arid tropics and the middle latitudes. Some crop yields will rise; yet others in the tropics will fall, increasing the risk of starvation in those areas. There will be more flooding as rain falls more heavily even in the otherwise drought affected areas. Hurricanes like Katrina will get stronger and heatwaves will increase with accompanying fires and droughts. People will migrate in search of scarce resources, provoking conflicts; there are few remaining of the sort of vast empty spaces to which humans migrated in the past, shedding much blood (for example in Tasmania and Newfoundland when they did so). When climate change was debated as a security issue at the UN, some of the African countries that took part expressed their present worries about groups in their countries buying weapons already for use in future resource wars.

The IPCC has observed that each notch upwards in the average global temperature produces another set of severe problems in addition to those already recorded. At a warming between 2°C and 3°C, all the risks get much greater. There are more floods, more heatwaves, more extensive droughts, more hunger, the bleaching of most of the world's coral, species extinction, higher sea levels with faster melting of Greenland's ice, the shrinking and maybe loss of high mountain glaciers, inundation of coastal areas and small islands, ever stronger hurricanes and perhaps a reduction in monsoon rains. Go a degree or two higher still and catastrophe beckons, with near-total melting of the Greenland and Western Antarctic ice sheets, accelerated warming as parts of our ecosystem produce rather than soak up carbon (an example of 'positive feedback'), more flooding, falls in food production, and deaths – many, many more deaths. The outlook becomes so bleak that it is hard to imagine allowing it to come about: hard but not impossible. The evidence is all there. We can easily join up all the dots. Will we?

What should encourage us is the understanding that it is not impossible to put together a programme that would prevent disaster. Unfortunately we cannot now avoid a temperature rise of about 2°C over pre-industrial levels. The most serious risks crowd in on us beyond that point, so the closer we can hold things to the 2°C figure the better. If we are lucky, we may be able to put the ceiling there; if we are unlucky, then we will find ourselves in the danger zone beyond 3°C. So the task is to ensure that greenhouse gas emissions peak within fifteen years and fall to half their present levels by the middle of the century. Without any technological breakthrough, scientists – including Britain's Sir David King – have shown how you can do this with a combination of fuel economy in cars, fuel efficiency in buildings and appliances, carbon capture and storing in coal-fired power stations, the use of alternative energy sources like solar panels and wind turbines, an end to deforestation, new planting of trees in the tropics and an increase in nuclear power. The target can be achieved, if the will exists.

It should encourage us that we have dealt successfully with another major threat to the planet, namely the depletion of stratospheric ozone which shields us from ultraviolet radiation. The problem began with the invention in the 1930s of Freon, the first of the chlorofluorocarbons, by the research chemist Thomas Midgley. (Poor Mr Midgley did the double: he was also the man who discovered that lead in petrol cut engine knocking in cars and enhanced engine performance.) Freon replaced some of the dangerous gases that had been used before in refrigeration. It made air-conditioning possible and was also useful in solvents and spray propellants. Unfortunately, as CFC use increased after the Second World War, it became clear that the emissions were thinning the ozone layer. Small holes were created over Chile and Australia. Increased ultraviolet radiation brought the risk of cataracts, skin cancer and the suppression of immune-system responses. Skin cancer rates in Chile, which includes the world's most southern town, Punta Arenas, have soared. We could count ourselves lucky about one chemical feature of the damage – that it was the chlorine in CFCs that did the harm. Had we used more generally the interchangeable but more expensive bromine (which goes into the halons that are used for fire-suppression systems and which destroys ozone faster and in far greater quantities), we would have torn the ozone layer apart.

The growing evidence of a link between CFCs and ozone depletion in the 1970s was initially discredited by Du Pont and other chemical manufacturers. But the proof of a connection grew and so did public disquiet, not least when pictures of the hole in the ozone layer were shown on television. Beginning with the Vienna Convention in 1985, the international community acted to protect the planet's sunscreen. The Montreal Protocol of 1987 has been toughened twice in 1990 and 1992 to phase out the production and use of CFCs and halons. I chaired the London meeting in 1990, when much of the running was made by the American delegation. It insisted that we should act on the precautionary principle in our understanding of the science – moving in other words on growing evidence rather than waiting for final, unequivocal proof – and accepting that developed countries should move first, bringing developing countries along later with the assistance of technology and resource transfers from richer signatories to the protocol. The crucial moment at the conference came when China and India agreed to go along with this approach. China, for example, was given until 2010 to phase out CFC production. The success of the agreement can be measured only by what happens to the ozone layer. So far, the results are encouraging with evidence, for example, that the ozone hole over the Antarctic is closing. The reason for covering this agreement at some length is that the process began with denial, went on to the criticism that nothing was put on the table except good intentions, and eventually secured its objective with American leadership and Chinese and Indian cooperation. It is an encouraging model when we look at the far more complicated issue of global warming and climate change.

We should now be moving towards the end game in securing a binding international agreement on this issue. The starting point is the Kyoto Protocol, technically an amendment to the UN Framework Convention on Climate Change (UNFCCC). It was agreed in 1997 and came into force in 2005. Over 170 countries have ratified it. Since the change of government in Canberra in late 2007, this group now includes Australia. The US administration under President Bush was implacably opposed to the agreement. The Protocol distinguishes between developed countries, which have largely created today's problems, and developing countries, which need assistance to avoid creating tomorrow's. Developed countries undertake between 2008 and 2012 to reduce their greenhouse gas emissions to 5 per cent below 1990 levels; for EU countries, for example, this means a cut of 15 per cent below the 2008 figure. The Protocol also establishes a carbon emissions trading scheme, under which the developed countries or industries within them could trade emissions – an excessive emissions producer purchasing credits to cover what it does from an emissions reducer. This is called 'cap and trade'; countries accept caps and can purchase their way to meeting them if they cannot take sufficient domestic measures to hit their own targets. They can buy from one another or from the developing countries, for example by funding projects under the Clean Development Mechanism which reduce emissions (like a forestry scheme or carbon sequestration from a coal-fired power station). The Protocol is recognized to be a first step. But it establishes the infrastructure for further, stronger agreements under which countries set binding caps on emissions, establish a global scheme for trading carbon emissions with a realistic price set for carbon, and accept an equitable and common responsibility for reducing the greenhouse gases caused by burning fossil fuels.

Efforts to hammer out a stronger agreement to build on and succeed Kyoto did not get very far in 2007. A December meeting in Bali, attended by a throng of negotiators, hangers-on, NGOs and journalists, accepted that the problem was serious and that the world needed a deal before the end of 2009 so that a new and binding framework would be in place when Kyoto runs out in 2012. But, partly owing to very unpopular blocking tactics by the American delegation, progress beyond this was slight. A scheme to compensate developing countries for conserving their forests was agreed, and delegates accepted that they should try to hammer out a comprehensive deal by the end of 2009. They agreed on a road map (not, in the circumstances, the best metaphor) for future talks. The Americans, under pressure, agreed to participate in them. Then all 10,000-plus members of the climate change caravan flew home, living to fight and fly another day – admittedly (which is some sort of small blessing) with the future purpose of negotiating an overall agreement. A UN Conference in Poznan, Poland in 2008 was no more successful than Bali. Hopes turned towards the 2009 Copenhagen meeting, though expectation of the recent greening of America's political class may be considerably exaggerated.

The main thing they will fight about in future is the best means of limiting climate change. We should not allow this debate to be distorted by ideological disputes. There is some truth in Nicholas Stern's argument that the pumping of vast quantities of carbon into the atmosphere represents a huge market failure. Human activity responds to price signals. We do not charge enough for carbon – indeed in much of the international economy we do not charge at all for it – so more carbon dioxide goes into the atmosphere. The more expensive the carbon, the less we would be likely to use it. In addition, markets usually find cheaper and more efficient ways of achieving socially desirable objectives such as adequate housing or increased investment in energy. Put those arguments together and the way ahead looks simple. We raise carbon's price, having set limits on how much greenhouse gas can be emitted, and we allow the market to do the rest, thus putting the main weight on the market aspects of the 'cap-and-trade' scheme. The trading of emissions of carbon dioxide is certainly a valuable tool and the EU has also made good progress in developing a carbon market. This was the sort of approach used successfully by the US in the mid-1990s to cut sulphur dioxide emissions and reduce acid rain. However, the initial difficulties in running the carbon scheme showed the importance of the context within which the market operates. In the beginning, the EU handed out too many emissions permits to industries like electricity generators, cement manufacturers and metal makers. This drove down the effective price of carbon and made permits virtually worthless. In order for the market to work effectively, the carbon price has to be driven up by using caps to force acceptable emission levels down. You can trade emissions by all means, but there have to be increasingly tough restrictions on what quantity of emissions is acceptable.

Government regulation has to go hand in hand with the use of market instruments. It is this very need for regulation that produces knee-jerk reactions of hostility among some market ideologues. I suspect that the view is sometimes taken that having successfully fought socialism, we should not allow more central controls and regulation of our lives to be allowed in through the green door. Some of the quasi-Orwellian solutions proposed for global governance of environmental issues (referred to later) deepen these anxieties. Yet regulation has always been required, preferably applied with a light touch, to ensure that markets do not damage the collective or individual welfare. We stopped the use of lead in petrol. We tightened the emission standards for petrol fumes and raised engine performance levels. We restricted smoking so that non-smokers were not obliged to inhale other people's tobacco fumes. We used public-health inspectors to ensure that the food people ate did not poison them. We applied efficiency standards to electrical appliances and insulation regulations to homes and offices. We obliged the private and public providers of our water to make certain that what we drink is safe. Regulation is not necessarily hostile to markets: it can help markets to work better. There will not be a successful accord on global warming without ever-tighter caps. We are more likely to reduce our emissions to levels below those caps if we use the price mechanism sensibly. Setting and enforcing caps worldwide is much more difficult than refining carbon-trading mechanisms and applying globally what has worked moderately well on a national and regional basis.

What should be the main pillars of a post-Kyoto agreement? First, we require a global target to hold warming at between 2°C and 3°C if we possibly can. This will require interim targets for 2025 or 2030 on the way to a mid-century cut of 80 per cent of emissions on 1990 levels. In order to achieve a global target, we will naturally require national targets, which is where the real diplomatic and political hassle gets going seriously and noisily. The national figures will need to take account of historic responsibility for current levels of greenhouse gases, the amount of emissions per head of population, the overall level of a country's emissions, its capacity to change, its wealth and its vulnerability to climate change threats.[10] There will also need to be an agreement on the starting point for the process. Since the 1990s saw rapid growth in the US and an economic slump in Russia, taking a 1990 base-line for cuts requires a huge effort from America and gives Russia a big bonus. There are then arguments about how the responsibility is allocated between industrial sectors and between groups of countries. How should we deal with aviation and shipping? Should we assign responsibility here to the flag of the carrier, the departure point, the port of arrival, or the nation of the majority of passengers or freight being carried? Most difficult of all is the allocation of responsibility between developed and developing countries, an issue which is above all a matter of how the balance is struck between the US and China. China in total now emits more carbon dioxide than the United States. But look at emissions per head of population and the American figure is almost five times the Chinese one. There are also the issues of historic responsibility and relative wealth. Any proposal to put all these elements together will have to encompass different starting points, convergence dates, industrial targets and, conceivably, relate the targets directly to economic growth in order to put as much weight as possible on fuel efficiency. There will also need to be financial and technology transfers from the rich to the poor, and assistance towards the costs of mitigating the effects of global warming, for example helping poor countries to build up their coastal defences.

Of all the main actors in the environmental negotiations ahead, the European Union – without any smugness or complacency – should probably be the best placed to achieve tough targets. At present the EU accounts for just over 30 per cent of the world's GDP and is responsible for 15 per cent of global carbon emissions. This should fall to below 10 per cent by 2050. The EU has, of course, been, with the US, the main carbon dioxide culprit in the past. At a European Council (heads of government) meeting in 2007, the EU committed itself to reducing emissions by 30 per cent on 1990 levels by 2020, provided other developed countries did the same; in any event, without any firm international agreement, an independent European cut of 20 per cent was pledged. The Council argued that developed countries should aim to make cuts of between 60 and 80 per cent by 2050, which is what is required to keep global warming between 2°C and 3°C. To accomplish these ambitious though essential targets, the EU has set a number of objectives, for example for use of renewable energy and for investment in effective low-carbon technologies. The EU has kept more or less to these overall plans though there has been a bit of back-sliding under pressure from parts of industry, like car makers, and from those politicians like Mr Berlusconi who claim that developed economies cannot cope with both a recession and tougher environmental standards.

There are several reasons why the EU is more advanced than others in making these forward commitments. First, there is a more developed sense of the threat of climate change (especially among young voters) in Europe than elsewhere. This does not mean that turning Europe into a low-carbon economy will be politically easy. Politicians in most countries are still nervous of embracing policy positions that may be electorally awkward (like environment taxes and putting up the cost of travelling by road and air). The idea of sustainable economic development has not emerged easily into regular political discourse or the campaigning narratives of most mainstream parties. Nuclear power – a clean energy source – still spooks many voters in Europe (except, apparently, in France, which is heavily dependent on nuclear power) and is a subject that tends to repel rational argument. My own view is that nuclear power in Britain and globally is an essential energy source if we are to abate global warming. With very few exceptions, European politicians and controversialists, whatever their caution about policy prescriptions, are not inclined to challenge the scientific consensus on climate change and its human causes. Those who do, like the Danish statistician Bjørn Lomborg, tend to enjoy a rather brief notoriety largely because they satisfy a natural public delight in doubting and kicking against the consensus.

European countries are welfare democracies with high standards of living and a developed sense of communal responsibility (at the expense, some argue, of individual entrepreneurialism). They are conservative about change, which probably encompasses worry about the massive changes that global warming would bring, even if these might be less severe in Europe than in any other continent. There is a tradition of environmentalism with strong minor parties that define themselves almost entirely in terms of green issues, and which have been strong enough from time to time to unnerve the mainstream parties. Partly as a consequence of Europe's welfarism as well as of the nineteenth-century development of our cities and rural areas, there is a strong public transport system with good train services in much of Europe (excluding, alas, the UK). We also depend more on gas than other economies, which gives us, as we saw in the last chapter, strategic problems partly of our own making in dealing with Russia but which is good for our environmental record: 41 per cent of the carbon dioxide in the atmosphere comes from coal, 39 per cent from oil and only 20 per cent from gas. Some of our oldest, most polluting industries were closed down in the wake of the collapse of Russia's east-European empire; they were bankrupt as well as filthy. Some European industries still create problems. Chancellor Angela Merkel has to fight to get the German automobile industry to improve the fuel efficiency of its gas-guzzling vehicles. These efforts have been seen by some firms as the imposition of a heavy disadvantage on them in comparison with the more fuel-efficient cars from Italy and France. But Merkel has been prepared so far to fight for tougher fuel regulation, making the point that lower emissions will prove a competitive selling point for vehicles. Europe has been in the vanguard of efforts to put an effective carbon-trading scheme in place. There are still mountains to climb if Europe is to meet the targets it has set. But the task can be achieved, and the best way of encouraging others to act is for Europe to have the confidence to do so itself, whatever others do in the short term. European politicians are often searching for a vocation for their union of nation-states. What is Europe for in the twenty-first century? What should it do? How can it demonstrate the vision and relevance that will motivate its citizens? Much windy rhetoric is expended trying to answer these questions. The best answer would be to take responsibility for leading the way in international efforts to save our planet.

The first summit that President Bush attended with the EU was in Göteborg, Sweden, in 2001. It was before 9/11 and he was still feeling his way towards giving his presidency a sense of definition and purpose. He was not yet what he was tragically to become: the 'War President'. Nevertheless, one thing was clear already. He did not see eye to eye with his European opposite numbers on the environment. At the press conference after the summit he slyly drew attention to the problems some Europeans were then having in meeting their emission reduction targets. His father, the first President Bush, had told the world at the time of the 1992 Rio conference that the American way of life was not up for negotiation. He himself went further. One of the first acts of his presidency was to announce that the United States would not ratify the Kyoto Treaty (which had been signed by his predecessor though with nil chance then of Senate approval). Kyoto, he announced with more satisfaction than accuracy, was 'dead'. At one stroke he was able to ditch the policy of the previous administration, which was so closely associated with Al Gore, the man he had defeated in the courts for the presidency. He was also appealing to his base in the Republican Party, which thought that the whole climate-change kerfuffle was bogus, got up by the forces of darkness who wanted to allow the UN to run America and international law to constrain its testosterone. Moreover, he wished to avoid doing anything that might be unpopular with energy companies, polluting industries, taxpayers, car drivers, automobile companies, or financial backers. He led a party to whose right-wing members Governor Mitt Romney, when campaigning unsuccessfully to inherit the Bush battle standard, was to appeal by claiming that global warming had nothing to do with the US. If the globe thought it was warming, then the globe could get on and do something about it, but leave Planet America out of it. For President Bush initially this was pretty much the word from Washington, conveyed with only the slightest arching of an eyebrow by Secretary of State Colin Powell. Let Washington get on with the real environmental agenda trying to rewrite legislation on clean air, clean water and endangered species, relaxing pollution limits and chopping down more of America's forests. Denying America's great record of environmentalism – from Benjamin Franklin through Henry David Thoreau to Teddy Roosevelt – President Bush's approach deeply depressed all those friends and admirers of the US who know that these environmental problems can be solved only with American participation, and believe also that they *can* be solved if the US gets involved. Like President Putin, Mr Bush believed that the economy came first, the environment second – if not rather lower than that. Let the rest of the world go hang, and if there was a problem for future generations then let them, with God's guidance, do what they wanted about it, in the margins presumably of paying off the debts run up on his watch.

All this was doubly curious and reprehensible. The United States had in the 1970s been a world leader in energy efficiency and conservation and in developing alternative energy sources. This was a positive response to rising energy prices in an economy much of whose previous virility had depended on cheap fuel. But the emphasis for many politicians rather curiously shifted. As the evidence about greenhouse gases accumulated, American politicians and lobbyists began to pooh-pooh the idea that there was a problem, because if one did exist then the figures made clear that more radical change in America had to be at the heart of solving it. At first President Bush's administration denied the science, queried it, undermined the institutions that enunciated it and diluted their conclusions whenever they emerged. Later it moved into diplomatic damage limitation, seeking to embroil others in initiatives that offered a pain-free and change-free alternative to Kyoto. Washington was assisted in this disreputable enterprise by John Howard's Australian government, which joined in promoting the Asia–Pacific Partnership. This purported to offer a way forward on 'clean development and climate'. According to the Climate Institute of Australia, it would have led to at least a global doubling of greenhouse gas emissions by 2050.

What was so deplorable about the Australian behaviour was that they, as much as or more than anyone else, should have been sympathetic to the need for radical measures of international cooperation on climate change. The environment in Australia is extremely vulnerable. For a start, Australia suffers from infertile and saline soils, with low and unpredictable rainfall. The introduction of rabbits and foxes by early British settlers proved as disastrous as subsequent subsidized clearance of vegetation and overstocking of sheep. This has led to what are called man-made droughts. Australia's fragile environment has been further threatened by real drought in the Murray river basin and in the main grain-growing areas of the south-west. One of the most attractive tourist destinations in Australia, the Great Barrier Reef, is threatened by coral bleaching as a result of rising sea temperatures. Australia was also one of the countries most affected by ozone depletion, and quite properly was an enthusiastic advocate of global measures to reverse it. Back in those days, Australia did not excuse inaction on the grounds that developing countries were being let off taking the early action demanded of the industrialized countries that had done most to create the problem.

Yet this was the excuse for doing nothing trotted out by Mr Howard and his ministerial colleagues during our EU discussions with them in the early 2000s. They claimed that Australia could not be expected to act on climate change before developing countries did so, because heavy carbon-intensive industries (whose electricity charges were in fact often subsidized by Australian domestic electricity users) would relocate to Indonesia if their carbon use was restricted or priced any higher. Moreover, they argued that Australia's size increased the use of transport fuel, ignoring the fact that 60 per cent of this fuel is used in urban areas. By the tired end of his administration Mr Howard had been driven by growing Australian public concern about the environment (motivated partly by continuing droughts) to accept that more should be done internationally to combat climate change. His role as chief Pacific bag carrier and bottle washer for President Bush had not proved popular either when it took him to Iraq or carried him away from Kyoto. One of the first acts of his successor, Kevin Rudd, was to sign the Kyoto Treaty. This brought Australia, which has the biggest emissions per head of any industrialized country and whose emissions have been growing faster than those of any OECD country, into the mainstream of the fight against climate change. This is where most Australians clearly think their country belongs.

Canada has behaved little better than the Howard government, missing targets for emissions reductions and ducking and weaving at Bali to avoid commitment in principle to hard caps. Greenhouse gas emissions per head in Canada are only a little below those for the US and Australia. This is not what might be expected of a country which sets so much store usually by its role as a good global citizen.

The sort of public concern that had started to move Mr Howard (one example of which was the best-selling success of the Australian scientist Tim Flannery's excellent book *The Weather Makers*) has recently been matched in the United States. At the city and state level, from Florida to California, America has begun to move, embracing targets for greenhouse emissions, introducing regulations on fuel efficiency and promoting carbon neutrality (for example in Austin, capital of the president's own state). Companies like Wal-Mart and General Electric joined the demand for action, taking initiatives themselves as well as supporting national measures. One sector in particular that attracted growing American support was the encouragement of the use of biodiesel and ethanol produced from plants and vegetation which have absorbed carbon dioxide when growing and simply emit the same gas when burned. The US has in particular supported with huge subsidies corn crops used for the production of ethanol as a vehicle fuel mix. This has already had a detrimental effect on the price of corn. Others have successfully used other crops, for example sugar in Brazil, where ethanol is a substantial energy source. Biofuels can be a very helpful alternative to fossil fuels, but their production can also have damaging environmental consequences, as the European Union has argued. Rainforest and other forms of natural vegetation have sometimes been cleared in Latin America and South-East Asia to make way for ethanol-producing crops. Wetlands and grassland as well as forest have been lost and the production of biofuels can involve fossil-fuel driven tractors, nitrogen fertilizer and heavy use of water. Nevertheless, if they are properly regulated biofuels could represent a helpful way forward in meeting transport needs in a more sustainable way.

A change in official American attitudes to global warming is central to any chance of success and fortunately this seems to have arrived with President Obama's election. He promises to bring strong political leadership on the environment, in a country that will have to adjust its lifestyle and in which many have been encouraged by politicians and lobbyists to disbelieve the scientific evidence on climate change. The new President himself was certainly not in denial on the science, indeed he picked several distinguished scientists to serve in his administration, like Steven Chu as Energy Secretary. Chu had previously been working on solar energy at Berkeley. John Holdren, the Harvard physicist and expert on climate change, became a senior adviser. President Obama's fiscal stimulus package included measures on clean energy and energy reduction; two of his first executive orders were to set a federal fuel economy target by 2012 and to instruct the Environment Protection Agency to reconsider a decision made in 2008 which had prevented California from setting tougher targets for greenhouse gas emissions from cars. His administration also set about working to establish a cap and trade system for carbon emissions but it confronted formidable difficulties in getting comprehensive environmental legislation through Congress. President Obama clearly understood that American leadership was crucial if there was to be any global agreement. Furthermore, he recognized – a point pursued by Secretary of State, Hillary Clinton, on her first trip to Beijing – that at the heart of any deal there would need to be an agreement between the United States and China. China will not move without America, and America will not move without China. They are locked together. An agreement between them is vital to saving the century.

Focusing on China does not mean that we can forget about other developing countries. Later this century, for example, the Indian population will exceed China's. But India's carbon emissions, whether measured in aggregate or per head, are only a third of those in China, reflecting China's much greater manufacturing success. If China will move, so will other emerging economies, even though some (India is in fact a conspicuous example) do not want to think too much about the subject for the present, save to assert the importance of basing the diplomacy leading to an agreement on past responsibility and present population size and economic strength. China's economic growth has been the biggest change agent in the world, and it inevitably has huge environmental implications for China itself and for the rest of us.

China's population is about one fifth of the world's total. Fifty years ago, 38 million people died in China's famine years, which were mostly a consequence of Chairman Mao's delusions. All that is a grim and distant past. Today, China's 1.3 billion people have made their country into the world's workshop. They have the highest production rates of steel and cement. They make a large number of whatever products you are likely to buy, from trainers to tracksuits, from televisions to laptops, from microwaves to children's toys. My father spent much of his life cherishing in vain the English middle-class ambition to own a Rover car. Once only made in Birmingham in the English Midlands, MG Rover cars are now manufactured in Oklahoma by the Nanjing Automobile Group. Where not long ago we asked a little quizzically whether this Chinese 'thing' could possibly continue at its present rate, we came to depend on it continuing, not least so that the proceeds of all this Chinese growth could bail out our banks and make up for the calamitous consequences of our asset-inflation and asset-invention in the West.

China has paid a high price for this roar-away, rip-along growth. It has the highest consumption of coal and fertilizers as well as tobacco. It is the biggest consumer of timber. Seven thousand new cars drive out every day onto China's vastly increased road network and this increase will continue unabated until 2030. Air quality is dreadful; according to the Chinese Academy of Environmental Planning 380,000 people are likely to die prematurely each year by 2010 from respiratory ailments. Soil is eroding and desertification spreading. Water quality is bad and the quantity of water is falling (not least as glacier melt affects the flow and the level of rivers). As for China's main rivers, the Pearl, the Yangtze and the Yellow, it is now quite common for them to stop flowing for parts of the year. Of China's 668 largest towns and cities, 400 are believed to be short of water, and the incidence of water rationing is growing.[11] Urbanization puts an increasing strain on the environment. The growth of cities is a worldwide phenomenon, but one especially marked in China. In 1900 about 225 million people worldwide lived in cities; this had risen to 2,900 million by the end of the century. The rise of cities creates a range of environmental problems and is directly associated with the exploitation of fossil fuels.[12] Chairman Mao did not much like cities, but since his departure and the reforms begun by Deng Xiaoping peasants have been flooding into cities to work in the new factories there. At the time of the communist takeover in 1949 there were five cities in China with a population of over 1 million; by the end of the century there were forty. There are six in Japan. By 2050, it is reckoned that 1 billion Chinese will live in cities. Sixteen out of the twenty most polluted cities in the world are in China.

The Chinese leadership seem to understand perfectly well the scale of their environmental problems, which are already a heavy drain on the economy and which have the potential to derail it. In 2006 the party boss in Shanghai, Chen Liangyu, was sacked partly because of his opposition to the Beijing leadership's attempt to rein in economic growth, to make it more equitable and to clean up heavily polluted industries. They know the arrogant folly of Mao's slogan 'Man must conquer nature', which overturned the traditional Chinese belief in harmony between nature and mankind.[13] But however much President Hu or Premier Wen may appreciate the need for sweeping changes to save China's environment, how much can they actually make such reforms stick at the local level? How far beyond Beijing's beltway does the writ of today's emperors run? Moreover, how are Chinese leaders to incorporate environmental concern into their main legitimizing project, which is premised on spreading prosperity? They may fear that environmental problems could create political turbulence; they also surely worry that the slowing down in the helter-skelter growth of the economy risks destroying the credibility and rationale for an authoritarian political system, Communist by name but bruisingly capitalist by method. This is not an academic conundrum for the rest of us. Finding a Chinese solution is a main key to saving the planet.

Back in 1928, Mohandas Gandhi said presciently, 'God forbid that India should ever take to industrialism after the manner of the West

. . . If an entire nation of 300 million took to similar economic exploitation, it would strip the world bare like locusts.' Subtract the nostalgic vision of a peasant economy and the sentiment is one that is relevant to all the emerging countries, not just India. What happens to the world if 1.3 billion Chinese decide to live like Americans and Europeans (a state to which it would not be unreasonable for them to aspire)? How does one planet survive when it appears to consume enough for two? What sharpens the dilemma for the Chinese is their heavy dependence on coal. The search for domestic oil in the 1970s and 80s having proved largely abortive, the growth since then – begun by peasant entrepreneurialism – has been fuelled largely by coal, of which China possesses an abundance. This argues for stepping up the efforts, already begun by the EU, to work with China on the development of an affordable technology for carbon capture and storage. Put simply, this involves taking the carbon dioxide created by burning fossil fuels and burying it before it gets into the atmosphere. The IPCC reckons that between approximately a third and two thirds of global emissions of carbon dioxide from power generation could be captured and stored by 2050 with about a third of emissions saved from other big polluters in industry.

In addition to the other problems detailed here, in 2008 China had to cope like everyone else with growing food prices. These were in part the result of rising demand for a more varied diet and in part the result of drought and higher grain prices in Australia. The Chinese leadership could have been forgiven for thinking that the tangled climate change quandaries dwarfed any of the other problems confronting them.

As I said near the beginning of this chapter, solutions to the problems of global warming are primarily issues of politics, not economics or environmental policy, and politics should provide the answers to negotiating a successor arrangement to Kyoto that ties in China and the United States. Sir Nicholas Stern has argued rather optimistically that 'as the science of climate change is widely accepted, public attitudes will make it increasingly difficult for political leaders around the world to downplay the importance of serious action'. Unfortunately, politics rarely functions in this rational way. If frogs could vote, would they manage to choose to turn off the gas ring before the warming water in the pot boiled them alive? I mean no disrespect to environmentalists and scientists in saying that the argument on global warming should no longer be seen as a 'green' issue driven by boffins. If hammering away at it in this way was going to deliver results, presumably Vice-President Gore would have won the American presidency rather than the Nobel Peace Prize. For all the environmentalists' hostility to President Bush, he was elected twice – well, made president twice, anyway – and was never nudged into doing something more helpful for the planet than his preferred inert and foolish inactivity. Global warming is about foreign and security policy; it is about trade and business; it is about opportunity and development; it is about stewardship; it is about the 70 per cent of those alive today who are still likely to be alive in 2050. It is an issue for generals, priests, tycoons, trade union leaders, lawyers, farmers, civil servants, doctors and our emergency services, not just environmental NGOs. It is about making changes in all our individual lives with often benign consequences that we cannot always ourselves detect or even measure. It is about balancing political action and technical fixes using market mechanisms more effectively wherever we can. It is not just a mainstream issue, it is *the* mainstream issue. It has to be dealt with realistically as well as boldly.

That means putting aside thoughts of a worldwide anti-carbon dictatorship which would move on remorselessly from controlling every carbon footprint to trying to control the number of the world's feet, in other words how much we are allowed to breed. It is going to be difficult enough to construct a global architecture that involves international oversight of national policies, building dispute-settlement machinery and ensuring national compliance with the arguments made. Going beyond these vauntingly ambitious goals is simply preposterous. We could do all these practical things, difficult as they are, and we could put in place without too much cost or turbulence the policies that would save us and successive generations. It will require all the resources of a committed and hopeful politics from Washington to Beijing, from Moscow to Canberra. There is, however, not much time to agree a treaty that will transform our lives and save our planet. For the nation-states involved in the venture, it will be much tougher than Versailles. It needs to be a lot more successful.

13

Coughs and Sneezes

Wherever the European has trod, death seems to pursue the aboriginal . . .

Charles Darwin, on board *The Beagle*, 1836

Improvement in health is likely to come, in the future as in the past, from modification of the conditions which lead to disease, rather than from intervention into the mechanisms of death after it has occurred.

Thomas McKeown, medical historian, 1976

The microbe is so very small,
You cannot make him out at all,
But many sanguine people hope
To see him through a microscope.

Hilaire Belloc,
'The Microbe', 1912

I had a little bird,
Its name was Enza,
I opened the window,
And in-flew-Enza.

Children's skipping rhyme,
dating from the Spanish flu pandemic in 1918

Whatever else we say about international politics, we are all at this moment fully engaged in our longest, most vicious, brutal and unfair war. The best outcome we can expect is survival. The enemy, always there, is disease.

We often forget the impact of disease on our history and on the development of the communities in which we live. Field Marshal Bernard Montgomery, one of Britain's great heroes of the Second World War, told the House of Lords in 1962 that 'Rule 1, on page 1, of the book of war is "Do not march on Moscow..."' This wise advice was a reference not only to Hitler's more recent experience but to Napoleon's catastrophic advance on Russia's capital in the summer of 1812. Napoleon set out for Moscow with over half a million men. By the time he fought the Battle of Borodino the number had been heavily reduced. By the end of the year as many as 400,000 French and allied troops had died, less than a quarter in battle. Marching through the heat of summer, they drank dirty water and even urine left in the tracks of the horses. They suffered from dehydration, malnutrition and increasingly from dysentery. Regiments, trudging through the excrement and the stink of those who had gone in front of them, were wiped out. The return journey saw the once Grande Armée cut to ribbons by starvation, cold, tuberculosis and typhus. The French losses amounted to over 300,000 men out of a population of 27 million; this is comparable to a loss of 700,000 from today's population. Marshal Ney wrote that it was not Russian bullets that conquered the army but 'General Famine and General Winter'. It was also 'General Typhus and General TB'.[1]

We noted earlier the impact of the Spanish conquistadors, beginning with 'Stout Cortez' and his 600 men, on the New World. Hernando Cortez conquered Mexico; Francisco Pizarro the Inca empire in South America. Disease ravaged their Amerindian foes. Native populations who, unlike Eurasians, had not spent several thousand years co-evolving with animals and their diseases, were pounded by epidemic after epidemic. Smallpox, measles, influenza and typhus were the biggest killers, but there were plenty of diseases (diphtheria, malaria, mumps, plague, yellow fever) which followed. Between the early sixteenth and the early seventeenth century the indigenous populations in America declined by 90 per cent. Advanced and complex societies, with cities and monuments, were reduced inside a few generations to nomadic hunting and gathering. Social breakdown was so devastating

that people often forgot that it had been their ancestors, a few generations before, who had actually built the dead cities and monuments
whose ruins they could see around them. Hernando de Soto, who in
1540 marched through what later became the south-eastern United
States, often came across recently abandoned cities. Spanish-borne
disease introduced at the coast had preceded de Soto's march by some
years. By the time the French arrived a century later the only evidence
of the Mississippians were the monumental mounds they had left
behind.

It was not only invasion, military campaigns and conquest that
were shaped from Mexico to Moscow by disease: so too was culture.
William H. McNeill argues that disease helps explain the triumph of
Spanish culture and Christianity in Latin America as well as the ease
of Spain's military conquest.[2] Very few Spaniards ever crossed the
Atlantic to the New World. Yet the culture of the Iberian peninsula,
brought with them in the case of so many of the conquistadors from
poor, oven-hot towns and villages in Extremadura, was firmly im-
planted for ever on a whole continent whose inhabitants – at least
those who survived – abandoned their own religions and rituals for
the Gospel of the missionaries. They had seen their own armies, their
own commanders, cut down by European diseases. They assumed the
superiority of their Spanish conquerors' God: a God who destroyed
the foes of those who worshipped Him, even while their own gods
deserted them. Apostasy must have seemed sensible and precautionary
to Aztecs and Incas. So now we can, as I noted earlier, give thanks in
the Royal Chapel in Granada for God-given contagion.

Disease can also lay claim to helping to impel the development of
political authority and state governance in fifteenth- and sixteenth-
century Europe. Black rats, fleas and maritime commerce brought the
Black Death to western and northern Europe from its presumed starting point, the armies of a Mongol prince who were besieging the
trading city of Caffa in the Crimea in 1346 and who flung plague-
infected cadavers over its walls. The infection, spread by flea bites and
coughing and sneezing, was lethal. Between 1346 and 1350 it is
reckoned that about a third of Europe's total population was wiped
out from Greenland to the Mediterranean. The demographic shock
lasted for more than a century. The fightback against disease began

in the northern Italian city-states, which started to put in place some of the minimum requirements for the betterment of public health – sanitary regulations, improvements in civic hygiene and controls to prevent contagion. Venice and Florence established boards of health in 1348. Ragusa on the Adriatic introduced quarantine regulations on shipping, an example that was followed elsewhere. Milan and Mantua brought in controls on commerce by land. Many cities established *lazaretti* – isolation hospitals. Large states – Henry VIII's England, Philip II's Spain and later Catherine the Great's Russia – followed suit. In response to the threat of plague and epidemic disease, political authority was concentrated in a few hands that could manage and contain disasters. Moreover, states competed beneficially with one another to demonstrate their ability to protect the welfare of their citizens.[3] Fighting disease was a formative element in the early growth of the European state.

Yellow fever in the United States had a similar galvanizing effect on the development of public health services (from laboratories to urban sanitation), reflecting a growing community-based social solidarity in fighting epidemics. Yellow fever was a major killer in US cities in the eighteenth and nineteenth centuries: in a single outbreak in 1793 the mosquito-borne disease killed 5,000 people in Philadelphia, one tenth of the population, despite the burning of tar in the streets. New Orleans was very badly hit in the following century. The final epidemic of the disease in the US broke out in 1905, but it continues to kill in Africa and South America. There were outbreaks in Kenya and Senegal in the 1990s and the first urban case in the Americas for fifty years occurred in Bolivia in 1999.

We require effective government and strong community involvement to fight disease. Again and again disease has shaped our societies. Very often humankind has simply been unable to fight its corner against infection: the struggle against viruses and bacteria is not a symmetrical contest fought by the Queensberry Rules.

Each of us – humans and the enemy – has different evolutionary strategies. Humans are very robust, very resilient creatures, but viruses and bacteria have more manoeuvrability and adaptability; they exploit openings mercilessly, much more so than do most humans. We tend inevitably to have a comfortably human-centred world view in which we exist in some kind of balance or equilibrium with disease. So clean humans, for example, fight dirty MRSA (an antibiotic-resistant bacterial infection) in hospitals that should be free of it. MRSA is in fact all over the place (including our own bodies), with unfortunately the best growth opportunities in hospitals where people are at their weakest. While the idea of balance may make sense in our heads, 1.7 metres off the ground, diseases whose entire being is defined by a desperate struggle for existence do not recognize such a thing as equilibrium. Darwin's theory of evolution was shocking not so much because it overturned a Christian world view (with God resting, exhausted by six days of hard creating, on the seventh) but because it overturned a human world view, positing that dynamism not equilibrium was the essential characteristic of the world. Dynamism is the music of life. Unfortunately, one result is that since every battle we win redoubles the pressure on diseases, they appear to fight back for their own survival with everything they have.

As humans, we possess a powerful cognitive capacity and its corollary, empiricism. We are not especially rigorous or consistent in our application of this attribute, even in securing our own survival. We are actually lousy at sticking to what we know and can readily discover, allowing other myths, narratives and stories to overwhelm our capacity for apprehending and combating disease. This makes it harder to fight it, something we have found out all too often, for example in the battle against AIDS. The AIDS pandemic sank its claws into the gay communities of San Francisco and New York partly because in the late 1970s those communities were still emerging from a long, bravely fought and only partially successful battle for equality and tolerance. For several years, into the mid-80s, the empirical understanding that the disease was sexually transmitted played second fiddle to a community narrative in which free love was the epitome of resistance to oppressive social and cultural norms. Early efforts to control the disease were sometimes seen as part of a wider, longer campaign of repression. Similarly, ongoing efforts to control the pandemic are inhibited by a wide variety of compelling, but irrelevant, moral qualms. Similar problems covering disputes about science as well as moral anxieties are encountered again and again in attitudes to the MMR vaccine in Britain, in the fight against polio in West

Africa and in opposition to the papilloma (HPV) vaccine. The idea of inoculating the young against a sexual disease (papilloma) that is thought to affect over a quarter of American women aged 14 to 39, strikes many people apparently as more horrifying than women dying of preventable cervical cancer which papilloma can cause.[4] While Alexander Pope in his eighteenth-century *Essay on Man* described us as 'great lord of all thing', he went on to remark: 'Sole judge of truth, in endless error hurl'd; / The glory, jest and riddle of the world!'

Epidemic disease has had a long and lasting impact on the evolution of human communities. But so long as human populations remained widely scattered and relatively isolated, they remained a rather low-priority target. That said, it is possible to imagine that an occasional mutation here or there in a bacterium, virus or fungus may have wiped out entire communities. This would have been a dead-end for the disease as well as for the community. From an evolutionary stand-point, disease is liable to be most deadly when it first develops the means of succeeding against our immune systems. After that, the selection process will push for sustainability, that is for a disease which can spread itself efficiently. Many of our oldest enemies like malaria and tuberculosis possess this characteristic. As 'recent' diseases go, AIDS is actually quite extraordinary in that it came ready-equipped with a long time-lag between the contraction of the disease and the first sign of its symptoms. Combined with the power to deconstruct our immune systems and an extraordinary adaptability, this latency probably makes AIDS as threatening a disease as has ever confronted mankind.

Some diseases are epidemic; others are endemic to human populations. Epidemic diseases represent a contact with something that is new, challenging expectations, placing a heavy and sudden selection pressure on human populations to develop resistance, change behaviour or find means of palliation or cure. This encounter can be disastrous, turning an epidemic into a pandemic, that is a situation in which multiple waves of the same disease or kind of disease begin a self-sustaining march back and forth across human populations. But some diseases fizzle out at this stage. The 'Picardy sweats' (similar to sweating sickness in fifteenth- and sixteenth-century England, though accompanied by a rash and less likely to be fatal), which swept France in the eighteenth century, came and went like wildfire. This mysterious disease has not recurred since 1861.

Some diseases, however, make an evolutionary leap to become endemic; they develop the means to spread themselves efficiently in human populations. Sometimes efficiency means not killing the human host, at least not immediately. Both tuberculosis and malaria have carved out their own evolutionary niche in humankind; they have become endemic, increasingly virulent though not always fatal. Malaria has been around for perhaps 50,000 years, but in most cases the transition from epidemic to endemic disease has been relatively recent. The origin and transmission of disease have been influenced by three factors: contact with animals, particularly domesticated animals; the development of agriculture and the rise in populations and subsequently in urbanization which this entailed; and the development of trade and migration networks by land and sea.

All this has made Eurasia historically the great hothouse of human disease. Not only are there numerous river valleys where agriculture has flourished, it has also been home to a wide variety of animals which could be and have been domesticated. Largely because of this domestication, Eurasia accounted for the majority of global trade and inter-civilizational mingling for many thousands of years. Eurasians had access to cows, horses, goats, pigs, numerous kinds of fowl, camels, donkeys, dogs and so on. The range in the New World was much more limited, and Eurasia's animal people-carriers – like horses – were largely absent, which helps explain why Inca, Aztec and Mississippian civilizations all managed to coexist in the New World without apparently making contact with one another. Thousands of years of human–animal and human–human contact meant that a wide and terrifying range of diseases was endemic to the Europeans who made contact with the indigenous populations of the New World: measles, tuberculosis and smallpox from cattle, influenza from pigs and ducks, pertussis (whooping cough) from pigs and dogs, and malaria probably spread by birds. Long proximity allowed Eurasians to build up a degree of resistance to some of these, but the result of the New World's encounter with them was cataclysmic.

Disease then cuts continually across human history. The plague epidemics which swept across Europe in the late Middle Ages and early Renaissance raised the relative price of labour, generating their own miniature industrial revolution: the social and economic institution of serfdom collapsed, cities grew and there was a major incentive to utilize animal, wind and water power in order to increase productivity. The landscape painting of England, Holland and France of the seventeenth and eighteenth centuries often depicts the mills and mill-races constructed a couple of centuries before. Malaria was the greatest barrier to exploration and development in sub-Saharan Africa, until the discovery of the utility of quinine as a prophylaxis,[5] and continues to place sub-Saharan countries at a major disadvantage economically. It was introduced by Europeans to Central and South America, where it also became an impediment to development. Meningitis was the scourge of Japanese children in the nineteenth century, killing four of Emperor Komei's six children (a fifth died of other causes) and helping to bring Emperor Meiji to the Chrysanthemum Throne. As diseases mutate, evolve in response to selection pressures or die out, it is not simply their own destinies which are involved: human communities are thrown down or raised up in the same struggles.

Attitudes to disease, especially in richer countries, have been filtered through a rosy-hued viewfinder. Science advances; fortunes are spent; health services are established and expanded; disease recedes. But that is only the first paragraph of the story. Over a century ago, in his novel *The Sleeper Awakes*, H. G. Wells predicted a world in which disease had been defeated. Medical science has made spectacular advances since then. We have vanquished previously fatal diseases. Insulin, penicillin and antibiotics have prolonged and improved the lives of countless millions. Vaccines and progress in surgery have prolonged life. Average life expectancy across the world has increased, with a particularly welcome fall in child mortality. By the middle of the last century improved public-health measures appeared to have overwhelmed the old threat of infectious disease in the developed world and we were hopeful about making progress in the same battles in developing countries. But by the turn of the century infectious diseases like HIV/AIDS, BSE/variant Creutzfeldt-Jakob disease, legionnaires' disease, SARS and a virus influenza seemed to be making a comeback in many parts of the world.[6] The World Health Organization (WHO) believes that there are now nearly forty diseases that were not known a generation ago. Old diseases like tuberculosis and cholera have also re-emerged: Latin America had been free of cholera for more than a century until in the early 1990s a pandemic raged across the region. By 1995, 1 million people were affected and over 10,000 had died. The breakdown of the economy in Zimbabwe, under a brutal and corrupt government, led to an outbreak of cholera in 2008 which killed up to 4,000 people and affected many more. True to form, President Mugabe denied what was happening.

We should not be too surprised: we are engaged in a continuing struggle. The Italian physician and poet Girolamo Fracastoro, a class-mate of Copernicus in the sixteenth century who wrote a moralizing poem about the symptoms and treatment of syphilis, noted in his treatise *De Contagione*, 'There will come yet other new and unusual ailments in the course of time. And this disease [syphilis] will pass away, but it later will be born again and be seen by our descendants.' Several developments have contributed to the change in fortunes in coping with disease. There has been increasingly rapid urbanization, especially in developing countries (where most of the largest cities are found today). In Nigeria, for example, the urban proportion of the population rose by the 1990s from a fifth to over a third in less than thirty years. Ever since the first cities developed they have been by-words for dirt and squalor as well as monumental magnificence. Dealing with excrement has never been easy. In Victorian London in the middle of the nineteenth century one in twenty homes had piles of human dung in the cellar. Cities make it easy to transmit disease by air, water, direct contact and through vectors such as insects. Changes in land use, for example forest clearance on a large scale, can also disseminate infections in better-off as well as poorer countries. Lyme disease, spread by ticks, reached epidemic proportions in the United States in the 1990s and Germany suffers from tens of thousands of cases each year. It is generally associated with suburban developments in reforested semi-rural country. Forest clearance in West Africa disrupted the breeding places of one species of mosquito only to see it replaced by a more aggressive one that spread a more malignant malaria.[7] Driving more roads through forested areas increases contact with disease-bearing animals, birds and insects. Lumberjacks in Central and South America have been infected with yellow fever by the mosquitoes that live in the tree canopy; the workers take the disease back to the cities when they go home. The IPCC, whose work was discussed in the last chapter, believe that global warming is increasing the threat from diseases such as malaria whose life cycle is supported by higher temperatures. Rainfall affects the breeding sites of mosquitoes which lay their eggs in standing water. The British government has warned that malaria could return by 2020 to the English countryside as mosquitoes move northward with a warming climate.

Increased trade and travel spread disease with brutal speed. In 2006 over 2 billion airline passengers flew around the world; some carried disease as well as their luggage. The dengue virus, whose original home was tropical West Africa, has been carried from one continent to another. This fever can lead to fatal haemorrhage. Dengue epidemics have affected millions of people from Latin America to South-East Asia. In each of the last four decades the average annual number of cases has doubled.[8] Speculation about the spread of SARS has touched on the likely results if the virus had been carried on a plane to Durban, where public-health surveillance and disease isolation would have been at best sketchy, rather than Toronto, where the health authorities dealt quickly and competently with the disease.

New agricultural methods also open fresh opportunities for disease. The main carrier of E. coli, the leading cause of kidney failure in children, is contaminated beef, though anything coming into contact with faecal bacteria may also serve as a vector. E. coli can also be spread by person-to-person contact or by drinking infected water, for example in swimming pools. It is robust, resistant to acid, salt and chlorine; it can live in moist environments for weeks; and it can withstand freezing or very high temperatures. The bacterium was known in the 1980s, but the disease became a much bigger problem in the following decade, by the end of which there were reckoned to be 73,000 cases annually in the US with about sixty fatalities. Modern practices of cattle rearing and slaughtering are a big part of the problem: cattle are often transported for long distances to feed-lots where they commonly wade hock-deep in manure and consume badly contaminated food and water prior to their transfer, which may involve another long-distance journey to the slaughterhouses where the hides and digestive tract are removed, a process which may contaminate – or more accurately cover in faeces – large quantities of meat. The meat is then dispersed through a vast and efficient distribution system so that a single infected animal can contaminate 32,000 pounds' weight of ground beef. The US Drugs Administration (USDA) reckons that between 1 and 50 per cent of cattle may carry the dangerous E. coli bacterium in their gut depending on the season: the summer is the worst period. Modern distribution provides a highly efficient means of propagating a bacterium which left to itself is not apparently especially well equipped to rage through human populations. Nor is the situation helped by the employment of large numbers of migrants – legal and illegal – in the unpleasant work. This leads to shoddy practices by workers who are poorly educated in food hygiene, poorly paid and so overworked that they are liable to make mistakes, and – when illegal – in terror of governments to whom they are extremely unlikely to report glaring problems in labour relations or industrial processes.[9] The problem is made worse by inadequate monitoring. Comprehensive food safety standards to combat *e.coli* only began to be adapted in parts of the United States in response to the 'killer lettuce' outbreak that affected much of the country in 2006. The health threat of BSE/variant CJD is a similar story; in this case the epidemic was probably caused by normally herbivorous cattle being fed the remains of other cattle. Fancy another beefburger and fries?

Among the other reasons for the emergence and re-emergence of disease probably the most potent is the collapse of rudimentary health services in some countries because of war and conflict as well as economic failure. The contrast here between Asia and Africa is stark. While there are still huge difficulties in some Asian countries (India, for example, has wretched statistics on child mortality despite its recent economic growth), on the whole the success stories in most of them are both a cause and a result of greatly improved healthcare. We have seen already that wars in African countries have led to sharp increases in the incidence of killer diseases. Crudely applied structural adjustment programmes in the 1980s and 1990s, under which poor countries cut back on social programmes or introduced inappropriate user fees for health treatment of patients and education of children, in return for loans and grants from donor countries and international financial institutions, also played havoc with skeletal programmes of healthcare. Among the developed countries, Russia provides an ominous lesson in how not to introduce market economics. Its healthcare system disintegrated in the 1990s leaving high death rates, particularly among men. AIDS, syphilis and other sexually trans-mitted diseases have spread fast, and tuberculosis rates in Russia have increased by 80 per cent since 1990. The Red Cross estimate that eighty people die in Russia from tuberculosis every day.

Malaria is still a ubiquitous killer spread by mosquitoes, of which there are more than 3,500 species. They can travel long distances and smell a possible meal at a range of up to thirty miles. The bite of malaria-carrying mosquitoes causes anaemia, headaches, sickness and sharp changes from intense fever to chills and back again. The para-sites that teem through the blood sometimes attack the brain.[10] In 2004 it was estimated that there were between 350 and 500 million cases of malaria worldwide. The disease kills about a million people a year, mostly in Africa. It is the main cause of death in young African children; it accounts for 18 per cent of the deaths of all African children under the age of five. Every thirty seconds a child dies of malaria. In addition to the direct slaughter, malaria is believed to contribute to the deaths of another 1.7 million people. It loses countries in sub-Saharan Africa about $12 billion a year. It eats up 40 per cent of the region's expenditure on public health.

The fight against malaria is an example of well-intentioned inter-national efforts to save the poor in particular from the most common fatal diseases, both epidemic and endemic. A Global Fund to fight AIDS, Tuberculosis and Malaria was launched in 2002 following discussions at the previous year's G8 Summit. It is a public-private partnership to which President Bush's administration and the Gates Foundation were particularly generous donors, and is funding a variety of initiatives including the development of a vaccine and the provision of insecticide-impregnated bed nets. (President Obama's own ambition, set out at the Clinton Global Initative forum at the end of 2008, is to put an end to malaria deaths in Africa by 2015). While the inclusion of malaria alongside AIDS in the campaign may initially have been incidental, there are in fact medical connections between the two as there are between AIDS and TB. Those infected with HIV are more likely to suffer from malaria, and the malarial parasite increases the virus particles in those with HIV.

The story of the campaigns against HIV/AIDS demonstrates even more clearly than the issue of malaria how interrelated are both the causes of disease and the ways in which it can be successfully combated. AIDS also brings into sharp focus some security questions that have always been part of the debate about disease. I will deal with them later in the chapter. First, however, we can see how we need to operate at both the national and the international levels to cope with the global AIDS epidemic.

HIV is a virus that hides in the body's immune system. It is one of the many diseases that has jumped the species barrier from animals to humans, in this case from African monkeys. The exact cause of transmission is widely debated: was it first caught from a monkey that had been killed, from contamination of vaccines or needles, or – signs of prejudice here – from some so-far undiscovered ritual sacrifices involving monkey's blood?[11] I am not sure that it really matters very much how the species leap was made. The key questions are why has it spread so fast and how can we stop it?

Cases of AIDS had been occurring for several years in Africa and Haiti, without the inadequate health surveillance systems in those areas detecting what was happening, before the chance discovery of the disease in the US by epidemiologists at the Centers for Disease Control and Prevention in 1979–80. They were investigating the large number of requests for antimicrobials to treat a rare form of pneumonia. I first became really aware of the disease myself when working as a development minister in Africa in the mid-1980s. Visiting Kampala, for example, most of the beds in the main hospital were occupied by people who were plainly suffering from AIDS (whatever the illness listed in the hospital records) and research suggested that a large number of the medical staff were HIV-positive. Even at that time, many of the features of the subsequent debate about AIDS were present. First, throughout eastern and south-eastern Africa the disease was principally associated with lorry drivers and prostitutes. In Zambia they called it 'SKANDIA', after the trucks whose drivers were believed to spread the disease as they drove across the continent, just as sailors carried syphilis around the Mediterranean in the six-teenth and seventeenth centuries. Most African governments refused to take seriously what rapidly became a pandemic, and which they variously regarded as a Western hoax or even a conspiracy. It showed the West's contempt for Africans, and in Europe and the US we fanned these flames by assuming that the sexual cause of transmission was a reflection of allegedly greater African promiscuity. The stigma associ-ated with the disease encouraged officials to hush it up. A brave WHO official, Jonathan Mann, struggled to get African governments to face up to what was happening. Tragically, he was killed with his wife in an aeroplane accident in 1998. Uganda's Yoweri Museveni was one of the few African leaders who took AIDS seriously, unlike, for example, President Thabo Mbeki of South Africa, who long ques-tioned whether HIV was the sole cause of AIDS. As early as 1986 Museveni launched a 'Zero Grazing' campaign which discouraged concurrent sexual relationships. The president argued that taking precautions against AIDS was a patriotic duty, and he started an AIDS control programme focused extensively on providing safe blood products and educating young people about the risks of HIV/AIDS.

To understand how best to fight the disease in Africa, it is important to recognize that Africans are not in fact more promiscuous than Westerners. In the West, promiscuity is serial: people tend to have one sexual partner at a time. In Africa, surveys do not suggest that people have more partners than in Europe or the US, but that they appear to have partners concurrently. So the 'Zero Grazing' advocated by President Museveni aimed to deter multiple relationships at the same time. This also explains why it was wrong to regard the disease as the result of a network of lorry drivers and sex workers. The causes of transmission were in fact more complex. They certainly included transmission by travellers, in particular men migrating to work in the mines and on the farms of South Africa. Living there in all-male communities away from their families, those migrant workers would return home from time to time, sometimes bearing infections picked up by casual or commercial sexual activities. Fighting the disease needs to build on local community understanding of what is happening and the social solidarity that has been evident in the successful cam-paigns in Uganda.[12] We have often imposed our own customs and assumptions on the organization of the AIDS campaign in Africa, and even our own moral views. There has been a fight between those advocating abstinence-only programmes and those who believe (rightly) that since many will ignore this well-intentioned advice the provision of condoms would keep down HIV infection rates. 'Zero Grazing' is still the right message, but where the grazing does occur the use of condoms is wise. It would also make sense to encourage circumcision: rates of HIV/AIDS are much lower in West Africa, where there is a higher incidence of circumcised Muslims, than in East Africa.

Sexual grazing across continents, but particularly in Africa, has led to horrifying results. Over the last quarter-century nearly 65 million people were infected with AIDS and about 25 million have died from AIDS-related illnesses. The WHO reckoned that at the end of 2007, there were 36 million people living with HIV, 3.2 million were newly infected and 2 million had died that year from AIDS. The figures were worst in Africa, where almost two-thirds of those infected with HIV lived and where 1.5 million died in that year. The figures were also particularly bad in Asia – comparable figures were 5 million with the infection and 380,000 fatalities. Globally there has been some progress since 2006, with the rate of infection slowing and mortality dropping. The prevalence of HIV in sub-Saharan Africa has also fallen a little. But even though coverage by antiretroviral drugs has increased almost exponentially, there are still enormous gaps in the coverage – for instance, fewer than 40 per cent of pregnant women infected with HIV receive them. The epidemic alters the demographic structure of many societies; in Malawi, for example, about a third of all children are orphans. Demographic change is mainly a result of the increase in the deaths of young adults, which also has a major economic impact in cutting the already low economic growth rates. Recognizing that the disease has created one of the biggest development crises in history, the international community at the UN and through the WHO has resolved to act nationally and internationally to deal with it. Growing amounts of money have been poured into the fight against AIDS in low- and middle-income countries – about $10 billion in 2007 – on drugs, nursing and hospital services, education and counselling. This is said to be not much more than half what is required.

The WHO is at the forefront of the global campaign against AIDS and other infectious diseases. Established in 1948 as an agency of the UN, it built on the work of the Health Organization which had been created under the auspices of the League of Nations in 1920. There is a long history of international collaboration on disease control. By the middle of the nineteenth century it was accepted that the protection of health was a proper subject for international discussions. Agreements on cholera and plague notification and control followed later in the century. The epidemics of typhus, cholera, smallpox and dysentery as well as the influenza that had ravaged Europe and other parts of the world after the First World War led to the creation of the Health Organization. The WHO has policed increasingly tough international security regulations. The latest and most comprehensive set of rules was agreed in 2005 after the SARS outbreak of 2002–3 and with warnings of avian flu increasingly alarming public opinion.

SARS – severe acute respiratory syndrome – is a new variety of pneumonia which is highly contagious and very dangerous. It first appeared in southern China in November 2002 but, practising the obsessive secrecy that has long been a feature of Communist China, the authorities covered it up. Any bad news is regarded as a potential embarrassment for the system – from famine to riots to contaminated milk to the 55,000 Chinese commercial blood and plasma donors (mostly in Henan) who were infected with HIV. In the case of the emergence of SARS there was another problem: the new Chinese leadership, President Hu Jintao and the Politburo Standing Committee, was being installed in the early spring of 2003. Nothing should be allowed to take any of the shine off this event. Thanks to the surveillance work of the Global Pandemic Initiative, a collaboration between the US Centers for Disease Control, the WHO and several other groups including IBM, and thanks as well to a brave doctor retired from a Chinese military hospital, Jiang Yanyong, who blew the whistle about the cover-up, international action was taken that prevented an epidemic turning into a pandemic. As it was, there were over 8,000 cases with more than one in ten fatalities. The figures could have run into millions. There was a big economic impact on Asia, with business and spending losses that are thought to have totalled $60 billion. The result was a renewed understanding of the crucial importance of good global health surveillance and transparency in reporting the outbreak of infectious diseases. The new International Health Regulations in 2005 obliged governments to cooperate with the WHO and its director general, now the former Hong Kong public health official Margaret Chan, and to report potential pandemics immediately.

Margaret Chan has a lot of relevant experience to draw on. She had to cope with the avian flu outbreak in Hong Kong in 1997, during which she ordered the slaughter of 1.5 million birds, and the SARS outbreak of 2003. She knows the importance of getting good information in time and of being able to lead public opinion. That has always been and remains a problem. The public need to understand the threat to their health; they have to tolerate marginal disruption of their lives and rights; they have to accept that the actions taken are necessary. None of these conditions seemed to be present in northern Nigeria when the polio vaccination programme was boycotted in 2003; there was a lack of trust in the health authorities and bizarrely a fear that mass vaccination was a Western plot somehow associated with the Iraq war. The number of confirmed polio cases in the area rose sharply as a result of opposition to vaccination.[13]

Margaret Chan and her senior colleagues plainly hope that the new regulations that have been promulgated will help them prevent an outbreak of avian flu turning into a mass global killer. Influenza pandemics have swept the world on average three times a century for the last 500 years. There were outbreaks in 1957 (Asian flu) and 1968 (Hong Kong flu); much the most serious was the so-called Spanish flu in 1918–20. The first cases were not Spanish at all; they were actually recorded on the other side of the Atlantic at Fort Reilly in Kansas. The pandemic broke across the world in three waves that carried off tens of millions. It used to be reckoned that 40–50 million died. Recent estimates suggest that the figure may have been far higher, certainly many more than perished in the fighting of the First World War. The French poet Guillaume Apollinaire and the German sociologist Max Weber were among the fatalities. It was the most vicious killer flu ever, attacking healthy young men and pregnant women more than the old and sick. It is odd that it did not have more impact on our folk memories. We appear to know more about medieval plagues like the Black Death.[14]

Since the first identification of the H5N1 strain of bird flu in Hong

Kong in 1997, the world has focused quite effectively on the risk of it mutating in a way that would allow it to be transmitted from person to person rather than from bird to person. There is no evidence yet of this mutation having taken place. It has nevertheless caused considerable alarm. The UN's and the WHO's senior coordinator for avian and human influenza was so worried in 2005 that he forecast that avian flu could kill between 5 and 150 million people, though so far fewer than 200 have died from the virus. Anxiety seems to have abated considerably with better surveillance and reporting, monitoring and slaughtering of poultry flocks, the stockpiling of drugs and billions of doses of vaccine to use against a range of flu viruses, and much more research. Countries in South-East Asia, including notably Thailand and Vietnam, have become more effective in identifying and isolating human cases and managing their poultry flocks. So far at least international efforts appear to be working. An epidemic has been kept at bay. But it is far too soon to declare victory, if indeed that is ever possible or wise. The reason for caution was underlined by an outbreak of a hitherto unknown flu, H1N1, comprising a mix of human, avian and swine influenza in Mexico in the spring of 2009. It rapidly spread to the US and other countries. Though some patients died, the strain of the virus did not seem as dangerous as had first been feared; but there were anxieties that it could return in a more aggressive form as had happened with Spanish flu. Moreover, there appeared to be a worldwide lack of adequate supplies of flu vaccine.

The threat of disease today, and its past impact on our history, mean that inevitably it has come to be thought of as a security issue in which the developed world is marked out from poor countries and yet is at the same time inescapably linked to them by the ubiquity of epidemics. It is a subject for generals and security experts, not just doctors and epidemiologists. On the one hand, a key feature of the developed world and part of the foundation of its power is the capacity to avoid, contain or treat most diseases. On the other, disease helps to cause systemic underdevelopment socially and economically, particularly but not exclusively in Africa, and further threatens some countries with total collapse. By the end of President Clinton's second term disease was on the security agenda.[15] In the context of the 'war on terror', disease and biosecurity advanced up this agenda. The 9/11 atrocities, and the anthrax attacks which followed hard on their heels, generated new concerns about the use of chemical and biological weapons and moved healthcare itself firmly into the security arena. There is also more generally a concern over disease as a complicating factor in military interventions or even a barrier to them. Diseases like malaria have always been a major obstacle. This is one of the reasons the United States has chosen not to be an imperial power. Explaining America's 'limited' security ambitions in the Middle East, one unnamed CIA agent shortly after the Iraq invasion said, 'We don't do diarrhea.' Numerous instances of violent psychotic episodes amongst members of the armed forces as a result of having to take anti-malaria drugs have also deepened the reluctance to send troops into areas where malaria is endemic.

There are three interconnected issues in the renewed concern about the relationship between health and security. First, there is the extent to which fighting disease and developing healthcare take on the characteristics of a security task. There are orders, lists, rules, and restrictions or interventions in normal daily life. This has been so ever since the public health interventions by ruling authorities in the Italian city-states. The second factor is the prevalence of the sort of small but dirty wars that we have discussed previously. There are, third, the special challenges associated with HIV/AIDS. The US cited concerns over this disease as a reason for refusing to contribute peacekeepers to some operations.

Turning disease into a security issue could have benefits, since we often regard security as a higher priority than healthcare. This prioritization is questionable, as the comparison already made between the deaths from Spanish flu in 1918–20 and the fatalities in Europe in the previous four years of war makes clear. Nevertheless, the fatalism that can easily affect the public approach to disease and healthcare has probably been circumvented recently by nervousness about the threat of bioterrorism. We recognize that we do have to care more about public health. Security is one of the few issues left in the West in which community is given explicit priority over the individual. Countering terrorist threats has led to curtailment of individual liberties. Where public health is concerned, the treatment of the individual is not an end in itself, it is the way in which you protect the community. That also entails other tough security measures such as the aggressive imposition of quarantine, which is really a prudent way of shutting the infected up together and letting fate sort out who lives and who dies. The experts who write about pandemic scenarios – building up stocks of Tamiflu vaccine to deal with avian flu, for example – tend to skirt round the fact that, confronted with a massive and deadly pandemic, the Western response would almost certainly have a military, security-oriented quarantine and damage-limitation component. Citizens would not be able to go about life normally, shopping, travelling, going to work, attending a football game or visiting the cinema. We need to think about what this would mean and, in advance of such a situation arising, exactly how it would be handled.

There is also a decisive connection between the spread of disease and the lack of security as a fundamental public good. Several new strains of HIV, for instance, seem to have emerged from Burma and the Congo. Why these have become hotspots for HIV remains unclear. But both locations, precisely because they are war-torn, destitute messes, have been good places to spread new strains of HIV globally: Burma because it is a big exporter of drugs as well as prostitutes; Congo because it is a major importer of armies from across Africa in addition to peacekeepers.[16] Where prostitution, rape, promiscuity, destitution and drug use are rife, and where standards of healthcare are shocking, it may be that multiple infectious contacts provide the breeding ground for new HIV strains. Those waiting for an HIV vaccine should not allow their hopes to soar.

There is a real link between the spread of disease, particularly perhaps HIV/AIDS, and the degradation of state capacity. We noted earlier in general terms the demographic and economic shock caused by the disease. The long latency period of HIV/AIDS means that infections which are picked up in the late teens or twenties will kill in the late twenties or thirties, the time when adults add the most value in terms of economic output and offspring to societies. The rate of HIV/AIDS infection is therefore one of the most important predictors of the long-term health, productivity and stability of a state. The *CIA World Factbook* includes, hardly surprisingly, figures on HIV/AIDS prevalence, which must have given some of the CIA African-country

experts in Langley a few sleepless nights. Figures for the overall prevalence of the disease understate the problem in certain sectors of the
population, above all the military, where infection rates are usually
between two and five times as great as in the general population.
There are two obvious consequences. First, the deployment of peacekeepers to a region may result in a high rate of disease transmission.
Second, in conflict zones, the disease may spread through casual sex
or rape (in certain conflicts, for instance in Sierra Leone and Rwanda,
deliberate infection through rape seems to have taken place). In either
case HIV/AIDS ensures that the consequences of fighting continue to
reverberate long after the conflict itself has passed. More generally, it
means that what should be one of the central institutions of state
stability – the armed forces – is eroding rapidly.[17]

One of the problems with treating disease and healthcare as security
issues is that this immediately imposes hard national boundaries on
what is plainly a global issue. The imperative, for instance, to contain
and treat an outbreak of a deadly new strain of avian influenza might
be impeded by nation-states jealously hoarding their strategic reserves
of antiviral medication. The adrenaline-pumping rhetoric of national
defence, applied to diseases, may be capable of containing an emergency, but may at the same time impede efforts to head off an emergency altogether. International cooperation is also threatened by
far-fetched suggestions that the diseases we confront may be connected to terrorism or germ warfare. There were, for example, crazy
innuendos that SARS was part of a covert conspiracy.

What is to be done? 'Germ governance' requires actions both
between states and within states. Yet, however important it is to look
at the global and intergovernmental aspects of disease because disease
is a global problem, there is a danger that we may ignore fundamental
deficiencies in health infrastructure in the states where suffering populations are the proposed targets of international policy solutions. We
know that there is a lack of basic health infrastructure in the global
south. As I know from personal experience, if all the trappings of a
developed health system from drug distribution to magnetic-resonance
imaging were suddenly dropped into many African countries, a lot of
them would go to waste. The nurses needed to take blood samples,
the lab technicians needed to analyse them, the doctors needed to

respond to the analysis with a diagnosis and treatment, the pharmacists needed to provide the treatment – these would simply not be there. Many would be working for the health services in rich countries. Coping with global health crises is not simply about access to goods like drugs or technology; it is also about the capacity to utilize or distribute those goods. This capacity is linked to a wide range of economic and political factors within states. Campaigns aiming for distributive justice, railing against the evils of pharmaceutical companies or American imperialism, often paper over major local failings within states, allowing them to point the finger abroad despite having failed to develop even the most basic foundations of effective healthcare or having allowed such foundations to fall to pieces. The states that have been most aggressive about licensing generic drugs, such as Brazil, have also been those who do place a high value on developing their health infrastructure, and which have achieved significant gains in this sector over recent years. The fact remains that compulsory drug licensing – allowing poorer countries to produce their own generic medication – is relatively useless as a policy tool if there is no capacity to produce the drugs that are licensed, distribute them, and use them consistently.

In 1899 Rudyard Kipling advised the United States (in the Philippines) to 'take up the White Man's burden' and to 'fill full the mouth of famine and bid the sickness cease'. But rich donor countries today cannot simply take on, with a generous surge of neocolonialism, the provision of healthcare in the south. Sovereignty is not so outmoded that we can sign up to the provision of healthcare on a global basis. We do need to provide more assistance – as the Gates Foundation is doing – to the development of health infrastructures in poor countries. This should be done in ways that work with local groups, developing patterns of communal solidarity, as happened in the campaign against HIV/AIDS in Uganda. This is all long-term work requiring commitment, patience and the willingness to learn as well as teach. It may satisfy emotional requirements to press for the rich north to do a great deal more – though exactly what is not always clear. That is hardly a satisfactory response to what amounts to a calamity in many countries where successful intervention against disease may be closer to social work than medical.

The question of increasing the access to vital medication leads to a lot of not very helpful name-calling. African countries account for between 1 and 2 per cent of a very profitable pharmaceutical market worth well over half a trillion dollars. Issuing compulsory licences for drug manufacture or using generic drugs to combat infectious diseases is not going to make much of a dent in the profitability of drugs firms, particularly as so many of the potential customers would not have been able to afford the goods provided by international pharmaceutical companies in the first place. A large amount of drug research and development (R&D) is sponsored by universities, charitable foundations and Western governments, which suggests that the use of generic drugs will not substantially influence R&D decision making. Having said that, it is also true that the majority of R&D is devoted to treating the sort of chronic conditions which affect Westerners, for example obesity, rather than treating infectious disease. While it is convenient to blame pharmaceutical companies for failing to address the ills of the Third World, there is an inadequate incentive structure to develop drugs or treatments for that purpose. Yet not only is the developing world an extremely challenging research environment (as I have seen while visiting Oxford University researchers in several countries), it is also from the point of view of licensing, litigation and public relations characterized by some pretty murky and shifting boundaries. Disease is not the only creature stalking the developing world. There can also be opportunistic journalists and lawyers, sometimes parasitic governments, and even occasionally – heaven forbid! – jealous NGO workers. The rules and standards are liable to change unexpectedly. The Trovan case, involving the trial of an antibiotic by Pfizer in Nigeria in the mid-1990s, is an example of what can happen in a prevailing culture in which 'the corporations' (remember *The Constant Gardener*?) are immediately assumed to be conspiratorial, evil and in cahoots with the government. The case has detonated an avalanche of legal actions.

It is wholly reasonable to suggest that life-saving drugs should be made available to people in developing countries regardless of what they are able to pay. The WTO has tried to adjust its agreements on trade and intellectual property to ensure that the latter does not take precedence over public health. This has been a particularly sensitive issue in relation to antiretroviral AIDS drugs. Several countries – including Brazil, India, China, Thailand and South Africa – have established thriving generic drug industries producing cheaper medicines, and bigger countries like Brazil have been able to use their economic and political clout to drive down the price of more sophisticated treatments. However, there is still some way to go before price has been eliminated as a barrier to treatment of disease in poor countries, and even as progress is made on that, distribution of the drugs will often remain a difficulty.

While we are a long way from global coordination of health research or the pooling of global health resources, we have noted already the progress made by the WHO, not least regarding disease surveillance and the issuing of warnings. Fears about SARS gave the organization a lot of political impetus. It is understandable that the WHO should be giving more attention these days to the lifestyle killers that often accompany economic progress – obesity and smoking, for instance. More than 17 million people die from heart attacks or strokes every year. But for the foreseeable future, the WHO's main task will be to help protect the world from epidemic disease. I fear that 'foreseeable' may turn out to be a very elastic adjective. SARS did show that it is possible to take decisive action to deal with infectious disease. Coping with AIDS and malaria is different and more problematic. They are chronic, endemic diseases. They infect broad swathes of the population everywhere. They are generally 'old news' despite the fact that they are just as terrifying (or more so) than SARS. They bring about a long, slow deterioration in health, frequently terminated not by the disease itself but by some other opportunistic infection. A long struggle lies ahead.

During a major cholera outbreak in London in 1854, a doctor named John Snow wandered about the city cataloguing cases of the disease and plotting them on a map.[18] He concluded that the entire epidemic could be traced to a single contaminated water pump, which the local council duly closed by removing its handle. This ended the epidemic. Snow's approach – the use of geography, statistics and policy – represented a radical departure in medicine. Medical treatment was not just about the health of the individual body and the treatment of bodily symptoms; it was also about the health and behaviour of populations. With this departure we began to apprehend the nature and logic of disease itself, rather than simply cataloguing its manifestations and responding to them. We began to understand the chance encounters, the opportunities taken and missed, which had produced disease. We have always responded slowly to the knowledge gleaned this way – because disease does not respect justice or morality; it does not refrain from slaughtering sacred cows; nor does it spare the righteous or pay reverent regard to cultural practices or personal preferences. It takes tremendous courage to face up to the realities of disease because, confronted by our smallest adversaries, most big ideas break down.

Just in case we doubt the dread rhythms of disease, we only have to remember the Aztecs, the Incas, the Mississippians whose entire universes were systematically annihilated by murderous infections. Confronting disease demands a lot more than a 'cure'. Sometimes this 'cure' might as well be a magical amulet, however much we wave it about. Men and women in white laboratory coats with tubes and bottles will not necessarily solve diseases, any more than John Snow solved cholera. A comprehensive approach to disease demands both personal and public responsibility and honesty. It demands that people should be capable of taking measured risks and making informed choices. It demands fidelity to empirical observation, medical research and clinical practice. Much of the threat of international disease is held up as an example of how outdated and outmoded sovereignty has become. However, it seems to me that the things I have just listed are precisely the sorts of broad public goods which sovereignty is supposed to nurture and even provide. Much of the debate about sovereignty in recent years has centred on the duty of governments to protect their citizens, not abuse them. Sovereignty is about more than running a chunk of geography and about more than exercising jurisdictional authority over people. It is also about responsibility for the well-being of the people governed, and that includes fighting effectively the diseases that kill and incapacitate them.

14

'Let Freedom Ring'

What we demand in this war, therefore, is nothing peculiar to ourselves. It is that the world be made fit and safe to live in; and particularly that it be made safe for every peace-loving nation which, like our own, wishes to live its own life, determine its own institutions, be assured of justice and fair dealing by the other peoples of the world as against force and selfish aggression. All the peoples of the world are in effect partners in this interest, and for our own part we see very clearly that unless justice be done to others it will not be done to us. The programme of the world's peace, therefore, is our programme . . .

Woodrow Wilson, prelude to the Fourteen Points, 1918

Personally I feel happier now that we have no allies to be polite to and to pamper.

King George VI to his mother, Queen Mary, June 1940

The growth of this place is really unbelievable. And you know, I like to think that I had something to do with it.

Richard Nixon, on returning to Hangzhou, 1993

Our growing interest in the physical universe has provided one of the current clichés of geopolitics. We investigate protons and Big Bangs, marvel at hydrogen's conversion in such a precise way to helium, get excited about what pebbles and rocks can tell us about geological eras, examine with enthusiasm the home life of lichen, and wonder at the emergence of life itself from the sea and the prehistoric ooze. But it is the crunching movements of the earth's crusts – hidden, grinding, inexorable – that give us the metaphor of the day. We are witnessing in global affairs the shifting of tectonic plates. What new leadership should we look to? What new combinations of power are emerging? How effectively are the democracies of the world tackling today's problems, and what answers do they have to China's challenge to the idea of democratic universalism? What shifting alliances, values, perceptions of national interest, institutions of regional or global governance are available to cope with the issues dealt with in this book? Who and what will help us to muddle through and above all in the year ahead to prevent a global recession turning into a slump?

I mentioned earlier that for many people 9/11 signalled the beginning of a new age, and that at the very least the events that day were horrors that we all recall witnessing. Sometimes the gates of history seem to open and close fast and with a great clang. 'It is not the same world as it was last July,' the US ambassador in London told President Wilson in October 1914. 'Nothing is the same.' Other times, change creeps up on us like the competitors in the childhood game Grandmother's Footsteps. One moment they are at the other end of the room, the next they are tapping us on the shoulder. The ascent of China (or do we mean Asia?) has been rather similar. The mood in the West has gone from surprised if disdainful interest to gee-whiz obsession and even anxiety, often driven by a shallow, nationalist view of economics. First, we noted where the microwaves and the laptops were made. Then we counted the contribution that China made to our good fortune – the lowered prices, not to mention (in the United States) the lower interest rates. Next we started to notice the jobs that were lost and the medium-sized businesses that closed down. There followed the foreign exchange billions, the cap-in-hand begging by our mendicant banks in Beijing and elsewhere in Asia, and the increase in prices for the food and other commodities we buy because the Chinese want them too. So we began to ask ourselves whether the no-longer Red East was a threat rather than an opportunity, especially when economic clout began to translate into political muscle, with a direct if downplayed challenge to the principles of liberalism that we thought had conquered the world. Suddenly China was the story, with a splashy Olympics the parade ground for its undoubted achievements. Just in case we thought the Asian story was all Chinese, we also watched with some surprise as Indians bought up what once were considered to be unshakeably British industries such as Jaguar motors and took commercial control of a game that we – well, 'we' if, like me, you are English – had always thought of as our own (however indifferently the national side had come to play it): cricket. Is nothing sacred?

For me there have been scores of moments when the world in which I grew up has seemed to alter profoundly, to have been drawn like the water in Bishop Berkeley's bucket towards the distant galaxies of Asia. Occasionally the change has been illusory. I was in Tiananmen Square in 1989, days before normal service was resumed, mistakenly believing that the world was witnessing the most profound and far-reaching of all peaceful democratic revolutions. On other occasions Beijing's bucket has contained real change. Am I marked more by the cranes in every Chinese city constructing half the buildings that will be erected in the world between 2000 and 2030, or by the fact that on my last visit to China's capital the young diplomat who greeted me off the plane was wearing tasselled loafers? Which impresses me more, the fact that my newest 'Italian' silk tie was actually made in China, or that I recently had a serious discussion without party-speak with Chinese officials about Africa and North Korea, or that I have just presided in London over a public discussion of modern Chinese novels? India sends its own often more nuanced messages of its arrival in what we in the West thought was 'our' world: the global Indian brands, the software engineers, the back-office outsourcing in order to complete America's tax returns and calculate many of the West's pay cheques. The young tell us what to expect. As I write, a quarter of the MBA students at Oxford University's business school are Indian; over a third of the mathematicians doing undergraduate or postgraduate work at the university are Chinese. Doors open for many, certainly, but for whom do they shut? Maybe only for those who shut their own.

Woodrow Wilson's Fourteen Points of 1918 – four more than God had needed, as the French premier at the time, Georges Clemenceau, observed – dominated the twentieth century. They were a liberal internationalist's response to Lenin, Trotsky and the Bolshevik revolution, with its initial certainty that the working classes of the world would rise up as one, copying their Russian cousins' example. President Wilson's commitment to free trade, self-determination and democracy turned eventually into America's strategy for the age, though not without a false start. For the Wilson strategy to stand a chance of working, the US had to go out into the world, be a part of it and a model for it.[1] In the words of the anthem 'America', freedom should ring 'from every mountain-side' in the 'sweet land of liberty', and the bells should be heard not just from Boston to San José but from Hamburg to Moscow to Hanoi. Unfortunately in the wake of the Versailles Peace Conference at the end of the First World War, America turned in on itself; the world could go hang; and hang it did, with the US predictably having to deal in the 1940s with some of the consequences. The Wilson approach was still there as an idealized strategy and this time it was taken off the shelf and implemented. Empires fell to self-determination, communism was buried by democracy (though not before 100 million casualties of that utopian virus had perished) and poverty and autarky were put to the sword in many parts of the world by free trade. There were blunders and there was stupidity. Cambodians were bombed by big American planes or murdered by their own crackpot dictator; Palestinians languished in a hopeless no-man's land between European guilt, Arab folly and Israeli insecurity; too many poor and wretched men and women became pawns in other people's fights or were abandoned to the merciless greed of their rulers. But what better formula has there ever been for peace and prosperity around the world than Wilson's, with the addition of Roosevelt's vision, Truman's courage and Kennan's intellectual clarity? 'Let freedom ring' was a better message than Lenin's notion that freedom was so precious that it needed to be rationed.

Wilson's programme for the world was freighted with an idea that has often been dressed up as a theory of international relations whose practical conduct is challenged by yet another theory. 'Democratic peace' theory goes head to head with 'democracies can't do foreign policy' theory: in the blue corner, Immanuel Kant; in the red, Alexis de Tocqueville. Kant's ideas (far the best thing ever to come out of Königsberg (now Kaliningrad), the Russian oblast trapped by history in gloomy poverty on the Baltic coast) launched the idea exaggerated by its cruder proponents that democracies do not fight one another. The theory provides much sport for those who cannot think about international relations without seeking some all-encompassing hypothesis into which to try and squeeze the events they are often reluctant to study in any historical depth. You can debate what is meant by democracy and what constitutes a war; sufficient perhaps to say that neither world war provides knockout evidence for Kantian theory. Nevertheless, by and large our modern experience is that democracies make the best neighbours, especially when the democracies in question do more than allow an occasional ballot. De Tocqueville in the other corner argued strongly in *Democracy in America* that democracies have difficulty sticking to long-term undertakings, 'are more prone to impulse rather than prudence', often discover that foreign policy is distorted by public opinion, and always find it difficult both 'to start a war and to end it'.[2]

Authoritarian regimes can make quick decisions in secret. They are not plagued by the necessity of telling people what is going on (a point frequently made by Henry Kissinger), though the Soviet Union does not seem to have benefited much from this in the long term. Precisely because of the problems identified by de Tocqueville during the 1830s, the US Constitution allocates greater powers to the presidency in making foreign policy, and in the UK the executive has more say on its own in foreign policy than in other branches of policy. While it is true that the cabinet and Parliament were informed and theoretically consulted, the British decision to go to war in Iraq despite the millions of protestors on the streets was very much Mr Blair's own call. It led to cross-party agreement in 2007 that in future no British government should be able to declare war without parliamentary approval. However, this will not change the fundamental truth that in foreign policy popular democracy can usually be kept at arm's length from its elected servants. Democracies nevertheless often do rather a good job of punishing those who stray too far and too long from prevailing public opinion, as Mr Bush and Mr Blair were to discover.

In the case of a century's, or more accurately half a century's pursuit of democracy and freedom, Wilsonian policy has not always been pursued with consistent rigour. The big game was played against

Soviet communism, and its self-serving and usually half-hearted manifestations elsewhere. Communism lost by a knockout in a fight that left little blood on the gloves of either protagonist – there was no war between NATO and the Warsaw Pact – however much was spilt by surrogates. Containment was simple and clear, and Soviet behaviour in the last days of the 1939–45 war and in its aftermath – for example, the rape of 2 million German women – made it easier to keep an anti-communist alliance in line. The consistency rather wavered elsewhere. The United States helped those it thought were anti-communist, democratic or not, and it underwrote stability where it thought some aspect of its national interest might be involved, such as securing Middle Eastern oil or protecting (democratic) Israel, regardless of what sort of autocracy it was required by these objectives to back. The policy was on show with former President Bush, who on his early 2008 swing through the Middle East to the not noticeably democratic Kuwait, Abu Dhabi, Saudi Arabia, Egypt and Bahrain trod only lightly on the democracy accelerator. His national security adviser, Steve Hadley, explaining the trip, assured the world that 'these folks are onboard with the freedom agenda, and are pursuing it in their own fashions'. 'Their own fashions' do not appear to embrace allowing men and women to vote for whomever they wish to govern them. There are several ways of giving democracy a bad name; from Florida on, the presidency of George W. Bush managed to find most of them.

American economic leadership after the Second World War helped to establish a global emporium with a stable international currency, a corporate model of how best to do business and an increasingly open market into which the rest of the world could sell its products. American consumers, debts and all, deserve our gratitude. After the Europeans, the next to take advantage of these conditions were the East Asian Tigers beginning with Japan and then moving on to Taiwan, South Korea, Hong Kong and Singapore. Other ASEAN states followed. There was a time when Japan was regarded in the US as 'the threat': its exports, for example of cars, mushroomed; its business models were copied; its reserves grew; its investment in US real estate and corporations soared. Japan flattered to deceive – or frighten. By the end of the 1980s six of the world's top ten banks in market value were Japanese. In 1986 the Sumitomo Bank bought a chunk of Goldman Sachs. Then came the economic slump in the 1990s, with the bursting of Japan's property and stock-market bubble. Bad loans rose to about a fifth of GDP. Japan lost a decade with a political leadership that was big on pork and small on policy reform. The worry had swiftly become not booming Japan but sagging Japan. Elsewhere in east Asia progress was sustained, based on a winning combination that I described in my book *East and West* almost ten years ago – political stability, investment in education and health, agrarian reform, the encouragement (with varying degrees of state support and patronage) of private enterprise and exports. No one else was quite as faithful to market principles as Hong Kong, but right across east Asia economies grew, the middle class increased and the number of the poor fell.

In the 1960s and 70s, the United States threw itself and its young into a very nasty war to save South East Asia from the advance of communism. By the time of the US defeat in Vietnam, communism was anyway on the way to the scrap heap, corroded from within by ideological failure and economic incompetence. As a system, communism had been tried literally to death; all that was left behind – except in the miserable wastes of North Korea and the peeling boulevards of Cuba – was the husk of autocracy, Leninist politics sustained by varieties of proto-capitalism. It was not perfect; the prison cells were still there to accommodate dissent; but it was better than what had gone before. America lost the Vietnam war, yet won the post-Vietnam peace.

Nowhere did we see that more dramatically than in China, where the leadership stumbled into the right policy. Failing to find enough oil domestically in the 1970s to pay for the implementation of the Ten-Year Plan, and faced with a growing economic crisis engineered by the madness of the Mao years, Deng Xiaoping and his chief economic adviser Chen Yun relaxed restrictions on agricultural production and the peasants took matters into their own semi-liberated hands. Once the economy began to roll, the puzzle was not really how spectacular economic growth was being achieved, but how it had been avoided in the past. What we were witnessing was the resumption of China's weighty place in the world. Until the Industrial Revolution

China had accounted for about a third of the world's output (counting in India too, the proportion went up to about half, though the figures for per capita wealth were much lower than in the west). Then came the misery of the declining Qing dynasty and the wars that followed it. China was ransacked by the colonial powers (not least Britain) in the nineteenth century; and in the twentieth it was torn apart by warlords and the fighting between communists and nationalists, pillaged by Japan, and then united under a dictator revered for pulling it together even while his manias kept it poor and in chains. For the workforce at the plants in China owned by the Taiwanese contractor Yue Yuen making sports gear for Nike, Puma and Adidas, for the employees of Hon Hai manufacturing parts for Hewlett Packard, Dell and Apple, for the 240,000 people working on the assembly lines of the Foxconn works in Shenzhen, for the Chinese families who have just bought a Chery car, a flat or a DVD player, all that is ancient history. In the last few years, for the first time in two centuries, there is a feelgood factor in China; Deng and his successors deserve the credit for that, and what has been good economically for China has been pretty good for the rest of us too.

China has stormed the world's markets by making goods quickly and cheaply (though occasionally – from lorry tyres to toys to tooth-pastes – the goods turn out to be unsafe too). Many companies, on the whole quite small, are used as outsource manufacturers for foreign companies. The global brands, which outsource the production, and their retailers make most of the profit. There are few well-known Chinese brands – maybe Lenovo which bought the Think Pad brand from IBM, and the brewer Qingdao (whose products are well known to me, and also to Helmut Kohl, to whom I once introduced them). There is no very obvious economic reason for this industrial progress not to continue, provided that the present recession is fairly short-lived. Labour supply is not a problem with more than 700 million still living in the countryside; many of these peasants are as keen as the young beauty in Dai Sijie's charming novel *Balzac and the Little Chinese Seamstress* to escape rural drudgery and poverty and go to work in the city. Nor is there likely to be any slow-down in productivity growth, provided the state continues to push the companies it still owns into the private sector, where productivity and returns on investment are so much higher. The key here is to depoliticize credit, a point that I will return to in its more political context.

As for moving up the value-added technology ladder, China does admittedly lag behind India, for example in innovation, and loses 70 per cent of the million young Chinese who go abroad each year to study and after their university courses choose to stay in their new foreign homes. So far China has circumvented all this in three ways. First, it buys in the technology needed, such as the engine for the Chery car. Second, it acquires technology – from semiconductor manufacturing to turbines and generators – through joint ventures. Third, it has a reputation for intellectual property theft even worse than America's in the nineteenth century (when Charles Dickens grumbled about the cheap pirated editions of his works on sale there). James Kynge recalls the story of the Japanese company Yamaha (dominating an industry that the British used to think belonged to them) which worked for years to produce a cheap motorbike for the Chinese market. Within months of the Jinbao model being manufactured and put on sale in 1995, exact replicas were being made in thirty-six factories at a third of the cost.[3]

The sheer size of China, the scale of the investment that still pours in – approaching $90 billion a year – despite lower returns than are achieved elsewhere in Asia, the amount of catch-up that China still has to do to make good the lost decades, the hard work and raw entrepreneurial zest of its people, all suggest that the years of double-digit helter-skelter growth should be able to continue provided that its export markets revive and remain open. China, partly by virtue of its numbers and its hitherto benign business environment, has been the largest economy in the world for eighteen out of the last twenty centuries. It would be no surprise if it was the largest again later in this century, though it will not be as rich as the United States or Europe in terms of per-capita wealth and its workforce, unlike India's, is ageing fast – by 2040 a third of the population, 400 million people, will be over the age of 60. It also has to steer a passage through hazardous political waters with no very clear chart.

Chinese leaders make much of their claimed tendency to think in the far longer term than the rest of us. There is a touch of 'Middle Kingdom-itis' about this. Beyond the Wall, horizons are said to be foreshortened; on its Beijing side, visionaries look into the far distance and even way beyond. One of the many anecdotes, probably apocryphal, which sustains the tendency to take Chinese leaders at their own estimation, concerns Chou En-lai, China's premier under Mao, and a more sophisticated and urbane leader than his boss (which was not much of an achievement). Asked about the results that might have stemmed from the French Revolution, he is said to have responded that it was too soon to tell. I have never understood why this should be regarded as a wise understanding of history's long pulls. After all, we know very well what happened as a consequence of the French Revolution; we have suffered enough from romantic nationalism and utopianism to fill a thousand volumes with the answer. Today, much as I admire the intellectual capacity of leaders like the two premiers of recent years, Zhu Rongji and Wen Jiabao, it does not seem to me that anyone at the top in Beijing looks any further ahead than most of their peers elsewhere; in other words, they concentrate on getting through today's thing until they are obliged to focus on getting through tomorrow's thing. Maybe the country is too large, its governing philosophy too muddled, its problems too immense, to be able to do anything else. Demand for commodities like wheat together with disease among the pig herd are pushing up prices for the workers – how do you get by without political disturbance? Stage managing the Olympics with over 20,000 foreign journalists roaming the country threatens disruption – how do you keep the lid on politics? Confronting growing Western protectionist sentiment menaces exports – how do you calm things down in America's Congress and Europe's parliaments? Tibetans protest against their oppression – how do you get more armed police into Lhasa and keep TV cameras out?

I have mentioned already the understandable concerns in the Chinese leadership about social equity and environmental calamity. In China, the economic as well as the real sun rises in the east; and China's boom times roll inland from the maritime provinces. But parts of the country still lag far behind, while some of those that flourish cough and splutter in the polluted air. Heavy pollution is believed to cause a rising number of birth defects in newborn babies in coal-mining areas, and the environment is given as one of the reasons for rising figures for cancer deaths, up to 1.5 million a year according to health officials. It will certainly be more difficult to solve either of these two big problems if, as most predict, economic growth falters; however, growth itself will not provide all the answers. Moreover, growth raises China's great existential question, which no amount of clever if constrained debate in China's think tanks seems capable of solving. The question emerges from the argument between the hard-line opponents of going too far, too fast with market reforms, and those who want to continue to push back the frontiers of state control. The hard-liners argue that if the party continues to give up control of the economy – allocating credit according to market rather than politi-cal criteria, allowing more enterprises (and therefore senior manage-ment positions) to move out of state ownership and control, encouraging a bigger role for foreign multinationals in the economy – then sooner or later the party will lose control of the state. The reformers argue that unless market forces operate across a wider swathe of the economy, foreign investment will flag, productivity increase will slow, growth will stutter, and jobs will be lost: in those circumstances, the party will certainly lose control of the state. China's historic dilemma, in whose peaceful solution we all have a direct interest, is that both arguments are correct. China's leaders simply do not know which way to turn. They manufacture slogans, sometimes supported by policies, to deal with other anxieties. President Hu Jintao's approach to equity and the environment goes by the names of 'harmonious society' and 'scientific development'. But these slogans have no way of answering the fundamental, indeed existential ques-tion. Nor do they provide an answer to the social consequences of growing unemployment as recession-hit factories close and their employees trudge home jobless to their villages. The leaders' political compass (the real one was originally invented in China) has no mag-netized needle.

There is no Marxism left in China, though there are bits of Leninism. The revolutionary proletariat, in the shape of leaders who are often the prince's children of an earlier generation of leading cadres, dictate policies that bear little resemblance to any known form of socialism. It's true, however, that the conditions in many of the factory dormitories of the outsourcing industries and in the villages that growth has left behind are similar to those that mothered and

fathered socialism in the first place. Socialism with Chinese characteristics means nothing. Potemkin façades of political philosophy are just
for show. Market capitalism with Chinese characteristics is at least
the beginning of a debate. I was once asked to lecture in China on a
theme dear to the hearts of the Peter Mandelsons and Dick Morrises
among us: 'politics in a post-ideological age'. Post-ideological for
some, maybe – but not for those of us stubbornly attached to the
belief that economic and political liberalism are always eventually
found to be joined at the hip. I am not post-ideological; I am hostile
to authoritarianism and to the abuse of human rights, wherever that
takes place. There is no denying that the people of China are far better
off and far more free, far more able to lead their own lives without
interference, than they have been for decades. But to allow that process
to continue, is it essential to retain a system that suppresses dissent?
Can China thrive only if the Communist Party, whose core belief is
now the immortality of the Communist Party, continues: impregnable,
unquestionable, immovable? Is history – the history that is presumably
still waiting to tell us what the French Revolution led to – on the side
of that proposition? It seems to be rather doubtful. Man is born free
– except in China?

Answers to these questions are hatched in China's academies and
party think tanks. The Chinese intellectual is not an extinct species.
Mark Leonard has carefully and fair-mindedly assembled some of
the thoughts offered today by intellectuals to the party (note the
circumscription of the audience).[4] 'What does China think?' Mr
Leonard asks; one assumes that the answer must go well beyond the
content of his pages, interesting though they are in demonstrating that
intellectual enquiry and argument are not dead in China. There are
the usual scratchings about that seek to find some meaning for democracy that does not actually involve being able to choose who really
governs you. Experiments in village democracy are discussed: so are
a wider choice in party elections and broader policy consultations and
participation in decision making. (Departing colonial powers – the
British in India, for example – used to engage in equally futile efforts
to hold back the tide.) But discussions about subjects like the rule of
law and the impact of technology on pluralism tend to peter out rather
hopelessly, simply leaving the proposition that democracy is not all

that it is cracked up to be, that most of those who brag about it do not always practise what they preach, that it has huge imperfections (heaven rot those wretched Floridian hanging chads), that pretty rum people often win elections, and that what democracy really spells is ... CHAOS. And all this is perforce turned into an assault on Wilsonianism. That is the real threat to the US and the West: not booming exports but the dooming of democracy – persuading other countries that shopping malls and humming factories require a spot of Leninism to get them going. What rate of GDP growth can be guaranteed by locking up your opponents and gagging journalists?

We surely do not need to be told over again that democracy has many faults. We know that story. Plato disliked democracy; it put the greedy and the idle in charge, who invariably finished off those like Pericles (actually he died in the plague) who had given them democracy in the first place. For Renaissance thinkers it unleashed tumult, and in the Enlightenment it was seen as a threat to virtue. America's Founding Fathers believed it would lead to the equalization of property, and those who resisted its development in Britain worried lest they imported the horrors of revolutionary France. Yet for all its imperfections, we have come to see it as the best guarantee of human rights and stability and the most likely environment for the sustained improvement in the human condition. That has been the evidence of the twentieth century, inconvenient though it is to those who dislike its sometimes random distribution of penalties and rewards.

'Go out' has not only been China's approach to its need for commodities, it has also been the accompanying message to the world that has reflected its denial of the case for fundamental change at home. 'Go out' and tell them how China has thrived without democratic impediment. 'Go out' and tell the world's authoritarians that the basic human right is to prosper, not vote. 'Go out' and say – first, economic development; only then perhaps political reform. 'Go out' and tell the world that Westphalia still rules, that states have rights that come before those of their citizens, that no one should intervene in China's affairs or in the internal affairs of any other sovereign state. 'Go out' and remind the world of America's and Europe's hypocrisy. 'Go out' and recall what happened in Russia when it put political reform before economic. Is that the wreckage that the West wants to see elsewhere, turning so many blind if democratic eyes to the mess that its political ethics beget?

China has companions in arms, notably Russia. Its economy until recently pumped up by the price of gas and oil, its national morale inflated by big-mouthed bullying, Russia sides with China in arguing that capitalist success does not require or result in the sort of democracy championed in the West. Set up against Wilson is the idea of illiberal capitalism. Russia claims that it is a democracy, a 'sovereign democracy' where once it was a 'people's democracy'. It is a good rule of thumb to assume that whenever the word democracy is preceded, as a definition of a form of government, by some descriptive prefix then one thing it is not is democratic. The Shanghai Cooperation Agreement binds China, Russia and the states of central Asia together in an institutional show of solidarity against – among other things – the transatlantic community's previous domination of the global agenda. At the UN, China works quietly with Islamic and other states to water down the authority of the Human Rights Council and to bowdlerize its criticisms. In the Security Council, China and Russia protect states (like Sudan, Burma and Zimbabwe) often regarded as pariahs by the US, Europe and their allies and partners. Here China has perhaps begun to play its hand with a greater awareness of the interests of a big power in stability, and the perils of a public diplomacy that leaves too many bad smells behind. China has nudged its troublesome client North Korea into a dialogue reluctantly and belatedly accepted by the US on nuclear weapons. It has supported UN peacekeeping more frequently and contributed its own people in large numbers to UN missions. It has counselled caution and dialogue in Khartoum. It distanced itself a little from Zimbabwe's mad dictator Mugabe (while continuing to deliver arms to him) and suggested that talks rather than tanks are the best way for Burma's generals to preserve their hold on power. China has become more adroit at conducting diplomacy whose core purpose is at odds with the world view for which Americans, Europeans, Canadians, Australians and their partners have argued, worked, sacrificed and died.

What do we – we in the West – do? Here is by far the most successful example of a country that has thrived in the last few years in the political and economic environment created principally by the United

States but still declines to accept the ethical foundations of the whole enterprise. We cannot, for a start, simply ignore the consequences of a shift in the economic scales. America's share of world trade has slipped, Europe's seems to have increased only marginally. As a debtor nation, the US has had to sue for Gulf and Asian bail-outs. Still, the US remains the world's only military superpower; and much of its 'soft power', which is tied up, for example, with the attraction of America to students and migrants, remains intact despite its dissipation during the last few years. America, moreover, is the only country that matters everywhere, on every continent. America is also the only country with the confidence and experience to give a lead to multilateralism, to the hunt with others for solutions to regional and global problems. But the rise of China, and of India too, means that the US will have to work with those Asian countries in shaping the policies and reviving the institutions required to deal with the problems raised in this book. America will need to work with China without sacrificing its Wilsonian ethic. It will need to incorporate principle with more coherence and consistency into the pursuit of policy objectives. The hazards of making foreign policy in an open democracy require a narrative that describes the purpose of what is being done in a way that is compelling in aligning the national interest with the interest of asserting and pursuing liberal, democratic, pluralist values. President Bush was not wrong to have a freedom agenda; it is simply that the way he pursued it was cack-handed and self-defeating. In the end, both America's national interest and the values it purports to sustain were both damaged.

President Obama came into office clearly determined to follow a very different approach, in which public diplomacy was best conducted on the basis of setting an example. The new president clearly understood, for example, that if you want to promote democratic values, pluralism and the rule of law abroad, you must begin by clearly practising them at home. You do not condone torture or split hairs about what it means; you simply stop it, as Obama did immediately on taking office. You abide by the international agreements you have made. You do not circumvent due process. You do not incarcerate people in a no-man's land beyond the reach of the law. You do not suppress the sense of outrage that animates the conscience of democracy. For all its failings – the power of money, the influence of lobbies, the peculiarities of its electoral process – there can be a majesty about an American presidential election that captivates the world. The 2008 Democratic and presidential campaigns kindled enthusiasm on every continent. There have been few better examples of America's soft power. Is what lifted the spirits of so many people outside the US – observing democracy in action – wholly irrelevant to government in their own lands, at best no more than its equal, at worst an inferior article?

Fixing what happens at home should be the easy part of the agenda. To promote freedom and democracy abroad, it is essential to recognize that this is not a 'pick and mix' policy. You cannot be in favour of democracy in India but not so interested in it in Pakistan; you cannot say that you will fight for it in Afghanistan but ignore it in Uzbekistan. You have to be consistent, though that does not require you to abandon your national interest or insist on a standard – or forced – model for democratization. A consistent policy on democracy incorporates three principles. First, you treat those who share your values differently from those who do not. However much we want and need to engage constructively with China, for example, there is bound to be a qualitative difference in the West's relationship with democratic India, Brazil or South Africa. Second, you talk to everyone but do not indulge in self-censorship when meeting those whose values are different. A polite but firm statement of your position on human rights is not, for instance, a way of losing business. If it were to lose business, it is as like as not the sort of business you can do without. Earning respect is important in international relations. Third, you need to make clear in all you say and do that pluralist democracy and the protection of human rights is not a Western prescription to be imposed on others. These things have worldwide roots and are universally valid.

There are well-known instruments for promoting freedom. There are educational programmes and funds for building institutions, civil-society organizations as well as governmental ones. There are schemes for sustaining a free media (something in which I was involved as a European Commissioner when we helped pro-democracy newspapers and a radio station in Milosevic's Serbia). There are aid projects that

condition development assistance on progress in improving governance. We know that what does not work is to try to install democracy
through armed invasion. That of Iraq was supposed to spread democracy from Syria to Saudi Arabia, as Senator McCain, among many
others, argued. I doubt whether that approach will be tried again. It
also helps if you can close down issues that inflame global opinion
against you and make it seem as though you are applying double
standards in what you say about freedom and democracy. That is a
problem that the US faces in the Middle East and particularly in
helping settle the bitter dispute between Israel and the Palestinians.
Paradoxically, it is an issue where a democratic state is surrounded
by what were, at least until fairly recently, implacably hostile authoritarians. It is an issue which magnifies Muslim and especially Arab
hostility to the US for reasons that can be both genuine and hypocritical. It is also an issue that demonstrates the wisdom of de Tocqueville's
observation about the problem of conducting foreign policy in a
democracy.

The Israeli–American special relationship has a number of foundations, some strong, others shaky or ephemeral. Europeans have tended
to hover between often uncomprehending criticism of the relationship
and tremulous prostration at the prospect of challenging it. The result
has been that, despite individual efforts like that of the EU's high
representative Javier Solana, Europe has counted for next to nothing
in efforts to resolve the bloody mess. We have been more reluctant in
Europe to criticize Israeli policy than are many Israelis and nervous
about distancing ourselves from the United States. We have written
cheques for the Palestinians and wrung our hands about the continuing bloodshed. From 2000–8, European Commission funding to
Palestine, the West Bank and Gaza, totalled nearly 3 billion euros.
About 50 million euros was spent in Gaza on physical infrastructure.
Much of it was blown to smithereens by the Israeli Defense Forces
during the assault on Hamas and Gaza over the New Year period in
2008–9. The onslaught over, Europe offered to spend large amounts
rebuilding from the rubble without any guarantee that new investment
would not be reduced to a burial ground of twisted metal and shattered concrete in its turn.

Europe's most significant initiative in the Middle East was the so-called Road Map for Peace in 2002, drafted initially by the Danes, backed by the rest of Europe, the US, Russia and the UN. It introduced the notion of parallelism rather than sequentialism into the efforts to secure a settlement. Both sides would be required to act at the same time, rather than excuse inaction on the grounds that the other side had not kept to its side of the deal. In practice the Road Map led nowhere, mostly because Europe was as reluctant as the other supporters of the initiative (the so-called Quartet) to insist on Israeli as well as Palestinian movement. So Israelis have been denied the security for which many yearn, and Palestinians the statehood that would give them the peace and prosperity they deserve. It is a horrible tragedy, with poisonous consequences.

America's 'special relationship' with Israel is by no means unique. Diaspora populations and shared institutions and ideas mean that the US has close ties with a wide variety of states around the world. That said, the 'Israel lobby' does exercise unique influence, and there are elements in the Israeli–American bilateral relationship which are distinctly unhealthy.[5] Historically, this relationship was conditioned by Zionism (the desire for a Jewish homeland, which after the Holocaust was undeniable), by Cold War efforts to contain communist influence in the Middle East, and by decolonization with the revolt in the Middle East against the West. America did not at first regard Israel as a natural ally in the region and did not treat her as such. Circumstances – the rise of Arab irredentism, the collapse of European power regionally, the emergence of the Cold War in the area – conspired to push them together. For all the concern about oil supplies, the US ended up aligning itself with almost the only state in the region without this commodity. Rather than spreading American influence in the region (a US objective in opposing the Suez debacle), Washington signed up as best buddy with the one state guaranteed to limit it. The Six-Day War in 1967 brought pan-Arabism crashing down; Israel's brave victory in that war, against much stronger (and Soviet-backed) adversaries, won the overwhelming sympathy and admiration of the American people and of most Europeans.

The rise of the culture wars in the US in the 1970s and 80s divided the country between the often self-described 'silent' majority and the noisy left, which was sometimes though not always liberal. There were those who in July 1969 turned up with their families and picnic baskets to watch the launch of *Apollo 11* which put the first man on the moon, and there were those who the next month went to muddy Woodstock to listen to rock and rhetoric. At such a time, wounded and humiliated in Vietnam, many Americans regarded their position in world affairs as one of slow decline, in which enemies were numerous and friends few and far between. Dirty Harry, taking on a ring of evil hippy revolutionaries in *The Enforcer*, was a hero for all those fearful if silent citizens. At least Israel was there, speaking to a variety of traditional American values and ideas: democracy, freedom from oppression, flight from (European) injustice, the battle against jealous and land-hungry neighbours.

But it was an Israel that was changing fast, with the often urbane and socialist European Jewry of the Ashkenazi making way for the Sephardim Jewry of the Middle East and the new immigrants from Russia and the Warsaw Pact countries. Politics became more religious and more hard-line with the rise of Likud and their victory in the 1977 elections. Before the end of the Cold War, Israel had been a valuable ally because she acted as a counter-balance to Arab radicalism and Soviet influence. After that, Israel's main diplomatic value rested on resolving the Palestinian problem, the Arab–Israeli hostility which it triggered, and the broader effects of this on the relations between the West and the Islamic world in the years of the 'war on terror'. In this period, Israeli intransigence, provocation, disproportionate responses to terrorist outrages and foot-dragging whenever diplomacy has sought to proceed through confidence-building, have proved a burdensome liability. The fault is not all on one side. When in 2000 Ariel Sharon visited the Haram al-Sharif (the Temple Mount religious site in old Jerusalem) under heavy police escort, his intention seemed to be to blast apart any prospects for an early settlement: so it turned out. Hamas and the Al-Aqsa Martyrs Brigade launched the Second Intifada, or uprising, though they were surely not obliged to react in this Pavlovian way, a point that would have been understood by Gandhi, Mandela and Havel. These events were part of a seemingly never-ending sequence. The Palestinians react to what the Israelis did yesterday, and the Israelis then react tomorrow with much greater force to what the Palestinians have done today. The latest round in these bloody exchanges came when, in response to rocket attacks on southern Israel from Hamas-controlled Gaza with deaths and injuries among innocent civilians, Israel responded with a mighty display of force which left 1,300 Palestinians dead, thousands wounded and homeless, and one in seven of the territory's buildings completely or partially destroyed. It may have been an accident that the attacks coincided with an Israeli election campaign (which saw an increase in support for the far Right) and the dying days of the Bush presidency before the inauguration of President Obama. In any event, most of the rest of the world regretted the heavy loss of life, criticized Hamas for being the author of the Gaza tragedy, and expressed the pious wish that the conflict could be over and that such moderates as were left could come together and end the killing and destruction: business, in other words, as usual. 'An eye for an eye' had seemingly left behind only the politically blind.

It is pretty straightforward to construct peace plans. It is being done all the time, not least by brave peace activists on both the Israeli and Palestinian sides. The devil is less in the detail than in the politics of the whole business. How does one ever break the bloody circle? The US has the best chance of doing so, and also has a stake that is not much less than that of the combatants. Unfortunately, every time a rocket hits an Israeli settlement, or a bomb mangles and maims the passengers on a Tel Aviv bus, Americans see in their mind's eye the Twin Towers crashing down. Israel's battle against a terrorist enemy is identified with America's own security. On the other hand, whenever an Israeli rocket or tank blows up a home in Gaza, whenever a child's funeral cortège wails its way through the West Bank, Al-Jazeera's viewers see the Stars and Stripes. There is a horrid symmetry that de Tocqueville would have observed with interest.

There are two things that the new Obama American administration might do. First, it should look more critically at its support of Israel. Should the United States turn a blind eye to Israeli espionage? Should it support the Israeli defence industry which has gleefully sold on high-tech kit to China and others? Should the administration surreptitiously give Israelis the impression that they do not really have to make any concessions for peace (a point made more explicitly by Congress from time to time)? The amount of pressure that Washington can put on Tel Aviv may be more limited than outsiders sometimes suppose, but it cannot be good for America that the pressure applied in the other direction appears so telling. Second, America should be prepared to speak out when Israel is plainly making the wrong policy choices. This is true when there are disproportionate Israeli military responses to Palestinian aggression as in the recent attack on Gaza, and it is true over the consolidation and extension of the settlement activity – the creation of colonies – on the West Bank. That is a key issue in any negotiations. The former Israeli prime minister Levi Eshkol is said to have remarked that Israelis loved the dowry but hated the bride – they wanted to keep the West Bank but did not much like the Arabs who came with it. It should be an aim of US policy to provoke as open a debate in Washington about policy options as there is inside Israel. The long-term security of Israel would be the beneficiary.

None of that is easy. There are domestic constraints on the ability of any American president or Congress to take Israel to task for its various sins. While there may be some exaggeration of the point, the Israel lobby certainly does wield substantial influence as it did in the early days of the Obama administration when a senior intelligence appointment was blocked because the nominee had in the past criticized Israeli government policy; the lobby pursues its goals very aggressively. So do the anti-abortion, pro-choice, pro-gun and other single-issue lobbies, and they are particularly effective when their specific issue seems to be plugged into the sort of culture war that was first identified so clearly in the late 1960s. All these lobbies draw their strength ultimately not from their resource base or their tactics so much as from their ability to construct bridges between voters and elected officials. I noted earlier the perceived similarity between traditional American and Israeli values. Israeli actions against the Palestinians have tarnished that image in much the same way that the constant use of the slur 'anti-Semitic' by the Israel lobby against any criticism of that country's policies has tarnished its own reputation. But many of those core values still resonate for Americans. There is no kindred feeling for Arab values which, as it happens, emphasize strong families, community solidarity, business ownership and religiosity. There is also a strong sense in the United States that Europe does not have any moral authority on the Palestine–Israel issue at all. The Israeli government plays skilfully on these sentiments, denying that there is ever a Palestinian leadership that can combine credibility both as a partner for peace and as a true representative of its people, encouraging the absurd and counter-productive American policy of not talking to those it does not like (including those democratically elected Hamas leaders whom the US and Israel have conspired to destroy)[6] and claiming that Europe is still in the grip of Holocaust-era anti-Semitism. Sooner or later a brave and resourceful American president will have to take this issue on, and I do not accept the cynical view that even such a bold gesture would be greeted around the world with jeers. It would surely delight America's friends of whom there are far more than it has become fashionable to reckon, and it would help bring lasting peace and security to Israel. At least President Obama began his term by showing a greater commitment to securing a peace deal than had his predecessor. He chose as a special envoy to the region Senator George Mitchell, a Lebanese American, who had distinguished himself by his patient diplomacy in support of the Belfast Peace Agreement, that was made possible in part by talking to those who had once been terrorists and bringing them in to the political process.

Who is to help America carry the burdens of leadership in a changed world where that leadership is more likely to be questioned, and where it will need to be shared from time to time, place to place and issue to issue with a variety of others? Who are the Greeks? Not, that is, the real ones – they are still where they have always been – but the pretend ones. Talking about Britain's relations with the US, Harold Macmillan told the Labour politician Hugh Dalton, 'We are like the Greeks in the later Roman Empire. They ran it because they were so much cleverer than the Romans, but they never told the Romans this.' There is a popular, patronizing view that Britain still stands shoulder to shoulder with the United States (or maybe, like a triumphant Roman general's Greek slave, shoulder slightly behind shoulder) at the heart of an Anglosphere that has made the world and can still run it. A Protestant work ethic, a common language, a commitment to liberty under law, the reconciliation of individual freedom internally and a strong state externally, a belief in free trade – all these things have made the English-speaking peoples an unstoppable force from Wellington to Washington, from Vancouver to Sydney, from London to Los Angeles (where the description 'English-speaking' might admittedly be questionable). This is not entirely twaddle, although it does run the risk of rummaging through the history books, seeking to find some reflection there of current American concerns.

There is certainly a social component to the institutions that make democracy and capitalism viable; to work well, they require a commitment to liberal values in some form or fashion. But the institutions that are established to sustain pluralist democracies are quite diverse, so there are large differences between the various English-speaking democracies around the world. The Canadian Liberal Party, moved south, would find it tough to win an election in San Francisco, let alone South Dakota. A British Conservative is practically socialist compared to a High Plains Conservative from New Mexico. The semi-dynastic Indian National Congress would seem pretty out of place in Australia (though there have been times over the last year or two when it might not have looked so far adrift from American politics). The discussion of social and cultural affinity can bring back to mind those unpleasant late-nineteenth-century reflections that America was starting to dilute her British blood and turn into a 'mongrel race'. A lot of people in the US admittedly feel a warm glow when they think of Britain and their British heritage, but many others feel equally enthused when they recall the Irish, Norwegian, Latvian, German, Turkish or even Kenyan blood that courses through their arteries. During the violent disturbances surrounding the Kenyan presidential election in 2008 Barack Obama put in a telephone call to candidate (and later prime minister) Raila Odinga, who is from the same tribe as Illinois' famous son. Britain and the United States have long-term institutional ties, for instance in military and intelligence cooperation. As liberal societies they share a high regard for the rule of law and property rights. There is a strong tradition of educational and economic exchange. They invest heavily in each other's countries, and they invest elsewhere too – from France to South Korea. The US and Britain negotiated much of the post-Second World War set-up, but not as a giant racial project, and both countries defend their national interests. That is what Keynes did at Bretton Woods and Truman at Potsdam. When the gypsy violinist starts to play, we should get a little nervous. We survived the candle-lit Thatcher/Reagan years in pretty good shape; the mood music between them did not drown out the hard-headed conduct of business, even if it sometimes distracted the media from their (genuine) disagreements. The Blair/Bush affair was more problematic; there is blood on the carpet and bills still to pay and America's highest honour, the Medal of Freedom, pinned to Mr Blair's lapel.

The United States should be able to look to the EU as its main partner, which is what Washington always wanted from the years when, though the fighting still raged in Europe and Asia, politicians and diplomats were starting to plan the post-war order. The European Union is an extraordinary development, if a contingent one. This historical accident is one reason for doubting whether it can be a model for other regional groupings in the next few years. Others might learn from the practical consequences of pooling sovereignty in defined areas and of accepting supranational systems of binding dispute settlement (one of the EU's triumphs). But ASEAN countries, the countries of Mercosur (the South American cone), of the Andean Pact and the San José group (covering Central America), of the Maghreb and of the African Union are unlikely to travel very far or fast in the EU's organizational direction. Moreover, the rightly praised quality of life in Europe – the balance achieved between individualism and social solidarity – is hugely attractive, but it has required a sustained and value-added economic performance which might itself be under strain for demographic and competitive reasons in the future. So while it is flattering to be told, as some do tell us, that Europe is a model for the world, the wave of the future, I rather doubt whether we are actually a manifesto for how the world should organize itself in the twenty-first century. We in Europe are today what we are because of what we were, which was not latterly a happy story; and we tend to duck the question of exactly what we now wish to be, because we either do not know the answer or, knowing it, do not wish to confront its implications.

The reason for the EU is clear, reactive, romantic, brave and visionary. The EU came into existence because of ethnic nationalism, the nationalism that convulsed the European continent in two world wars and through its ethnic component hatched the Holocaust. The EU was not like the federal United States of America; the comparison made by President Giscard d'Estaing between his work on the aborted European constitution and that of the Founding Fathers in Philadelphia was misconceived. In Philadelphia sub-national entities were creating a nation. In Brussels – from the Rome Treaty onwards – we have seen nation-states engaged not in burying individual national sovereignty but in transforming it. The EU does not subvert national sovereignty, it transcends it.[7] Each nation-state remains sovereign except where it agrees on a broader sovereignty – and the stress is on the verb 'agrees'. The American Constitution begins with the words, 'We, the people'; the latest treaty defining the institutional relationships within the EU begins, 'His Majesty the King of the Belgians . . .', and goes on to list in alphabetical order the heads of state in all the other EU countries. 'We, the people of Europe' are not the source of legitimacy and accountability. 'We, the people of such-and-such a country' validate the EU and provide its authority.

The EU initially sought to accomplish political objectives through prosaic economic means. To secure Europe against war, for example, two of its principal sinews – coal and steel – were managed by a community of nations. The prosaic has become, at least in size over the years, almost heroic and that has naturally had political results. Europe created a customs union, then a single market, then a single currency which circulates in its heartland. In trade policy, in the environment, in corporate regulation, as an economic bloc, Europe is a great power – a great civil power that stretches from the west coast of Ireland to Byelorussia. Its soft power has been a magnet for democratic reforms, as it has expanded to take in countries blighted by authoritarianism of the right and left and to spread pluralism, welfare capitalism and the rule of law. Europe is self-satisfied with some justification. It is wary of the change required to make it more competitive because it is so comfortable with its present lifestyle though this will come under strain in the recession and its aftermath, as will some of the successful policies pursued by the EU to integrate the economies of its member states.

Foolishly, Europe invests far too little in research and development and higher education; this would not be a tough issue to tackle. As a proportion of its national wealth it spends less than half as much as the US on higher education, and in too many countries governments interfere excessively in the management of their universities, which as a result are badly run with high drop-out rates. German universities were once a model for the foundation of research-based American ones; typically today German universities have about one fifth of the budget of Stanford and double the number of students. Academic drift to the US is not surprising. There have been five German Nobel Prize winners in the past decade or so; four are working in the US. All this will matter increasingly as Europe competes in the future in knowledge-based industrial sectors with the US, China and India. Yet so far Europe has managed to keep up with the competition and, partly because of the export performance of German industry, Europe has held or even slightly increased its share of world trade. The idea that Europe is exhausted and risk averse, that it has lost its way, and that it will inevitably find itself slipping into the competitiveness relegation zone, an irrelevance for the emerging giants of Asia, is a caricature, though there are certainly reforms that EU states need to pursue in the welfare, labour market and R&D areas in particular.

The biggest problem that Europe actually faces is largely one of civic identity, a point that I raised in a global context at the end of the second chapter. Europe does a lot of things very well – both through intergovernmental approaches and through accepting when necessary binding, sovereignty-sharing solutions, what I and other Europe geeks call supragovernmentalism. Both approaches are necessary and can work. Some policy areas are out of bounds for supragovernmentalism because they are regarded as the preserves of nation-states – tax policy, health services, welfare entitlement programmes and so forth. Some, like energy policy, require greater European-ness – more supra-governmentalism – if we are to be able to cope better with Russia and other energy exporters, matching our policies on energy and climate security. But there is no narrative that explains what we in Europe are doing, no real sense of Europe's present vocation or feeling of much need to work one out and explain it. All this is partly because there is too little democratic politics in Europe, not too much.

Of course, there was at the outset a surge of popular identification with the reconciliation of political leaders who had been erstwhile enemies. The sight of Chancellor Kohl and President Mitterrand hand in hand at the cemeteries and ossuary in Verdun in 1984 was a focus of public sympathy and understanding. What would constitute a European moment today? We all know that there is a European Parliament, condemned to wander from Strasbourg to Brussels and back again, where European sentiments are frequently expressed. The European Parliament does not have European moments, but long, long European hours. To what effect? Many of its members do good work; others, like parliamentarians everywhere, industriously collect the perks that they vote themselves; others (principally the British Conservatives) turn denunciation of the whole European project into a cottage industry subsidized by the taxpayer. There is this largely anonymous politics of the Parliament and there is the politics of ministers in the no longer smoke-filled conference chambers and corridors. But there is no popular politics about the whole business, a parliament but no people, elected representatives but no *demos*. One of the least creditable examples of this was the effort to wing Europe's not-a-constitution past its not-an-electorate. French and Dutch voters put an end to this game. Europe today faces a nasty paradox. We talk about 'one Europe' but see the greatest enthusiasm in some countries channelled into sub-nation-state ethnic nationalism – Scottish separatists, the Basques, the Catalans, the Bretons. Yugoslavia has broken up into its ethnic parts. What price holding together the Flemish and the Walloons around Europe's hearth? In the Brussels suburb where NATO's headquarters stand, spoken French is barely tolerated. And how do these ethnic groups present themselves? They offer, they say, what is both possible and desirable because citizens can identify with their ethnicity but remain part of the big and prosperous club. So Europe is becoming the escalator for ethnic ambition. It must surely have a grander role than this and one that its citizens help to shape, to take up or – such is the nature of democracy – reject if they do not want it.

First, European rhetoric must be brought into line with European reality. So much of the European blah-blah-blah simply whistles past those to whom it is addressed, not least because political leaders say in the abstract things they would never dream of doing in the particular. Opening up the ministerial council meetings in Europe to public view would have a salutary effect in joining up what politicians say in public with what they battle over in private. The anthem 'Ode to Joy' morphs into something much more humdrum when money and national interests are being discussed. The gap between rhetoric and reality is on most embarrassing show when it comes to the area where part of the burden-sharing with the US is most notable – in foreign and security policy.

I am in no doubt that medium-sized European countries can make a bigger impact on international events when they work together, adopting common positions and common strategies. The record of trying to do this is at best mixed. This is partly because foreign and security policies go right to the heart of what it means to be a nation-state. Will you agree to shoot and be shot at for your country? Perhaps. Will you do it for Europe? Very unlikely. Efforts to co-ordinate European foreign policy also have to cope with the fact that there are as many foreign ministers as member states – and as many prime ministers, too, many of them second-guessing and overruling their foreign ministers. A still larger issue than this is just how big a sacrifice Europeans are prepared to make as taxpayers or as citizens or as fighters for other parts of the world. Europe is the biggest aid donor in the world – the financing of soft power through development assistance is quite generous and it is beyond much political argument. The same is not true when it comes to military boots on the ground, or airlift capacity to move those wearing the boots to the next trouble-spot, or helicopters to support these soldiers when they are in theatre. So many of the problems discussed in this book require military assistance from time to time – protecting the serially abused, putting broken states back together, dealing with piracy, terrorism, the consequences of natural disasters, climate change and resource conflicts. The sort of conventional war for which NATO was designed is mostly – fingers crossed – a matter for historical study. But we still need soldiers – to support the international rule of law, to end conflict, to prevent atrocity, to feed the starving. Europeans do not like to be reminded of this: guns cost money and guns go bang, often with the intended results.

This point is well made by American commentators. American political commentator Robert Kagan likened Europeans to Venus rather than America's Mars, a fair enough point, though he should perhaps have conceded more explicitly that we are post-Martian in Europe, because we saw what the God of War could do when released from his cage.[8] James Sheehan has more recently argued that Europe may be a super-civilian state but is disqualified from becoming a superpower by inadequate expenditure on defence, lack of harmonization in defence procurement and indecisive nervousness about deploying the force that Europe actually does have. European defence budgets have shrunk; Germany spends, for example, only 1.6 per cent of GDP on its military, and two-thirds of this budget goes on personnel, including 130,000 civilian employees.[9] My father's generation wanted the Germans to spend less on their armed forces; so did my grandfather's. Today we want them to spend more, without doubt a preferable situation. European countries have made very useful contributions to peacekeeping operations. But heavier fighting, as in Afghanistan, stretches resources and the willingness of some countries to commit their forces in more dangerous war zones. The troops sent to Afghanistan have lacked sufficient helicopters and other equipment, and many of those who were airlifted to the country had to fly there in leased Ukrainian planes.

The contribution in Afghanistan and elsewhere would probably be under even more pressure if NATO did not still exist. NATO's main role ended with the fall of the Berlin Wall. Where today in Europe is NATO's front line, and where is its enemy? The Russians clearly worry that Americans and Europeans still see them playing that role; even critics of Tsar Putin would not go that far. So is NATO principally a relic of the past success of transatlantic cooperation that we are nervous to wind up for fear of creating a security void? Partly, it is. For me, getting rid of NATO seems an unnecessary leap in the dark; without it, I suspect that Europe's contribution to military solutions would be much weaker. The EU would certainly be hard pressed to undertake those occasional exercises in which its superpower ally does not wish to take part. In those instances the Europeans would not be able to tap into the assets that the US makes available to NATO as the organization's main military pillar. It is no longer unthinkable to consider Europe without NATO, but it would be very unwise – a risk too far.

Europeans need to confront the consequences of wishing to strut on the world stage as a major player while not being prepared to pay for much of that role. We cannot grumble quite so justifiably about American unilateralism in security matters when we are not prepared to dig as deep into our pockets to pay for our military as Americans are. Moreover, we need sometimes to see ourselves as the US is inclined to see us – Monday-morning quarter-backs, the courage of whose convictions does not always stretch to paying for them. We shall soon see how Europe is prepared to act now that there is a committed multilateralist in the White House. There are, however, at least two roles that we can play globally that should help America take the lead in international partnerships and assist the world as a whole to solve our common problems. These are collectively the sort of issues that may provide Europe with a new sense of vocation. They would certainly help to define who we are and what the EU can do.

First, Europe has to accept the responsibilities that attach to its role as a civilian power. There are two vital areas in which that plays out. We have to act more generously and creatively to reduce global inequities. This cuts to the heart of trade and agricultural policy. Europe cannot lead if it remains instinctively protectionist in some areas. The EU should also go out ahead of other countries and group-ings in the commitments made to abate global warming and climate change. If the issue is as important as I believe and as I have argued, European governments should place it at the head of the Union's agenda.

Second, the EU must recognize the crucial sensitivity of its handling of the question of further enlargement and in particular the Turkish application for membership. Provided that Turkey completes the pol-itical and economic reforms that it has begun, its negotiations for membership will deserve a happy ending. For Turkey to become an EU member would change the Union, a point that we should not seek to hide from our citizens. The European *demos* has to be party to the deal, and it should not be impossible to convince the public of the Turkish case if we try. A Turkey with a population of rising 90 million with a vibrant economy and young workforce would help to vitalize Europe's economy as the west-European population ages and declines. A democratic Turkey, secular and Muslim, would assist in preventing the cultural divisions and clashes that we sometimes appear intent on provoking around the world. A militarily professional Turkey would give the EU more credibility as a civilian power able to act occasionally with an effective military smack. Reject Turkey and the EU will have chosen to write a much smaller part for itself in the history of the twenty-first century, and having been so successful in promoting stability around our borders we may find ourselves doing the reverse.

Europeans will need to work with the US to draw Asian powers and the other big emerging economies into discussing and resolving the world's main problems. Like the US, the EU is bound to have a different relationship with those who are democratic than with China, where Europe is a huge investor and trade partner. For many Europeans India provides the most obvious example of this difference, a point which Europe has to make with great care in its dialogue with that country. For understandable reasons, Indians do not want to be seen as geopolitical pawns in a long-term struggle with China. That would be an absurd and dangerous way for the West as a whole to think, let alone to play its hand.

For an Englishman, even an Irish-Englishman like me, there is an extravagant romance about India born in part of tales from and before the Raj. At my Oxford college I was a couple of years behind the Nawab of Pataudi, one of India's greatest cricketers. Handsome, dashing, brave, he took on the mighty West Indian fast bowlers in the Parks at Oxford and dismissed them with lots of swash and quite a bit of buckle. (Years later our daughters appeared in the same daringly political Bollywood film.) India has always dazzled me – dazzled and often shocked. I recall on my first visit to Delhi the sense of wonder as I walked into the Herbert Baker Government Secretariat buildings there; they exemplified such a pride in mission, albeit one that would be indefensible today and one that left behind many scars. That complicated the West's – and particularly Britain's – relationship with India after our long drawn-out struggle to postpone the inevitability of independence and the botching of final departure. For the years that more or less coincided with a miserable economic performance – the years that Indians themselves called with a resigned shrug those of the Hindu rate of growth – India was run by an elite that was often both Westernized and anti-Western. It was not difficult to understand why that should have been. Indoctrinated with Fabian socialism, India's leaders alas tried to put it into effect with similar consequences to those experienced elsewhere in developing countries.

Today it seems different. Policy change and the development of industries that emerged away from the shadow of old-fashioned regulation and control have seen India escape from what was called the 'licence Raj'. The Indian economy has joined those celebrated by Goldman Sachs as the world's present and future stars with growth predicted to grow exponentially. But there is a caveat and a worm in the bud. The caveat is that India has to go on developing and improving its presently terrible infrastructure, opening up its market and relaxing its labour laws. Those are all objectives towards which government policies limp and creak. The worm is that India's party political structure has been crumbling. It becomes ever more difficult for either the Congress Party or the opposition Bharatiya Janata to form a government without the support of a kaleidoscope of regional and caste-based parties. While democracy has generally helped to hold ethnically diverse India together in an extraordinary manifestation of the power of elective accountability, it has also made decisive reform more difficult to carry through. India has a strong cross-party consensus for weak reform, whose potential benefits are constantly diluted by the vote-buying bargains struck with individual lobbies. The poor suffer most, the poor whose wretchedness provides most of the shocks for every visitor. More successful economic management is a victim too. Electoral bribes and baubles have pushed the fiscal deficit up towards 7.5 per cent of GDP and the cat's cradle of handouts secures, in the words of Prime Minister Manmohan Singh, 'neither equity nor efficiency'. The development budget is curtailed because of this; important social equity programmes are squeezed to make way for subsidies. The economy also suffers from corruption – too often the man with the key is not available until a few rupees change hands. Worst of all, to secure power, caste and ethnicity are sometimes brought into play. The anti-Muslim riots in Gujarat in 2002 were the most reprehensible example of this, though to their credit parts of the media exposed the official connivance in what had happened.

This is part of what really shines in India. It is a free society under the rule of law, however awesome the problems that the country faces.

It has a growing middle class; it is training a bright generation of engineers, doctors and business leaders; it has created conglomerates with global brand names; it is innovative and imaginative. Whatever the challenges India faces – as a presently much poorer country than China – it will never have to answer China's existential question. The political structure is solidly built, not a spider's house. India's politics can accommodate economic and social change. If India continues to grow and prosper, it will be a vital partner in the search for solutions to the twenty-first century's problems. Success should help give it the confidence to play a more assertive and self-assured international role.

What is it that will lure India out of its tent to join global efforts to solve global problems? India is not being offered a permanent seat in the UN Security Council. A place at the table with maybe the Chinese, South Africans and Brazilians, before or after the annual meeting of the G8, goes little way to recognizing twenty-first-century realities. Moreover, with a third of India's population struggling to survive on less than a dollar a day, and with others intent on securing a toehold in the ranks of India's middle class, how much can we expect them to listen to our call to arms worldwide – on proliferation, trade or the environment? Similar considerations echo in China, where some leaders translate our own Western environmental aspirations into a plan to have them deny their own citizens a fraction of the prosperity that we take for granted and on whose delivery probably depends the survival of their own political system and authority. Meanwhile, in Europe we are nervous about how to protect without disruption our beleaguered prosperity; in America the loss of jobs, stagnant pay, growing social inequality and international financial humiliation all nurture a sense of grumpy hostility towards an ungrateful world. Should the US not forget the unappreciative whingers, and take care first and foremost of No. 1? Is it still prepared, in President Kennedy's words, to 'pay any price, bear any burden, meet any hardship, support any friend, oppose any foe, in order to assure the survival and the success of liberty'? The prevailing economic mood in the transatlantic community does not provide the ideal backdrop to re-establishing the sort of leadership that the world needs, not at some indeterminate future moment but here and now. So will we all get it?

15

And So . . .

When a young man I worked for Lord Carrington, the former British
foreign secretary; it was much the most important part of my education. After the tangled complexities of a problem had been spelt out
lucidly for him, Lord Carrington had the genial habit of raising an
eyebrow and saying, 'And so . . . ?' The 'And so . . . ?' question does
rather elbow its way on to the page at the end of a book that has
sought to spell out some, though by no means all, of the major
problems facing the world today. My intention when I started to
write this book, challenged in part by the hopeless and dangerous

unilateralism of the first years of the Bush administration, was to demonstrate that nation-states had to work together to cope effectively with the problems that crowd in on us all. At the same time I wished to demonstrate that, for all my experience in working for the most successful example ever of political and economic integration, the EU, nation-states were not about to collapse as the best means of governing communities. Nor should they. What they need to do is to transcend conventional sovereignty in order to transform it into something that works more effectively. Yet sometimes tackling common problems better requires not simply more international cooperation. More effective domestic policies and better government at home are often needed to deal with global problems. The ineffective domestic policies on drugs in many developed countries keep the warlords in business in Afghanistan; the skeletal public-health services in some poor countries provide a breeding ground for the epidemic diseases that threaten them and rich countries too. The financial crash did not simply arrive, an inexplicable global tsunami, thrown into terrible motion somewhere over the horizon. It was based on bad policies in individual nation states whose effects were spread like a contagious disease by global financial institutions and the integration of the world's market place. Overall, the best governments seek to extend the freedom of their citizens; we should not want them to wither away but to maximize individual choice while standing guard over a sturdy infrastructure of institutions and services. What they do within their (permeable) borders is reflected in what they should seek to do outside, increasing the range of the free choices that people can make. Far from there being a clear difference between domestic and foreign policy, they are now frequently one and the same. What is the biggest foreign-policy issue of our time? Global warming and climate change – an issue that cuts to the heart of how we manage our lives, our households, our societies.

I realize that describing, one after another, the world's problems may engender a certain lowering of the spirits and the trajectory of the argument can spiral into melancholy. Pile problem after problem onto mankind's shoulders and it is easy to feel that we are tottering towards the precipice of an outsized, world-shaped earth-wreck. So how should I conclude? Should I go back after all on my initial reluctance to set out a prospectus for world-saving change? Should I offer a few blithe prescriptions with the strained cheerfulness of a doctor who knows a goner when he sees one? That would not convince me, so why should it convince you? What I can do, however, is to offer a little hopeful context, warn against blind alleys and culs-de-sac, indicate some priorities and offer a few thoughts on how we can behave as citizens.

First, when we take stock of our situation we should acknowledge that many of our problems are the by-products of our success as a species, especially in the past century, and not of our enduring failures. We rightly worry about nuclear proliferation, but long gone are the days in the 1950s and 60s when the nuclear strategist Herman Kahn speculated on the precise necessities of civil nuclear defence. One of his specialities was not how to send the rockets up, but what to do when they came down. How were we all to survive? The hollow mountains; the secure bunkers; the control rooms with all their meticulous preparations in Britain down to alternative broadcasting sites for BBC radio (broadcasting to whom, precisely?); the instructions to the commanders of nuclear submarines in the event of a nuclear exchange to try to tune into the *Today* programme on Radio 4 before opening their 'end the world' instructions from the prime minister;[1] the forgotten caches of guns and medical supplies which construction workers happen on now and again, all this which could have been the tomb of our civilization has become instead a curious part of our archaeology. Of course, we fret that others – less reliable, we assume, than we were – might develop these doomsday weapons, that a terrorist group might buy or steal one, but these should be manageable and resolvable fears and threats. They are shadows in the light of dawn, not the pitch-black of the Cold War's night.

Second, in some respects the world is changing less than might at first appear. Epidemic disease is hardly new, after all. What *is* new is our ability for the first time as a species to make common cause across the world and to pre-empt outbreaks and new diseases, rather than to fight the symptoms as best we can. Our anxiety about epidemic disease is really the result of a new opportunity, not a new threat. Of all the changes in the world, the damage we are doing to our environment is perhaps the only one which is truly new in nature and in scale, the only remotely existential challenge that we face. Here is the true test of our new-found common sentience: can we agree that the threat exists? More to the point, can we convince people to take the action necessary to deal with it and halt the damage?

This brings me to a third moderately optimistic conclusion. Even this planet-changing climate problem is not insoluble. We know the sort of things that will have to be done. They are not riddles or mysteries. Looking at one problem after another – proliferation, money laundering and crime, the Middle East, energy security, lootable resources, civil conflict – the answers are usually pretty clear. The puzzle is not 'What is to be done?' but rather 'Who is to do it and how?' The issues are mostly matters of will. We know why action on this or that is needed. We know, usually, how to act, what to do. The capacity to act is the problem, not the comprehension of what we should be doing. Given our ability down the millennia to muddle through, I find that mildly reassuring.

Fourth, it is true that the international system in which states exercise their sovereignty on the basis of juridical equality has cracks and deep potholes. There are states that are nothing more than hollow shells protecting criminal or terrorist outfits. There are those which do little more than provide token legitimacy to vicious warlords hawking their countries' wealth to the highest bidder. There are states whose main defence of their own sovereignty is to obstruct and repel outside concern about the random or organized abuse of their citizens. But we should not take too rosy a view of the past. The long journey of statehood has not been a procession of virtue. Consider empire, the idea of which enjoyed a revival in popularity during the early Bush years. Whether European empires, for example, were enlightened or not is rather beside the point. Proud as I am of many of the things achieved abroad in my own country's name, the truth is that European empires were enlightened when it suited them and utterly murderous when it did not. The British built plenty of railways in India, true; in 1919 they also gunned down at least 379 Indian civilians in cold blood at Amritsar and then lionized the man who ordered his soldiers to open fire. It was a different world then, maybe a more ordered world in some ways – but a better world?

We are witnessing in our own age something unprecedented in

human history. Most men and women have already achieved, or are moving towards, political responsibility, ownership of their own lives. There have been missteps and diversions along the way, landslips and burnt bridges; there have been legions of crooks, tyrants and demagogues to defeat; there have been terrible atrocities by neighbours against neighbours which erode our belief in human decency. However, despite all of the evidence so regularly provided that the conduct of human affairs can be a sordid mess, we should pause to reflect that there are more people living in what in less free days we called the 'free world' than ever before. Many more are desperate to join us. For every failed state there are numerous liberalizing others quietly getting on with the business of building free and secure institutions in prosperous, plural societies.

For liberal democracies, especially those with the responsibilities born of wealth and privilege, there should be what President Bush called 'a freedom agenda'. Criticize the man by all means, lament the damage he did to such a good cause, but the cause itself is right and its adherents are slowly but surely winning. So do not become too obsessed with the problems, the perils, the pitfalls, and do not forget about all those places that are succeeding against the odds in becoming liberal democracies. We do not win every battle or even every war. We should still have faith in our strength and the sources of our strength, in our democracies, in our free markets, in our free institutions, in our civil societies, in the rule of law and the functioning of impartial justice. For the first time ever, free institutions are not a dream or an idyll. They are not the subject of utopian fiction or romantic poetry. They are not the vague memory of a dead civilization. They are a clear reality or a clear possibility for everyone alive today. In the grand sweep of history, that yearning to breathe free, that spirit of the possibilities of pluralism, matters much more than the grim headlines of the daily news. Governments still shoot opponents in Tibet; still starve them in Zimbabwe; still rob and jail them in Russia. But the spirit that buried communism will bury its autocratic successors too. 'There have been tyrants and murderers,' Gandhi said, 'and for a time they seem invincible, but in the end they always fall.' To be sure, there are great challenges before us, but they are not the balance of power, the scramble for empire, the racial diplomacy of old. We should remember that and pause for a moment to look on the past and see how far we have come. As we grasp for common awareness and common cause, and as we cast our eye over potential solutions to some of our problems, we should take heart. There are many, many things plaguing us. But we have already got many of the big things right, successfully securing and spreading the mandate of Woodrow Wilson. So the glass is not just half full, it is being filled further.

How do we continue that task? Is it to be accomplished at the great international conferences that will crowd the calendar, for example the Kyoto follow-up in Denmark in 2009 and the Nuclear Non-Proliferation Review Conference in 2010? These dates will be ringed in the diary of Barack Obama, the first claim on whose political energy and credit will alas be how to wean Americans without too much pain off the unfortunate practice of living on credit provided by banks living on credit sustained by credit-backed markets floating on credit-backed funds. Everyone assured us that it worked in the model, and there were bonuses to show that it worked in practice too. How much time will Barack Obama be able to take off from picking up the pieces after the model's spectacular crash to attend to the world's other major common problems? Will he have the political skill and conviction to keep faith with free trade, to resist protectionism and return to the Doha agenda, to see off the snake-oil salesmen who claim that Americans automatically get poorer when the Chinese get richer? Maybe when the global economic fall hits the bottom of the trough and we bounce back, quickly or slowly, we shall pass into a period dominated by homely, traditional virtues. We will approve of prudence and fiscal rectitude, expect our bankers to be boring and cautious, acclaim real engineering rather than its flashier financial relative. But greed and foolishness will one day emerge again. As Gustave Flaubert said at the time of the Franco–Prussian war, 'When this is over we shall still be stupid.'

I am unconvinced that the right place to sort out all our toughest problems is at some great international jamboree. First, much of what needs to be done internationally should be the outcome of what is first done at home, a point to which I will return. Second, the great international conferences that reshaped the world have a pretty problematic pedigree. Their results have not, admittedly, always been as short lived as those of the meeting on the Field of the Cloth of Gold, close to where the Channel Tunnel now emerges into French daylight, between Henry VIII of England and Francis I of France in 1520; within a year the agreement had been cast aside and the English and the French were doing once more what they used to enjoy doing best, scheming against one another. (The English have always loved France, but resented the fact that it is full of Frenchmen.) Nor does a conference always promote instant amity; the Peace of Westphalia itself did not succeed in bringing the 176 plenipotentiary negotiators together under one Christian roof. The Catholics stayed in Münster, the Protestants thirty miles away in Osnabrück. It is true that the Congress of Vienna (1814–15) drew a line under the Napoleonic Wars, but the Congress of Berlin (1878) laid the foundations for future trouble, marking Germany's emergence as the greatest power in continental Europe and setting the Balkan nations off on their pursuit of violent solutions to the problems that had not been solved by distributing them among the 'Great Powers'. 'Peace with honour', Disraeli called it; he was not the last person to use the phrase. Versailles in 1919–20 began with the highest hopes, and ended not by inseminating Nazism (a far-fetched criticism) but by confirming how little could be achieved when the once-great powers were in most cases no longer so great, and when the greatest of them, which was becoming ever more powerful, absented itself from the rest of the world's affairs.[2] Moreover, it showed how difficult it can be to cool and curb the passions let loose by religion and nationalism.

Yalta has a special resonance for me. I once went to a meeting with the Ukrainian president Leonid Kuchma and his government in the Livadia Palace in Yalta, the tsars' summer resort. It was the same venue that had housed the famous three-sided summit between Stalin, Roosevelt and Churchill in 1945.[3] Here, looking down on the Black Sea, they had carved up the post-war world, giving Poland and eastern Europe to the Soviet Union, Greece and western Europe to the transatlantic democratic sphere of influence, bits of Asia to Moscow as a prize for entering the war against Japan (which it would anyway have done), and returning countless Russian POWs and allegedly Soviet citizens who had fought for Nazi Germany to their deaths or incarceration in Stalin's gulags. Churchill too described it as 'peace with honour' in the first draft of a parliamentary speech (the words were wisely excised by his private secretary), and the Munich appeasers in Britain's House of Commons voted against it in a sort of conscience-clearing gesture. On my visit to the Kuchma summit we were served a lavish banquet in a marquee in the palace garden. By each setting at table there was an industrial-sized tub of caviar and a carafe of ice-cold vodka. I almost warmed to the president, otherwise a man of undiscovered charm. Halfway through our meal the president's mobile phone rang. It was the president of Russia, Mr Putin, calling to wish Kuchma a happy birthday: a call but no card. Nevertheless we knew that both men were sending the EU a message about Russia and Ukraine. It was not very nuanced.

The most positive thing to emerge from the original Yalta conference was Stalin's reluctant endorsement of Roosevelt's proposal to establish an organization of embryonic world government, the United Nations. Conceived in wartime Washington, the UN was born at the San Francisco Conference in 1945. It carried with it the hope that war could become something studied by historians. Peace would be secured and policed by the Great Powers – the US, Russia, Britain and China (in its nationalist shape at first), to whose number France was generously added. A Military Staff Committee would oversee the direction of forces placed at the disposal of the Security Council, where the Big Five would all hold a veto over decisions. There would be an Economic and Social Council to alleviate the poverty that so often bred conflict: a Trustees Council to oversee the progress to independence of colonies; and a World Court to adjudicate international disputes. Envisioned by Roosevelt, it was midwifed on the president's death by his successor Harry Truman for whom it represented the fulfilment of one of humanity's long-held dreams. Truman carried around in his wallet a rather awful Victorian poem by Alfred, Lord Tennyson[4] called 'Locksley Hall' which contained these lines:

> In the Parliament of Man, the Federation of the World,
> There the common sense of most shall hold a fretful realm in awe,
> And the kindly earth shall slumber, lapt in universal law.

As my mother used to say, 'Chance would be a fine thing.'

In his address at the final plenary session of the San Francisco Conference Truman called for a 'just and lasting peace', to be achieved partly by international cooperation to correct the economic and social causes of conflict. He wanted to see the removal of artificial and uneconomic trade barriers and an international bill of rights to safeguard human rights and fundamental freedoms. The aim was to bring about, through the worldwide rule of reason, an enduring peace 'under the guidance of God'. The aims were noble, the product of reason whether divinely inspired or not. The delivery inevitably was all too mortal, its components cut from humanity's crooked timber.

Truman's objectives are still all too relevant today. So is that the clinching argument that the UN has failed? Whenever I hear that proposition, I wonder first how things would have been without it, and second I think of some of what it has still been able to do despite all the encumbrance of human frailty. I also remember some of those who have worked and died in its name for a better and more rational world. In the first list are the UN High Commissioner for Refugees (looking after 20 million people driven by conflict from their homes in South America, Asia and Africa), the UN Development Programme (with its pioneering work on governance, gender and education in the Middle East), the UN Children's Fund, the bodies within the UN family like the International Atomic Energy Agency (IAEA), the World Food Programme and the WHO. And there are the peace-keepers from the Congo to East Timor. Surprisingly, most UN casualties in recent years have not been among military peacekeepers but among their civilian cousins. One such example was the Brazilian Sérgio Vieira de Mello, who died in a bomb blast in Baghdad in August 2003.[5] I had known him when I was in Hong Kong and he was working for the UNHCR, helping us to cope with the Vietnamese boat people whom we were not 'allowed' to call refugees lest we accept too many obligations towards them. On a visit to Iraq after the 'mission' (according to President Bush) had been 'accomplished', I visited the shattered building of the Canal Hotel where Vieira de Mello had died, buried under the concrete rubble. He was there because the US had pushed the UN into blessing its occupation of

Iraq, and wanted a UN mission to help establish an interim Iraqi government. Despised though it was by much of the Bush administration, the UN was seen to have its uses. With the death of Vieira de Mello, the UN lost one of its best, a good and brave man who exemplified its highest standards and aspirations.

It is fair to say, however, that the UN has fallen well short of the hopes of those who saw in its creation the prospect of their world slumbering peacefully 'lapt in universal law'. At the outset, it showed our determination that there would be no more Dresdens, Hiroshimas, Burma Roads or Buchenwalds. As the Cold War froze a polarized world into hostile camps, it remained an investment in hope to set against the fear of nuclear Armageddon. What went wrong? First, it was – how could it not have been? – a creature of its time, with its principal institutions reflecting the world order at the end of the war. It was in a sense seen as a continuation of the wartime alliance, and the 'exceptions and loopholes'[6] that were subsequently exploited to its detriment, in terms of both morality and practice, were the result of bargains between the powers who had fought Germany and Japan into the ground. The wielding of the veto, or the threat to wield it, has regularly discredited and incapacitated the UN, though it has also probably persuaded the Great Powers who wield it not to abandon the organization in a geo-political huff.[7] The vetoes of Soviet Union ambassadors helped to drain away American enthusiasm for the organization, as did the UN's identification with hostility towards Israel: in 1975, the UN General Assembly passed a resolution branding Zionism as a form of racism and racial discrimination. (This was revoked in 1991.) The UN's bureaucracy was thought to be Byzantine, inefficient and corrupt; its Secretary Generals, with the exceptions of Dag Hammarskjöld and Kofi Annan, a pretty unexceptional lot, usually wanted more as secretaries than generals, though in the case of Kurt Waldheim it transpired that the organization had acquired for a whole decade a leader who had been, if not a general, certainly a decorated wartime German officer. He also economized with the truth, to use a charitable euphemism. This did not help build the UN's reputation.

In Waldheim's time, from 1972 to 1981, the UN found that its role had changed significantly. It was no longer mediating principally between combatants but between the rich world and the poor countries in the south of the globe.[8] The poor demanded a New International Economic Order which would have made them and everyone else much poorer; the wrongs suffered by them under the old order were to be reported by the Western media under a New World Information and Communications Order, which would remove freedoms from newspapers and broadcasters in developed countries that had already been routinely taken away from many of them in the developing states. These were not good times for reason. Perhaps inevitably, the US became ever more reluctant to accept that the UN could constrain its use of power, and the more this happened the more the majority at the UN saw itself as a countervailing force to the world's only superpower. The scene was set for Iraq; the part written for Ambassador John Bolton, the outrageous pantomime dame in this sad story.

Where do we go from here? Most of the problems described in this book would be easier to solve if the UN operated today as it was originally intended to do. I do not believe that we should resile from trying to reform the UN. But it makes no sense at all for all else to wait on this happy day. Take, for example, the central organizational issue of how you can apply the power and resources of the biggest states to dealing with problems faced by all states. The role of the Security Council at the heart of the UN is inhibited by its rules of procedure and its membership. The use or threatened use of the veto hampers effective and fast responses to problems like Darfur. China and Russia block most attempts to get around Westphalian notions of sovereignty; the US gives an automatic thumbs-down to anything that looks like criticism of Israel. Efforts to limit the veto to matters of high national importance to the country wielding it, and to report the veto's use for debate in the General Assembly, get nowhere. Equally, any adjustment to the membership seems doomed; the permanent members are still the wartime Allies, though the communist government in China replaced the nationalist regime in Taiwan in 1971. What chance of Germany joining the Council when Italy wants a place too, and when France and Britain hang on to their post-war seats, reluctant to give up these manifestations of sovereignty for, say, a single European seat at the table? (When I was European

Commissioner, three European representatives used to turn up at the UN for meetings of the Middle East Quartet – with the UN, Russia and the US – thus making that body what conker buffs would call a 'sixer'. How do you make four equal six? Invite to a meeting the EU member-state President of the Council, the High Representative for Common and Foreign Policy and a Commissioner.) How do you get Japan onto the council if China blocks its path, and if there is no Japan, can India join please? And if India joins, what about Brazil and Mexico, let alone Pakistan and Argentina? How do you leave out Egypt? Which African countries will join when Nigeria and South Africa become members? On top of which, would we really have wanted President Mbeki on the Security Council given his spineless behaviour over Zimbabwe? Maybe we would be better served if Africa could be represented by those dock workers in Durban who refused to unload weapons in April 2008 from a Chinese ship bound for China's clients in Harare. Reorganizing the Security Council is like playing three-dimensional chess in a darkened room. Maybe one day the game will be played and concluded. And maybe one day, in W. H. Auden's words, 'the salmon will sing in the street'.

The reform of the UN bureaucracy will proceed, though probably more slowly than global warming melts the permafrost. But we should not exaggerate the scale of the problem. The Iraq oil-for-food scandal showed up some of the failings in UN management, horribly damaging the authority of Kofi Annan in the process. The problem lay in fact as much in the court of member states, whose own bureaucracies are often shot through with corruption and incompetence. How do we wish to speed up and clean up the UN? Send in a team of Russian or Angolan civil servants? Or, if I am allowed a moment's parochialism, perhaps we could parachute in a hand-picked team of British officials from the ranks of those who have tried to computerize the National Health Service or to hold secure the private details of British citizens' lives?

I guess that we can at least expect in the future the positive re-engagement of the US in the UN; that on its own would send a sigh of relief through the better parts of the organization and perhaps produce a more positive atmosphere for pushing through some of the reforms that would threaten the more defensive views of national sovereignty by making the organization more effective. An example of where truculent intransigence got the US in its Bolton years is the composition and remit of the new Human Rights Council, in which any serious critique of a member's human-rights record can be blocked by countries that sit on the Council while massively and serially abusing human rights themselves and which has been given the excuse to turn a deaf ear to criticism by being offered too many 'double standards' targets by the US in recent years. The end to logic-chopping in the White House about waterboarding will enable democratic countries to apply more pressure on those states where torture is an almost routine part of interrogation, especially when they work on what Vice-President Cheney in 2001 called 'sort of the dark side'.[9]

Before the World Summit at the UN in 2005, Kofi Annan put forward a set of sweeping reforms for changing the organization and for tackling development, human-rights abuses, peacekeeping, disarmament, terrorism and security issues. It was thoughtful and ambitious; by the start of the summit it had been gutted and by its end only one really big new idea seemed to have survived, though even this global endorsement was subsequently denied. This was the notion of the responsibility to protect, or 'R2P', as it had come to be called; it was an attempt to address in a way acceptable to powers great and small, rich and poor, Westphalian and post-Westphalian, the question of how in future the world could ensure that 'never again' was not simply a hopeless response to the latest atrocity but a way of preventing the next one.

I should come clean. The conflict prevention and resolution organization which I co-chair, the International Crisis Group, and its recently departed president Gareth Evans, a former Australian foreign minister, have been centrally involved with the creation of and advocacy for this concept. Atrocities were its parents. The world had stood by while 800,000 Rwandans were slaughtered in a hundred days in 1994. Never again: except that the following year 8,000 Bosnian men and boys, sheltering in what purported to be a UN-guarded safe haven in Srebrenica, were murdered by the forces of the Serbian general Ratko Mladic. There had, of course, been military interventions which had worked in the past to prevent atrocities (India in what was then East Pakistan in 1971, Vietnam in Cambodia from 1975 to 1979, Tanzania in Uganda in 1979 and 1981) and there had been interventions which had not worked (Somalia in 1992–5). Politicians and others began to hunt for a formulation which would conceptualize, justify and legitimize action to prevent or stop genocide, atrocities and ethnic cleansing. Bernard Kouchner, who had started the organization Médecins Sans Frontières and was later to be UN high representative in Kosovo and French foreign minister, began the debate with his advocacy of a right to humanitarian intervention. Tony Blair took the argument further in a famous speech in Chicago in 1999 after a NATO-led coalition had intervened to protect Kosovo against Serb repression. The problem with Mr Blair's formulation, and different variants of it, was that it went down better with rich Western countries than with others, it seemed to attach greater importance to powerful UN members than to the weaker ones and it was a straightforward assault on the traditional notion of national sovereignty. I have some sympathy with the Blair argument. What he was trying to describe was something that would work, albeit he was doing so in Gladstonian language that would never be supported these days – at least in Britain – by an equivalent weight of Gladstonian power. But it was not easy to see how it could get the support of a consensus of the weak as well as the powerful and therefore achieve legitimization through the UN. Kofi Annan's own attempt to draw a neat distinction between national sovereignty and individual sovereignty, asserting that individuals have rights too which are not the monopoly of states, did not quite take the trick. Surprisingly the concept of R2P seemed to do so.

The idea of the responsibility to protect emerged from a family tree of high-powered international commissions through which a common thread was the membership of Gareth Evans. It sought to deflect criticism with a concept that reversed the principle of the right to intervene. The responsibility of states to protect citizens, not least against atrocities, covered the duty to prevent these things happening in the first place (for example through economic measures, diplomacy or institution building), to react effectively to them if bad things did happen, and to rebuild societies where atrocities had taken place. Advocates of R2P were at pains to argue that military intervention was not always necessary or appropriate, that the concept was not just humanitarian intervention in camouflage, and that it was not a blast of neocolonialism. Where other issues on the Annan wish-list for global reform in 2005 largely fell by the wayside, R2P survived. It represents one of the few hopeful developments in international cooperation in recent years, though we should not allow ourselves to be carried away. Transports of enthusiasm are not yet in order, despite Pope Benedict's endorsement of the concept in his eloquent address to the UN in April 2008. Now we have to make R2P work. First, although it could be argued at a stretch that elements of R2P had been used in defusing the Kenyan post-election crisis in 2007–8, this was closer to a piece of old-fashioned mediation as some of the underlying and destabilizing problems in Kenya lingered on. There is a tendency to describe anything that helps damp down a potential conflict as 'R2P'. Second, the real test will come when – and, alas, it will happen – another state falls apart in ethnic turmoil. I doubt myself whether we have yet come near to forging a consensus about definitions of and limits on state sovereignty. Third, when a 'never again' situation arises once more requiring military as well as other forms of intervention, are we closer to a situation where the Security Council will be prepared to legitimize it and provide the means to do the job properly? Fourth, the rich-versus-poor, strong-versus-weak polarization still exists in and outside the UN and will continue to bedevil efforts to deal with failed and failing states from Zimbabwe to Burma.

The problems thrown up by questions like humanitarian intervention and responsibility to protect encourage some to think that we should not pile all our eggs into the UN's basket. We should not, they say, resile from the UN, but since we apparently cannot remedy its deficiencies we should establish a narrower organization, an Alliance of Democracies, with the power and the will to act in defence of freedom. It would be like NATO writ large, including not just richer non-transatlantic countries like Australia, New Zealand and Japan but developing country democracies like India and the more developed but not-yet-OECD countries such as Brazil and South Africa. First, whatever the intention, any such grouping would of course wreck the UN and destroy any further efforts to reform it. The UN would become an even louder lobby for the South against the rich North. Second, why should India and Brazil or South Africa want to join? They would be hitching their stars to states that exemplify (fairly or unfairly does not matter) a colonial past and a selfish present which they deplore. As a result, they too are deeply suspicious of post-Westphalian ideas about sovereignty. Third, the challenge is not how to shut China (and Russia) out of global leadership but how to get them to accept a more responsible role in exercising it. Would we deal more effectively with global warming or nuclear proliferation, with Iran or North Korea, with China and Russia on the outside of the tent looking in? Fourth, how would a smaller grouping of countries provide the legitimacy – for military actions, for instance, or for tough sanctions – which is refused by an organization that represents not the few but everyone? The answer to the UN's problems is not to give up on the organization but to work patiently and consistently to try and make it work better. Where sensible outcomes cannot be achieved through the UN, then it will be necessary from time to time to put together alternative partnerships and occasionally to use other instruments such as regional organizations, with some diminution in legitimacy. We should always try first to work through the UN to help sort out global problems. That is what it is there for. While it will not always work, the UN is more likely to do so if we make a habit of regularly giving it our best shot, a far better approach than what was well described as John Bolton's joyless enjoyment in rotting it off.

The blocking capacity of bigger states – or in some cases formerly bigger states – in the Security Council inevitably opens the UN to the criticism that it tilts global governance in the interests of the powerful and disenfranchises the poor. Since I do not believe that we stand on the threshold, or even at the gates of the drive, of an era of global government under which all states are treated as equals under a common authority, or where accountability for global government is owed to individual global citizens (presumably regarding themselves above all as citizens of the world rather than America or China or Paraguay), I cannot see that aspect of the UN changing. Given my views on nation-states, their survivability and their necessity, I regard dreams of world government as just that. Why allow ourselves to be distracted by fairy tales? And would we anyway want to live in a world where final authority was so far removed from the individual citizen that it could not possibly be truly democratic? The great French philosopher and political scientist Raymond Aron hated utopian thought and totalitarianism alike. The first often turns into the second and I think this is a danger as soon as one starts to contemplate the practicalities of world government. I am far more sympathetic to the notion of equity in the institutions established as part of the post-war settlement for the purpose of global economic management, the World Bank and the IMF. They need to operate with greater transparency and to be more accountable to their principal customers in the developing world. Since their establishment, the US has laid claim to the presidency of the World Bank and Europe to the top post at the IMF. The heads of both organizations should be appointed according to merit and there should no longer be a political carve-up of these two most senior posts between the transatlantic partners. The attempts to deal with the global recession, and to prevent the repetition of some of the errors that had led to it, highlighted the importance of reform of the economic institutions set up at Bretton Woods.

The question of global equity will throw an ever longer shadow across traditional foreign and security policy discussions; not least as the recession's impact hits the poorest countries. The 'bottom billion' are not going to get suddenly better off, nor are they going to disappear. Their numbers will indeed increase just as population figures in better-off countries and better-off groups stabilize; the further the very poor are left behind, the more of them there will be. They will be able to see more of our comfort; we will witness more of their misery. There will have to be substantial resource transfers from rich to poor, though this should be done in a hard-headed way. Sensible conditionality is not the last hurrah of colonialism. The developed countries should not renege on their aid commitments because of the need for belt-tightening at home. Particular priorities should be education (not neglecting the needs of girls and young women), the management of water resources and access to clean water, and the development of healthcare systems which are soundly based in the community. This is one of the lessons from the success of the AIDS campaign in Uganda. Donors should work better together and accept common standards and arrangements for monitoring success. We should spare poor countries the bureaucratic burden of endless inspections and surveillance by everyone who gives them money. We need to convince China, now such a large aid donor in Africa, that good governance matters. They will be reluctant to associate this with democracy, but may at least be prepared to accept that it covers corruption, the rule of law and transparency in managing public accounts. The Extractive Industries Transparency Initiative deserves wide support if the resources of poorer countries are to be used for development and are not to be salted away in private bank accounts. Transparency in identifying the provenance of resources should also be extended beyond timber and diamonds, and in the post-Bush, post-Bolton era that beckons we should try again to monitor and regulate effectively the trade in small arms.

We all know that trade is more important to developing countries than aid. This was meant to be at the heart of the WTO's latest attempt to secure a further liberal multilateral trade deal, the so-called Doha Round. It was supposed to demonstrate that a more open trading system could benefit rather than disadvantage the poor. But progress has so far been dashed on the rocks of agricultural protectionism, nervousness about the impact of further elimination of trade barriers, and a lack of political will, which is itself partly a result of the absence of much lobbying by industry and commerce. There seems to have been a mood of general exhaustion about trade liberalization. The big danger is that, having lost forward momentum, the American recession and economic slow-downs elsewhere will throw the whole process of opening up markets into reverse. Protectionism looms, and the rhetoric of the American presidential election was hardly a paean to the benefits of free trade. If only the debate had been more about how to encourage savings, the real way to deal with the US trade deficit. The world must hope that President Obama will not in office bow to populist, protectionist pressures. In his first weeks in office, he seemed prepared to stem the tide, refusing for example to accept an ill-considered 'buy American' provision in his economic stimulus package. But domestic economic and financial difficulties will not make such resistance easy. When people are losing their homes and their jobs, when they feel that their standard of living is falling, it is not easy to convince them of the need for further bold market opening, let alone to think more about the problems faced by the whole world.

So America's new president will find it difficult (however hard he tries) to put together an imaginative and adequate policy position on global warming in the first months of power when so many domestic economic issues are hammering on the Oval Office door. Yet the ambition is to negotiate a planet-saving deal at the conference in Denmark before the end of 2009. Desirable, even vital, though I think that may be, it is at present difficult to see how it will be achieved. What is important is that such a conference should mark distinct progress in negotiating a final deal, and for that to happen we need to recognize the central political issue. No deal is likely to be sufficient or deliverable if it is simply the input to debate. The issues are so profound that you cannot depend, as in negotiating most other international issues (though not, as it turned out, Versailles), on negotiating a deal and going home to try to put it into place. A climate-change agreement will have to be the output of debate. It needs to reflect the common understandings that have been reached throughout the world. Policy has to be the outcome of politics, not the other way round. That is more or less the position we have reached in Europe, though even here there are signs of backsliding as some of the big polluting industries squeal about unfair competition and the uniqueness of their problems. But why should we think that gas-guzzling, high-emission cars, for example, demand a special place in our public affections? Their manufacturers should see their own future competitiveness in terms of their more limited environmental impact. The right to drive a large SUV or gas-guzzling saloon is not a hallowed part of European civilization. Having taken a responsibly bold position on global warming, it would be disastrous for the EU to start quibbling about our own targets being wholly dependent on others doing the same. Others are more likely to do the same if Europe is prepared to blaze the trail. Moreover, climate change should be seen as an area in which the EU really can demonstrate global leadership, making up for our lack of political will and effectiveness elsewhere.

At the heart of any effective global agreement on climate change will be a settlement between the US and China, a hugely difficult enterprise on both sides. How can the Chinese recalibrate their growth model without aborting the drive for greater prosperity that legitimizes their political system? Even if they know how to do this, how can what is decided at the centre be made to stick way out beyond

Beijing's walls? This has always been a problem for China's rulers, as the Confucian Book of Odes recorded:

> We get up at sunrise
> At sunset we rest.
> We dig wells and drink.
> We till the fields and eat.
> What is the might of the emperor to us?

Or the might today of the Politburo of the Chinese Communist Party? Among the problems for the American president will be to convince US citizens that an agreement with China, which will inevitably look at the start like a transfer of economic advantage to America's biggest long-term competitor, is the overwhelmingly correct thing to do. It will involve burying the false but dangerous thought that the century ahead is going to see an inevitable hegemonic struggle between China and the United States. This fulfils for some people in the West the requirement that there should always be barbarians at the gate. Having sent the last lot packing, we look around nervously for the next bunch so that we know where to direct our fire. So must China play barbarian, the superpower set to bury us first in Wal-Mart special offers and next in its geopolitical ambitions, whatever they may be? Momentous as I believe China's rise has been, it is both premature and dangerous to hold China up as the menacing new champ. I set out earlier some of the huge challenges that China faces, among them the myriad problems of governance that arise when a creaky, shadowy autocratic state starts trying to run like a pro. As a general rule I find it hard to accept that a state entity that has to work quite so hard to survive is a superpower. Beating up, imprisoning or shooting political critics, protestors and dissidents does not seem to me a mark of quietly self-confident authority. If the Chinese are to become a superpower, they are going to have to square a lot of circles, solve a lot of problems, in the coming century. America's interests (and China's) would be best served by acting as China's partner in confronting those dangers, and building as a result a better and more prosperous world. The US should see itself as a collaborator of China, albeit with a presently different set of values, rather than as a rival.

Where else do we find barbarians? We can make out their shadows in the dark world of transformational Islamic terrorism, and some claim to see them too in whichever west-Asian countries are believed to thwart America's will and challenge Israel. With Saddam Hussein dispatched, his old adversaries in Iran are regarded by many as the main threat in their region, especially as they are thought to harbour the dream of having their own nuclear weapon. Within two years of taking office the new American president will be one of the primary actors at the 2010 Nuclear Non-Proliferation Treaty Review Conference. I spelt out earlier the importance of the United States and its nuclear allies in particular taking the steps that would help create an atmosphere in which toughening up the verification and monitoring arrangements made under the treaty might be more acceptable to the non-nuclear powers. That should be a key part of the approach to Iran, alongside the extension of the powers of the IAEA so that it can act as the world's nuclear fuel banker for civil nuclear power. If there was ever a measure of the degree to which America's problems in the world are self-inflicted, Iran is it. Whether or not the Iranians want an atomic bomb is debatable. What they clearly want is legitimacy, for which read talking to America, something which President Obama seems to countenance. Iran's antics have been in direct proportion to America's refusal to engage with it. Talking to Iran, trying to draw the country out of sometimes (though not always) irresponsible isolationism, would assist Europe in circumventing dependence on Russian oil and gas networks, connecting the EU directly through Iran with central Asia.

The political interconnections in the Middle East are plain. You cannot get a deal on Palestine that does not involve both Fatah and Hamas. No deal on Palestine is likely without a resolution of Israel's arguments over the Golan with Syria, which would also make possible a political as well as military ceasefire with Hezbollah in Lebanon and a return to peaceful development in that tragic entrepôt land. Engagement with Iran would help to unlock the puzzles in Syria and Lebanon. A peace deal between Israel and Palestine, especially if incorporated in a regional security pact, would cut back the growth in support for transformational terrorism. Sensitive handling of Turkey's negotiations to become a member of the EU would also help to abate some of the rage in parts of the Muslim world against what are believed to be the double standards, the neocolonialism and the brashness of the West. Unfortunately the United States and Europe are invariably seen at their most materialistic in the East, where, for example, oil fortunes often purchase huge, prefabricated, tasteless lumps of Western lifestyle viewed through the Armani shades that peek out under numerous hijabs. And the West, of course, talks freedom while supporting autocracies so long as the oil and gas continue to be pumped.

The rise of political Islamism, in both its more and less extreme forms, has prompted a surprisingly vicious backlash against all religion. Where religion was said until fairly recently to have become irrelevant in modern politics, it is now often blamed truculently for all our predicaments, the cause of so much misery in the Middle East and beyond. Much of the attack is repetitious and unoriginal; fundamentalist secularism meets fundamentalist religion. Do we really need another visit to the archives of the Inquisition or more laboured jokes about the belief in miracles? Must we look again at those religious fundamentalist websites – Christian, Jewish, Muslim – which put retribution ahead of love and charity, which turn a literalist faith into the great foe of reason? All those familiar assaults on religion neglect something basic to its role in contemporary society. Lech Walesa credited the visit of Pope John Paul II to Poland in 1979 with inspiring him to found Solidarity. The Pope's visit in 1981 forced the communist regime there to free the imprisoned Walesa for a papal audience. By standing alongside Solidarity, John Paul II placed his own body between the individual conscience and the oppressive power of autocracy, protecting the one, challenging the other. The Catholic Church was not waging war against the Soviet Union, nor were the Lutheran groups in East Germany. What they did was to provide a foundation from which many people in the Warsaw Pact countries were able to reconstruct a civil society. Yes, Catholicism and Lutheranism were important, but important alongside trade unionism, and the commitment to a humanistic set of values – freedom to assemble, organize and speak out. When totalitarians are forced – for example by Buddhists in Burma or China – to acknowledge that there are boundaries and limits under the sun, then the entire totalitarian system, the terror, the false values are dealt a mortal blow. In its affirmation of what is just and humane, and in its willingness to sacrifice everything for that affirmation, religion may set lasting and powerful limits on what may otherwise appear to be limitless temporal power.

The role of religion in parts of western and central Asia looks in some respect like a consequence of temporal power being pretty well absolute. The modernity of societies there is superficial. The glamour of the West has been brought in without its anguish, its troubles, its muddle, its creativity, its cultural liberty. Governments offer anything and everything except political freedom and real pluralism; the totalizing ideological force of religion in this region reflects the general destruction of civil society. The demand of religious believers is unequivocal: they say to the state, 'Keep out of our lives or there is going to be trouble.' Paradoxically, that has the ring of civil libertarianism about it. In this sense, Islam like Christianity or Buddhism retains the seed within itself of a functioning civil society. But where there is no wider civil society, where state authorities struggle to keep the lid on their civil societies, the danger is an explosion of Muslim dissent. This is why so many Westerners talk up freedom and democracy in general, but are nervous about seeing much of either in Muslim countries. Do we tell Mr Mubarak in Egypt to make way for free and fair elections? To what would they lead? What are our messages from Algeria to Saudi Arabia? Yet the longer civil society is marginalized or suppressed, the more likely it is that the debate will polarize, with Muslims forced to make a decision between the secular state or Islam. That could become a rolling disaster. The modern age had its roots in the discovery by growing states that they were in danger of cracking their teeth on Christianity. We should try to avoid corrupt, stagnating, autocratic states cracking their teeth on Islam.

I am constantly struck by how often the real answers to problems 'over there' lie 'back here'. Successful foreign policy is frequently successful domestic policy, and the reverse. The conditions and the degree of prosperity abroad are closely connected to our trade and economic policies at home. Our domestic policies on drugs are not winning the so-called war against them; with no apparent end in sight, murder and devastation are visited upon those who produce and trade drugs overseas, and in most of the West we fill our prisons with those who use them; this miserable market does not shrink. The problems of the international arms trade have much to do with how we manufacture and distribute weapons. The threat of epidemic disease is partly related to pharmaceutical research and development, to licensing and litigation at home. Global warming happens because of the cars we drive, the domestic appliances we use, the homes we live in, the jobs we do, the way we produce and use energy. None of which is to argue that there is nothing to be done abroad. But if we think we can solve all our problems by tackling them abroad, out there, without trying to face up to them right here, we will fail.

It goes far wider, touching those issues that we think show our sense of global humanism like demography and human rights where it is so much easier to preach than to act. As we sermonize about peace and love to Kurds, Shias and Sunnis, how well do we treat our own migrants and minorities? Is it any wonder that so much rhetoric about human rights is regarded as cant? I have experienced this in my own country, for example on the night when I was holding a crowded public meeting in Northern Ireland about the reform of policing. 'It's much easier for you to come over here from London and give us lectures about reconciliation than it is for us to practise it,' said one female questioner. So it is: easier for us to call for tolerance in other lands (the further away the better) than it is for us to make the same pitch right here at home, convincing people to treat migrants and asylum seekers decently. There is a danger of Western politicians trying to have it both ways, lecturing foreigners on this or that virtue, while listening first to pollsters and focus groups at home, calling for another crackdown and talking tough as old boots. I do it myself. I think I know more about Guantanamo Bay than about the condition in Britain's prisons or asylum holding centres. How much harder it is to confront our own monsters than to point to those elsewhere.

There is, finally, a temptation to call for bigger and better citizens, with bigger and better leaders. Here, grumpy old men join ex-politicians in the saloon bar. Everything is going to the dogs (as absurd – to be noted in passing – as the notion that the young are so much more idealistic than the rest of us). We are on the skids. There's no hope. Look at them all, rings in their ears and no buckles on their shoes. All, as General Dumouriez said, is lost. Even the greatest and wisest of us can wander off, tut-tutting and head-shaking, down this path. At the end of *Sketches from a Life* George Kennan, who as much as any other mapped the transatlantic community's strategy for defeating Soviet communism, fell into a routine denunciation of the materialism, greed and decadence of modern society, calling for 'true spiritual leadership and environmental preservation as the primary aims of civilization'.[10] Mind you, he knew really that none of this was going to happen. I should like to join in denouncing materialism, greed and decadence, thoroughly bad things I say; but I hope that Mr Kennan did not go depressed into the night that this is pretty well all that has been achieved in the West he helped to save. There are today individual freedom and choice (more widely spread than ever before), free intellectual inquiry, laughter, aspiration, generosity, love of family across the generations, sacrifice for others and maybe a greater sense of our common humanity. What I would hope there may be too is at least the stirrings of an understanding that to live in a better world, a world that is not just the same as today, requires a more active democratic citizenry, a sentiment inherent in Barack Obama's American presidential campaign oratory. Many criticized his slogan, 'Yes, We Can'. Do we really want leaders who tell us, 'No, We Can't'? As citizens we can hope for and expect a better world because, after all, it is finally we who are sovereign: the point underlying Mr Annan's speech on humanitarian intervention. This is where the hunt for sovereignty should begin and end.

Commentators have often spoken of the end of sovereignty as though it meant the beginning of an exciting new era of people power. The end of sovereignty is not upon us, because we as individuals, as citizens, are the ultimate holders of sovereignty. We place that sovereignty in the government of our nation-state as a matter of trust. That nation-state, as I argued at the outset, is not a quaint and anachronistic holdover but a compromise written in blood that just about managed in the second half of the last century to bind the demons that attend power to a peaceful and progressive policy. Those nation-state governments can and should work themselves and with others to exercise that sovereignty that we have invested in them. For them to turn round and tell us that sovereignty has evaporated is like our bank manager telling us that the savings that we deposited have vanished. To what purpose then are claims like the 'end of sovereignty' made? That is my sovereignty that is being talked about. If sovereignty is ended, gone in a puff of political science, then the problems outlined in this book cease to be our problems, and if they cease to be our problems then we cease to be able to do anything about them. There is, on the contrary, plenty we can do, not believing ourselves omnipotent but recognizing that both on our own and together we – that is the family we, the nation-state we, the European, Asian, Latin American, North American, African or Australasian we, the global we – can go on muddling through, sometimes solving, sometimes managing, sometimes simply enduring our common predicaments, the hazards of sharing this planet.

What is the reason for thinking that, the reason for raising the somewhat tattered banner of optimism? At school I learned by the yard the work of the English poet John Masefield – Britain's poet laureate in the middle decades of the last century – especially the maritime exploits of the 'quinquereme of Nineveh', 'the stately Spanish galleon' and the 'dirty British coaster'. Masefield spanned the centuries. He often sounded like Kipling. He had spoken to men who had fought at Waterloo. Much of his vocabulary (drawn from his shipboard adventures) was obsolete: flying jibboons, dead-eyes, paunch-mattings and laniards.[11] Masefield is not very well regarded these days, being among other things comprehensible at least when not up the mizzenmast. Sometimes what is so easy to understand in his work is admittedly a little trite, trite but true. His memorial stone is in Poets Corner in Westminster Abbey. There is no epitaph written on it, but in a way he had written his own in a 1926 novel, *Odtaa* (an acronym for 'one damned thing after another'), about a fictional South American state:

> I have seen flowers come in stony places
> And kind things done by men with ugly faces,
> And the gold cup won by the worst horse at the races,
> So I trust too.

Why is it regarded as prudent to say we are all doomed, a statement which has never been true? In a world still capable of rationality, creativity, generosity and kindness, I guess that phrase of Masefield's is alpha and omega for me, the beginning and the end. 'I trust too.' After all, for a grandfather, what on earth is the alternative?

Notes

1 Introduction

1. Richard Haas, 'State Sovereignty Must Be Altered in Globalized Era', *Taipei Times*, 21 February 2006.
2. Benedict Anderson, *Imagined Communities* (Verso, 1991).
3. Anna Reid, *Borderland* (Phoenix, 1997).
4. Martin Rees, *Our Final Century* (Arrow Books, 2003).
5. Thomas J. Biersteker, 'State, Sovereignty and Territory', in Walter Carlsnaes, Thomas Risse and Beth A. Simmons (eds.), *Handbook of International Relations* (Sage, 2002), pp. 157–77, here p. 161.
6. Kenneth N. Waltz, *Theory of International Relations* (McGraw-Hill, 1979), p. 88.
7. Institute for National Strategic Studies, Washington, DC, 'Strategic Assessment, 1999', p. 250.
8. Lawrence Wright, *The Looming Tower* (Knopf, 2006).
9. Jorge Luis Borges, 'Story of the Warrior and the Captain', in Borges, *Labyrinths* (Penguin, 1971), p. 163.
10. Winston S. Churchill, *The World Crisis* (Scribner's, 1923–31), vol. 1.1, chapter 11.

2 The Journey So Far

1. Frances Stonor Saunders, *Hawkwood: Diabolical Englishman* (Faber and Faber, 2004).
2. Quoted by Charles Tilly, *Coercion, Capital and European States, AD 990–1992* (Oxford, Blackwell, 1992), p. 84.
3. Geoffrey Parker, *The Military Revolution* (Cambridge University Press, 1988; repr. 1996).
4. C. V. Wedgwood, *The Thirty Years War* (Cape, 1938; repr. NYRB Classics, 2005), p. 460.

5. Parker, *The Military Revolution*.

6. Jessica T. Matthews, 'Power Shift', *Foreign Affairs*, Jan.–Feb. 1997, p. 61.

7. Anthony Quinton, in A. Kenny (ed.), *The Oxford Illustrated History of Western Philosophy* (Oxford University Press, 1997).

8. Henry Kissinger, *Diplomacy* (Simon and Schuster, 1994), pp. 20–21.

9. William H. McNeill, *The Pursuit of Power* (University of Chicago Press, 1982).

10. Christopher A. Bayly, *The Birth of the Modern World* (Blackwell, 2004).

11. Linda Colley, *Britons: Forging the Nation, 1707–1837* (Random House, 1992).

12. Milan Kundera, *Life is Elsewhere*, trans. Peter Kussi (Faber and Faber, 1986).

13. Piers Brendon, *The Dark Valley* (Pimlico, 2001).

14. World Bank Report No. 32205, 'Democratic Republic of Congo: Economic and Sector Work, Governance and Service Delivery', 30 June 2005.

3 Les Big Macs and the Crash

1. Michael Veseth, *Globaloney* (Rowman and Littlefield, 2005).

2. Adam Gopnik, *Paris to the Moon* (Random House, 2001).

3. Giuseppe di Lampedusa, *The Leopard* (Everyman's Library, 1991).

4. Nayan Chanda, *Bound Together: How Traders, Preachers, Adventurers and Warriors Shaped Globalization* (Yale University Press, 2007).

5. Angus Maddison, *The World Economy: A Millennial Perspective* (OECD, 2007).

6. Martin Wolf, *Why Globalization Works* (Yale University Press, 2005).

7. Chanda, *Bound Together*.

8. Thomas Friedman, *The World Is Flat* (Allen Lane, 2005).

9. Martin Wolf, 'Will the Nation-state Survive Globalisation?', *Foreign Affairs*, Jan.–Feb. 2001.

10. Robert Keohane and Joseph Nye, *Governance in a Globalizing World* (Brookings Institute Press, 2000).

11. Veseth, *Globaloney*.

12. William Greider, *One World, Ready or Not: The Manic Logic of Global Capitalism* (Simon and Schuster, 1997).

13. Wolf, 'Will the Nation-state Survive Globalisation?'

14. There is an excellent discussion of this issue in Chanda, *Bound Together*.

15. Wolf, 'Will the Nation-state Survive Globalisation?' Martin Wolf is extremely good at itemizing examples of rich-country hypocrisy on trade issues.

16. John Ralston Saul, *The Collapse of Globalism* (Atlantic Books, 2005).

17. David Held and Anthony McGrew, *The Global Transformations Reader* (Polity Press, 2003).

18. 'The End', Michael Lewis, *Portfolio.com*, December 2008.

19. Ibid.

20. 'The Reckoning', Eric Dash and Julie Cresswell, *The New York Times*, 23 November 2008.

21. Keohane and Nye, *Governance in a Globalizing World*.

22. Anne-Marie Slaughter, 'Governing the Global Economy through Government Networks', in Held and McGrew, *The Global Transformations Reader*.

4 Skies of Flame

1. Address to a Joint Session of Congress and the American People, 20 September 2001.

2. Audrey Kurth Cronin, 'Behind the Curve', *International Security*, 27, 3 (Winter 2002/3).

3. Louise Richardson, *What Terrorists Want* (Random House, 2006).

4. Paul Bowles, *The Spider's House* (Random House, 1955; repr. Abacus, 1991).

5. Ivo Andric, *The Damned Yard and Other Stories*, ed. Celia Hawkesworth (Forest Books, 1996).

6. Lawrence Wright, *The Looming Tower* (Knopf, 2006).

7. Ibid.

8. Ibid.

9. Fareed Zakaria, *The Future of Freedom: Illiberal Democracy at Home and Abroad* (W. W. Norton and Co., 2003).

10. Wright, *The Looming Tower*.

11. Bowles, *The Spider's House*.

12. Amartya Sen, *Identity and Violence: The Illusion of Destiny* (Allen Lane, 2006).

13. Paul Wilkinson, Memorandum for the House of Commons, Foreign Affairs Committee, June 2003; Jane Corbin, *The Base* (Simon and Schuster, 2002).

14. Walter Laqueur, *No End to War: Terrorism in the Twenty-First Century* (Continuum, 2003).

15. Bruce Hoffman, 'Rethinking Terrorism and Counterterrorism Since 9/11', *Studies in Conflict and Terrorism*, 25 (2002).

16. Cronin, 'Behind the Curve'.

17. James Fallows writing in the *Atlantic Monthly*, September 2006.

18. Adam Roberts, 'The "War on Terror" in Historical Perspective', *Survival*, 47, 2 (Summer 2005).

19. Robert Thompson, *Defeating Communist Insurgency: Experiences from Malaya and Vietnam* (Chatto and Windus, 1966).

5 Mushroom Clouds

1. Jonathan Schell, *The Fate of the Earth* (Cape, 1982; repr. Stanford University Press, 2000).

2. J. Cirincione, J. B. Wolfsthal and M. Rajkumar, *Deadly Arsenals* (Brookings Institution, 2005).

3. Robert Hutchinson, *Weapons of Mass Destruction* (Cassell, 2004).

4. Joachim Krause, 'Enlightenment and Nuclear Order', *International Affairs*, 83, 3 (2007).

5. Thomas Graham, Jr, *Commonsense on Weapons of Mass Destruction* (University of Washington Press, 2004).

6. Quoted ibid.

7. Quoted in Hutchinson, *Weapons of Mass Destruction*.

8. Lawrence S. Wittner, *The Struggle against the Bomb*, vol. 2, *Resisting the Bomb* (Stanford University Press, 1997).

9. Coordinating Committee for Multilateral Export Controls (COCOM), Comprehensive Test Ban Treaty (CTBT), Cooperative Threat Reduction (CTR), Senior Defense Group on Proliferation – NATO (DGP), Fissile Material Cut-off Treaty proposal (FMCT), Initiatives for Proliferation Prevention (IPP), Material Protection Control and Accounting Programme (MPC&A), Nuclear Cities Initiative (NCI), Non-Proliferation Treaty (NPT), Nuclear Suppliers Group (NSG), Proliferation Security Initiative (PSI).

10. Krause, 'Enlightenment and Nuclear Order'.

11. Chaim Braun and Christopher F. Chyba, 'Proliferation Rings: New Challenges to the Nuclear Non-proliferation Regime', *International Security*, Autumn 2004.

12. International Crisis Group, 'The State of Sectarianism in Pakistan', April 2005, www.crisisgroup.org.

13. Guarav Kampani, 'Second Tier Proliferation: The Case of Pakistan and North Korea', *Non-Proliferation Review*, Fall–Winter 2002.

14. Braun and Chyba, 'Proliferation Rings'.

15. I have told this story in some detail in *Not Quite the Diplomat* (Penguin, 2005).

16. Jaswant Singh, *A Call to Honour* (Rupa and Co., 2006).

17. Strobe Talbott, *Engaging India* (Brookings Institution Press, 2004).

6 A Hundred Million Rifles

1. *Human Security Report, 2005* (Human Security Centre, University of British Columbia/Oxford University Press, 2005).

2. Paul Collier, *The Bottom Billion* (Oxford University Press, 2007).

3. Jeffrey Boutwell and Michael T. Klare (eds.), *Light Weapons and Civil Conflict* (Rowman and Littlefield, 1999).

4. *Small Arms Survey, 2006* (Graduate Institute of International Studies, Geneva/Oxford University Press, 2006).

5. Moisés Naím, *Illicit* (Heinemann, 2006).

6. Rachel Stohl, 'Fighting the Illicit Trafficking of Small Arms', *SAIS Review*, Winter–Spring 2005.

7. A full account of this affair can be found in Kathi Austin, 'Illicit Arms Brokers: Aiding and Abetting Atrocities', *Brown Journal of World Affairs*, Spring 2002.

8. Ibid.

9. Neil Cooper, 'What's the Point of Arms Transfer Controls?', *Contemporary Security Policy*, April 2006.

10. Ishmael Beah, *A Long Way Gone* (Fourth Estate, 2007).

11. 'The Usual Suspects', report by Global Witness, 2003, www.globalwitness. org/media_library_detail.php/96/en/the_usual_suspects.

12. Martin Meredith, *The State of Africa* (The Free Press, 2005).

13. 'Moldova, the Country that Europe Forgot', Economist.com, Correspondent's Diary, 18 May 2007, www.economist.com/daily/diary/displaystory. cfm?story_id=9173421.

14. Cooper, 'What's the Point of Arms Transfer Controls?'

15. Sarah Percy, *Mercenaries* (Oxford University Press, 2007).

16. Rajiv Chandrasekaran, *Imperial Life in the Emerald City* (Knopf, 2007).

7 Greed, Conflict and the 'Bottom Billion'

1. Tim Butcher, *Blood River* (Chatto and Windus, 2007).

2. Paul Collier, *The Bottom Billion* (Oxford University Press, 2007).

3. David Landes, *The Wealth and Poverty of Nations* (Little, Brown, 1998).

4. Jeffrey Sachs, *The End of Poverty* (Penguin, 2005).

5. Martin Meredith, *The State of Africa* (The Free Press, 2005).

6. Michael Klare, *Resource Wars* (Henry Holt and Co., 2001).

7. William Reno, 'Shadow States and the Political Economy of Civil Wars', in M. Berdal and D. M. Malone (eds.), *Greed and Grievance: Economic Agendas in Civil Wars* (Lynne Rienner, 2000).

8. Much of the detail in the next few paragraphs is taken from another outstanding report by Global Witness, 'Same Old Story', published in 2004, www.globalwitness.org/media_library_detail.php/118/en/same_old_story.

9. Keith B. Richburg, *Out of America: A Black Man Confronts Africa* (Basic Books, 1997).

10. Collier, *The Bottom Billion*.

11. P. T. Bauer, *Equality, the Third World, and Economic Delusion* (Harvard University Press, 1981).

12. Sachs, *The End of Poverty*.

13. Ibid.

14. William Easterly, *The White Man's Burden* (Penguin, 2006).

15. Collier, *The Bottom Billion*.

16. Robert Calderisi, *The Trouble With Africa* (Yale University Press, 2006).

17. Collier, *The Bottom Billion*.

18. Landes, *The Wealth and Poverty of Nations*.

8 Blood and Water

1. Emily Arnold and Janet Larsen, *Bottled Water* (Earth Policy Institute, 2006).

2. United Nations Development Programme, *Human Development Report 2006* (UNDP, 2006).

3. Marcus Moench, 'Water and the Potential for Social Instability', *Natural Resources Forum*, 26, 3 (2002).

4. United Nations Development Programme, *Human Development Report 2006*.

5. James Kynge, *China Shakes the World* (Weidenfeld and Nicolson, 2006).

6. United Nations Development Programme, *Human Development Report 2006*.

7. 'Climate Change and Agricultural Vulnerability', report prepared by the International Institute for Applied Systems Analysis, 2002.

8. Moench, 'Water and the Potential for Social Instability'.

9. Michael Klare, *Resource Wars* (Metropolitan Books, 2001); Peter H. Gleick, 'Water and Conflict', *International Security*, 18, 1 (1993), and 'Environment and Security', in Gleick, *The World's Water 2006–2007* (Island Press, 2007); Thomas F. Homer-Dixon, 'Environmental Scarcities and Violent Conflict', *International Security*, 19, 1 (1994).

10. Gleick, 'Environment and Security'.

11. Gleick, 'Water and Conflict'.

12. Homer-Dixon, 'Environmental Scarcities and Violent Conflict'.

13. Klare, *Resource Wars*.

14. The water problems of central Asia have been extensively covered in Eric W. Sievers, 'Water, Conflict, and Regional Security in Central Asia', *New York University Environmental Law Journal*, 10, 3 (2002), and in two reports by the International Crisis Group, 'Central Asia: Water and Conflict' (2002) and 'The Curse of Cotton' (February 2005).

15. Klare, *Resource Wars*.

9 Stuff Happens

1. R. T. Naylor, *Wages of Crime, Black Markets, Illegal Finance and the Underworld Economy* (Cornell University Press, 2004).

2. Louise Shelley and John Picarelli, 'Methods not Motives: Implications of the Convergence of International Organized Crime and Terrorism', *Police Practice and Research*, 3, 4 (2002).

3. Stephen Flynn, 'Beyond Border Control', *Foreign Affairs*, Nov.–Dec. 2001.

4. Manuel Castells, *End of Millennium* (Blackwell, 2000). Castells has an excellent chapter on the global criminal economy.

5. Ibid.

6. Claire Sterling, *Thieves' World: The Threat of the New Global Network of Organized Crime* (Simon and Schuster, 1994).

7. Misha Glenny, *McMafia* (The Bodley Head, 2008).

8. Moisés Naím, *Illicit* (Heinemann, 2006).

9. Shelley and Picarelli, 'Methods not Motives'.

10. Castells, *End of Millennium*.

11. Naím, *Illicit*, provides extensive coverage of the trade in counterfeit goods and of other forms of criminal activity.

12. Nancy Scheper-Hughes has written very well and widely on this subject, for example at http://sunsite.berkeley.edu/biotech/organswatch/pages/cannibalism.html.

13. Andrew Nichols Pratt, 'Human Trafficking: The Nadir of an Unholy Trinity', *European Security*, 2004.

14. David A. Feingold, 'Human Trafficking', *Foreign Policy*, Sept.–Oct. 2005.

15. William F. Wechsler, 'Follow the Money', *Foreign Affairs*, July–Aug. 2001.

10 Hooked

1. Kal Raustiala, 'Law, Liberalization and International Narcotics Trafficking', *International Law and Politics*, Fall 1999.

2. Jung Chang and Jon Halliday, *Mao: The Unknown Story* (Cape, 2005).

3. Jonathan P. Culkins and Peter Reuter, 'Reinventing US Drug Policy', *Issues in Science and Technology*, Fall 2006.

4. Ibid.

5. Steve Coll, *Ghost Wars* (Penguin, 2004).

6. Transnational Institute, Drug Policy Briefing, January 2005.

7. Richard Gibson and John Haseman, 'Prospects for Controlling Narcotics Production and Trafficking in Myanmar', *Contemporary South East Asia*, April 2003.

8. Moisés Naím, *Illicit* (Heinemann, 2006).

9. 'The Nexus among Terrorists, Narcotics Traffickers, Weapon Proliferators, and Organized Crime Networks', study prepared for the Library of Congress, December 2003.

10. Hans T. van der Veen, 'The Trans-Mediterranean Drug Complex', *Mediterranean Policy*, 9 (Autumn 2004).

11. Peter Reuter and Alex Stevens, 'An Analysis of UK Drug Policy', report prepared for the UK Drug Policy Commission, 2007.

12. Misha Glenny, *McMafia* (The Bodley Head, 2008).

13. 'Drugs: Facing Facts', report by the Royal Society of Arts Commission on Illegal Drugs, Communities and Public Policy, March 2007.

11 Filling the Tank

1. Matthew R. Simmons, *Twilight in the Desert* (John Wiley and Sons, 2005).

2. David Frum, *The Right Man* (Random House, 2001).

3. Alan Greenspan, *The Age of Turbulence* (Penguin, 2007).

4. Susanne Peters, *Coercive Western Security Strategies* (Routledge, 2004).

5. Jeremy Legget, *Half Gone* (Portobello Books, 2005).

6. Paul Roberts, *The End of Oil* (Mariner Books, 2005). Roberts argues this point about peak and plateau very convincingly.

7. Ibid., citing the work of geologist Colin Campbell.

8. Carola Hoyos, 'The New Seven Sisters', FT.com, 11 March 2007, www.ft.com/indepth/7sisters.

9. Jan H. Kalicki and David Goldwyn, 'Energy, Security and Foreign Policy', in Jan H. Kalicki and David Goldwyn (eds.), *Energy and Security: Toward a New Foreign Policy Strategy* (Johns Hopkins University Press, 2005).

10. Joe Barnes and Amy Myers Jaffe, 'The Persian Gulf and the Geopolitics of Oil', *Survival*, 48 (Spring 2006).

11. 'Who are the Islamists?', International Crisis Group, September 2004, www.crisisgroup.org/home/index.cfm?id=3021.

12. 'Can Saudi Arabia Reform Itself?', International Crisis Group, July 2004, www.crisisgroup.org/home/index.cfm?id=2864.

13. Speech by Senator John Kerry, Seattle, 27 May 2004.

14. Anna Politkovskaya, *Putin's Russia* (Metropolitan Books, 2004).

15. Flynt Leverett, 'The New Axis of Oil', *The National Interest, Inc.*, Summer 2006.

16. Derek Brower, 'Checkmate Gazprom', *Prospect*, July 2007.

17. James Kynge, *China Shakes the World* (Weidenfeld and Nicolson, 2006).

18. Ian Taylor, 'China's Oil Diplomacy in Africa', *International Affairs*, 82, 5 (2006).

19. Henry Lee and Dan Shalmon, 'Searching for Oil', working paper, Harvard University John F. Kennedy School of Government, March 2007.

20. Josh Kurlantzick, 'Beijing's Safari', *Carnegie Endowment*, November 2006.

12 Hotting up

1. John McNeill, *Something New Under the Sun* (Penguin, 2000).

2. Tim Flannery, *The Weather Makers* (Text Publishing, 2000).

3. A. M. Mannion, *Global Environment Change* (Addison-Wesley-Longman, 1997).

4. Rachel Carson, *Silent Spring* (Houghton Mifflin, 1962; repr. Mariner Books, 2002); Bill Moyers, 'Welcome to Doomsday', *New York Review of Books*, 24 March 2005.

5. McNeill, *Something New Under the Sun*.

6. William Rees, 'Degradation', paper presented at the Trudeau Conference on a Climate of Reconciliation, Calgary, 5–17 November 2007.

7. Jim Hansen, 'The Threat to the Planet', *New York Review of Books*, 13 July 2006.

8. McNeill, *Something New Under the Sun*.

9. Gabrielle Walker and David King, *The Hot Topic* (Bloomsbury, 2008).

10. Ibid., for much the best analysis of the problems faced by individual countries when the negotiations get under way.

11. James Kynge, *China Shakes the World* (Weidenfeld and Nicolson, 2006).

12. Clive Ponting, *A New Green History of the World* (Vintage Books, 2007).

13. Jonathan Mirsky, 'China's Assault on the Environment', *New York Review of Books*, 18 October 2001.

13 Coughs and Sneezes

1. Adam Zamoyski, *1812: Napoleon's Fatal March on Moscow* (Harper-Collins, 2004).

2. William H. McNeill, *Plagues and Peoples* (Anchor Books, 1976).

3. Paul Slack, 'Introduction', in Terence Ranger and Paul Slack (eds.), *Epidemics and Ideas* (Cambridge University Press, 1992).

4. Infection rates from the *Journal of the American Medical Association*, 28 February 2007.

5. Fiammetta Rocco, *The Miraculous Fever Tree: Malaria and the Cure that Changed the World* (HarperCollins, 2003).

6. Robin Weiss and Anthony McMichael, 'Social and Environmental Risk Factors in the Emergence of Infectious Disease', *Nature Medicine*, December 2004.

7. Arno Karlen, *Man and Microbes* (Simon and Schuster, 1995).

8. 'A Safer Future', report by the World Health Organization, 2007.

9. Eric Schlosser, *Fast Food Nation: What the All-American Meal Is Doing to the World* (Penguin, 2001).

10. Helen Epstein, 'Death by the Numbers', *New York Review of Books*, 28 June 2007.

11. Tony Barnett and Alan Whiteside, *AIDS in the Twenty-first Century* (Palgrave Macmillan, 2006).

12. Helen Epstein, *The Invisible Cure* (Viking, 2007).

13. Ayodele Samuel Jegede, 'What Led to the Nigerian Boycott?', *PLoS Medicine*, March 2005.

14. Karlen, *Man and Microbes*.

15. Michael Mandelbaum, 'Foreign Policy as Social Work', *Foreign Affairs*, Jan.–Feb. 1996; Samuel Berger, 'A Foreign Policy for the Global Age', *Foreign Affairs*, Nov.–Dec. 2000.

16. Laurie Garrett, 'The Lessons of HIV/AIDS', *Foreign Affairs*, July–Aug. 2005.

17. Stefan Elbe, 'HIV/AIDS and the Changing Landscape of War in Africa', *International Security*, 27, 2 (2002).

18. Steven Johnson, *The Ghost Map* (Penguin, 2006).

14 'Let Freedom Ring'

1. John Lewis Gaddis, *The Cold War* (Allen Lane, 2005).

2. Alexis de Tocqueville, *Democracy in America* (1835–40; repr. Signet, 2001).

3. James Kynge, *China Shakes the World* (Weidenfeld and Nicolson, 2006).

4. Mark Leonard, *What Does China Think?* (Fourth Estate, 2008).

5. John Mearsheimer and Stephen Walt, *The Israel Lobby and US Foreign Policy* (Farrar, Straus and Giroux, 2007).

6. David Rose, 'The Gaza Bombshell', *Vanity Fair*, April 2006.

7. David Marquand, 'Verdun, Auschwitz and the Future of Europe', Adam von Trott Memorial Lecture, Oxford 2008.

8. Robert Kagan, *Of Paradise and Power: America and Europe in the New World Order* (Knopf, 2003).

9. James Sheehan, *The Monopoly of Violence* (Faber and Faber, 2008).

15 And So . . .

1. Peter Hennessy, *The Secret State* (Penguin, 2002).

2. Margaret Macmillan, *Peacemakers* (John Murray, 2001).

3. David Reynolds, *Summits* (Allen Lane, 2007).

4. Stephen Schlesinger, *Act of Creation* (Westview Press, 2003).

5. Samantha Power, *Chasing the Flame* (Allen Lane, 2008).

6. Gabriel Kolko, *The Politics of War* (Random House, 1968).

7. Paul Kennedy, *The Parliament of Man* (Allen Lane, 2006).

8. James Traub, *The Best Intentions* (Bloomsbury, 2006).

9. Philippe Sands, *Torture Team* (Allen Lane, 2008).

10. George F. Kennan, *Sketches from a Life* (Norton Paperback, 2000).

11. Peter Vansittart, *In the Fifties* (John Murray, 1995).

Index

He just wanted a decent book to read ...

Not too much to ask, is it? It was in 1935 when Allen Lane, Managing Director of Bodley Head Publishers, stood on a platform at Exeter railway station looking for something good to read on his journey back to London. His choice was limited to popular magazines and poor-quality paperbacks – the same choice faced every day by the vast majority of readers, few of whom could afford hardbacks. Lane's disappointment and subsequent anger at the range of books generally available led him to found a company – and change the world.

'We believed in the existence in this country of a vast reading public for intelligent books at a low price, and staked everything on it'
Sir Allen Lane, 1902–1970, founder of Penguin Books

The quality paperback had arrived – and not just in bookshops. Lane was adamant that his Penguins should appear in chain stores and tobacconists, and should cost no more than a packet of cigarettes.

Reading habits (and cigarette prices) have changed since 1935, but Penguin still believes in publishing the best books for everybody to enjoy. We still believe that good design costs no more than bad design, and we still believe that quality books published passionately and responsibly make the world a better place.

So wherever you see the little bird – whether it's on a piece of prize-winning literary fiction or a celebrity autobiography, political tour de force or historical masterpiece, a serial-killer thriller, reference book, world classic or a piece of pure escapism – you can bet that it represents the very best that the genre has to offer.

Whatever you like to read – trust Penguin.